# LOST VOICES

*The Untold Stories of America's*
*World War I Veterans and Their Families*

## MARTIN KING AND MICHAEL COLLINS

Guilford, Connecticut

An imprint of The Rowman & Littlefield Publishing Group, Inc.
4501 Forbes Blvd., Ste. 200
Lanham, MD 20706
www.rowman.com

Distributed by NATIONAL BOOK NETWORK

British Library Cataloguing in Publication Information available

**Library of Congress Cataloging-in-Publication Data available**

ISBN 978-1-4930-3164-1 (hardcover)
ISBN 978-1-4930-3165-8 (e-book)

♾™ The paper used in this publication meets the minimum requirements of American National Standard for Information Sciences—Permanence of Paper for Printed Library Materials, ANSI/ NISO Z39.48-1992.

Printed in the United States of America.

*This volume is dedicated to all veterans of all wars.
We will never forget you.*

# CONTENTS

# Acknowledgments

Thank you first and foremost to my wife Freya for her continued support despite all the adversity, and posthumous thanks to my late grandfather, Private 4829 Joseph Henry Pumford, who fought at Passchendaele in World War I and provided invaluable inspiration for my early interest in military history. He was promoted to corporal but then demoted for punching out a sergeant. He was unique in managing to terrify both sides in that particular conflict. Also, and not forgetting, offspring Allycia and Ashley Rae, brother Graham, sisters Sandra and Debbie, brother-in-law Mark, nephews Ben and Jake, and niece Rachel. My respected Maori clan in New Zealand, Parei, Clifford Julian, and Josef Barnard. Treasured long-time friends Andy Kirton, Commander Jeffrey Barta (ret'd), General Graham Hollands (ret'd), Professor Carlton Joyce, Ray Wheatley, Steve Highlander, and Betsy Jackson, for their wonderful support and encouragement. Grateful thanks to my dear friends at the United States Embassy Brussels, and the wonderful Protocol Team, thanks to Mr. Roland Gaul formerly of the National Museum of Military History, Diekirch, Luxembourg. Thank you also to Dan and Judy Goo in Hawaii, Mrs. Carol Fish and the staff at the United States Military Academy, West Point; Rudy Beckers and Greg Hanlon at Joint Base McGuire, Dix, Lakehurst, for their wonderful ongoing support. Many thanks to Joseph Schram American Legion Flanders Field, Doug McCabe, former curator of the Cornelius Ryan Collection, Ohio University; my friends Brian Dick, John Taylor, and the excellent SHAPE kids; World War II veteran John Schaffner and former Madam Ambassador Denise Campbell Bauer. Also grateful thanks to literary agent Roger Williams, Rick

Rinehart, Evan Helmlinger, and the tremendous staff at The Rowman & Littlefield Publishing Group, who continue to inspire me.

—Martin King

Thank you first to my amazing son, Daniel Edward, for continuing to make me realize how important it is to preserve history for future generations. To my coauthor, Martin King, for your support, patience, and friendship throughout the writing of this book. My agent, Roger Williams, for his patience and guidance throughout the publishing process. To my parents, John and Joanne Collins, for your continued support in my writing endeavors. My brothers John and Chris, my sisters-in-law Melissa and Maria, nieces and nephew, Morgan, Katie, Keira, Margo, and Henry. To the King family for their support and understanding during the writing of this book. My friends Michael Aliotta, Christopher Begley, Patrick Healy, Howard Liddic, Mike Edwards, John Vallely, Sean Conley, Christian Pettinger, Mark Weber, Dirk De Groof, Rudy Aerts, and all those who support me during my many travels. To Kathleen Reilly and Ann-Marie Harris and the staff in the Local History Department at the Berkshire Athenaeum who continue to support my research endeavors. Thank you to Rick Rinehart, Lynn Zelem, and all the staff of The Rowman & Littlefield Publishing Group. In loving memory of my grandmother, Kathryn Riordan.

—Michael Collins

# Preface

Mike Collins and I have written five books together so far, all about forgotten heroes or historically neglected US divisions that participated in World War II. We had mutually agreed that it was time to take on something else, but we weren't entirely sure what that "something else" would be. It all started during one of our many transatlantic Skype calls.

"Surely everything that can be written about World War One has been written," I said to Mike when he first proposed the idea of switching our attention from World War II books to writing something about World War I. In all honesty, I wasn't particularly enthused at the prospect of tackling the First World War. "What's the point, unless we can bring something new to the table?" I said. "You're right; I agree with you," he replied, then added, "But wait until you see what I've found."

That was the spark. That was the impetus to present something different about the Great War, something that has the *Wow, I didn't know that* factor.

There is nothing more enthralling or invigorating for a historian than rummaging through old archives and casting one's eye over documents unseen for many decades. In this case it was letters and newspaper articles discovered by Mike, most of which had been buried under dust for almost one hundred years. The language and dialogue alone puts one right back to the time when these items were written. These are the things that give us goose bumps and completely engage our attention for the duration.

The battles and campaigns of World War I have been covered and meticulously studied from all angles by innumerable historians around the world. There would have been very little that we could have added. If we were going to broach the subject of America's involvement, then it had to be from an entirely new and different perspective. Our previous volumes always gave precedence to the voices of those who experienced war firsthand, and were largely transcribed from direct interviews with surviving veterans. The purpose of this volume is to provide a similar platform for those previously unheard voices whose lives were affected and impacted by US involvement in World War I, also known as the Great War.

My grandfather fought with the King's Own Yorkshire Light Infantry in World War I. He lost two brothers in that horrendous conflict, and was wounded at the Battle of Passchendaele. Again, this is a battle that has been analyzed and scrutinized from every perceivable angle. The first book that I read about the Great War was Sir Basil Liddell Hart's *A History of the First World War.* He served in the same regiment as my grandfather, and wrote a riveting account that was both scathing and highly informative. I was gripped from the first page.

Many historians take the stance that America's involvement in the Great War was minimal, but it cannot be underestimated by any means. US participation brought Germany to its knees and forced them to accept a punitive armistice, achieving a victory of sorts over the German forces and their allies.

We hope that this volume will take you right back to these seminal moments in time when the world was thoroughly embroiled in a devastating conflict that devoured empires and consumed lives on an industrial scale. This "war to end all wars" struck at the sanguine heart of humanity and coldly ripped it out. It was the end of the age of imperial dynasties, unprecedented in the slaughter, carnage, and destruction it inflicted on humanity. This great watershed of twentieth-century geopolitical history caused the deaths of nine million soldiers, with a further twenty-one million wounded or maimed for life. By the end of the war many countries had sacrificed the flower of their youth to this unprecedented conflict.

Many agree that the title "World War I" is a misnomer in some respects—not because of the global nature of the conflict, but because

| Country | Men Mobilized | Killed | Wounded | POWs + Missing | Total Casualties | Casualties in % of Men Mobilized |
|---|---|---|---|---|---|---|
| Russia | 12 million | 1.7 million | 4.9 million | 2.5 million | 9.15 million | 76.3 |
| France | 8.4 million | 1.3 million | 4.2 million | 537,000 | 6.1 million | 73.3 |
| GB + Empire | 8.9 million | 908,000 | 2 million | 191,000 | 3.1 million | 35.8 |
| Italy | 5.5 million | 650,000 | 947,000 | 600,000 | 2.1 million | 39 |
| USA | 4.3 million | 126,000 | 234,000 | 4,500 | 350,000 | 8 |
| Japan | 800,000 | 300 | 900 | 3 | 1,210 | 0.2 |
| Romania | 750,000 | 335,000 | 120,000 | 80,000 | 535,000 | 71 |
| Serbia | 700,000 | 45,000 | 133,000 | 153,000 | 331,000 | 47 |
| Belgium | 267,000 | 13,800 | 45,000 | 34,500 | 93,000 | 35 |
| Greece | 230,000 | 5,000 | 21,000 | 1,000 | 27,000 | 12 |
| Portugal | 100,000 | 7,222 | 13,700 | 12,000 | 33,000 | 33 |
| Total Allies | 42 million | 5 million | 13 million | 4 million | 22 million | 52 |
| | | | | | | |
| Germany | 11 million | 1.7 million | 4.2 million | 1.1 million | 7.1 million | 65 |
| Austria | 7.8 million | 1.2 million | 3.6 million | 2.2 million | 7 million | 90 |
| Turkey | 2.8 million | 325,000 | 400,000 | 250,000 | 975,000 | 34 |
| Bulgaria | 1.2 million | 87,000 | 152,000 | 27,000 | 266,000 | 22 |
| Total Central Powers | 22.8 million | 3.3 million | 8.3 million | 3.6 million | 15 million | 67 |
| | | | | | | |
| Grand Total | 65 million | 8.5 million | 21 million | 7.7 million | 37 million | 57 |

some claim that it never really ended. The seeds of discontent and disillusion sown in 1918 led to World War II, and, more importantly, the war never ended in the hearts and minds of those who survived.

In the following pages you will hear some new perspectives on the Great War, along with the long-silenced voices of those who were directly involved—those who suffered and fought, and were never heard.

### Prayer of a Soldier in France (1918)
By Alfred Joyce Kilmer, 165th Infantry Regiment
(1886–1918)

My shoulders ache beneath my pack
(Lie easier, Cross, upon His back).
I march with feet that burn and smart
(Tread, Holy Feet, upon my heart).
Men shout at me who may not speak
(They scourged Thy back and smote Thy cheek).
I may not lift a hand to clear
My eyes of salty drops that sear.
(Then shall my fickle soul forget
Thy Agony of Bloody Sweat?)
My rifle hand is stiff and numb
(From Thy pierced palm red rivers come).
Lord, Thou didst suffer more for me
Than all the hosts of land and sea.
So let me render back again
This millionth of Thy gift. Amen.[1]

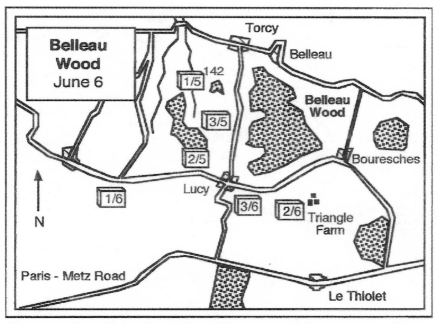

This map indicates the positions of the US Marines during their advance on the German positions. *COURTESY OF JOSEPH SCHRAM, POST COMMANDER, THE AMERICAN LEGION FLANDERS FIELD POST BE02*

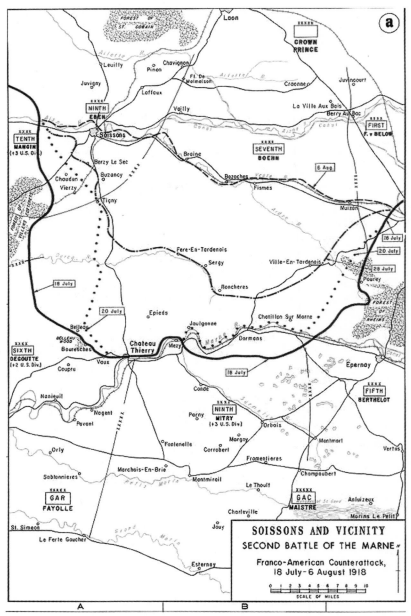

This map shows the location of the French and American troops during the counterattack in the summer of 1918. *COURTESY OF JOSEPH SCHRAM, POST COMMANDER, THE AMERICAN LEGION FLANDERS FIELD POST BE02*

The US 4th Division lines are illustrated on this map during the Aisne-Marne offensive, which took place in late July 1918. *COURTESY OF JOSEPH SCHRAM, POST COMMANDER, THE AMERICAN LEGION FLANDERS FIELD POST BE02*

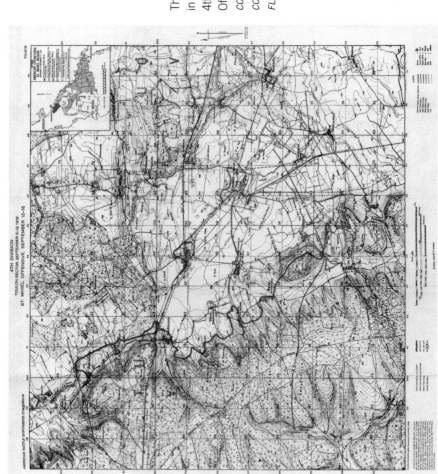

This map shows the front lines in the Toulon Sector of the US 4th Division during the St. Mihiel Offensive in September 1918. *COURTESY OF JOSEPH SCHRAM, POST COMMANDER, THE AMERICAN LEGION FLANDERS FIELD POST BE02*

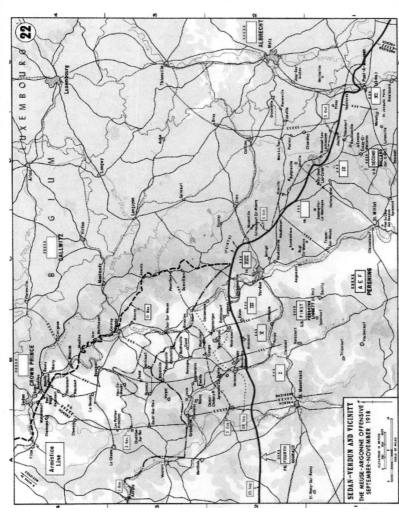

This Meuse-Argonne Campaign map during September–November 1918 shows the US front lines up until the Armistice on November 11, 1918. *COURTESY OF JOSEPH SCHRAM, POST COMMANDER, THE AMERICAN LEGION FLANDERS FIELD POST BE02*

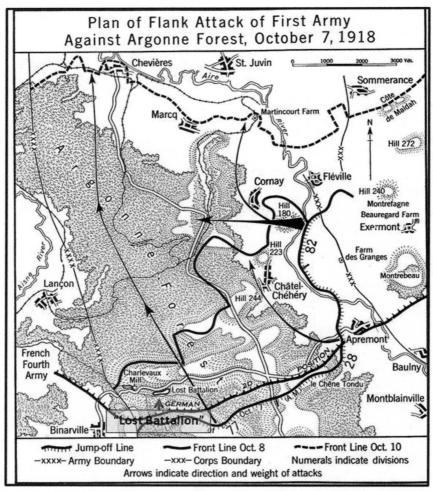

Plan of Flank Attack of First Army Against Argonne Forest, October 7, 1918

This map illustrates where the "Lost Battalion" was located in the Argonne Forest on October 7, 1918. *COURTESY OF JOSEPH SCHRAM, POST COMMANDER, THE AMERICAN LEGION FLANDERS FIELD POST BE02*

# Introduction

AMERICA WAS NEUTRAL—THERE WAS NO QUESTION ABOUT THAT. It had been neutral since the end of the American Civil War, and had no intention whatsoever of being drawn into this latest European debacle. Soon after President Woodrow Wilson's government had been officially notified by Germany of that nation's declaration of war against Russia, and once they had been officially notified by Russia regarding her status, Wilson, the descendant of Scottish Presbyterians and a staunch idealist, officially declared that America would indeed remain neutral. The people of the United States had expected him to issue this American proclamation of neutrality, and he delivered.

Wilson's government had drawn the conclusion that Germany, Russia, and the Austro-Hungarian Empire were all significant naval and maritime powers. A conflict involving these three nations, even if England, France, and Italy were not involved, would soon raise questions concerning the rights of neutrals and their property on land and sea; furthermore, the attitude of Americans toward the combatants also needed to be considered.

The declaration of neutrality that America had issued previous to this was in 1904, in response to the Russo-Japanese War. When the formal declaration of war between those two nations was made on February 10, 1904, President Theodore Roosevelt wasted no time in issuing his neutrality proclamation the very next day. Previous to that one, there had been the Franco-Prussian War. This declaration of war was dated July 15, 1870, but President Grant did not issue the American proclamation of neutrality until August 22, only nine days before the pivotal Battle of Sedan, which in effect crushed France and decided the outcome.

All of these proclamations of neutrality were practically the same, save for a few minor adjustments that referred to the countries at war.

# Part I

# The Road Once Traveled

## CHAPTER ONE

# Our Allegiance

MOST YOUNG AMERICANS HAD NO IDEA WHAT BEING IN THE GREAT War would entail. For some, it would lead here.

## MARINO BALLARDINI, BATTERY F, 134TH FIELD ARTILLERY, 82ND DIVISION
**Berkshire Evening Eagle,** *January 13, 1925: "Takes Own Life with Gas at Home"*

> *On August 22, 1918, Private Marino Ballardini sailed with his organization for overseas service, and while in France participated in the Pannes Offensive and the Bois de Bonseil engagements. He returned to the United States on March 31, 1919, and received his honorable discharge on April 30, 1919, at Camp Devens, Massachusetts. In 1919, while visiting Italy, he married Miss Rachele Menici in Brescia, Italy. Marino Ballardini was found dead at his home on 14 Third Street in Pittsfield, Massachusetts. Ballardini, age thirty-two, died from inhaling gas. He had been in ill health for a few weeks, and Dr. Criscitiello, his attending physician, said that he had been despondent.*
>
> *It was reported as a case of suicide, as the cocks on the gas stove and on a gaslight were found turned on, and the room, filled with gas. When Mrs. John Ballardini, cousin of the victim, went to the home for a visit at 11:30 a.m., she found the man seated on a chair near the kitchen stove. Dr. Criscitiello was called and the police were notified. The poor man apparently was dead when discovered by his cousin. Mr.*

*Ballardini had made his home in Pittsfield for many years. He served with the United States Army during World War I, and since that time had been employed as a bricklayer there. He left a wife and son.*[1]

At the turn of the twentieth century America was still busy impressing its identity on the world stage. It was still a fresh and volatile country, a compendium of contradictions that had already experienced one violent and destructive war in living memory, and fully understood the devastating implications of armed conflict. It was a country resolute in professing its identity but unsure of its place in the world. Frequently beset by internal struggles, it sought to impose compromised ideologies and laws on a public that was not always receptive. It extolled virtuous principles even though these were seldom observed and applied in the many multiethnic communities, which were equally fervent about retaining cultural and traditional ties to their old countries. America would emerge from World War I self-assured, self-reliant, confident, and the envy of the free world.

Toward the end of the nineteenth century, America had sought to engage the process of state building with the intention of remaining on a par with other long-established industrial nations. If this implied asserting its capacity to project its interests abroad, then so be it; but there were limits. In 1898 a commission led by excellent administrator but negligible politician, William Howard Taft, embarked on creating an American-style model of imperial governance in the Philippines, seized as a collateral asset in the war to free Cuba from oppressive Spanish rule. Not every politician agreed with Taft's expansionist policies, or his empirical assertions, but they were unanimous in recognizing America's desire to lead by moral example—to be globally perceived as a country that intended to serve humanity as a whole by presenting a distracted world with its version of "liberty for all mankind" through its enlightened systems of law and temperate justice.

Global opinion mattered to America, and there were fears that these firmly held values would be compromised if the country agreed to participate in the latest European war that had started in 1914.

Years before he entered the White House, President Woodrow Wilson had worked hard to formulate distinctive views regarding America's position in the global community. While he proclaimed the country's virtues, he was worried that if the nation acted irresponsibly abroad, this would only serve to compromise these hard-won democratic values. During his first July 4 address as president, he remarked: "America has lifted high the light which will shine unto all generations and guide the feet of mankind to the goal of justice and liberty and peace."

Extolling liberty for all mankind was one thing, but practicing what one preached was entirely another. Scant reference was made to the fact that there was a lot of inequality in America at that time. Life expectancy for the average white American was just forty-eight years, roughly the same as that of a peasant on the Indian subcontinent. This devolved to a mere thirty-three years for African Americans, who, despite President Abraham Lincoln's Emancipation Proclamation, remained a maligned people, subject to widespread prejudice.

In the early twentieth century endemic racial oppression and segregation escalated across the United States, prompting civil rights activist W. E. B. Du Bois and other black leaders to distillate their activism by founding the Niagara Movement in 1905. By 1909 white reformers augmented this organization to form the National Association for the Advancement of Colored People (NAACP). Early in its fight for equality, the NAACP used the federal courts to challenge disenfranchisement and residential segregation. The eventual impact of World War I on race relations in American history was nothing short of cataclysmic, and the aftereffects were destined to resonate way beyond the trenches of the Western Front. This war would instill a new perception of what democratic America should aspire to be, rather than what it had previously believed itself to be.

President Woodrow Wilson was stridently opposed to any American intervention from the outset, and he intended to do everything within his power to preserve and protect the neutrality of the United States, its citizens, and persons within its territory. On January 22, 1917, he addressed the Senate and staunchly advocated *Peace without victory*, regarding the warring European nations while simultaneously imploring his fellow Americans to *stay impartial in thought as well as actions*.[2] Soon after war broke out in Europe, Wilson outlined the position of the United States, its rights, and its obligations as decreed by international law. Furthermore, in order to prevent any inadvertent violation of the country's laws and treaties, his administration declared that the act of April 20, 1818, generally known as the "Neutrality Law," was to be stringently observed, with no exceptions. This act expressly prohibited a number of activities that could potentially assist the belligerents.

In 1913, one year prior to August 19, 1914, when US president Woodrow Wilson addressed Congress and publicly proclaimed the US policy of neutrality, a reunion of more than 21,000 American Civil War veterans had been held at Gettysburg. The name of that monumental battle, along with Antietam, Fredericksburg, Bull Run, and many others still resonated with the public. Overt animosity between the North and the South may have diluted over the intervening years, but it was still present. Neither side harbored a desire to sacrifice its sons again, particularly to a conflict thousands of miles away from American shores.

During his address, Wilson warned US citizens against taking sides in the current European war, for fear of endangering the wider US policy. He made his position very clear:

*The effect of the war upon the United States will depend upon what American citizens say and do. Every man who really loves America will act and speak in the true spirit of neutrality, which is the spirit of impartiality and fairness and friendliness to all concerned. The spirit of the nation in this critical matter will be determined largely by what individuals and society and those gathered in public meetings do and say, upon what newspapers and magazines contain, upon what ministers utter in their pulpits, and men proclaim as their opinions upon the street. The people of the United States are drawn from many nations, and chiefly from the nations now at war. It is natural and inevitable that there should be the utmost variety of sympathy and desire among them with regard to the issues and circumstances of the conflict. Some will wish one nation, others another, to succeed in the momentous struggle. It will be easy to excite passion and difficult to allay it. Those responsible for exciting it will assume a heavy responsibility, responsibility for no less a thing than that the people of the*

*United States, whose love of their country and whose loyalty to its government should unite them as Americans all, bound in honor and affection to think first of her and her interests, may be divided in camps of hostile opinion, hot against each other, involved in the war itself in impulse and opinion if not in action.*

*Such divisions amongst us would be fatal to our peace of mind and might seriously stand in the way of the proper performance of our duty as the one great nation at peace, the one people holding itself ready to play a part of impartial mediation and speak the counsels of peace and accommodation, not as a partisan, but as a friend.*

*I venture, therefore, my fellow countrymen, to speak a solemn word of warning to you against that deepest, most subtle, most essential breach of neutrality, which may spring out of partisanship, out of passionately taking sides. The United States must be neutral in fact, as well as in name, during these days that are to try men's souls. We must be impartial in thought, as well as action, must put a curb upon our sentiments, as well as upon every transaction that might be construed as a preference of one party to the struggle before another.*[3]

In time Wilson's rhetoric would change dramatically, but for now he was sticking to his guns. He wanted to ensure that the previous Grant and Roosevelt neutrality proclamations would guarantee America's future neutrality. All stipulations therein were to be articulated and stringently observed. The following would be strictly forbidden:

- Accepting a war commission from either belligerent.
- Enlisting in the private service of either belligerent as a soldier or seaman on board any warship or privateer.
- Hiring another person to enlist or to go beyond the jurisdiction of the United States to enlist in the service of either belligerent. This, however, does not prohibit the subjects of either belligerent, who are merely temporarily in the United States, from enlisting or retaining another subject to enlist aboard a belligerent warship which may happen to arrive in American waters.

- Fitting out, or attempting to fit out, any ship for the service of either belligerent. Issuing a commission within the jurisdiction of the United States to any ship to act as a belligerent.

- Increasing or improving the armament of any belligerent warship within the jurisdiction of the United States.

- Setting on foot or fitting out within the jurisdiction of the United States of any military expedition against the territory of either belligerent.[4]

President Grant's second proclamation, issued on October 8, 1870, was later incorporated into the Roosevelt proclamation. This was intended to further augment the previous stipulations by declaring that "the use of the waters of the United States by belligerent armed vessels, whether public ships or privateers, in order to prepare for hostile operations or to keep a watch on the ships of the other belligerent lying within jurisdiction of the United States, must be regarded as an unfriendly act."

Treaties and proclamations were one thing, but attempting to appease a young man's fervor to participate in the "great European adventure" was another thing entirely. Arthur Empey was a young American living in New Jersey when war broke out in Europe in 1914. Enraged by the sinking of the *Lusitania* a year later and the subsequent loss of the lives of American passengers, he prepared to join an American army that would combat the Germans. When America did not immediately declare war, Empey boarded a ship to England, enlisted voluntarily with the 1st London Regiment Royal Fusiliers in the British Army, and went on to serve in the 56th London Division on the Western Front—first as a bomber, and then as a machine gunner. It was a clear violation of America's neutrality laws, but no one appeared to have been too bothered at the time. Further enlistments of Americans occurred when Sir Sam Hughes, Canada's minister of militia and defense from October 1911 to November 1916, authorized the creation of a recruitment organization called the "American Legion." Canadian recruiters went to the United States and recruited American volunteers to fight in the Canadian Expeditionary Force (CEF). The number is uncertain, but some estimates put the number of volunteers recruited during this drive as high as 16,000.

Meanwhile, Arthur Empey was soon manning a trench on the front lines. He survived his experience and published his recollections in 1917. He could have warned American soldiers what they were getting into: This war had no precedent. This was a gargantuan clash of empires, and killing had been elevated to an industrial scale. New cynical means and methods of mass murder had been devised by the combatant nations using state-of-the-art machine guns, heavy artillery, and despicable chemical weapons. During the war, the Germans produced 38.6 million tons of gas shells; the British, 8.3 million tons; and the French, 5.3 million tons. Up to 800,000 soldiers became victims of gas.[5]

Shortly after Arthur Empey had been made a member of a machine-gun crew, he was sitting in a British trench while a comrade observed the German lines through a trench periscope. This was an optical device that soldiers used during World War I to observe the ground in front of their trenches and fortifications, without taking the risk of raising their eyes above the parapet and creating a target for enemy snipers. Suddenly the all-too-familiar alarm was called: "Gas!" Arthur knew instinctively that the weather conditions were conducive for a possible enemy gas attack, and the warning had been passed along in an effort to be vigilant.

## PVT. ARTHUR GUY EMPEY, 1ST LONDON REGIMENT ROYAL FUSILIERS

*We had a new man at the periscope, on this afternoon in question; I was sitting on the fire step, cleaning my rifle, when he called out to me: "There's a sort of greenish, yellow cloud rolling along the ground out in front; it's coming." But I waited for no more; grabbing my bayonet, which was detached from the rifle, I gave the alarm by banging an empty shell case, which was hanging near the periscope. At the same instant, gongs started ringing down the trench, the signal for Tommy to don his respirator, or smoke helmet, as we call it. Gas travels quietly, so you must not lose any time; you generally have about eighteen or twenty seconds in which to adjust your gas helmet.*

*A gas helmet is made of cloth, treated with chemicals. There are two windows, or glass eyes, in it, through which you can see. Inside there is a rubber-covered tube, which goes in the mouth. You breathe through your nose; the gas, passing through the cloth helmet, is neutralized by the action of the chemicals. The foul air is exhaled through the tube in the mouth, this tube being so constructed that it prevents the inhaling of the outside air, or gas. One helmet is good for five hours of the strongest gas. Each Tommy carries two of them slung around his shoulder in a waterproof canvas bag. He must wear this bag at all times, even while sleeping. To change a defective helmet, you take out the new one, hold your breath, pull the old one off, placing the new one over your head, tucking in the loose ends under the collar of your tunic.*

*For a minute, pandemonium reigned in our trench—Tommies adjusting their helmets, bombers running here and there, and men turning out of the dugouts with fixed bayonets, to man the fire step. Reinforcements were pouring out of the communication trenches. Our gun's crew was busy mounting the machine gun on the parapet and bringing up extra ammunition from the dugout.*

*German gas is heavier than air and soon fills the trenches and dugouts, where it has been known to lurk for two or three days, until the air is purified by means of large chemical sprayers. We had to work quickly, as Fritz generally follows the gas with an infantry attack. A company man on our right was too slow in getting on his helmet; he sank to the ground, clutching at his throat, and after a few spasmodic twistings, went West [died]. It was horrible to see him die, but we were powerless to help him. In the corner of a traverse, a little, muddy cur dog, one of the company's pets, was lying dead, with his two paws over his nose. It's the animals that suffer the most, the horses, mules, cattle, dogs, cats, and rats, they having no helmets to save them. Tommy does not sympathize with rats in a gas attack.*

*At times, gas has been known to travel, with dire results, fifteen miles behind the lines. A gas, or smoke helmet, as it is called, at the best is a vile-smelling thing, and it is not long before one gets a violent headache from wearing it. Our eighteen-pounders were bursting in No Man's Land, in an effort, by the artillery, to disperse the gas clouds. The fire step was lined with crouching men, bayonets fixed, and bombs near at hand to repel the expected attack. Our artillery had put a barrage of curtain fire on the German lines, to try and break up their attack and keep back reinforcements.*

*I trained my machine gun on their trench and its bullets were raking the parapet. Then over they came, bayonets glistening. In their respirators, which have a large snout in front, they looked like some horrible nightmare. All along our trench, rifles and machine guns spoke; our shrapnel was bursting over their heads. They went down in heaps, but new ones took the place of the fallen. Nothing could stop that mad rush. The Germans reached our barbed wire, which had previously been demolished by their shells, then it was bomb against bomb, and the devil for all.*

*Suddenly, my head seemed to burst from a loud "crack" in my ear. Then my head began to swim, throat got dry, and a heavy pressure on the lungs warned me that my helmet was leaking. Turning my gun over to No. 2, I changed helmets. The trench started to wind like a snake, and sandbags appeared to be floating in the air. The noise was horrible. I sank onto the fire step; needles seemed to be pricking my flesh, then blackness. I was awakened by one of my mates removing my smoke helmet. How delicious that cool, fresh air felt in my lungs. A strong wind had arisen and dispersed the gas. They told me that I had been "out" for three hours; they thought I was dead.*

*The attack had been repulsed after a hard fight. Twice the Germans had gained a foothold in our trench, but had been driven out by counterattacks. The trench was filled with their dead, and ours. Through a periscope, I counted eighteen dead Germans in our wire; they were a ghastly sight in their horrible-looking respirators. I examined my first smoke helmet; a bullet had gone through it on the left side, just grazing my ear, [and] the gas had penetrated through the hole made in the cloth. Out of our crew of six, we lost two killed and two wounded. That night we buried all of the dead, excepting those in No Man's Land. In death there is not much distinction; friend and foe are treated alike. After the wind had dispersed the gas, the RAMC got busy with their chemical sprayers, spraying out the dugouts and low parts of the trenches to dissipate any fumes of the German gas, which may have been lurking in same.*[6]

Initially there was absolutely no ambiguity regarding the American position, but in time that would change. It would be a gradual change influenced by an irrevocable sequence of events that would inevitably draw the United States into this latest European conflict. Meanwhile, Wilson refused to strengthen the country's armed forces, "lest such action might give a wrong impression to the great warring powers."[7] Former president Theodore Roosevelt took an entirely different stance when he asserted, "Unpreparedness has not the slightest effect in averting war. Its only effect is immensely to increase the likelihood of disgrace and disaster in war."[8] Roosevelt called for the immediate strengthening of the armed forces, the formation of a reserve corps, and the provision of military training for every American youth.

One of Teddy Roosevelt's biggest regrets was that he was not able to lead the United States as its president during a major conflict. When World War I erupted across Europe in 1914, Roosevelt wasted no time in asserting his opinion, immediately advocating that the United States join England and France to fight against Germany. He vehemently attacked Wilson for his policies of pacifism and neutrality, which led to a frequently acerbic relationship between the two for the duration. This was exacerbated by Roosevelt's constant undermining of the Democrat's policies, which occasionally made it difficult for President Wilson to execute the duties of his office.

While Wilson remained intransigent in his opposition to American involvement by flatly refusing to strengthen the country's armed forces, Roosevelt persisted in his call for a strong military when he said that the Wilson administration's refusal to prepare for war against Germany had led to "the murder of the thousands of men, women, and children on the high seas." He was referring, among other things, to the callous sinking of the RMS *Lusitania* in 1915 by a German U-boat torpedo, which resulted in the deaths of 1,195 persons, including 128 US citizens, and caused outrage on both sides of the Atlantic. Broadway composer Jerome Kern had planned to sail on the *Lusitania*, but missed the ship because he overslept when his alarm clock didn't go off.

In time the unrestricted submarine warfare waged by German U-boats against other nonmilitary ships and civilians inevitably induced American sympathies to veer toward the Allied cause. As these raids against American ships became more blatant, tensions mounted, which led to further calls for the United States to enter the war. While heated exchanges continued in Congress regarding the sinking of the *Lusitania*, on March 24, 1916, a German U-boat torpedoed and severely damaged another passenger ship, the British vessel, SS *Sussex*, which resulted in twenty-five American civilian casualties (out of a total of eighty casualties, including fifty fatalities).[9]

As a direct response to continued German naval aggression, Wilson addressed Congress on April 19, 1916, vigorously condemning the German actions. During the course of his speech he made a direct threat: "Unless the Imperial German Government should now immediately declare and effect an abandonment of its present method of warfare against passenger- and freight-carrying vessels, this Government can have no choice but to sever diplomatic relations with the Government of the German Empire altogether."[10]

German reaction in the wake of Wilson's speech was swift. Five days later, on April 24, 1916, it temporarily abandoned its U-boat campaign, which was mainly directed around Britain and the Mediterranean at the time. The Reichstag issued a statement declaring that from that day on, passenger ships were to be left unmolested, and merchant ships would be thoroughly searched before being sunk.[11] Secretly Germany was infuriated that Allied armed merchant ships had been actively using American ports since 1914 for the transport of American manufactured war materials in significant quantities. Immediately after the outbreak of war in August 1914, US company Bethlehem Steel accepted major arms orders from the Allies. From France, they received orders for the production of guns and grenades, and similar orders from Britain.

In October of that same year, Charles Schwab, director of Bethlehem Steel, personally visited Lord Kitchener and Lord Fisher of the Admiralty. They agreed, among other things, that his factory would surreptitiously produce twenty submarines for the British, albeit at an inflated price. The construction of these vessels was in flagrant violation of US and international laws, but that wasn't going to be an issue. Schwab was a well-connected businessman with friends in high places, and thanks to his astute machinations, Bethlehem Steel circumvented these laws by establishing manufacturing facilities in Canada.

During the first years of World War I, Bethlehem Steel had a veritable monopoly on contracts to supply the Allies with certain kinds of munitions. During this period Schwab made many visits to Europe in connection with the manufacture and supply of munitions to the Allied governments. The parts for these military contracts would be produced in the United States and then assembled in Canada. In 1915, the submarines were ready to be shipped from Canadian harbors. These materials and subsequent "war loans" substantially revived the US economy, as exports to Europe increased dramatically—from five hundred million in 1914, to no less than three and a half billion by 1917.

Britain still had the most powerful navy in the world, and on the orders of the Admiralty this powerful navy acted provocatively by frequently seizing cargo ships that left American ports bound for Germany, while simultaneously doing everything possible to prevent the Central Powers from receiving any form of assistance material from the United States. Consequently, Germany was repeatedly denied access to these potential financial and material resources, which eventually led to vehement protest in the Reichstag. But it was all to no avail. The fact that the Americans, through their loans and deliveries, were already in clear breach of international law was enough to provoke the Germans to eventually abandon any attempt at appeasement, and proceed with their indiscriminate submarine warfare.

By January 1917 the situation in Germany had deteriorated. During a wartime conference that month, representatives from the German Navy convinced the military leadership and Kaiser Wilhelm II that a resumption of unrestricted submarine warfare would help to defeat Great Britain within five months. German policymakers argued that such resumption would directly violate the "*Sussex* Pledge." This pledge was a promise made in 1916 by Germany to the United States prior to the latter's entry into the war.[12] Previous to that, early in 1915, Germany had conducted unrestricted submarine warfare, allowing armed merchant ships, but not passenger ships, to be torpedoed without warning.

The crisis point arrived when the United States was directly accused by Germany of supplying munitions and financial assistance to the Allies, and could therefore no longer be feasibly considered a "neutral party." Germany also believed that the United States had jeopardized its neutrality by acquiescing to the Allied blockade of Germany.

German chancellor Theobald von Bethmann-Hollweg believed in prudence and caution when he stated that resuming submarine warfare would inevitably draw the United States into the war on behalf of the Allies. He also firmly believed that this would ultimately lead to the defeat of Germany. For many in the German government, in theory at least, there had been a de facto state of war between the two countries since the beginning.

British "First Lord of the Admiralty" Winston Churchill was scathing in his comments about Woodrow Wilson's delay in entering the war: "What he did in April 1917 could have been done in May 1915," he wrote. "And if done then . . . in how many millions of homes would an empty chair be occupied now?"[13]

Once the United States officially entered the war in 1917, all four of Theodore Roosevelt's sons volunteered to serve. Roosevelt asked permission to head a volunteer division for service in France, but Wilson exacted a little personal revenge on that occasion by having Secretary of War Newton Baker flatly refuse this request.

Nonetheless, America would eventually become embroiled in the bloodiest conflict to date, and Wilson's pacifist orotundity would transpose from passionate refusal, to participation in a European war, to complete, unrestricted inclusion. But precisely what would this mean to those at home, and those fighting abroad?

In 1917 America was still a relatively young country, and still the prime destination for thousands of European immigrants, many of whom were escaping persecution, and had long sought to establish their own communities in various regions across the United States. It didn't matter if the person was an indigenous American or an immigrant: Once they signed up to become an American citizen, that is what they would be—in name, at least. From 1836 to 1914, over thirty million Europeans immigrated to the United States. The peak year of European immigration was in 1907, when no less than 1,285,349 persons entered the country. German-American immigrants emulated other ethnic groups who came to the United States, settling in various enclaves where they could enjoy their own language and culture. Theodore Roosevelt persisted with his clamorous opinions on the subject of American involvement when he said, "We have been culpably, well-nigh criminally, amiss as a nation in not preparing ourselves, and if with the lessons taught the world by the dreadful tragedies of the last twelve months, we continue with soft complacency to stand helpless and naked before the world, we shall excite only contempt and derision when disaster ultimately overwhelms us."[14]

As early as 1915, following the sinking of the *Lusitania*, the mood in America had begun to change. Public opinion against Germany was further incited in early 1917 by acts of ostensible German espionage, and the infamous "Zimmermann Telegram." This message, intercepted by British code-breakers and released at a rather opportune moment for the Allies, suggested a Mexican, German, and even Japanese alliance against America. If their plan was successful, it implied the potential return of Texas, New Mexico, and Arizona to Mexico.

The newly appointed German foreign minister Arthur Zimmermann dispatched the telegram on January 16 to his Washington ambassador, Count Bernstorff, for the purpose of forwarding it to Heinrich von Eckardt, the German minister in Mexico City. The telegram stated in no uncertain terms that if the United States entered the war, Eckardt was authorized to offer Mexico an alliance in which the two countries would fight side by side, Germany providing financial aid and consenting to Mexico regaining the territory it had lost to the United States after the war of 1846–1848. Eckardt was also told to encourage the Mexican president, Venustiano Carranza, to invite Japan to change sides.

The document was transmitted in the German diplomatic code and by three different routes. The first means was via a wireless message sent directly from Germany to a receiving station on Long Island that the Americans had permitted to remain open. The second was via the "Swedish roundabout"—the Stockholm foreign ministry, which permitted German telegrams to be sent along its cable to its representatives in the Americas. The third method of transmitting was via the Americans' own diplomatic cable service between their Berlin embassy and the State Department, a special facility made available to the Germans by Wilson when he was trying to mediate, although it wasn't intended to be used for organizing a coalition against him. British naval intelligence in London successfully intercepted all three messages and had the means to decipher each one, thanks to a codebook they had managed to procure from the luggage of a German secret agent operating in Persia.

Wilson never doubted the veracity of the telegram, and decided to release the details to the press on March 1, 1917. He was outraged that the Germans had so openly flouted the use of a cable that he had specifically allocated to be at Berlin's disposal. The episode reinforced his growing conviction that the existing German rulers could not be trusted. The most important result of the telegram's publication was the media's almost zealous clamoring that a war with Germany should be declared as soon as possible. A psychological barrier had been spanned; the Zimmermann Telegram had reinforced the German security threat, making it almost palpable to all sections of American society.

There were disconcerting whispers at the time among congressmen that the telegram could have been concocted by the Allies to draw America into the war on their side, but these were dismissed when Zimmermann himself later admitted sending the damning communication. Moreover, for their part the Germans made no concerted attempts to dilute or deflect the situation. Soon after the telegram was published Germany committed a sequence of overt acts of provocation against the United States. On March 16, 1917, the American vessel *Vigilancia* was sunk without warning, and fifteen merchant seamen lost their lives. Other ships soon followed as German naval aggression persisted, and increased. Berlin and Washington were now heading for an unavoidable collision.

All of these elements combined contributed to increasing xenophobia and animosity toward Germans, along with a growing fervor among American citizens to get physically involved in the European war. Theodore Roosevelt was aware that a significant number of recent immigrants hailed from German backgrounds, but that didn't detract from his often pugnacious opinions in the slightest. Six years after leaving the presidency he was still a very influential force in American politics. He took a different view of the war in Europe. In a speech that he delivered in New York City on October 12, 1915, he made a scathing reference to the immigrant communities when he said: "There is not room in this country for hyphenated Americanism. Our allegiance must be purely to the United States. We must unsparingly condemn any man who holds any other allegiance."[15] It was an inimitable sideswipe at those who considered themselves German Americans, or anything else but pure American, by birth or decree.

The United States finally declared war on Germany on April 6, 1917. Immediately after this, measures were enacted that would directly affect—and afflict—German-speaking communities. One of the first acts was to seize all German-registered ships berthed in American ports. Domestic German-language newspapers printed in the United States were consequently shut down or lambasted so adversely that advertisers abandoned them and they were forced out of business. At that time there were no less than 522 different German-language newspapers in circulation in the United States. Schools that included German-language studies in their curriculum were compelled to remove these lessons completely.

Churches that had been founded as German-speaking or bilingual were told in no uncertain terms by the Methodist Synod to discontinue their German-language services forthwith. From April 16, 1917, on, all males older than the age of fourteen who were still "natives, citizens, denizens, or subjects" of the German Empire became regarded as "alien enemies." The ascendant tide of anger directed toward Germany was rising rapidly. When Congress declared war, there were over 2.8 million German-born people living in the United States. The Justice Department had actually been keeping many of them under surveillance since 1915. With the declaration of war, presidential proclamations were almost immediately targeted at "alien enemies," or Germans who had not yet completed the process of naturalization.

All bets were off, and it appeared that America was gearing up to go to war. Both French and British forces had experienced a punishing year in 1917: first, the failure of concerted French and British offensives on the Western Front, and second, the success of Germany's U-boat offensive. These predators of the seas torpedoed millions of tons of commercial shipping and incited great alarm in the British government. Then in October the Austrians inflicted a resounding defeat on the Italian Army at Caporetto, forcing a precipitate retreat that threatened to completely drive Italy out of the war. Writer Ernest Hemingway referred to this battle in his novel *A Farewell to Arms*, but didn't actually participate in it. When he heard the Red Cross was taking volunteers as ambulance drivers, he quickly signed up and was accepted in December of 1917. He was sent to an ambulance unit in the town of Schio, where he worked driving ambulances for the Italian Army. On July 8, 1918, only a few weeks after arriving, Hemingway was seriously wounded by fragments from an Austrian mortar shell.

In 1917 the Bolsheviks had seized power in Russia and immediately sought a separate peace with the Central Powers. The Allies understood the implications of this completely, and help couldn't come soon enough. After precisely 976 days of neutrality, on April 2, 1917, President Woodrow Wilson—the man who had been so vociferously opposed to joining the European war—addressed Congress, and asked for the very thing that he had gone to great lengths to avoid: a solid declaration of war against Germany:

*We have no selfish ends to serve. We desire no conquest, no dominion. We seek no indemnities for ourselves, no material compensation for the sacrifices we shall freely make. We are but one of the champions of the rights of mankind. We enter this war only where we are clearly forced into it, because there are no other means of defending our rights.*[16]

He went on to say:

*The world must be made safe for democracy. Its peace must be planted upon the tested foundations of political liberty. We shall be satisfied when those rights have been made as secure as the faith and the freedom of nations can make them.*

*Just because we fight without rancor and without selfish object, seeking nothing for ourselves but what we shall wish to share with all free peoples, we shall, I feel confident, conduct our operations as belligerents without passion and ourselves observe with proud punctilio the principles of right and of fair play we profess to be fighting for.*[17]

Only 56 of 531 congressmen and senators objected to the motion.

Soon after war had been officially declared, on April 6, 1917, French and British governments hurriedly dispatched delegations to the United States to coordinate assistance and offer practical advice on how best to organize American involvement. The only factor that unified the British and French apart from fighting a common enemy was the fact that America could, and would, make a substantial difference, eventually tipping the balance in favor of the Allied cause—but first the country had to effectively mobilize for war.

By the time America joined what President Wilson would famously describe as "the war to end all wars," forty-one declarations of war had been enacted. The American declaration of war was the forty-second in a row. In the course of World War I, more would follow, and countries such as Panama, Cuba, Guatemala, Nicaragua, Costa Rica, Haiti, and Honduras—countries that were in most cases politically or economically dependent on the United States—would be coerced into reviewing their neutrality. A neutral state could be regarded as a potential ally to the Central Powers, providing shelter for German submarines, which could take on fuel in their harbors. The war effort of these countries was generally regarded as dismissive, or, in most cases, merely symbolic. This was after all an unprecedented global conflict that would eventually entail no less than sixty-two declarations of war. This didn't include an additional five countries that severed all diplomatic relations with Germany.

## C. HAROLD FLOYD, 107TH INFANTRY REGIMENT, 27TH DIVISION

*War was declared in April, 1917, but it was July before the country was ready to use the National Guard. In the meantime, we of the Guard had worked incessantly to bring our organizations up to war strength and train the large number of new men who joined. In the 7th Regiment of New York, as in most of the regiments, the old, experienced men were dropping out every day to go to the Officers' Training Camp at Plattsburg. Sergeants, corporals, and privates went away, to come back in three months [to] visit us as commissioned officers, thereby making those who had not gone somewhat dissatisfied with their lot.*

*As first sergeant of Company I of the old 7th Regiment of New York, I spent practically the whole time in the Armory in New York City, getting out the paperwork, interviewing applicants for enlistment, and filling out the blanks for those accepted. Then came the President's Call on July 15, 1917, and we were mustered into Federal Service. Less than a month later, on August 5, the whole National Guard of the country was drafted, and we became federal soldiers without state affiliations. Everyone worked with a will to be recruits, to fill the few remaining vacancies, and at last, we were at full war strength, an old regiment, extremely proud of itself, proud of its record and anxious to add a new and glorious chapter to the long history. Then came an order to send six hundred men to the 69th Regiment to fill them to a new war strength. It was hard to part with those men. Many were in tears as they marched out of the Armory for the last time, leaving the regiment that some had served in for years, and all honestly believed to be the finest organization in any army. And this in spite of the great admiration we all had for the 69th.*

*Recruiting was much harder after that, but we redoubled our efforts and finally filled the gaps. The men reported early every day, drilled in the morning and afternoon in Central Park, and in the evening, except for a small guard, were excused and allowed to go home. In the meantime, the Up-State Regiments had moved to the city and gone into camp at Van Cortlandt Park. One day, the whole New York Division marched down Fifth Avenue in a great farewell parade, through a long line of observing relatives and friends. We had only two officers with us at the time, and I therefore commanded the 2nd half company and found it very tiresome, with the frequent necessity for halting or marking time, due to delays ahead. Nevertheless, it was a very impressive and inspiring event, and made you feel, if you never did before, that serving your country in wartime was the most really worthwhile thing a man could do. A short distance back of us was the Sanitary Detachment with doctors and stretcher-bearers. "Ah, here comes the sad part," said one sympathetic lady on the curb as she saw this detachment approaching. The sad ones were a bit uncertain whether they had been complimented or insulted.*[18]

The Great War incited a major upheaval in the US Army, which was compelled to reinvent itself, from a relatively negligible force of around 300,000 domestic active servicemen and reserves that fought small wars close to home, to a modern military fighting machine capable of dispatching literally millions of men across the precarious Atlantic Ocean to engage in a heavily mechanized, industrial, and, on occasion, strategically flawed conflict.

The challenges faced by US military authorities were staggering. The US Army had to recruit and train infantry soldiers and select competent instructing officers, along with instructing engineers and the medical troops required to support combat operations. Then there was the building of training camps, equipping these troops and transporting them overseas where they would finally confront the reality of fighting a war that had thwarted the best military minds throughout the previous three years.

## BEN ALLENDER, COMPANY G, 168TH INFANTRY DIVISION

*After about a month's drilling at the armory, on July 1, 1917, the company was ordered to encamp. July 1st was Sunday, so we did not go into camp until Monday. Sunday was spent in fixing us up with the odds and ends of uniforms and equipment, which the state had in reserve, which sure were keen. We met at the armory Monday morning, packing up all [the] things we received for camp, and we left immediately after dinner for Camp Andrew. This sure was an ideal place for a camp, located on a hill about three-quarters of a mile beyond the Crout Hill car line. We pitched our tents and were issued some cots, or those who were fortunate got one.*

*We were in the command of Captain Stellars and Lieutenant Nelson, with Phil Binks for our top soak. I was in a tent with eleven others, with Bill Veach as our "Corpal." The nights were exceedingly cold for July. We started to drill right away and kept busy from 5:30 a.m. until 6:30 p.m. While in this camp we received three shots in the arm for typhoid prevention. We also received a vaccination for smallpox.*

*We drilled very hard at Camp Andrews, and we soon looked like a real company [rather] than a bunch of rookies. We only had about 108 men at this camp, as there was not enough tents to accommodate the rest of the company. On July the 15th we were called into Federal Service and the balance of our company was called into service, stationed at the armory. We put on a guard mount with the 1st Cavalry band at the Country Club and it was great. Later we put on a guard mount at the camp and had an unusually large crowd. We took our final examination and were mustered into service by Captain Smith of Co. M, 1st Iowa, on July 25th. Only a few were turned down, and we had to discharge six men, as we were only allowed to carry 150 men, which was war strength at that time.*

*On August the 13th our regiment was selected as one of the four regiments of infantry for the Rainbow Division, which was supposed to be the pick of the National Guards. On August 15th we received orders to break camp and to be in Des Moines by Friday, August 17th. Immediately after breakfast Thursday morning we broke camp and started to packing. By noon everything was packed and ready for the trucks. On Friday morning August 17th at six o'clock we met at the armory. We were lined up and then assigned to our squad again. We then marched to the City Park where we had our picture taken by Chgo [officer in charge] Shaw. We then marched to the dip [and headed] by the home park of the 1st Cavalry band, the enlisted men having left on Wednesday noon before Grinnell.*

*November 30: There sure is a storm tonight. The waves are going clear up on the deck. Just a minute ago, one hit the hatch, and water went all the way through the ship. No doubt many of us will be feeding fish before morning. I have been lucky on both trips, as I have not been sick so far.*[19]

Many of the conscripts who were herded into the training camps were illiterate, and the vast majority had never even crossed their state lines, let alone been overseas. This wasn't unusual for the time, when it was possible to leave school at the age of ten. While access to formal education improved dramatically for most of the population of the United States during this time, there were still many who remained illiterate.

As the trains from the South brought the men into the camps during November 1917, it was observed by more than one military official that they were an incongruent collective of all sizes, ages, and colors. Many hailed directly from the cotton- and cornfields, or from the lumber and mining districts; more importantly, most of them had scant idea as to why they were being assembled, and many probably cared little about the reason. The officers who received them were often themselves fresh from the training camp. The task of making soldiers out of such raw material presented a gargantuan challenge to the military authorities, to say the least.

These raw recruits were immediately introduced to the rudiments of elementary army training, while the officers organized daily drill schedules and conducted lectures on the simple rules of better living and army sanitation. The officers of the 92nd Division were resolute in their determination to make fighting men out of this group—men capable of occupying a larger place in the community at the same time that they were making soldiers of them, fitted to fill the place in a modern fighting machine such as was being built by the United States Army.

Without exception the men showed that they were eager and willing to learn. Thorough military instruction soon removed the stoop from their spines and the shamble from their gait, as they drilled incessantly, along with learning to read and write their names. On the first payroll of one regiment of the 92nd Division, around 90 percent of the men were illiterate or semiliterate. Five months of night school gradually eradicated this deficiency and replaced it with smartness in drill, cleanliness in billets, discipline, a pride in the uniform, respect for the flag, and the ability to confidently sign their names to the payroll.

When that same division was on its return trip south to be mustered out of the service, Red Cross workers in two cities marveled at the improvement in the men's appearance, some even doubting that they were the same men who had passed these points going into the draft. Every single one of those same men provided a receipt in his own handwriting for his final pay, and many of them were even capable of correcting any clerical errors.

However, officers and NCOs tasked with the instruction and training of newly acquired conscripts noticed a certain reticence from some who proved less malleable than many army officials had hoped, contesting a whole host of army policies and practices while they served. The sheer number and the army's clear dependence on these new recruits forced many army officials to show a certain willingness to make notable concessions to their wartime force when formulating a host of manpower, leave, and punishment policies. Reformers within the higher echelons also played an important part by establishing an official process to acknowledge soldier's opinions in the policymaking process by urging the army to establish a more cooperative and less coercive relationship with its new recruits. Called into federal service on July 15, 1917, the 27th Division organized an intense recruiting drive to increase its numbers. John Joseph Brennan and his friend were among those who answered the call.

## John Joseph Brennan, Specialist, 102nd Engineer Train, 27th Division

*July 23, 1917: Harry Willard and I decided to join the army. We started thinking about it at suppertime and continued until bedtime. Woke up in the morning thinking about the same thing.*

*July 24, 1917: We are still thinking, so at 9:00 a.m. we went over to the Armory at Troop B on New Scotland Avenue, since they are recruiting over there for the 102nd. Engineers. Harry was examined first and then came my turn. Behind me was H. R. Mack, owner of the Packard Car Agency. After looking me over, [they said] I was in good shape and condition, but terribly skinny, and many pounds underweight. Captain Mohler said to Lieutenant Keens that at camp I would put on weight. I am wondering how he thinks a pick and shovel man will put on weight unless he is not going to work as very hard. They gave me a quart of water to drink and told me to sit around for a while and then come in and get weighed again. This time, although I didn't put on any more pounds or look any different, I was accepted. When I was weighed the first time, I was 128 pounds; the second time I weighed 135 pounds. This is just the first day.*

*July 25–August 24, 1917: From the above dates, all we did was drill, and my, what wonderful long walks they would take us on around Albany. From early morning till night, that is all we would do, and we think it is terrible. I suppose later on when we are told to do something else and look back to these days we will say that we are never satisfied. For the past couple of weeks I have done more walking than I ever did in all [my] lifetime. I think I have seen more of Albany than I ever did. We got our uniforms today and [noticed] that a lot of us look alike in them.*

*July 1917: We are just a group of young boys, average age between twenty and twenty-four years old, just starting manhood. In civilian life you don't have as many bosses as you have in the army; neither do you have to salute as many people. To [us] that change is not hard; all you do is accept it. While in Albany we did an awful lot of walking and marching—supposed to limber us up. The people in our hometown were wonderful to us.*

*August 27, 1917: Yesterday and the days past were just another part of our past life. This morning we are in another city [New York City]; you might say an advanced step. From the morning that we arrived in New York City, until yesterday when we left it behind, we certainly did enjoy ourselves. The people were so good to us and showed such respect for both the man and the uniform. The day before we left New York City, Loft Candy Firm gave all of us a box of candy. The time in the city was so amusing to us. The trains underground, the trains overhead, the trolley cars, the buses, the tunnels under the rivers—all were exciting to us.*

*September 13, 1917: Arriving and being in Camp Wadsworth, Spartanburg, South Carolina, was the big change. That's where we became disciplined soldiers. Up until then we didn't take our officers seriously, e.g., the trouble with the officers in New York City. We never knew such times existed in our country as we saw here. A colored person steps off the sidewalk to let a white person pass, separate entrances on all railroad stations, public buildings and so forth. The poor people, white or black, live mostly on grits, okra, and yellow cornmeal. While in Spartanburg we had our fun time, but we did a lot of hard work and drilling, digging ditches, building roads, cutting down trees, and all other kinds of hard work. You don't complain, you just do as you are told. Yesterday we were in South Carolina, today Camp Stewart, port of debarkation, nearing the time to become fighting men.*[20]

President Wilson had briefed his chosen American Expeditionary Forces (AEF) commander, Gen. John J. "Black Jack" Pershing, on the importance of retaining complete autonomy for the American forces who were earmarked to go to Europe. Pershing was a West Point graduate and a career soldier who had a certain propensity for directness that endeared him greatly to President Wilson. Both men agreed that the preservation of independence in the field would put America in a better position once victory or peace had been achieved.

Ignorant of this instruction, British lieutenant general Sir George Tom Molesworth Bridges proposed the rapid mobilization of 500,000 Americans to ship to England, where they would be trained, equipped, and incorporated into the British Army. This proposal would be the first of many schemes that would attempt to integrate American battalions and regiments into one or other of the Allied armies.

As early as June 14, 1917, Pershing arrived in Paris to command the AEF. By November of 1917, only 77,000 Americans had physically reached France, and the initial euphoria that had greeted the first arrival of the "doughboys" in the summer of 1917 began to disintegrate. (There are many theories on the origins of the name "doughboys." Some historians claim that doughboys were named such because of their method of cooking their rations. Meals were often doughy flour and rice concoctions either baked in the ashes of a camp fire or shaped around a bayonet and cooked over the flames.) This caused some consternation among the high commands of the respective Allied forces, despite the fact that the AEF achieved a faster buildup of forces than both Britain and France had between 1914 and 1916.

The amassing of men and supplies for the AEF was largely achieved because during the period of neutrality, Allied arms contracts had expanded American munitions capacity, and the Council of National Defense, created by the 1916 National Defense Act, had already drawn up an industrial mobilization plan. American zeal for volunteering wasn't initially as fervent as had been experienced in Britain during the early stages of the war, but it soon gathered steam.

President Wilson had noted the British experience regarding hostility to conscription. To counter a possible similar reaction in the United States, he passed the Selective Service Act that came into effect in May 1917. By April 1917 the US army numbered only 5,792 officers and 121,797 men. There were a further 181,610 men in National Guard units. C. Harold Floyd was one such National Guardsman. His story captures the zeitgeist of many young Americans at the time.

## C. HAROLD FLOYD, 107TH INFANTRY REGIMENT, 27TH DIVISION

*On September 11, after weeks of drilling and waiting, we marched down the avenue again, but this time not to return until the Great War was over. We boarded Pullmans and tourist sleepers at Jersey City and started on the long ride to the training camp in South Carolina. It was a long, tiresome journey, but with so many men together, something amusing was going [on] every minute—principally card games and the telling of thrilling tales, which began with "When I was on the border . . ."*

*For once in my experience as an enlisted man, I was better off than the junior officers, [and] many non-coms. I took possession of the stateroom in the* company's car, while the lieutenants occupied uppers in the officers' car. It was a great pleasure to see the envious way in which they looked in the door as they passed by on inspection trips and to listen to their stories of discomforts when they stopped in to chat for a while.

After traveling for two days we came to Spartanburg, South Carolina, and detrained in a field a few miles beyond the station. The regiment was formed and we hiked over to what was to be our section of Camp Wadsworth. It was still very hot, and the men from the North felt very uncomfortable in their thick clothes and heavy packs, but the fields of cotton, the little cabins, and the queer Southern darkies working on the camp construction took all their attention.

When we reached our section, we found fine large mess shacks at the head of each company street and good shower baths at the foot, but in between was a grove of small trees and underbrush. At least, that was the experience of the companies of the Third Battalion. Some of the other companies were more fortunate and drew open land. Some were less fortunate and drew a hollow, which in wet weather became a watercourse. We set to work with a will and soon had a place cleared for the tents and the company street, leaving two rows of trees on each side for shade. It made a very attractive little street, and we were rather proud of it after we had seen some of the others.

In a very few days we were settled and the regular military routine was running like clockwork. All around us were the other regiments of the 27th Division. At retreat, we could hear a great chorus of bugles fading away into the distance in every direction. So confusing were all these bugles that we frequently obeyed the wrong one. It was very discouraging to roll out of bed at an unearthly hour in the morning and dress in a great rush and then find that you had gotten up with the next regiment, whose watches were ten minutes fast.

One night, shortly after midnight, we were startled by fire call. It was the first time many of the men had heard it, but by no means the last. Everyone fell in, though most of them did not know exactly what they ought to do, and some had to be stopped, as they were dashing out of the street in true civilian fire-alarm style. However, we were soon awaiting orders in column of squads at the head of the street, each squad carrying its water bucket and every man in place. It was a sorry-looking crowd; most of the men were half awake and in every conceivable garb, from a barefooted private in BVDs to another fully dressed and with a large part of his equipment on. And then it turned out to be a tent fire in another regiment, so there was nothing to do but crawl back into our blankets.

Camp Wadsworth was about four miles from the small city of Spartanburg, and thither the doughboy went whenever he could get off. Wednesday and Saturday afternoons and all of Sunday were holidays, and on those days the camp was deserted and Spartanburg correspondingly filled with soldiers. It was an attractive little city, and its inhabitants showed the greatest hospitality to the soldiers from the North. We were immediately welcomed everywhere, invited to dine and made to feel at home. When we were still new and without friends in Spartanburg, it was not at all unusual to be stopped on the street by some lady or gentleman whom we had never seen before and urged to come home for dinner. It never required much urging, and friendships thus made continued during the time we were at the camp. As a result one of our sergeants was soon engaged, and several other men became objects of suspicion.

The great trouble with Spartanburg was the difficulty in getting there from camp. Many went by the F & N, a cross between a railroad and a trolley line, which came within about a mile and a quarter of camp. Most, however, preferred the taxi; at a quarter a head, and as the crowd at the beginning and end of the holiday was far in excess of the taxi accommodations, it required strength, skill, and diplomacy to get a seat, and then you could always count on having at least one man on your lap.

Regimental orders allowed us to be away afternoons and evenings of holidays, but required us to be present at retreat at 4:30 p.m. The result was that just before retreat, a line of taxis would dash up to the head of the street, quickly disgorge as many khaki-clad figures as could be squeezed into them, who would rush to their places in line, answer "Here," or, more likely, "Yeow," and, five minutes later, tumble into the same taxis for the return trip to town.

But life was not all pleasure, by any means. Drills went on day in and day out—close-order drills, bayonet training, the throwing of grenades, gas defense instructions, and the various formations evolved during this war. Every day lines of men stood in the company street and signaled back and forth with semaphore and wig-wag flags. My tent was equipped with a buzzer, connected with the captain's tent in one direction and the Third and Fourth Platoon sergeants' tent in the other. We sometimes found that in trying to say *uncomplimentary things to each other, we had called up the captain by mistake. He was a good sport, however, and always signaled back that he was unable to read the message, whereupon it would be repeated in a very different form.*

*In October the 27th Division was reorganized. Men were transferred from one regiment to another to bring companies from a maximum of 150 to 250 men, and the organizations were renumbered. We became the 107th US Infantry, and to increase our size to the required strength, nearly all of the men and many of the officers of the First New York Infantry were transferred to us. The First was a fine old regiment with a long and honorable history, of which its members were extremely proud. To be broken up and transferred to a strange regiment was very discouraging, and the men of the First came to us with very bitter feelings. Later other regiments were broken up and more men came to us, until the men of the old Seventh were far outnumbered by the new arrivals.*

*Seventh men also began to feel that they were in a strange organization, although in reality it was the same regiment. Before the transfers took effect, the Seventh went out on the drill ground and had a farewell parade and review, the last parade under our old name. Then we prepared to give the new men a rousing welcome. When they arrived they marched by a cheering throng of Seventh men, and that night we gave them a special dinner. They were a splendid body of men from the large towns of Upstate New York and from the country districts, but it was a long time before the different groups were entirely amalgamated, and training was delayed in consequence.*

*In the various companies, men of all types and all classes lived together on the most intimate terms, and it did them all no end of good. They learned to know and appreciate each other and chum together in a way that would have been impossible in any other place than the army. One young private of wealthy parents served in the same company with another who had been a gardener for his family.*

*In place of Captain Hayes who had commanded old I Company for several years in the Armory and on the border, and made it the best-drilled company in the Regiment, we now had Captain Egan from the First New York. He was a big, good-natured man with an excellent knowledge of the game, and what counted very much with us, a habit of looking after his men's welfare.*

*We were soon organized as Company I of the 107th Infantry, and then training for France began in deadly earnest. An English sergeant major gave instruction in the setting-up exercises used in the British Army—physical jerks, the men called them—and for strict discipline and quick thinking, they were the best training we ever had. In the middle of some exercise, Sergeant Major Tector would snap out the command, "Get off the earth!" The whole class would make a wild dash for trees, tents, boxes, or anything else that would hold their bodies free of the ground. They fairly tumbled over each other to get there, too, because the last man was very likely to be sent running at full speed to the head of the street and back while the others rested. Some man at a distance would laugh at the performance, whereupon the class would be ordered to go get him. By the time he had been hauled and dragged back by a whole platoon, he was through laughing at the physical jerks forever after. The men enjoyed the work, especially the ready wit of the sergeant major and the sarcastic remarks with which he called attention to the slackers and lazy ones. As a result of this, and of the fear of having to do a special stunt because of being behind in obeying a sudden, unexpected command, the men were keenly alert every second, and therefore all got the fullest possible benefit from the exercises. They were a great contrast to the old Regular Army drill in which most of the men were half asleep while they mechanically waved their arms and legs about.*

*We also had tours of duty in practice trenches, built like those in France. These trenches were very realistic. There was a front line, support line, and reserve line, with numerous connecting trenches, deep dugouts and shallow dugouts, listening posts, and gas alarms. We entered at night, walking for what seemed like miles up one trench, down another, winding about until all idea of direction and position was lost to everyone but the guides and officers who had been there before. Nothing in sight but red earth all around, and a long, narrow streak of dark sky overhead. Each platoon was led to its position and took over from the platoon, which had been holding that part of the line.*

*Then began long hours of watchfulness; inspecting officers were everywhere in the darkness, trying to catch a sentry off his guard. One listening post, way out in No Man's Land, was surprised, and its garrison of two men captured and marched away by inspectors, without the front line immediately behind being any the wiser. Then there were gas officers walking about with real gas bombs, which they threw in among any unsuspecting groups found in a trench. If you were caught unprepared, it was guaranteed to nauseate even the hardened soldier. The trenches were knee-deep with a soft pudding-like mud, and Oh! So cold. Everyone was soaked and shivering. I slept most of the night sitting on a fire step with my feet in six inches of water.*

*Company I never gives up, even in practice, so we stuck it out. At the prearranged hour we marched out, so coated in red mud from head to foot that every regiment whose camp we passed on the trip home turned out in force to watch us go by and make numerous remarks on our appearance. But we were proud of ourselves nevertheless, [and] we were soon ready for the next adventure. On two occasions we marched twenty-four miles to the rifle range at Eagle Rock up in the mountains of South Carolina. In this beautiful little spot we shot at a long line of targets, at first close up, and then at greater distances, until the bull's-eye appeared a mere speck across the field. Some made wonderful scores, some would prefer to have their scores forgotten, but the great majority qualified as marksmen or better. On the last trip to the range we went over the top following a very real barrage sent over by our own artillery. As Christmas approached, it took the whole force of kitchen police to prepare the feast. The mess shack was decked in holly and anything else the woods afforded, as were also the tents.*

*Late in the evening of the night before Christmas, I heard music just outside my tent. Three Italian members of the company and one American, with a banjo and mandolin and four good voices, were serenading us with "Stille Nacht, Heilige Nacht [Silent Night]."*

*We called them in, and for the next hour, sang every song we knew and many that we did not. Christmas, itself, was a great success. About half the men had boxes from home filled with eatables, warm clothing, and many things useful and otherwise. The other half shared in everything. Then a three-course dinner, with army food conspicuous by its absence. Many of the men were allowed to go home for Christmas, and many more for New Year's. This was a great boon, for ordinarily a furlough for home was only give for exceptional reasons, such as sickness or death in the family, or to get married. No one got married more than once, but the mortality in the soldiers' families reached tremendous proportions as the months wore on, until the police up in New York State were requested to investigate some of the cases. A few mothers and sisters were quite shocked to learn that they were desperately ill, when they thought themselves quite well.*

*During the winter months, some of the men bought lumber and boarded in the sides of their tents to keep out the cold. I constructed a very comfortable little chateau, having a door with a window in it, a long shelf along one side for a desk, and a real stove bought in Spartanburg and paid for by a subscription taken up among the three residents of the tent. Still, the canvas roof let in cold air faster than the stove could take care of it, and we had a hard time on the cold nights. The good people of Spartanburg assured us that never before had they seen such cold weather, and we answered that we never had either. The officers built small houses the shape of a tent and laid out paths in front of them, making a very attractive little settlement.*

*Back of the officers' quarters we built an auditorium large enough to hold the whole regiment, the lumber being given by a friend. For a long time we were undecided whether to call this the Chapel, the Movie Theatre, or the Entertainment Hall. We finally compromised on Regimental Building, and it became the gathering place for those who liked to read, write love letters, or escape details. Movies and other entertainments amused the men in the evenings.*[21]

In an attempt to maintain the war economy, Congress delegated the categories of those regarded as working in "reserved occupations" vital to the war effort, such as agricultural and industrial workers, granting them deferments for the duration. Further exemptions were not statutory but were often made by recruiting boards and offices for most married men, along with those who had dependents. Conscientious objection, which had proven to be a passport to social exclusion and heavy punishment in the United Kingdom, was permitted with impunity in the United States. Exemption on religious grounds, and later, on secular grounds, was allowed. In those first few months a total of 2,738,000 men were inducted, and consequently, the army had no shortage of soldiers. What it didn't have was sufficient armaments and troop transport ships. Moreover, many of the ad hoc training camps were often not fit for their purpose when the recruits arrived.

## George E. Leach, 151st Artillery, 42nd Rainbow Division

*September 4, 1917: Broke camp at Fort Snelling at 2:00 p.m. and marched down the same road with the regiment that my father marched down with his to the Civil War, and at 6:30 entrained on our first leg of the journey to France. The regiment was carried in two sections.*

*September 5, 1917: En route all day with no events to record, except we received tremendous ovations in every town we passed through. Took the regiment out at Gary, Indiana, at 7:30 for exercise.*

*September 8, 1917: Arrived at Camp Mills, Garden City, at daylight in the rain. Called immediately on General Summerall, who is in command of the 67th F. A. Artillery Brigade. We are attached to the 42nd [Rainbow] Division.*

*September 9, 1917: The Second Battalion arrived from Fort Riley this a.m., and my regiment is now completely assembled, the Second Battalion having been at Fort Riley as a school battalion for the officers' training camp.*

*September 15, 1917: Received a twenty-four-hour pass this morning to go to New York and closed up some of my business. The regiment occupied with making camp.*[22]

The federal government attempted to manage the war economy without resorting to nationalization or to compulsory influences. It decided to respect the Allies' existing war contracts, so that orders for the AEF would be considered as additional to these. Accordingly, most of the AEF's weaponry was supplied by Allied industries. The US Army purchased almost ten million tons of supplies and equipment in Europe during the war, while only seven million tons were actually provided by the United States.

The external purchase of airplanes and field guns from France and Britain may have initially alleviated the pressure on America's war economy, but the War Department went into overdrive by going on a veritable spending spree.

## HILLIE JOHN FRANZ, COMPANY L, 34TH INFANTRY REGIMENT, 7TH DIVISION

*This 27th day of May 1918, myself and lots of others were sent to Marlin, Texas, the county seat of Falls Co., Texas. Here we spent the night in a hotel, and what a night it was—very little sleep, but a good and noisy night. We did mostly everything we were big enough to do, as we were now protected by the US government. The morning of May 28 we boarded a train for Camp Travis, San Antonio, Texas. On arriving there we were placed in quarantine in a recruit camp for three weeks. Here we learned that we didn't know hardly anything. We were taught how to keep in step or make right or left face. While we were drilled this way, we all took all kinds of shots and exams and tests for this and that. And some would really make us sick.*

*After being here almost three weeks, as we were having lunch one day at noon in a large mess hall, [in walked] a captain or major or some officer, as we didn't know his rank at this time. As he entered someone called out "Attention!" and each of us jumped to attention, as there were several hundred of us in this mess hall. And this officer spoke, asking if there were some that would like to go to Europe and get into the war over there, as they needed several hundred soldiers to fulfill the 7th Division, which was a regular army division, and was not up to standard in the amount of men, and all that would like to go to raise their hands. So you may know [that] I, for one, held my hand high. Of course I didn't realize what I was fitting myself in for.*

*Anyway, those of us that raised our hands were placed in a group and taken to someplace in camp, and here they got all our records and a lot of questions were asked and answered, and so on. Firstly we were placed here and there in different numbers. As for myself, I was placed in Co. L, 34th Regiment, 7th Division. When all this was completed, the 7th Division was sent to Camp MacArthur at Waco, Texas. Again we were all placed in quarantine, and those of us that hadn't got all of our shots and vaccinations got them, as we stayed another three weeks here. [We] would [get] shots and vaccines and at times the boys would fall out on the ground like flies after taking a shot, before they could get to their bunks, and [they] had to be carried in by others. It was real sad at times, and some of the old-timers that have been in the army for twenty-seven years laughed at us and bawled us out for being chicken, and would say you are now in the army. This went on for three weeks, [and] then we boarded a train for Camp Merritt, New Jersey. This was about the 27th day of July. This was a pleasant trip. Arrived at Camp Merritt, we drilled some and did most everything you could think of to get us hardened. On about the 17th day of August, we moved to Hoboken, New Jersey, ready to leave for France.*[23]

Congress stalled over introducing tax increases to compensate for the spending spree, but authorized Wilson's son-in-law, William Gibbs McAdoo Jr., to launch a $2 billion bond issue, the first of the "Liberty Loans," at a low, tax-free interest rate. When the United States entered World War I in 1917, it became immediately evident that an unprecedented effort would be required to divert the nation's industrial capacity away from meeting consumer demand and toward fulfilling the needs of the military. At the time of the congressional declaration of war, the American economy was operating at full capacity, so the requirements of the war effort could not be met by putting underutilized resources to work. The wartime population would have to sacrifice to pay the bill, and McAdoo understood this completely. Shortly after war had been declared, he delivered a speech that he later recorded for posterity: "We must be willing to give up something of personal convenience, something of personal comfort, something of our treasure—all, if necessary, and our lives in the bargain—to support our noble sons who go out to die for us."[24]

McAdoo found it easiest to cover his costs through borrowing, the low interest enabling him to contain the burden of debt service. To actually sell these bonds, even though banks rather than individuals were the main purchasers, he needed to mobilize and motivate the public. The authorities initially hoped to rely on basic patriotism, but the public was slow to respond. It was going to take a surprising degree of coercion and manipulation to motivate a society whose very cohesion had been regarded as questionable due to the substantial immigrant arrivals of recent decades.

Wilson fully appreciated and understood the need to persuade the public to support his scheme to raise funds. On the basis of this understanding, he created the Committee on Public Information (CPI) to promote the war domestically while publicizing American war aims abroad.

He further enlisted the help of an investigative journalist and writer named George Creel to lead the CPI. A devoted supporter of President Wilson, Creel had initially written an entire book in defense of Wilson's decision to avoid entering World War I. Now it was time to change tack, and Creel was charged with selling what was essentially America's first ideological war to the public. Although many historians have lambasted him over the years, he was the right man at the right time. Creel understood the power of the written word and how to manipulate the available mass media of the time. He was a skillful operator, and Wilson had made a wise choice in recruiting him for the job. Although Creel and the CPI would later be heavily criticized by journalists for releasing exaggerated accounts of events, and for hiding bad or unflattering news about the war by censoring the press, the overall public response to CPI-inspired publications and newsreels was favorable.

The CPI was innovative in the way it effectively merged advertising techniques with a sophisticated understanding of basic human psychology. Multilingual brochures and advertisements were published to persuade the American public to get behind the war effort. This was the first time a modern government had disseminated propaganda on such a vast scale. Creel knew precisely what he was doing, and he knew how to influence public opinion. The committee published the reasons why America had chosen to participate in the Great War, and used newsprint, posters, radio, the telegraph, cable, and movies to broadcast its message for public consumption.

The CPI played a number of roles for the American government during the war, including serving as an erstwhile propaganda ministry and establishing a model for extensive media consumption that would later influence the propaganda methods of infamous Nazi Joseph Goebbels. Creel rejected the claim that the CPI was a means to circulate propaganda when he wrote about the committee's rejection of the very term: "We did not call it propaganda, for that word, in German hands, had come to be associated with deceit and corruption. Our effort was educational and informative throughout, for we had such confidence in our case as to feel that no other argument was needed than the simple, straightforward presentation of facts."[25]

Further draconian measures to prevent media criticism of Wilson and the CPI's drive to mobilize the public were not always welcomed by other politicians. In 1917, Senator Robert La Follette from Wisconsin had quipped: "The purpose of this ridiculous campaign is to throw the country into a state of sheer terror, to change public opinion, to stifle criticism, and suppress discussion. People are being unlawfully arrested, thrown into jail, held incommunicado for days, only to be eventually discharged without ever having been taken into court, because they have committed no crime. But more than this, if every preparation for war can be made the excuse for destroying free speech and a free press and the right of the people to assemble together for peaceful discussion, then we may well despair of ever again finding ourselves for a long period in a state of peace. The destruction of rights now occurring will be pointed to then as precedents for a still further invasion of the rights of the citizen."[26]

With the war effort now gathering momentum Wilson summoned Gen. "Black Jack" Pershing to his office to discuss the forthcoming role of the AEF. The emphasis was to be complete independence for the American forces in Europe; they would neither be requisitioned nor divided among the other Allied armies on the Western Front.

John Joseph Pershing was born on September 13, 1860, on a farm near Laclede, Missouri. He began his career as a teacher, but later passed an entrance examination for West Point. Although he had no designs on forging a military career, he liked the idea of getting a West Point education. He had been an exemplary cadet, and even a member of the West Point Honor Guard that escorted the funeral procession of President Ulysses S. Grant. After graduation, Pershing served in the 6th Cavalry in a number of minor military engagements against the Sioux and Apache, led by Geronimo. In the Spanish-American War he commanded the all-black 10th Cavalry, and was later awarded the Silver Star. After the defeat of Spain, from 1899 to 1903 he was stationed in the Philippines. By this time, Pershing had earned the nickname "Black Jack" for his service with the African-American 10th Cavalry as they led the charge in the battle at San Juan Hill, but the name also came to signify his harsh demeanor and rigorous implementation of military discipline. Tragedy struck in late

1913 when his wife and all three daughters died in a fire; only his six-year-old son, Warren, survived. Pershing was devastated by the loss, and those who knew him said he never fully recovered. He distracted himself by becoming immersed in his work.

On March 9, 1916, Mexican revolutionary Pancho Villa and his men raided the border town of Columbus, New Mexico, killing eighteen American soldiers and civilians. In response, President Woodrow Wilson ordered Pershing to capture Villa. The expedition to achieve this objective began on March 15, 1916. Several skirmishes occurred, but the US Army never physically apprehended Villa. President Wilson became overly concerned about the situation and worried that it might provoke a war, so he ordered Pershing to stop the expedition. Consequently, the troops were recalled to their barracks between January and February 1917. A close ally and supporter of Woodrow Wilson's presidency, Pershing was a natural choice to lead the proposed AEF.

The General Organization Plan of the AEF was an essential part of Pershing's strategy to build and train an independent American army in France. He rejected French and British demands to amalgamate his troops into their depleted armies, and insisted on forming an independent American army before committing any US troops to the front lines. Wilson therefore gave Pershing a written order before his departure for Europe, forbidding him from amalgamating American forces. Pershing stubbornly maintained the stance that American forces would only fight under a completely American chain of command on a distinctly American section of the Western Front. There would be exceptions, and these would include the African-American divisions being dispatched to France. In a secret communiqué of August 7, 1918, concerning African-American troops sent to the French military stationed with the American Army, Pershing stated: "We must not eat with them, must not shake hands with them, seek to talk to them, or to meet with them outside the requirements of military service. We must not commend too highly these troops, especially in front of white Americans." Despite the tone of this message, it is difficult to categorize Pershing as either a racist or an egalitarian. He was a complex and often contradictory individual who changed his ideas on race at different times to suit his own purposes.

CHAPTER TWO

# The American Expeditionary Force

IMAGINE A WORLD WITH NO COMPUTERS, NO CELL PHONES, VERY FEW household appliances, no TV, and none of the other technological luxuries we enjoy these days. This was America in 1917, when America's working classes flocked to see silent movies, the year that Charlie Chaplin's best films were released, *East Street* and *The Immigrants*. Mary Pickford was known as "America's sweetheart," and jazz was becoming increasingly popular. In February of that year, the Original Dixieland Jazz Band cut their first record using two of their own tunes, "Livery Stable Stomp" and "Jazz Band One-Step." The spread of jazz from New Orleans was accelerated in November 1917 when US armed forces closed down Storyville, the notorious red-light district, because of disturbances between sailors and civilians. The jazzmen began to drift north, and found plenty of clubs anxious to cash in on their authentic New Orleans sound.

It was a time when poverty was rampant and medical care was almost nonexistent. One baby out of ten died during his or her first year of life. There were thousands of immigrants arriving daily, and roughly 14 percent of the US population was foreign-born. A century before, most jobs required little formal schooling, and most of the population had not gone beyond elementary or grammar school. High school graduates were a rarity; only an estimated 18 percent of the population above the age of twenty-five had completed high school. Average unemployment was at around 9.7 percent, and according to contemporary economic predictions, a recession was looming.

This was America in 1917, the year that it began to mobilize for active participation in a European war. Within a very short time almost all of the country's resources had been directed toward supporting the war effort. The persistent message that permeated all levels of society was as essential to victory as the action on the front lines. To this end, the United States government refused to tolerate any form of dissent or sedition. They introduced strict censorship controls on newspapers, and letters to and from servicemen. They also cracked down on groups believed to be intolerant or reluctant to support the national war effort. Progressive thinkers were convinced beyond a doubt that the war would contribute to a stronger sense of unity in the nation, and in this assumption they were on the mark. Hierarchical social contradictions would disappear and be replaced by fervent patriotism and service to one's beloved country. In a further effort to promote the American war industry, the War Industries Board was established. Although this was lacking significantly in organization, it enhanced closer cooperation between the big industrialists and the government. On August 5, 1917, the Engineer Train was mustered into federal service by Major Townsend, USA, at Troop B Armory, New Scotland Avenue.

## JOHN JOSEPH BRENNAN, SPECIALIST, 102ND ENGINEER TRAIN, 27TH DIVISION

*Some of us have coats large enough to carry the family washing home; the pants, especially the seats, are big enough for a couple of bread baskets to hide away in. The hats are dandy, big enough that we won't need any ear mufflers with them during the winter. The tailor who made these uniforms must have been paid for them by the yard, or else he thought this war was going to be fought by our grandfathers.*

*August 25, 1917: Received unexpected orders at the Amway [Troop B Shed, New Scotland Avenue] to move as soon as possible to New York City Armory at the corner of 99th Street and Park Avenue.*

*August 26, 1917, Sunday morning: Went to Mass and received Holy Communion and then ate breakfast. Will never forget how hard it was for me to say good-bye to my sister, Mary. Mama was down to Uncle Patrick's in*

Great Neck, Long Island, since she was sick. I stood on the steps of the front porch fully fifteen minutes before I got nerve enough to say good-bye and be on my way. At the Armory in the morning, P. N. Bouton, Miss Shaw, Mr. and Mrs. Campbell, and my sister came over to see me and to say good-bye. In the afternoon we had a wonderful farewell parade. Saw quite a few of my friends and said "So long." Somehow, for some reason or other, this parade gives me a different feeling than any other parade that I was in. There were great crowds out to see the parade, and everywhere we got great cheering. Ate supper and was kept quite busy on detail after the parade, and also with visitors. We left the Troop Shed about 9:30 p.m. for the railroad station. Talk about the feeling in the parade in the afternoon, this one has everyone stopped! Not a band or any kind of music at all. Just everybody along the curb hollering good-bye and sweet pappa, what a lot of pretty girls offering us a kiss, or plenty of them. I haven't seen anybody in line that had to be offered the same kiss twice. It if weren't for the rooters, this walk to the station would be next to marching at your own funeral.

At the railroad station yard it was one wild time. You would think that we were the missing link, the way everyone was looking for one of us. The sounding of the bells and the engine whistles and horns sure was some noise. Well, this grand old farewell that we are getting is about to come to an end. It is now about 12:15 a.m. and they are shouting "All aboard." Our feet and not more than one hand is on the train and the rest of us is either shaking hands with a boy friend or kissing a girl friend. The doors are closing and the train is heading for the bridge across the river. Good-bye, old Albany.

August 27, 1917: Arrived in New York City at 5:30 a.m. All during the night there was plenty of fun on the train. No time for sleep until about 4:30 a.m., and then at 5:30 a.m. was the first time that we got acquainted with "All out." Well, we sure do get plenty of handouts in the line of eating. To look around and see the women and children and elderly men coming over to give us some coffee and eats makes us wonder, where they all came from so early in the morning, and how they got the news that we were going to be hungry. After getting our eats we had to scramble together and get ready to go to the Armory at 94th. Street. We walked a short distance from the railroad station to the trolley cars and rode the rest of the distance.

As the war effort gathered momentum, industrialists and farmers bene-fited considerably from the imposed national homogenization, but it also contained significant obstacles. All potential dissenters and those vocifer-ously opposed to the war effort were treated with great suspicion by local and governmental authorities at large. This resulted in the dissemination of endemic, rampant fear of espionage and subversion throughout the nation. Everything that was deemed politically radical was considered potentially seditious by the authorities.

It became quite apparent early on that the organizing, training, and shipping of fresh US divisions to Europe was a costly and time-consuming operation. Paradoxically, up until 1917, the greatest American contribution to the war had been in the provision of materials and finan-cial arrangements with the Allied powers, but when it came to equipping its own troops, the United States fell short of expectations.

## C. HAROLD FLOYD, 107TH INFANTRY REGIMENT, 27TH DIVISION

*At last, after months of training for France and the battle line, we had reached our first objective. When we would reach the second was uncertain. For the present we had fairly comfortable quarters, as Brest's soldier population had not yet overgrown the available space. The Pontanezen Barracks was rather picturesque: a great bare parade ground, along one side of which was a row of ancient barracks formerly used by the French garrison, all vacant spots, except the parade ground, being covered with American pyramidal tents. The old French mansion of the camp commander was now an American military office building. All was surrounded by a ten-foot stone wall that even an American soldier could not climb, much to his disgust.*

*We were assigned to a row of tents where I placed my men, drew rations, a cook stove, and some wood, appointed an acting mess sergeant and two cooks, and they were settled. Then I found the tent in which I was to live, near the office building, and had a detail set up the French bed with which it was equipped: three planks resting at the end on iron stands that locked like old-fashioned towel racks. The second night I unpacked my army canvas-covered cot and had the French antique removed.*

*We remained at Brest three days and then started for the interior. Our bat-talion was now reduced to three companies, under Burtis as senior officer. The day before we left, I was saddled with the unpleasant job of battalion supply officer. Taking a detail of about a squad, I went into town to a big storehouse, run by the American Quartermaster Department, and drew three days' rations for each man in the battalion. Piles of canned beef, jam, bread, and canned fruit were laid out in front of us while I studied ration tables, figured how much I ought to get, counted boxes and cans, and signed receipts.*

*Our orders were to pile all these supplies beside the track where the train was to be on the following morning and leave a guard over them. We put everything on a truck and started for the aforesaid track. We visited more tracks than a city of that size was entitled to, but apparently no one in or out of the army knew anything about the proper one. Anyway, we had a pleasant ride, and I finally unloaded beside another similar pile of rations, belonging to another outfit, which was to leave at the same time with us, and presumably on the same train.*

*Very early the next morning, before dawn, in fact, we assembled our three little companies, had breakfast, and soon after daybreak, marched through the back gate in the great wall surrounding the barracks, and down to the station. As we passed through Brest, old Frenchmen waved at us. There were no young men at home, and women rushed out and shouted and tried to illustrate by savage gestures how we should treat the Hun when we got to him. They were poor women of the lower classes and they worked themselves into a frenzy, cursing the hated Boche, and trying to instill a like feeling in our men, who smiled back sympathetically.*

*At the station we found a long train of little boxcars waiting for us, a few third-class passenger cars on the rear end. Up forward was another passenger car for the officers. The men were very much amused at these little cars, which were like toys compared with the ones to which they were accustomed. On each boxcar was painted "8 chevaux, 40 hommes" (8 horses, 40 men), its capacity for military transport. The train was soon boarded, the rations were divided, [so] that each car had an equal amount, and we started.*

*My men, who had the few passenger coaches on the end, were intensely interested in the strange country, the little stone houses, great windmills of the type we call Dutch, and long lines of tall poplars along the roads. They wondered at the quaint old women in white caps and wooden shoes and the old men with their baggy trousers. We traveled all day and all the succeeding* night, arriving early in the morning at Tours, where a long stop was made. Then on through the picturesque countryside with its many châteaux, to the little city of Saint-Aignan on the River Cher.

Here we detrained and guides led us to the Classification Camp, the great clearinghouse from which replacements and casuals were distributed to the different units in all parts of France. As we marched on to the great bare field with its crowds of men and rows of unsightly wooden shacks, I prayed inwardly that our stop here might be short. But our orders in American had been to rejoin our regiment at the port of debarkation, and they had ignored those and sent us way down here. Apparently the orders from one headquarters were worthless in another, and we began to have misgivings.

I lined my men up on the field and turned them over to the authorities. As short a time as we had been together, I had become very much attached to those men and hated to leave them to be broken up and scattered all over France. Chums who had come from the same town and served in the same company [were] split up and sent in all directions. When I looked in on the field several hours later, those men were still waiting in line, sitting on their packs. I entered to protest at the camp office, and finally they were led away to be classified and billeted. The camp was about two miles from the City of Saint-Aignan and close by the station, which also seemed to have no particular relation to the town. The billeting officer gave me a little room, without windows, in a farmhouse near the river, and I settled down for the night.

Next morning I was formally released from command of my company, the papers having been found correct, and sent to the office of the camp commander. In order to get away as soon as possible, I started right in to tell this officer how necessary it was for me to get back to my regiment without delay. He asked me where my regiment was and I did not know, but thought it must be in Brest. The captain smiled and said that he would keep me until he had information that my regiment was in France, and I could work in the camp office. Burtis and Brundage had the same experience, and we became officers of the Classification Camp. I was ushered into the billeting office and told that I would have charge from 5 p.m. until the day force came on. A soldier must always obey orders cheerfully and without question.

Burtis, Brundage, and I tried to be good soldiers, but we all thought the best conceivable plan that we could think of, individually or collectively, was to *get sent back to our regiment. Where was the old regiment and all our friends? Sometimes we got news from men who had been sent to the hospital, sick, and were on their way back. I told the captain that my regiment was now in France, but he smiled and was not impressed. I was needed right here. Then came the great German drive and the agony of having to sit in a wooden shack office, winding and unwinding Regular Army red tape and wondering if my company was in the thick of it without me. Burtis wrote of our whereabouts to a major in the regiment and got reprimanded by the camp authorities. I made formal application for return and it was informally disapproved.*

*Through it all, however, a sense of duty made us work to the very best of our ability in spite of the temptation to make ourselves useless. My job was to assign to billets, in shacks and tents, the men arriving during the night, anywhere from two or three hundred to seventeen hundred, and to turn over to the evacuation officer the men scheduled to leave during the same period. Also to bring up-to-date the card index system which showed the location of every man at camp. Two youngsters came to me one day, looking as though they had just lost their last friend. In fact, they were about to lose him. They had stuck together through everything since entering the army, and orders had been issued which would send them in different directions and among entire strangers. They did not care where they went so long as they were together. Fortunately, I was a friend of the proper officer and I induced him to put them on the same roster. The most disgruntled man, however, was the one who had come out to fight and found himself detailed to repair shoes or act as clerk, coming to France to shoot Huns and ending up with this civilian job at one-fourth or less of his regular wages.*

*After a few days in my windowless billet, I got a much better room in the nearby town of Noyers in the house of Madame Bertrand, a fine old French-woman, who was only too anxious to work her head off to make me comfortable, and who insisted on talking French by the hour, until I finally began to understand a little of what she was saying. My room was a very pleasant one on the second floor of the little village house, with a French window leading onto a tiny balcony, which overlooked the garden. Another officer occupied the next room, while below was the barbershop of young M. Bertrand, a former soldier disabled by wounds. His father, a very old man, was a little peculiar, and the family could do nothing with him. Every morning at the first peep of dawn, and just after I had returned from the night job at the office, he sallied forth to look after the chickens. What he was doing to them, I could never discover. Looking out of the window, I could see him hobbling up and down the driveway, chasing them first one way and then the other and yelling "Allez vite" and other commands at the top of his lungs. Sometimes he brought out the family donkey and harnessed him to the big two-wheeled cart, making more noise about it than the crowd at a ball game. Sleep had to be postponed for the time being.*

*But the kindness of Madame made up for the eccentricities of Monsieur, and she was a wonderful cook too. We hired her to cook us a dinner one day and invited a friend to join us. The old lady from way down in the country produced a dinner [of several courses] that would have been hard to equal in any hotel, with delicious salads, roast rabbit, and many other delicacies. Every house had its rabbit coop in the yard, and these little animals seemed to be the favorite food of the inhabitants, though they were too frugal to eat them often.*

*Nearly every building, be it a house or barn, had all its spare rooms occupied by American soldiers. The upper stories of the barns, and sometimes of the house as well, were reached by ladders, and every evening the homecoming doughboy could be seen climbing the long ladders to his sleeping quarters. These [rooms] were made of a stone which was more like white chalk than anything else, and soon had a truly American appearance, [the] walls covered with initials and addresses, easily cut in their surface. Houses, which had lasted a century, were disfigured in a day by a custom which is hard to explain and impossible to defend. A less reprehensible custom was the renaming of many of the streets and marking them with well-lettered signboards. In Noyers, we had Copley Square, reminiscent of Boston, while the main highway from camp to Saint-Aignan was [renamed] Montana Avenue.*

When the United States entered the war, in an attempt to regulate the war economy the federal government was compelled to intervene directly or indirectly in many sectors. This entailed mobilizing labor forces; financing arms production; taking over railways and shipbuilding; and strict regulation of agricultural production, along with the control of food consumption. To avoid any threats caused by potential industrial unrest, they even went as far as organizing mediation between employees and bosses.

On May 18, 1917, Congress enacted what came to be known as the Selective Service Act. It boldly recited the military obligations of citizenship, and bestowed upon the president the quorate power of proposing regulations for the purpose of striking a balance between the country's industrial and economic needs on the one hand, and its military needs on the other. Among other things, it provided that men could be summoned for service in the place in which it would best suit the common good to call them.

Many believed that the country would not respond favorably to a draft upon the manpower of the republic. Under the first selective draft, 9,586,508 men between the ages of twenty-one and thirty-one were registered; of this number, 8,848,882 were white and 737,626 were African-American. It transpired that the total registration of citizens of African descent constituted almost 8 percent of the entire (racially composite) registration. By November 11, 1918, the AEF would number 4.1 million officers and men and 2.8 million conscripts.

## BEN ALLENDER, COMPANY G, 168TH INFANTRY DIVISION

*December 2, 1917: The storm which started Thursday is still raging, and it sure has been a great experience for us. I have heard stories about storms, and I thought that it must have been exaggerated, but I will never doubt them again, as we sure have seen some big ones. We were unfortunate enough to be located at the aft of the boat, and we got some awful rocks; the propeller is just beneath us, and it sure keeps up a beautiful noise. It has been raining today, and it, combined with the waves, makes it nearing impossible for us to stay out on deck. We have been running very slow since the storm started, making only four and five miles an hour, which will make us three or four days later in Liverpool, where we expect to land. We expect to meet the convoy tomorrow or Tuesday, and they will guide us through the war zone.*

*December 4, 1917: Finally the storm has broken up and we are entering the war zone, but we have not yet met the convoy.*

*December 5, 1917: Letters were written ready to be mailed when we land in Liverpool. We are in the war zone, but feel just as safe as if we were on land.*

*Under orders, we are sleeping in all of our clothes and our blouses and overcoats and lifesavers, ready for any emergency.*

*December 6, 1917: I was put on lookout guard; my post was on the bow of the ship, four decks above the main deck. My orders are to never raise my eyes off the water nor talk to anyone. I was on post from 1:30 a.m. to 3:30 a.m., looking for a sub, when I could not see the water fifty feet away from the boat. About three o'clock one of our own boats nearly ran into us, owing to the fact that we never [travel] in the same direction [for more than] nine minutes.*

*December 7, 1917: Early this morning we sighted land. At 2:20 p.m. we dropped anchor in the harbor just outside of Liverpool, which was not a very pleasing sight, except when the sun was shining. Then it was a beautiful place to look on. Everyone was anxious to dock and get off, but was unable to do it, so it was put off until tomorrow. We had an orchestra on the stern of the boat and had a stage dance; everybody seemed to be happy.*

*December 8, 1917: In the port of Liverpool and were taken off at 8:30 a.m. and loaded on a train made up of coaches, four compartments each, and eight men in each compartment. We left the station at nine o'clock, going through some beautiful farm country and seeing women doing men's work. We pulled into Birmingham about noon, where hot coffee was served to us. Before leaving the boat each man was given a box which was to him three meals. It included half a loaf of bread, a small piece of cheese, one can of corned beef, one boiled egg, and two small oranges. We passed through Oxford and arrived in Winchester about 5:00 p.m. [We] got off, and after marching through mud for about four miles, or so we arrived at a camp used for a rest camp before embarking for France.*

*December 10, 1917: We got orders to get things ready to leave the next morning. At the same time we lost nine men, who were transferred to the Quartermaster Department. Among these were St. Maus and corporals Nauman, Smith, and Vaughn, all of them fine fellows. We broke camp about 9:00 a.m. and marched to Winchester, where we [caught the train] to Southampton.*

*We see lots of women taking men's places at work. We were loaded on the* Marguerite *about 3:00 p.m. and pulled out in a short time down the bay. And this night was the worst I ever put in. There was no place to sit down or sleep. I laid down on the floor on top of some packs, and when I woke up there was four men laying on top of me. If we got up, someone would get your place, and you would have to stand up for a couple of hours. Some of the boys stood up all night. Finally, to our delight, the trip was ended, and we docked at [Le] Havre, France, about 2:00 a.m., Wednesday, December 12th. Before leaving the boat, each man got a cup of tea and a small piece of cheese, which was the first we had to eat for twenty-four hours.*

After the outbreak of World War I, one US regiment, the 34th Infantry, became a part of the 7th Division at Camp McArthur in Texas. On July 25, 1918, the 34th Infantry began its journey to Camp Merritt, New Jersey, setting off for France on August 18, 1918, on the troopship *America*. Upon arriving at Brest, France, on August 27, 1918, the regiment went into a rest camp for a few days at Pontanezen, prior to moving into the 15th Training Area near Ancy-le-Franc. In September the move to the Front was commenced, with short periods of training en route.

## HILLIE JOHN FRANZ, COMPANY L, 34TH INFANTRY REGIMENT, 7TH DIVISION

*We were loaded on a ship named* America, *once owned by the Germans as a passenger boat. We were eight thousand strong, the 7th Division and the ship's crew. Here we were drilled as to what we had to do if we were to be attacked on our trip. We were to go to our bunks or in the hole, as they called it. In other words, clear the deck of the ship as soon as possible. That was strict orders. Now after being out several days and nights, it really happened. Our big guns started firing and roaring, and the word was, get in the hole. But instead of going to the hole, we all rushed to get to the deck to see what all the shooting was about.*

*We seen some real subs trying to get to us and shooting at us, and our destroyers were out there like rabbits chasing around and around. In a little while it was all quiet again and the ship's captain called our major up and asked him what kind of soldiers he had there, as they didn't follow instructions to get in the hole. Our major replied to him he had regular army soldiers, and they were ready to fight and not run for holes. Well, after this we had a pleasant trip—lots of good singing, boxing, dancing, and several good movies, good cheer.*

*After being out ten days on the trip we finally landed at Brest, France. This was a large harbor for coming-in ships. Brest lies on a high hill, almost surrounded by a high rock wall, and here we began our life in France. After being unloaded and lined up with full packs, we were marched up a steep hill. As we struggled up this hill there were lots of French children and lots of old people along this route, begging for anything and everything they thought we may have to give them. And there were lots of young ladies trying to sell such [things] as grapes, nuts, and some candy. And of course, some of the boys tried to get friendly with these girls.*

*Private Goodman was one of the first ones to say, "Hello, there, young lady," and she answered him by saying "Nuts." And here and now is where the word* Nuts *got started, and it became slang among the army with us.*

*Now those of us that were added to the 7th Division to bring it up to full strength were still without any guns, and here we were, to fight a war. We finally got to the top of the hill and were ordered to pitch tents. But no sooner [had we done this than] there was another order that we would move on to [Pontanezen], what they called a rest camp, seven miles on further. And as we went on we would get word to give way to the right, to let trucks by. We reached the rest camp about dark, and we were all give out. And it was raining and orders were to pitch tents. So we did, in mud ankle-deep. To pitch tents, it was meant for two men to go together, as each man carried half a tent, and by putting them together we would have a small tent for two men to sleep under. No bottom; only ground, and this was mud for a floor. This tent is in size about six feet long, four feet wide, and about three feet in the highest place. You would crawl in and out at one end, and always [through] mud or water. Nevertheless, we would sleep in this way, as most of the time we were exhausted.*

*Some of the boys took awful colds, and some were sent to hospitals with pneumonia. Yes, this was a rest camp. We were put to work building and repairing roads and building barracks for sick soldiers. We remained here several days, then we marched on to [Ancy-le-Franc], an old cow barn, and believe me, here we made our beds or bunks on concrete floors in old cow stalls. Here some of the boys started to complain of bugs or something crawling. Here we began to realize it was real war. Here we drilled for a week, and then we hiked to another town named Shemey [sic], and drilled for several weeks here.*

*I must say the names of these towns may not be spelled right, as they were all burned out, or most of them were, and some of them were named by us soldiers.*

*There were a few French people living here, and when a soldier would try to buy anything from them, the answer was always "Finished, no got." This is where the slang "Finish, no got" got started among the soldiers. We had some rest here. On September 19 we were training for a short hike, twelve miles' march at dark, and at eleven o'clock we came to Reniers, a rail center. Here we went into tents again and stayed here till all the regiment got here that belonged to the 7th Division, our division. Now here we were loaded onto boxcars, like cattle. Here we found out what a box or cattle car rode like. Here in France we were shipped to a town named Cheuaex [sic]. We were forty men in one boxcar, and the cars were only forty feet long, with four wheels to a car. Some of the boys tried to sleep, but no use, for it was cold and raining, and [there was] no room to lie down.*

The American Expeditionary Force HQ was established in France as early as June 13, 1917. The 1st US Army chiefs of staff were James G. Harbord, James W. McAndrew, and again, James G. Harbord. Harbord was originally appointed AEF chief of staff in May 1917, when he efficiently helped to organize the successful dispatch of US forces to the Western Front, but in May of 1918, Harbord relinquished his position and chose to accept a field command as general officer commanding (GOC), 4th US Marine Brigade.

The first US troops arrived in June 1917, but were not deployed to the Western Front until October 1917. Owing to the fact that the proposed troop strength could not be reached by purely voluntary means, in 1917 a system of selective conscription was introduced. The other Allied armies complained on occasion about what they regarded as relaxed discipline in the AEF. This "new" army appeared to operate under a different set of rules, which wasn't initially transparent to the British and French. What they didn't know is that the most important transformation that occurred for the US Army during the Great War was the imposition of obedience on the new conscripts. Army officials no longer simply commanded obedience; they used coercion and relaxed discipline to negotiate it. Such negotiations had occurred within the ranks of other Allied armies along the Western Front, as troops set limits on the amount of violence they would accept in raids, daily shelling rituals, and pitched battles. Within the US Army, however, much of this negotiation over the meaning of obedience occurred behind the lines.

## ALFRED A. BLAIS, 301ST AMBULANCE COMPANY

*We left Camp Devens on July 10, and it was some happy crowd. We started out from our barracks at 1:30 in the afternoon and marched through Camp Devens. We were cheered by those who remained at Devens, and we entrained in camp, and at 3:30 p.m., out we started. There were more civilians who were looking on. Next [question] was, where were we bound for? Some said Hoboken, some New York, and all were fooled. Right through New Hampshire, we passed through most of the important cities in that state. We made no stops. We went along just as fast as the twentieth-century limited travels allowed. It was rather hard to see people in summer resorts having a great time, some bathing, some at swell hotels, and we were on our way to the unknown.*

*At eleven o'clock at night we all decided to try and get in a little sleep. I woke up around midnight and looked out and we were passing a little town, and the train seemed to be slowing up. There were quite a few people outside, and they told us that we were on the Canadian border. Sailed to Halifax. At 5:30 in the morning we found ourselves just outside the city of Montreal. We remained there until eight o'clock, when the train rolled into Montreal. We remained until 2:30 in the afternoon in a dockyard, and at 4:30 we left on a British transport for a sail down the St. Lawrence River. It was a fine evening, and sailing along slowly, everyone was singing and along the banks were crowds waving handkerchiefs and cheering as we passed by.*

*Canada is surely a pretty country, and we passed many important places, among them the city of Quebec with all its great fortifications. After sailing along for five days we landed in Halifax. We remained at Halifax for five days, awaiting other ships of our convoy, sleeping in hammocks, doing our washing with safe water, and being regular sailors. At Halifax we saw all of the ruins of the past winter's catastrophe. About every day of our stay in Halifax two or three ships loaded with American troops would come rolling in. On each ship was a band playing "Over There," so there was no opportunity for getting lonesome. Saturday morning when we rolled out of our hammocks we found quite a few new neighbors, among them a battle cruiser, which certainly looked good to us. The previous day our ship was reloaded with provisions and coal, so we had a suspicion that we would sail out in the morning.*

*Soon after breakfast the cruiser started out of the harbor, and was followed by twenty-two ships loaded with American troops, along with four torpedo boats. Airplanes went out a ways in the ocean with us, and at about noon we did not have either torpedo boats or airplanes with us, only a battle cruiser. Everything went along smoothly for a few days, then things began to get rough, and it was not a heavy sea either, but quite a few were seasick. At night no lights were allowed, and anyone caught smoking a cigarette was severely punished. On the way over I had a chance to see a whale and many other species of large sea creatures. After sailing along for thirteen days and nights, we woke up in the morning and found ourselves amid a nest of American destroyers, and they surely were welcomed. They were the first Americans we had seen since leaving Halifax.*

*Attacked by submarines: About 4:00 p.m. a sneaky little sub appeared, then disappeared. It fired a few torpedoes at us, but missed. Soon we found we were in a nest of them, and immediately a new course was taken. All ships turned their guns toward the subs, and after battling for half an hour, all subs had disappeared. None of our convoy was touched, with the exception of the damaging of one of the American destroyers. Later we heard that the Americans had sunk three German submarines in the conflict, and four in the early morning, making a total of seven for the day.*

*Around 5:30 p.m., when everyone was over the excitement, we came rolling into the Irish Sea. By this time our convoy had been split into three parts, and we only had seven ships with us. The old land looked good to us after being aboard ship and on the water for twenty days. There were few who went to bed that night. I was not so foolish, and got in an eight-hour snooze.*

*When I awoke in the morning I found we were in a little harbor in Wales, moving along slowly. Wales is one of the prettiest countries there is. After breakfast, I took my stand on deck for my morning air. About 9:00 a.m. we passed a little town named Barre [Barry]. It is a summer resort in Wales. Being the first American troops to pass through Wales, you can imagine what kind of a reception we got. The people cheered and waved. There were British flags everywhere, and once in a while Old Glory was floating in the breeze. At*

*Barre people were bathing and fine summer hotels were looking us in the face. Here is where all on board demonstrated what a happy crowd the Americans were. There were 100 nurses and 2,700 doughboys all singing "Over There." It made some noise, and we received many thanks from the people.*

*Reception at Cardiff: Still sailing, we struck another little town in Wales called Cardiff. We arrived about 10:30 a.m., finding in the docks American warships. Cheering started again, and this was the town where we were to disembark. The people knew of our coming and everywhere were American flags. A large crowd was on hand to see the first doughboys from the States land in their town. At noon orders came that the boys and nurses were to give a parade at 1:30 p.m. One company was to be held to unload the ship, and as we were the healthiest-looking crowd after the overseas journey, we were selected for the work.*

*At 1:30 the boys disembarked with packs, company colors, and American flags, followed by the nurses. You should rest assured those nurses received some reception, and were cheered all along the line of the march. The doughboys received their share also. After the parade they were given dinner, and according to their story, it was some feed. We did not know, as all this time we were in our shirtsleeves, unloading baggage, cartridges, barrack bags, etc. We worked until 11:30 p.m., unloading the ship, and everything was moved with an electric derrick so we did not do much lifting ourselves.*

*After unloading we washed up a bit and had something to eat. Then we started making our rolls, to make another move. By this time all other troops had left the ship, as every hour, from three o'clock on, a train carried them away, so that we were the only ones [left] in town. After 2:00 a.m., all tired out, we fell in and the sergeant gave roll call. All were present, and we entrained in dinky little railway cars, just like American Pullmans. After traveling until eight in the morning, we were pretty well tired out, as we did not get much rest, but no one complained.*

*We had crossed Wales and England and landed in Westminster, England, around 9:00 a.m. Here we slung packs and hiked five long miles, where we struck a camp and found breakfast awaiting us. After removing packs we were placed in small billets, holding about twenty-four men. Before anything we wanted something to eat, so we marched over to a large hall, where at least three thousand soldiers were eating a hearty breakfast. It was some hall, and there was some system there. And best of all we got plenty to eat—rice, jam, cheese, and a little stew. After breakfast we decided we would clean the barracks.*

What awaited AEF troops on the Western Front was going to be a shock to the system. The appalling conditions that the average soldier experienced during the First World War were unprecedented. A soldier in a frontline trench had to contend with mud, filth, lice, rats, and the overwhelming stench of death, disease, and macabre landscapes. These were the grotesque realities that made everyday life, at times, simply unbearable. It was these conditions, along with months of punishing attrition, that incited the French Army to revolt in 1917. After countless battles, their reservoir of moral courage had evaporated, and on May 5, 1917, the French 21st Division mutinied. It wasn't just the slaughter on the field of battle that had broken the French; it was the daily grind, the attritional nature of an industrial war, and simply the feeling of being expendable that had finally caused the situation. During the Battle of Verdun, when a unit of reinforcements found themselves marching past General Nivelle and his aides on their way to the frontline trenches, they protested by loudly bleating like sheep, as if they were merely lambs being led to slaughter.

American military authorities had noted this, and had no desire to emulate the French model. Consequently, all US soldiers had the right to challenge offensive or unpopular policies from the very first day they stepped into a military training camp. In their quest to mold army disciplinary doctrine along more acceptable lines, citizen soldiers did not hesitate to enlist help from their families, outside agencies, or even their political representatives to sway army decisions in their favor. The power of public opinion to shape disciplinary policy was evident throughout the war.

In contrast to the British forces, the US Army modified their use of the death penalty, which provides just one example of how outside civilian concerns intervened to influence disciplinary policies. In May 1918 President Wilson personally began reviewing the death-sentence convictions of two soldiers who fell asleep on sentry duty in a forward trench, and those of two others who refused to drill after being up all night on guard duty. After receiving numerous letters from concerned mothers expressing general anxiety for the welfare of their sons, Secretary of War Newton Baker urged the president to commute their sentences.

AEF commander General Pershing wasn't swayed at all, and personally recommended that the sentences be carried out, to "diminish the number of like cases that may arise in the future." Eventually the president decided that the American public would accept executions only for mutiny, desertion, espionage, rape, and murder, and commuted the sentences. Wilson's altruistic decision dramatically curtailed the use of executions as a disciplinary tool in the wartime army; the eleven AEF soldiers actually executed during the war were all convicted of murder or rape, crimes that also received the death penalty in civilian society.

Although executions were rare in the US Army in comparison to the British and French forces, they did occur, and were used to maximum effect. On July 5, 1918, forty thousand white troops and three thousand black troops at Camp Dodge, Iowa, were marched before a scaffold to watch the execution of three African-American soldiers who had been convicted of sexually assaulting a white woman. The purpose of the hanging was to serve as punishment for an incident that allegedly involved five African-American soldiers who were accused and convicted of raping a young white telephone operator. According to witness testimony, on May 24, 1918, the soldiers approached a young white woman and her fiancé while they were sitting on a hillside. The woman was raped repeatedly while her fiancé was beaten and restrained. Shortly after the incident, four of the soldiers were arrested; the fifth was never charged. Within five days of the incident, three of the four soldiers were condemned to death.

The forced witnessing of the event by the entire camp dispelled the confusion that had obscured the actual state of race relations in and around Camp Dodge. Official orders, if not macabre fascination, dictated that the event could not be ignored, and some of those who witnessed it were mentally scarred for life. The hangings ironically provoked widespread sympathy and acknowledgment of the humanity of African Americans, the likes of which hadn't been induced by any other event. Critics referred to these hangings as a "legal lynching," and the execution earned a prominent place in the wartime memories of these unwilling observers. *Des Moines Tribune* reporter Leslie Brooke described the chilling scene as the troops assembled and the death march began:

> *As the scaffold was approached, "God save my soul" rent the deathlike silence. "Have mercy," and "Oh Lord, save me." The cries of the condemned men echoed and re-echoed. Soon the shrieks of Negro soldiers, unwilling and terrified spectators, driven into a hysterical state, added to the sickening scene. It was terrible. There was no commotion. Fainting and frantic Negroes were promptly carried to the rear. One who had lost mental control ran straight for the gallows.*

In 1978, Lt. Russell B. Rathbun recalled the experience: "It was a very hot day with no wind. Thus the voices of the condemned men really reached the thousands of soldiers surrounding the scaffold. It was a horrible event. Most of us were not experienced soldiers, just ordinary young guys. . . . I was concerned that my recruits facing the scaffold might even panic. . . . I saw some of them weaving in ranks, trying to stand at attention." Rathbun found the incident as traumatic as anything he would later see in Europe. It was the first intentional death that these troops had encountered—at the hands of their own army, rather than the enemy's. For many it was as horrific as anything they would suffer on the Western Front.

American civilians were largely oblivious to the vast majority of ubiquitous wartime disciplinary issues that didn't require the death penalty. Throughout the war, American officials struggled to keep unauthorized absences, racial rioting, and work slowdowns among rear-area troops to a minimum. Behind the lines, the army adopted an array of persuasive and manipulative techniques intended both to coerce and deceive soldiers into conformity. To prevent soldiers from spending too much money on alcohol, for instance, the army set up mandatory savings accounts that effectively reduced the monthly pay given to each soldier. Giving soldiers less money preserved the facade of compliance with otherwise unenforceable orders regulating soldiers' visits to French cafes and other, less-reputable establishments. Persuasion was another popular technique, as camp officers undertook a massive propaganda campaign to convince enlisted men that saluting their officers was simply a sign of respect and not a symbol of subservience.

Another internal problem acknowledged by the AEF was the realization that American soldiers did not have a strong ideological commitment to the larger national purpose for declaring war. After sounding out the men in his unit, a second lieutenant concluded that "nine out of ten of our enlisted men do not even know what they are fighting for; the idea is simply to kill the Boche" (*Boche* being the vernacular used by almost all of the Allied troops when referring to the Germans). Throughout the war, the vague dedication that American soldiers exhibited to the objective of killing Germans and saving France troubled officials, who believed that troops would need stronger ideological motivation to continue fighting.

These same officials assumed that the war would continue well into 1919. Pershing remained steadfast in his conviction that political education and building morale remained the responsibility of unit officers. Stateside officials, however, deemed political indoctrination to be as important as marksmanship training for the modern soldier, and introduced systematic political education into the training camps. While officials at home and overseas disagreed over whether troops needed a sophisticated understanding of the war's causes and goals in order to perform well on the battlefield, they did agree unanimously that soldiers' views mattered to those at home.

Throughout the war, officials tried to resolve the logistical problems that prevented most troops from voting. In their arguments for collecting the soldier vote, high-ranking officials expressed complete faith that soldiers in the field would remain loyal and supportive of the war, even if civilians recoiled at the anticipated high casualties, and began to demand a negotiated peace should the war endure until 1919, or even 1920. The acting chief of the War College Division, Col. D. W. Kethum, said, "It is not unlikely that the time may come when our soldiers in the field, in the aggregate, may be able to see more clearly what the necessities of the situation require than do the voters at home. In such an event, they should not be deprived of their right of suffrage, not only because it is their right, but because their deprivation, at such a time, might seriously endanger the interests of the nation."

The Army War College was created as a solution to the military failings uncovered during the Spanish-American War. On November 27, 1901, Secretary of War Elihu Root established the Army General Staff and the Army War College to train staff officers. As an adjunct to the staff, the purpose of the college was to advise the president, devise plans, acquire information, and direct the intellectual exercise of the army.

The faith that American officials placed in their troops' commitment to fight until victory proved well-founded. Moreover, the wartime experience established the principle within the modern American military that soldiers' preferences mattered, and went some way toward eradicating the concept of unquestioning obedience to orders, regardless. For individual soldiers who served, these institutional legacies were less important than the personal impact of the war.

## CHAPTER THREE

# Johnnie, Get Your Gun

PRESIDENT WILSON SUSTAINED HIS EFFORTS TO MAINTAIN PUBLIC SUP-
port for his policies through propaganda as well as legal prosecution.
During 1917 and into 1918, Americans participated in countless parades
and commemorative events to demonstrate their support for the war. At
a time when many American homes had pianos and few had gramo-
phones, sheet music played an important role in popular culture. People
gathered in their living rooms to sing songs, or indulged in communal
singing when they heard them performed at music halls and parades.
After the United States joined the war, the government even turned to
songwriters to help promote the war effort.

The media and popular culture was significantly bolstered by America's entry into the First World War, and consequently, the mood of the
nation was reflected in these patriotic and often heavily jingoistic songs.
It's fair to say that America hit the ground running with the war effort,
and extolled a fervor and desire that at the time completely consumed the
nation. Composers scrambled to write songs about the war and America's
contribution to it. The music industry jumped in full force, and almost
every piece of sheet music published during 1917 and 1918 carried some
sort of patriotic or war-related message on the back.

The most popular song of the day was "Over There":

*Johnnie, get your gun*
*Get your gun, get your gun*
*Take it on the run*

*On the run, on the run*
*Hear them calling, you and me*
*Every son of liberty*
*Hurry right away*
*No delay, go today*
*Make your daddy glad*
*To have had such a lad*
*Tell your sweetheart not to pine*
*To be proud her boy's in line*
*Over there, over there*
*Send the word, send the word over there*
*That the Yanks are coming*
*The Yanks are coming*
*The drums rum-tumming*
*Everywhere*
*So prepare, say a prayer*
*Send the word, send the word to beware*
*We'll be over, we're coming over*
*And we won't come back till it's over*
*Over there*

While these lyrics are fervently pro-war, other songs had a slightly more sinister tone, and in some cases conveyed an openly hostile message, including songs like "What Kind of American Are You?," written by Albert Von Tilzer, who also composed the American classic tune, "Take Me Out to the Ball Game." Tilzer was born in Indianapolis, Indiana, on March 29, 1878. His parents were Polish Jewish immigrants. Lew Brown and Charles R. McCarron wrote the lyrics to "What Kind of American Are You?," which was published by the Broadway Music Co. of New York, New York, and released in 1917. On the front cover of the sheet music is a drawing of a pointing Uncle Sam, bearing more than a passing resemblance to Lord Kitchener on the famous British "Your Country Needs You" poster. A map of the United States is featured on the lower half of the cover.

*What kind of American are you?*
*It's time to show what you intend to do*

*If they trample on Old Glory*
*Will you think that they are right*
*Or will you stand behind your land*
*And fight with all your might?*
*What kind of American are you?*
*That's a question you'll have to answer to*
*If the Star-Spangled Banner don't make you stand and cheer,*
*Then what are you doing over here?*

Another popular American song during the Great War was written by Howard John and Percy Wenrich, titled "Where Do We Go from Here?"

*First of all, at the call, when the war began,*
*Pat enlisted in the army as a fighting man;*
*When the drills began, they'd walk a hundred miles a day,*
*Though the rest got tired, Paddy always used to say:*
*Where do we go from here, boys, where do go from here?*
*"Anywhere from Harlem to a Jersey City pier";*
*When Pat would spy a pretty girl, he'd whisper in her ear,*
*"Oh joy, oh boy, where do we go from here?"*

After April 1917, sheet music almost invariably supported the war effort. Songs were completely unambiguous in their straightforward appeals to men to enlist, and they often portrayed women as supporting the war effort from home. They even went so far as warning unenlisted men not to seduce soldiers' girlfriends.

One woman who joined the war effort was Alice L. Mikel Duffield; part of the US Army Nurse Corps, she was based in Fort Pike, Arkansas.

## ALICE L. MIKEL DUFFIELD, US ARMY NURSE CORPS
*War broke out, I think it was April, and I was still in training. And it had been raining, but it cleared off. It was warm, even then. [My] mother had a baby boy, born on my birthday, when I was twenty years old, and I didn't even see him, 'cause I wasn't there. But later, he got sick, and Mama wrote to me and she said, "Alice, I am just worn out. Your little brother has pneumonia, that's*

*what Dr. Means says. And I take care of him, day and night, and try to do the cooking, and everything else to keep the household running. If you could just get off for a short time and help me till I get rested, I surely would appreciate it." And Miss Tye said, "There's no reason why you can't go." She said, "What do you know about pneumonia?" I said, "Nothing." We had one man that had pneumonia. Now, we had people, doctors, lecturing on all these subjects. We got all our schoolbooks given [to us]; we didn't pay for them, they were given to us. And different things about different diseases. All of them, free. We got notebooks, pencils, everything furnished. Three meals a day, and a place to sleep. And our laundry was done. And that's the only way we could have [done] it.*[1]

Throughout this period, government at all levels, in addition to private organizations and individual citizens, used every form of communication at their disposal in an increasingly sophisticated and often unprecedented manner, in an effort to win over the hearts and minds of the nation. Propagandists quickly seized upon the potential of these emerging mediums to reach large, diverse audiences. This was the first time in the country's history that Americans had been so broadly and energetically encouraged to support a national war effort.

The emergent film industry also lent its weight to the war effort. Studios produced a succession of highly patriotic—even, at times, inflammatory—movies, which played to packed cinemas. Films such as *The Kaiser*, *Beast of Berlin*, *The Prussian Cur*, and *My Four Years in Germany* effectively fueled the public's hatred of Germany, while at the same time infusing audiences with patriotic fervor.

The US government simultaneously produced dozens of brief documentaries, the likes of which served not only to educate the public about the war effort, but also, importantly, to inculcate a sense of shared purpose within the country. This in time transposed the whole concept of what it truly meant to be an American, something that had never before been so passionately contested and openly extolled. Patriotism was induced both physically and psychologically on a massive scale. The dual purpose of government-sponsored propaganda was to garner support, but also to vilify those who, it was felt, were less than wholly committed to the national cause. German Americans, socialists, and pacifists, in particular, were denigrated, along with suspected draft dodgers, popularly referred to at the time as "slackers."

Although the federal government theoretically recognized the rights of conscientious objectors, its attitude was more inclined toward benevolent condescension than open sympathy. America's leaders simply couldn't comprehend the fundamentally unshakable religious beliefs of certain groups such as the Mennonites, who frequently had German names and, even worse, often spoke with German accents and blatantly refused to support the brave boys at the Front by participating in war bond drives. The suspicion and intolerance directed at these groups, as well as incidents of mob violence against them, was driven in part by their negative portrayals in the press and other media-based organizations. Meanwhile, doughboys were crossing the Atlantic.

## CHARLES GERWITZ, BATTERY B, 320TH FIELD ARTILLERY, 82ND DIVISION

*We left for overseas the first of May with a convoy of thirteen ships. The ship that I was on was a British cargo ship converted to a troopship called the* Excelsior. *When we were about eight days out, we had a terrible wind storm; the waves came over the deck all the time. We were all belowdecks playing cards, when all of a sudden there was an awful crash which startled everyone. They hollered "We were hit," so everybody rushed for the stairs, which was [sic] about 6 feet wide. It had a railing on both sides but it was built crossways the ship. When the stairs was all filled with men the ship rolled back and the stairs was straight up and down, and it dumped all of them on a heap on the floor. Some of them lay there quite a while before they could get up. Then the guard said that the anchor had come out of the hold too far—that it swung and hit the side of the ship and that all was well.*

*The first land we [sighted] was Ireland. We entered the Irish Sea; the water was calm when we got there about midnight, and when we dropped anchor the ship just trembled. We were in the forward end and many men who had been asleep in their hammocks thought we were hit. We later landed safely in Liverpool, England.*

*In the year of 1918 my Uncle Sam sent me to France. The 320th P.A. landed at Liverpool, May 13, 1918. Each one received a card of welcome and greetings from the King and Queen. We got off the boat at 8:00 a.m. and boarded a train for Worcester. The trains are the same as in France; the capacity of the freight cars is five or six tons. The country was very pretty, trees were in blossom, the fences were all hedges; it looked exceptionally good after having been on water [for] two weeks. The buildings were built of brick.*

*The people in England were unfriendly and acted as though they were doing us an honor to have us there. We had a great many fights with them the few days we stayed. While we were in camp there was a shortage of water. The water was turned on at mealtime, then shut off again. The English said it cost too much to pump the water to have it on all the time. We left for Southampton across the English Channel. We loaded seven carloads of mail on the boat. Some threw the bag out of the car, carried it to the boat, and dropped it into a hole on the deck; it fell a good ways down. Some of the mailbags were very heavy and they would burst when hitting the floor. The boat was very crowded. All standing room was filled. After dark the boat started out. By morning most of us were piled on the deck floor; some went to sleep, then others would fall over them. It seemed unnecessary to be treated that way. Others complained of the same treatment while crossing the Channel.*

*By daylight we docked at Le Havre, France. We were very glad to get off the boat, but it was hard to walk after taking such punishment. We got on a platform of a big warehouse, which was being used for a hospital. From there they took wounded soldiers over to England. We stayed there an hour, and had English hardtack and coffee. We left, carrying a full pack, for a long hike. The sun was shining and it was very warm. We landed in a camp at 3:00 in the afternoon. That night at retreat, we were told that they have air raids very often and when we hear the signal we should all come out in the groups we were in. Each group should go into a different direction so there wouldn't be so many in one spot. At one o'clock when everyone was nestled on Mother Earth, sound asleep, the whistle blew and we heard several airplanes and saw searching lights looking for the airplanes. Antiaircraft guns were popping out. Everyone was out by that time.*[2]

The conflict evolved into a struggle of competing resources, and Americans were radically reorganized to maximize efficiency. Among the results was the introduction of veritable armies of women into blue-collar jobs that had formerly been exclusively male territory, and the migration north of black workers to replace workers who had gone to war. The contribution the country was making to the Allied effort in men and resources would ultimately prove to be decisive, but first, all the parts had to be in place.

## GEORGE B. DEMPSEY, MEDICAL OFFICER

*December 7, 1917: A little recreation today. The whole company and most of the officers went on a rabbit hunt, each man armed with a club. A large circle was formed around the rifle range. The circle gradually closed and the rabbits ran hither and thither, trying to escape. On the final lineup, seven rabbits were accounted for. Five captured for the fourth platoon. Hurrah for platoon Nr. 4.*

*December 8, 1917: A real old-fashioned snowstorm today. Snow everywhere, two feet deep. The wind is howling around the barrack and the snow has drifted in through the cracks. I am officer of the day today and feel sorry for myself, and especially for the poor guards walking their posts. The newspapers at present are full of the Halifax disaster. Why do such things occur? We all believe in a kind Providence, and that most things that occur are all for the best. It is hard to see how a thing like that could be for anybody's good. Why does the Almighty allow such things to occur? Why, oh why, why does the war go on? Why does one man kill another? What is the whole thing about? Will the world be better [after] this war? After all, aren't the Allies and the German people fighting for the same things? Personal liberty, political liberty, and religious liberty. Liberty for all. There is a rumor that our unit may be sent to Italy. The danger is probably greater but the chance of serving is also better. Service is what we want. Service to the cause for which our country is fighting.*

*December 14, 1917: A foot of snow on the ground and the temperature around zero. Still living in temporary wooden barracks, not very favorable surroundings for military training. The military situation has probably not reached its crisis. If the Allies can weather the storm of the next few weeks, the chances of winning the war are good. The crisis means the period of darkness and the period of despair. At a time like this it is the duty of all to stick together and do all in his power to weather the storm. The Lilly Base Hospital is still aboard ship in New York Harbor, waiting convoy to "Over There." Reports are that convoys will leave New York on December 15th and again on December 27th. Perhaps we will be among the lucky to leave on December 27th.*

*December 25, 1917: Christmas Day spent in Fort Benjamin Harrison—that is, we called it Christmas. Last night everyone was blue and went to bed early. [In] the morning the barracks was cold and gloomy. At noon we had an excellent dinner. Mrs. Smith, Miss Parker, and two Smith children were present, adding greatly to the day. After dinner the boys gave a show—vaudeville stunts, singing, jokes, music, etc. In this way the afternoon was spent very well indeed.*

*December 29, 1917: Vague rumors are in the air that we will soon be moving. Where to? All equipment is now complete and the men are being inspected daily to see that they stay fit.*

*December 30, 1917: Ordered to Tenafly, New Jersey, to leave here at 4:00 p.m. tomorrow afternoon. Everyone busy now getting ready for the prospective move.*

*December 31, 1917: The last day of the year, and everyone is on the move. The quartermaster trains here are going east with us. At 2:00 p.m. all of our packing was done and we began loading. The boys carried their barracks bags to the baggage car; the rest of their equipment they carry on their backs. At 4:00 p.m. the first section of the train (twelve cars) began loading. At 4:15 p.m. the second section began loading. We occupied the last five cars of the second section. Our rations were supplied by the quartermaster, and were in the baggage car. The men were given tourist sleepers and the officers, Pullmans. At 5:00 p.m. the train pulled out and we were on our way. Oh what a relief, after four long months, to get away from that godforsaken spot.*

*January 1, 1918: On board special troop train bound east. How good it seems to be going east once more. Pullman car ice cold and no water to wash (some of the pleasures of traveling on a troop train). Bully beef and bread three times a day, a good diet for a fat man. Arrived at Buffalo at 9:00 a.m., stayed three hours, succeeded in getting a canteen full of coffee—cold, to be sure, but nevertheless, good. Pullman car changed, arrived at Syracuse at 7:00 p.m., and had hot coffee. Progress.*

*January 2, 1918: Arrived at Dumont Station at 7:00 a.m., unloaded the men, and marched up to Camp Merritt, Tenafly, New Jersey. Barracks all cold and weather outside at zero. We started fires in the stoves, and in about two hours began to get comfortable. Dinner at twelve—also bully beef. Our own quarters are heated with steam and are very comfortable; each man has a room to himself.*

*January 3, 1918: A day of readjustment, the men made comfortable and reorganized. This afternoon Captain Wilder and I took the company over to the palisades, quite a long walk but well worthwhile. Many of the men had never been out of the Midwest, so the view over the Hudson was quite a novelty to them. The men stood the trip well, only one of them falling out.*

*January 4, 1918: Had inspection this morning by a member of the Inspector General's department. He complimented E.H. 2 very highly. This evening I got permission to go home overnight. Left Camp Merritt at 1:00 p.m. and New York at 3:20. Arrived home at 6:00 p.m. and found a telegram there to return at once. Had supper at home and returned to New York on 7:00 p.m. train. I arrived again in camp at 12. My folks seemed to be pleased that I got home if only for a few minutes.*

*January 5, 1918: Rather unexpected orders have arrived to leave Camp Merritt tomorrow at 8:00 a.m. for Portland, Maine. Inspected by sanitary inspector this afternoon and complimented highly on the condition of E.H. 2. Today all the men were ordered to wash their dirty linen and bathe. Looks to us like a trip overseas is expected. The men are all excited at the prospect ahead of us.*

*January 6, 1918: Reveille at 4:30 this morning and breakfast at 5:00 a.m. Three busy hours spent in packing and loading baggage on trains. Men marched to Dumont Station at 8:00 a.m. We are traveling again with the quartermaster troops that left Fort Harrison with us. Again we occupied the last part of the second section. Only day coaches this time; I spent a miserable day as the car was cold. Arrived at Albany at 5:00 p.m. and got a Pullman to continue the journey.*

*January 7, 1918: Arrived at Portland, Maine, at 11:00 a.m. and debarked from the train in a snowstorm. After an hour we finally got all our men and baggage on board British steamer* Megantic *of the White Star Line; the steamer also has many officers of the R.F.C. on board. Traveling 1st Class, three officers to each stateroom, surroundings very good; our men are traveling 2nd class. Dining room and food are excellent. Steamer pulled out of the harbor at 3:00 p.m., and a short time later we had our last look at USA.*

*January 8, 1918: On the Atlantic Ocean, no land in sight. Ship rolling a little but not enough to be uncomfortable; not seasick yet. Boat drill at 10:30 a.m., each man being assigned to a boat; all lights are carefully covered at night. A very good library of books on board so will have plenty to read. Sighted land again at 2:00 p.m. and entered harbor of Halifax at 3:30 p.m. Passed through two submarine nets and a minefield; several large camouflaged steamers in harbor.*

*January 9, 1918: All day at the pier in Halifax, not allowed to land. A little of the destruction done by the explosion a month ago can be seen from the steamer. Some buildings have canvas spread on the roof and many of the windows are boarded up. Other buildings show large patches of new boards, probably covering holes. A vessel near ours is a minelayer being loaded with mines. Steamer has been taking on mail all day; hope we get started in the morning.*

*January 10, 1918: Left the pier this morning at about 8:00 a.m. and passed up the river to the Bedford basin. The basin is about five miles above Halifax, and is about three miles in diameter. In the basin are many ships waiting to be convoyed across.*

*January 11, 1918: Spent the whole day lying at anchor in the basin. Time would hang heavily on our hands if the surroundings weren't so good. Got a good book out of the library and have been quite comfortable.*

*January 12, 1918: Off on the great adventure. Raised anchor at 2:00 p.m. and passed down the river, led by the* Carmania. *Going down the river we saw the results of the great disaster [of] December 6th. Two large ships were almost entirely wrecked. Hundreds of houses more or less wrecked. We passed a British and American battleship in the river; arrived on the Atlantic Ocean about 3:00 p.m.*

*January 13, 1918: Steaming northeast at the rate of ten knots. Around us can be seen the other ships of the convoy, about a dozen in number. Bringing up the rear is a US battleship. The water is quite rough and the ship is rolling quite a bit. Had my first touch of seasickness, just nausea and dizziness. We are wearing our life preservers all the time, gives the ship an odd appearance.*

*January 14, 1918: Making good progress toward our destination and all is well. The sea is quite calm today and I am feeling fine. Gave some sitting up exercises on the deck this evening and spent considerable time in the open air; also passed most of the time playing checkers and reading.*

*January 15, 1918: Hit by a norther today and the sea is very rough. The huge waves breaking all around us is a glorious sight but a little hard on the stomach. Had to take [to] my bed today to keep down my breakfast. I estimate that we are about half of the [way] across, almost a thousand miles from home.*

*January 16, 1918: This morning one of the quartermaster men died of purpura hemorrhagica; he had only been sick two days. The wind has gone down but the sea is still roaring and the ship pitching.*

> *Sunset and evening star*
> *and one clear call for me*
> *and may there be no moaning of the bar*
> *When I put out to sea.*

*January 17, 1918: Having a rather uneventful time, ship going only about ten miles per hour and the weather is pretty rough. Reading Thackeray's* The Newcomes *to pass the time.*

> *Water, water everywhere*
> *Far, far from the brink*
> *Water, water everywhere*
> *Nor any drop to drink.*

*January 18, 1918: Every day is bringing us nearer to danger. However, I think we will be able to avoid the subs. I haven't any idea just where we are, but I imagine we are something more than halfway across. It will seem good to see a daily paper once more. Since January 6th we have been entirely out of touch with the world.*

*January 19, 1918: A case of C.S. [cerebral spinal] meningitis among the quartermaster troops. I hope it will stop with one case. This business of wearing a life preserver all the time is getting to be a nuisance; will surely miss it when we get on land.*

> *Break, Break, Break*
> *On thy cold gray stones, O sea*
> *And I would that my tongue could utter*
> *The thoughts that arise in me.*

*January 20, 1918: The clock is to be moved ahead 1 hr and 41 minutes tonight. That is London time. I take that to mean that we are now in the danger zone. Everything going on about the same, but under a little higher tension. Doesn't seem like Sunday, though we had church this morning in the dining room.*

*January 21, 1918: This morning our warship had disappeared, leaving us without protection, but this evening eight British destroyers appeared and surrounded the convoy. How much safer it seems with the destroyers around us. We will surely be picked up anyway if we are torpedoed. Hereafter will sleep with my clothes on until we reach the port.*

*January 22, 1918: It is a fine sight to see the destroyers racing back and forth around us. It must be exciting to work in the fleet. This evening the convoy was broken up; four of the fastest ships, ours included, went on ahead with four destroyers. We are making much better time now, about twenty miles per hour. It is rumored we will arrive in Liverpool on Wednesday night. Sea is very rough; have been in bed most of the day.*

*January 23, 1918: The sea is much smoother this morning. I imagine we are somewhere between Ireland and England, probably in Irish Sea. Passed a fleet of minesweepers at work; ship sailing by itself now, with one destroyer protecting it. Submarine sighted this morning, torpedo said to have passed close to stern. Arrived at dock in Liverpool at 8:00 p.m. and stayed on board ship for [the] night.*

*January 24, 1918: This morning I discovered that my baggage had been opened and quite a bit of clothing stolen. Debarked at 3:00 p.m. and immediately got on board a train. Passing out of Liverpool we received a great ovation from the people. The American flag was waved and women and children waved and cheered. Had an opportunity to see some of England we passed through. In passing through the country we frequently stopped at little country stations. At these stations everyone gave us a great welcome, and many wished us "Godspeed." The little girls acting as train guards came alongside the coaches and talked with us, always in a cheerful and inspiring manner. At one station a finely dressed old gentleman came alongside our compartment and asked if there was anything he could do for us. The spirit of all the people seemed to be, "You are my brother and come to give me a lift." Such a welcome was much inspiring to all of us.*

*Arrived at Winchester at 11:00 p.m. On debarking from the train at Winchester the men were all lined up in columns of four. It was a fine moonlit night. The men marched in silence through the streets of Winchester. Not a word was said. Nothing to be heard but the tramp of feet marching in cadence. Now and then a door or a window would be opened and someone would stick out their head and say nothing, or only "Good luck, boys," or Godspeed, boys." The whole march was very impressive to me, and gave me one of my first real thrills.*

*Far-called, our navies melt away*
*On dune and headland melts the fire*
*Lo all our pomp of yesterday*
*Is one with Nineveh and Tyre*
*Lord God of Hosts be with us yet*
*Lest we forget*
*Lest we forget.*

*January 25, 1918: After a five-mile hike from 11:00 p.m. to 1:00 a.m. we arrived at camp outside of Winchester. This afternoon I had an opportunity of visiting the city. Went through the cathedral, said to be the largest in England, and started about 1066. Went through castle built by "William the Conqueror," and in which many of the kings of England were born and lived. Saw the old gate and many relics in it.*

*January 26, 1918: Had the men out for a hike this morning and evening, saw considerable surrounding country. England seems to be very hard hit by the war. Food is very scarce, and most of the work is being done by the women and children. They are very cheerful considering the circumstances. Preparing to move again, this time, I hope, to France.*

*January 27, 1918: Up at 5:00 a.m. and men all in line for start at 8:00 a.m. On train at 9:30 and arrived at Southampton at 10:30. Stayed on pier at Southampton until 4:00 p.m.; in meantime, had dinner at Southampton Hotel. Embarked on* Prince George *at 4:00 p.m. and had supper on board. Started out of harbor at 8:00 p.m., Channel perfectly smooth and moonlight very bright. An excellent night for U-boats; however, we are protected by two destroyers. No sleep tonight.*[3]

Popular discontent with the progress of the war in Russia culminated in a decisive revolution that overthrew Tsar Nicholas in March 1917, and by November of that same year, transferred power to the Bolsheviks. Lenin's new government signed the armistice with the Central Powers on December 15, 1917. Now that the Russians had decided to abandon the war, in an attempt to address the potential imbalance, the Germans were able to redeploy many of their troops from the Eastern Front to the stalemate that existed in the West. The seemingly infinite supply of fresh American soldiers had the potential to address this problem, giving the Allies the advantage and demoralizing the Germans. When Pershing asked to be provided with a million men, Congress replied confidently that it could muster 420,000 by the spring of 1918.

As already stated, Pershing's ultimate intention and Wilson's express wish was that the AEF would be entirely autonomous, but throughout 1918 they were beholden to the other Allied armies. The paradox was that the US arms industries had provided weapons for both the French and British armies, but were unable to do the same for their domestic force, which relied heavily on French and British assistance to train, transport, and arm them for the duration. A skillful negotiator and, on occasion, quite intransigent, Pershing successfully deflected the French demand that the Americans simply provide fresh infantry troops for French divisions. Nonetheless, the majority of American troops spent a substantial amount of time training with French units, and until the fall of 1918 most American divisions fought as attached units to the French Army. Several divisions also fought and trained with the British Expeditionary Force (BEF).

The doughboys still preferred homegrown entertainment, though.

## C. HAROLD FLOYD, 107TH INFANTRY REGIMENT, 27TH DIVISION

*On another occasion we were cheered up by a visit from Harry Lauder, who sang and danced for us in an open field near the town, while a soldier accompanied him on a portable piano. At the end Harry gave us a long talk in a serious vein, in which he spoke of the death of his son, and suitable methods of greeting the Huns when next we saw them.*

*Finally our rest period came to an end, and we hiked over to Roselle and entrained for the Front. We had the same long train of boxcars, longer than ever this time, as it held the whole regiment, each car marked "8* chevaux, 40 hommes"*—"40 hommy cars," the men called them. This time the officers rode in boxcars as well as the men. Going around a curve, when the whole train was in sight, it seemed to extend off into the distance in both directions, while out of each door hung as many doughboy legs as could be squeezed into the space. Now and then the familiar cry would be borne back by the wind: "When do we eat?" and "Say, Frog, what town is this?"* Frog *was the army designation for a Frenchman.*

*Toward evening, we pulled into the bomb-torn station at Amiens, and late at night, passed through the ruins of Péronne. A short distance beyond Péronne we reached Tincourt and detrained. The darkness was black as ink, and in a few very short time, the battalion was in column and marching across a gently rolling country toward Allaines. At dawn, we were passing through a village which was nothing but a heap of brick and stone. A few bits of ruined arch showed where the church had been. Nothing else was recognizable.*

*A few miles beyond we came to another village much like the first. That had been Allaines, and was to be home of the Third Battalion until further orders should send it elsewhere. I found a small barn, half of which was still covered with a bit of roof, and took possession for Battalion Headquarters. Unfortunately the Regiment Supply Officer was able to prove that he had been there first, and B.H.Q. was turned out. Then we discovered a house, one corner of which was still standing, including a small room which was intact except for a few gaping holes in the wall. One end of the room became my bedroom, the other end held Sergeant Major Kunst, and in the daytime was all office. It was about nine feet by six in size. Three feet of the next room, all that was left of the house, with the help of a few shelter halves, was made into the Battalion Post Office. We felt fortunate in having the best-preserved house in that part of town.*

*One of the chief authorities on rumors in the battalion announced that Allaines had been captured and recaptured five times during the present war. I don't know the truth of this, but the place certainly looked it. An old line of German trenches ran near the town, and the country in every direction was littered with souvenirs of all kinds—rifles, canteens, clothing, grenades, flares,* signal lights, and everything used in warfare, not to mention a few dead Germans who had been overlooked by the burial parties. One of the latter was found by a party of doughboy explorers in a dugout. Knowing that the Germans had on at least one occasion placed a bomb under a dead body so that it would explode when the body was touched and kill the burial party, these boys took every precaution. A long rope was cautiously fastened to one leg and then the boys retreated to the other end and hauled on the rope. But they only succeeded in pulling the dead Boche about halfway out of the dugout, and finally gave it up. Another party came along, found the body with the rope attached, and pulled it a little further. Finally, a third group discovered the body and got it all the way out. The object of all this labor was not to bury the German but to see if he had any good souvenirs about him.

That night we had a celebration, which put an ordinary Fourth of July in the shade. Boche hand grenades were exploding in every direction; the sky was filled with all varieties of German signal lights, rifle bullets whistling through the air, and here and there, a great crash where some inventive genius had discovered a safe way to explode a whole box of bombs at once. I was obliged to send out a patrol in the interest of safety and quiet, to put an end to the celebration, after an English officer had complained that his men had had several narrow escapes. Under cover of darkness, however, an occasional signal light showed in the sky, while the patrol was at the other end of its beat.

The most annoying feature about Allaines from the point of view of Battalion Headquarters was the frequent night visits from hostile airplanes. As we could not block the holes in the wall of our office in such a way as to keep all light from showing, we were under the stern necessity of blowing out the candles every time the warning whistle blew. It seemed impossible to do more than fifteen minutes' work on the papers at one sitting once the searchlights caught a plane, and we were entertained with the spectacle of a white speck dodging and diving about in the sky, while the long beams of light chased it from side to side.

It was at Allaines that we got the detailed plans for the attack on the Hindenburg Line, between St. Quentin and Cambrai, which we were to make a few days later. Numerous maps and aerial photographs of the territory to be attacked were distributed, and officers' meetings were held to consider the details. There, too, we were joined by Lieutenant Hill, Intelligence Officer, and two sergeants of the Australian Expeditionary Force. We were much impressed *by the Australians, fine upstanding men and good soldiers. They made friends with our men at once and were usually the center of a group with which they were swapping yarns. Their orders were to put knowledge, gained by long experience, at our disposal and assist us in every way possible.*

*On September 26, to me a very welcome order came through, making me a first lieutenant, followed by an assignment as permanent battalion adjutant. Until then I had only been acting in that capacity, not having the rank required for an adjutant. Next day we left Allaines for the front line. It was a long hike, and we had the most serious work of our lives ahead of us, but the men plugged along in the best spirits, singing and joking. At one of the halts, the non-coms were assembled and given the plan for the big fight, with orders to instruct the men accordingly. They realized what it meant, but listened with a quiet, determined attitude and immediately entered into a discussion of any point that was not clear, in a way that showed that the success of the operation meant more to them than any personal feelings. While we were halting, ambulances were passing by filled with wounded men of the 106th Infantry, which was already in action.*

*Then we continued on with more songs running up and down the line. Toward evening we reached a field pitted with shell holes and stopped for supper. Some of our own big guns were firing from this neighborhood, and a few enemy shells were dropping at a little distance. It was quite dark when we started again. I was out attending to some matters connected with the rolling kitchens which were to remain behind, and when I returned, the battalion had started down the road. More time was lost trying to find where the orderly had taken my horse.*

*The road was choked with long lines of transports going in both directions. The darkness was that of a cellar without windows; and moreover, I soon came to a fork in the road with nothing to show which route the battalion had taken, and it was too dark to see the map. I guessed right, however, and by dint of following in the trail of wagons in the same direction and slipping by and ahead at every chance, I finally came up with one of our companies. To get by that, in the crowded state of the road, to dart in and out with a horse that required several minutes of belaboring before he would depart from the custom of always walking as slow as possible, was extremely difficult. This horse had been promoted from pack pony, after having been gassed, and long custom and a shortness of wind combined to make him believe that a slow walk was the only appropriate gait for all occasions. I finally worked up to the head of the column and was immediately ordered to go and see if everyone was present.*

*In the middle of the dark night, we marched into Ronssoy. The horses were sent back, and Captain Egan took the two front-line companies and disappeared into the darkness, going down to post them himself. We of Battalion Headquarters turned into the support line and stumbled along toward the place where we had been told that we would find a dugout suitable for headquarters. Very lights [signal flares] down front would occasionally light our way, and a few shells were falling here and there. I saw a man lying on his face in what seemed an unnecessarily exposed place and went to awaken him, but found he was dead. At last we found our dugout, a niche in the side of the trench about eight feet by ten and containing six bunks up two tiers. It was protected on top by a roof almost two feet thick, no protection at all from a direct hit. On the bunks were various articles of British equipment left there doubtless by men who had gone out on some mission and never returned.*

*Similar dugouts nearby were taken for the enlisted personnel of Battalion Headquarters, though to do so, as well as to get possession of our own, we had to rout out a number of men from one of the machine-gun battalions who had overflowed into our trench from a nearby position. The trench was so crowded that, when one young runner came to me and complained that he had no place to lie down in, it took several trips up and down the trench before I could find a place where, by making the occupants move, sufficient room could be made to hold the boy. As soon as the few necessary arrangements had been made, those not on duty dropped down into their selected spots and slept like logs until late in the morning.*[4]

# PART II
# OUR BOYS WILL FIGHT

CHAPTER FOUR

# He Will Not Prove a Traitor

WHEN LINCOLN SIGNED THE EMANCIPATION PROCLAMATION FREEING all slaves within the Confederate-controlled territory in 1863, the way was paved for the first black volunteer regiment to be formed in the Northeast, which would become known as the 54th Massachusetts. Most of these volunteers hailed from Maine, Massachusetts, Connecticut, Vermont, New Hampshire, Rhode Island, New York, Pennsylvania, Ohio, Michigan, Illinois, Indiana, Kentucky, Maryland, South Carolina, Missouri, Canada, and even the Caribbean. Most of the officers of the 54th were white men, diligent Harvard graduates who subscribed to abolitionist ideologies. On May 22, 1863, the War Department had initiated Order 143, the Creation of the US Colored Troops. This effectively allowed African Americans to enlist in the Union Army. Up until that juncture they had only been allowed to serve in the navy.

Once the black regiments were created, these men would serve in the same army and fight the same enemy, but they would not receive the same pay. Regardless of rank these soldiers were frequently maligned by their white counterparts and only received $7 per month for their service, while the lowest-ranking white soldiers were paid almost double that amount. When Sgt. William Walker complained of this disparity, refusing to fight along with other men in the 3rd South Carolina Volunteers, he was executed on March 1, 1864.

Many years later, in 1917, African Americans were among those willing young men who rushed to the recruiting stations, seeking to volunteer their services, but they were not accepted. A month later, the

Selective Service Act didn't exclude African Americans, and during the Great War almost three million were registered. The first Selective Service Act was passed by Congress on May 18, 1917, in response to the demands of World War I. The act required all men between the ages of twenty-one and thirty to register for military service. The US military continued to discriminate against African Americans by limiting their assignments primarily to labor battalions. Black men hoped to demonstrate their patriotism and loyalty by serving in combat units, fighting the Germans.

A booklet was released on April 13, 1917, titled "The New Negro's Attitude toward His Government." The subtitle further clarified the purpose of this document: "He will not prove a traitor to the cause of his country, nor a coward in the face of his enemies." The Honorable Mr. Charles E. Hughes, who would later oppose the Ku Klux Klan, anti-Catholicism, and anti-Semitism, wasn't regarded as being patronizing when he spoke to an African-American audience with these words:

*I am sure you don't want particular things done for you on account of Color. . . . No, the Negro is not asking special acts of government nor state for his special benefit. He is no longer a child and a ward. Fifty years of freedom, fifty years of actual contact with the business world, fifty years of commercial activity and education, have enabled him to develop into a full-grown man. And he wants only a chance to play a man's part in the material construction of things. He wants a chance to earn an honest living along all avenues and channels that are open to other men and women of his skill and ability. He wants to bear the burdens as well as enjoy the blessings of his country. He will not claim a country when it is enjoying peace and plentitude, and desert it in times of war and devastation. He wants fairness in every particular, and justice everywhere; in the courts, upon the lands, and upon the high seas; can he ask for more, and should he ask for less? He wants to shed his blood along with the blood of other citizens, when the shedding of blood is required to preserve and protect his country. He expects to give his life along with the lives of other loyal men, when life must be sacrificed to defend the flag, which protects him and his fellow men.*[1]

Military leaders persisted in their belief that African Americans had neither the physical, mental, nor the moral acumen necessary to withstand combat. At the time Native Americans and African Americans were not allowed access to most public schools and institutions of higher learning. Following the Civil War, some African Americans were at least allowed to learn how to read and write. However, segregation laws, whereby the African-American population was not allowed to share facilities that were used by the Caucasian population, were used to frustrate the development and growth of learning for this group, which meant that literacy among these recruits was considerably lower than their Caucasian counterparts.

Subsequently, the army assigned them to labor battalions, constructing wharves, docks, railroads, and warehouses. At that time the US Navy was becoming increasingly restrictive in its use of African-American sailors. African Americans were still confined to positions that involved such menial tasks as mess men, cooks, or coal heavers. When questioned about the limited positions available to African Americans on board US ships, Josephus Daniels, appointed by President Woodrow Wilson to serve as secretary of the navy during World War I, stated: "You are informed that there is no legal discrimination shown against colored men in the navy. As a matter of policy, however, and to avoid friction between the two races, it has been customary to enlist colored men in the various ratings of the mess man branch; that is, cooks, stewards, and mess attendants, and in the lower ratings of the fire room; thus permitting colored men to sleep and eat by themselves."[2]

Although technically eligible for many positions in the army, initially very few blacks got the opportunity to serve in combat units. They were actively prevented from joining the Marine Corps, Coast Guard, and Army Aviation Corps. Theoretically all branches of the army were open to them, but in practice, some 380,000 of the 400,000 black soldiers who served honorably in World War I were members of service or supply regiments, serving as drivers, engineers, and laborers. Even in these limited roles, they were subjected to an almost constant barrage of indignities and insults.

Back in 1917 there was no popular concept of racial equality, particularly in the Southern states of America, where institutional racism remained endemic. The hundreds of thousands of former slaves who had fought in the American Civil War definitely turned the tide in favor of the Union Army, but the victorious Northern capitalists reneged on their promise of equality. The power of the radical Reconstruction in the South, backed up by the military power of the Union Army, was soon splintered, and the freed blacks were politically expropriated, kept segregated, and economically relegated to the lowest echelons of American society. The triumph of reaction and the institution of official "Jim Crow" segregation was ultimately expressed in the segregated US armed forces that served and fought in World War I. *Jim Crow*—a derisive colloquial term for an African American—refers to any state law passed in the Southern states that established different rules for blacks and whites, based on the disreputable theory of white supremacy.

When the war erupted across Europe in 1914, African Americans who lived in the Southern states existed in a world fraught with hardship, at the mercy of white communities determined to repress any notions of equality. African-American soldiers served in the United States Army long before World War I. Free blacks and slaves enlisted in state militias, and had even served in the Continental Army during the American Revolution. The story of the black 54th Massachusetts regiment—based on the personal letters of Col. Robert Gould Shaw, and the novel *One Gallant Rush* by Peter Burchard—provided the backbone for the movie *Glory*, about one of the many black units that fought for the North in the Civil War.

The famous Buffalo Soldiers on the Western frontier were revered for their martial abilities, and Pershing himself commanded a unit of African Americans that fought in the Spanish-American War. But World War I marked a turning point. Black soldiers would eventually serve in cavalry, infantry, signal, medical, engineer, and artillery units, as well as serving as chaplains, surveyors, truck drivers, chemists, and intelligence officers.

Many African Americans saw World War I as a valid opportunity to gain respect from their white neighbors and prove their patriotism; unfortunately, they would face even further discrimination, and failure to fully comply with racial restrictions could be met with savage reprisals. Since the Emancipation Proclamation African Americans had been regarded as full citizens of the United States—in theory, at least—but those living in the South were denied their constitutional right to vote, among other things. This ensured that the Southern states remained a racial oligarchy, a contradiction to a supposedly democratic nation.

In 1916, fifty-four blacks (including one woman) were lynched in the South, the abominable practice of murder by extrajudicial action. In many cases this occurred in communities where African Americans were expected to enlist and serve a country that didn't protect them. Consequently, many of these repressed African Americans began to look to the North for the employment and freedom they so badly needed, and deserved. Eager to escape the racially oppressive social and political environment of the South, and lured by wartime industrial job opportunities, approximately 500,000 African Americans migrated to Northern cities such as Chicago, New York, and Detroit. What began as a dribble rapidly turned into a veritable tidal wave, as these people left the South to work in Northern-based industries, which, in turn, benefited greatly from this influx of blue-collar workers.

The year that America declared war, no less than seventy African Americans were lynched, summarily executed by white people. Meanwhile, the North became the location of violent race riots by white workers resentful of the ever-increasing black population. Whites attacked and killed or wounded more than a hundred black men, women, and children. Down south across the river in St. Louis, a wide-eyed eleven-year-old named Josephine Baker would remember these inequalities and the violence directed at her people for the rest of her life. She would leave America and settle in France, where she became one of the most feted and highest-paid entertainers throughout the 1920s and '30s.

When compulsory enlistment was introduced, the draft boards were comprised entirely of white men. Although there were no specific segregation provisions outlined in the draft legislation, blacks were simply told to tear off one corner of their registration cards so they could easily be identified and inducted separately. Rather than turning blacks away, the draft boards—those in the South, in particular—did everything within their power to sign them up for military service. The disparity that existed in Southern exemption boards was frequently blatant and uncompromising. One Georgia county exemption board discharged 44 percent of drafted white applicants on physical grounds, but exempted only 3 percent of blacks that corresponded to the same requirements. It was fairly common for Southern postal workers to deliberately withhold the registration cards of eligible black men and have them arrested for being draft dodgers. African-American men who owned their own farms and had families were often drafted before single white employees of large planters. Although comprising only 10 percent of the entire United States population, African Americans provided 13 percent of inductees.

The most difficult issue facing the War Department during World War I was the demand that African Americans should be trained as commissioned officers. Initially, the idea was insultingly dismissed as laughable. It was considered to be common knowledge that these men inherently lacked any leadership qualities. Only the resolve and insistence of the National Association for the Advancement of Colored People (NAACP), the Urban League, and such black newspapers as the *Chicago Defender* eventually changed War Department policy. An exclusively African-American officer training school was established at Fort Dodge, near Des Moines, Iowa, on October 14, 1917. In all, the school graduated and commissioned 639 African-American officers. However, the War Department had a strict rule that stated no African-American officer could command white officers or enlisted men. White men refused to salute black officers, and black officers were often barred from the officers' clubs and quarters. The War Department rarely interceded, and discrimination was usually overlooked, or even, on occasion, secretly condoned.

One solution to the issue of utilizing African-American officers and soldiers was characteristic of military racism of the time. General Pershing had little regard for his African-American divisions, and willingly consented to attach several of these to the Allied French Army for the duration. Col. William Hayward, commander of New York's 369th

Infantry, criticized Pershing for this erroneous decision. According to Arthur W. Little's 1936 book, *From Harlem to the Rhine: The Story of New York's Colored Volunteers*, Hayward felt that "[General Pershing] simply put the black orphan in a basket, set it on the doorstep of the French, pulled the bell, and went away."

One such African-American soldier, Brewster Garnet Wright, who preferred to be called Bruce, was born on December 26, 1895, in Springfield, Illinois, the son of two successful teachers, Willis and Mamie Drake Wright. Willis's father, Thomas Wright, was a freed black man who owned a substantial amount of land in the Springfield area. Mamie Drake Wright was of Mexican-Indian descent, and grew up in California. She met Willis on an Indian reservation.

When Wright's unit was mobilized between April and May of 1917, Company L was separated from the regiment and designated as the 1st Separate Company of Infantry, commanded by J. H. Pryor. It was then sent to Camp Greene, North Carolina, where it became Company L, 3rd Battalion, 372nd Infantry. Camp Greene, named after Revolutionary War hero Gen. Nathanael Greene, had been assembled in less than ninety days. Troops started arriving by the hundreds in September of 1917, then, in the thousands. At its peak, the camp hosted more than sixty thousand soldiers. At Camp Greene soldiers were assigned to eight-man tents raised on wooden platforms above the ground. In the bitter winter of 1917–1918, the most brutal in fifty years, those raw recruits endured frequent punishing snowstorms and ice storms.

## BRUCE G. WRIGHT, 372ND REGIMENT, 93RD INFANTRY DIVISION

*I joined Company L of the Sixth Regiment Massachusetts National Guard June 15, 1917, at Camp Darling, Framingham, Massachusetts. Spent the remainder of that month ( June) and all of July educating myself into the army routine; also drilled eight hours each day, except Sunday, which day was set apart to receive our friends in camp.*

*Late in July we got orders to break camp, which we did, and the next three days was spent in a cross-county hike from Framingham to Ayer, Massachusetts [Camp Devens], a distance of not over fifty miles. We reached there the third day, the thermometer registering about 98 degrees in the shade, tired and footsore, then pitched camps on the spot that was later known as Camp Devens. We had the next day to rest, but the days following during August we spent in hard drill eight hours a day.*

*L Company was the only colored company in the regiment. In fact, L Company was the only colored company in the whole Massachusetts National Guard, and was known as the state's best-drilled company. It was captained by Captain Pryor, and had lieutenants Seamon and Holmes. Colonel Sweetster was very proud of his regiment as a whole, and was just as good to our company as the white companies. The boys were all fast friends, and our evenings were spent together in the rest room, enjoying ourselves in numerous ways.*

*Late in August sad news came that the Sixth Regiment was to be split. That meant that each company would be detailed to do guard duty. Some would guard bridges, others, shipyards or arsenals. The day came for the breakup. It seemed that we all had hoped to stick together, [and] go to France and fight together. All the boys' faces grew long at the thought of being separated. We all marched to the train and on to Boston, the whole regiment, where we paraded; then each company went its way. L Company was detailed to guard the Watertown Arsenal in Watertown, Massachusetts. We all kind of liked that, as it was near home, and we could see our people every other day. But France was on our mind. France was where we wanted to go. That perhaps is why we could be content with guard duty at Watertown Arsenal. We had 150 good men, two of [whom] we were going to lose, as they had their choice of whether they wanted to stick in or not. They were discharged (Private Watkins and Private Guy), and two of my buddies squeezed in their place, Private Lemon and Private Goodman.*

*About the middle of October we broke camp and prepared to [go to] Camp Bartlett in Westfield, Massachusetts, where we soon learned to be Eskimos. The temperature some days was near the zero mark. We were joined by a colored company from the Connecticut National Guard who had been guarding the Springfield Arsenal. We were supposed to work and drill, too; some did, but the wise ones didn't. I was one of the wise ones. A couple of the companies of the 4th Massachusetts were also in this camp. Several regiments were made up here and sent overseas.*

*In November we broke camp to leave for the South. Arrived after a two-day ride in regular Pullman cars to Charlotte, North Carolina, at Camp*

Greene. *We were the first colored soldiers seen south of the Mason and Dixon line in full equipment since 1865. The colored people used us fine and everything went well for an hour or so. One of the crackers insulted one of our boys, and the war began right then for us. We got plenty of practice for the Boche, by fighting with the dirty crackers. The mayor of Charlotte sent orders to Captain Pryor to keep us in camp. The captain said he saw no reason why we should be imprisoned in camp, and in his speech to us at retreat the day he got the notice, he said, "Boys, here's an order from the mayor of Charlotte." (He read it to us.) "Now you see what you are up against. I'm not going to tell you to stay in camp, and I'm not going to tell you to go out, but if you go out, go prepared for anything. You all have your own guns and bayonets, and you know where the ammunition is. It's up to you." That night there was plenty of disturbances in the town of Charlotte, and several crackers were bumped off. We lost no men, but had some shot up, so we had to carry them back to camp. Two days later we were moved out of Charlotte farther north, to Camp Stuart in Newport News, Virginia.*

*At Camp Stuart several colored companies were combined with other regiments from Ohio, Connecticut, Tennessee, Maryland, and Washington, DC. We drilled together each day for about four months. Now [we were] ready to go to France—all glad to go and get a chance at real warfare, and glad to get out of this hellhole where so many had been shot up protecting themselves from the crackers.*

*Set sail for France on March 31, 1918, on the captured German boat, the* Die Susquehanna, *on the sea from March 31 until April 13. The night of the 31st we set sail from the harbor at Hampton Roads, Virginia, and when we awoke the next a.m., could see nothing but water. The day was clear and the water was smooth, and we all took great delight in hanging over the sides of the ship, looking into the water. A lot of the boys began to get seasick; I had a funny feeling myself. I had heard that if you eat plenty, that it would keep you from being sick, and from then on—which was my natural custom—I ate all I could get, and on that trip I got plenty, as many of the boys were in such a predicament that they gave their food away.*

*Then the fun began; every way you looked you could see someone with a shovel and a broom, cleaning up the deck in spots where those unfortunate soldiers had emptied their stomachs. My turn came late that afternoon on April*

*1. I had eaten so much that I was two hours trying to empty the load through my mouth. After that I ran and got another feed and was not sick from then on.*

*On April 2, the crapshooters and card players assembled, and we sported with one another the greater part of the day. Then came a boat drill. Every soldier had his life preserver to get and fasten around himself and get to a special lifeboat that he was assigned to when the drill signal was sounded. That took no more than a half an hour, and then we were again at our leisure. There were more well ones than sick ones in our bunch, so we found plenty of amusement in playing [against] one another, boxing and letting the crew tell us of their experiences in their previous trips across. We couldn't smoke on deck after dark, and reading was impossible, as the ship was all in darkness, so singing was our pastime after darkness had crept over the horizon.*[3]

The 92nd and 93rd Divisions were African-American, and collectively numbered around forty thousand troops. In the course of 1918 they would experience hard battle firsthand. Pershing willingly loaned the 93rd Division to the French Army. It was the only American division to serve exclusively under French command. Despite having to acclimatize to French methods of combat, and having to wear French-style uniforms with Adrian helmets, the division's four regiments performed exceptionally well, and received numerous commendations for valor.

Eugene Jacques Bullard was America's first black military aviator. Born in Columbus, Georgia, on October 9, 1894, one of ten children, he encountered violent racism during his formative years. Because of this he decided to leave America and go to France, where he had heard blacks were treated better than in his homeland. His father was known as "Big Chief Ox," and his mother was a Creek Indian. Bullard stowed away on a ship bound for Scotland to escape racial discrimination, later claiming to have witnessed his father's narrow escape from lynching as a child. Bullard noted many years later in his diary, "My father had told me in France there are not different white churches and black churches, or white schools and black schools, or white graveyards and black graveyards. People, colored and white, just live together and treat each other the same, and that was where I wanted to go."[4]

Discovered as a stowaway on a German freighter several days out of Norfolk, Virginia, he was put ashore in Scotland, finally settling in Liverpool, where he learned to box. Late in 1913 he left for France, where he first encountered a semblance of racial equality. In October 1914, during the early months of World War I, he enlisted in the French Foreign Legion. In November of 1916 he transferred to the French Flying Service, becoming a member of that unofficial brotherhood of American volunteers who flew with the French Lafayette Flying Corps. Bullard completed his training as an enlisted pursuit pilot the following August, and within a week he was flying combat sorties with a French squadron at the Front. He was assigned to 93 Spad Squadron on August 17, 1917, where he flew some twenty missions, and is thought to have shot down two enemy aircraft.

With the entry of the United States into the war, the US Army Air Service convened a medical board in August 1917 for the purpose of recruiting Americans already serving in the Lafayette Flying Corps. Although Bullard passed the medical examination, he was not accepted because African Americans were barred from flying in US service at that time. Of the 650 American aviators who served in the Great War, 110 were attached to the Lafayette Flying Corps. In addition, 33 pilots remained in French service, fighting in French squadrons until the end of the war. Others worked as instructors at aviation schools both in France and in America. Their mascots were two lions named Whiskey and Soda. One of Theodore Roosevelt's sons, Quentin, served with this unit, along with the grandsons of Ulysses Grant and George Pickett.

By November Bullard was credited with the destruction of one German aircraft and claimed a second, becoming the first black American to destroy an enemy aircraft in aerial combat. Bullard's career as a fighter pilot was cut short several months later after an altercation with a French officer, and he finished the war as an infantryman. He fought with distinction in the French 170th Infantry until he was seriously wounded at Verdun. He was then invalided out of the French Army.

Although never earning the distinction of "ace," Bullard still won many of his adopted country's highest military decorations, including the Légion d'Honneur, the Médaille Militaire, and the Croix de Guerre.

After the war, he would become close friends with flying legend Charles Nungesser and jazz luminary Louis Armstrong. Yet despite his acclaim in France, Bullard received virtually no recognition in America. Worse, after returning to the United States as a wounded combat veteran and an aviation trailblazer, he died on October 12, 1961, in New York, penniless and in obscurity.

No Medal of Honor was awarded to a black serviceman during World War I. But in 1988 the Department of the Army researched the National Archives to determine whether racial barriers had prevented the awarding of the nation's highest decoration for valor. The archives search produced evidence that Corp. Freddie Stowers of Anderson County, South Carolina, had been recommended for the award; for "unknown reasons," however, the recommendation had not been processed. Stowers was a squad leader in Company C, 371st Infantry Regiment, 93rd Division. On September 28, 1918, he led his squad through heavy machine-gun fire and destroyed the gun position on Hill 188 in the Champagne Marne Sector, France. Mortally wounded, Stowers continued to lead his men through a second trench line.

On April 24, 1991, President George H. W. Bush belatedly presented Stowers's Medal of Honor to his surviving sisters in a White House ceremony.

### Medal of Honor Citation

*Corporal Stowers distinguished himself by exceptional heroism on 28 September 1918 while serving as a squad leader in Company C, 371st Infantry Regiment, 93rd Division. His company was the lead company during the attack on Hill 188, Champagne Marne Sector, France, during World War I. A few minutes after the attack began, the enemy ceased firing and began climbing up onto the parapets of the trenches, holding up their arms as if wishing to surrender. The enemy's actions caused the American forces to cease fire and to come out into the open. As the company started forward, and when within about 100 meters of the trench line, the enemy jumped back into their trenches and greeted Corporal Stowers's company with interlocking bands of machine-gun fire and mortar fire, causing well over 50 percent casualties.*

*Faced with incredible enemy resistance, Corporal Stowers took charge, setting such a courageous example of personal bravery and leadership that he inspired his men to follow him in the attack. With extraordinary heroism and complete disregard of personal danger under devastating fire, he crawled forward, leading his squad toward an enemy machine-gun nest, which was causing heavy casualties to his company. After fierce fighting, the machine-gun position was destroyed and the enemy soldiers were killed. Displaying great courage and intrepidity, Corporal Stowers continued to press the attack against a determined enemy. While crawling forward and urging his men to continue the attack on a second trench line, he was gravely wounded by machine-gun fire. Although Corporal Stowers was mortally wounded, he pressed forward, urging on the members of his squad, until he died.*

*Inspired by the heroism and display of bravery of Corporal Stowers, his company continued the attack against incredible odds, contributing to the capture of Hill 188 and causing heavy enemy casualties. Corporal Stowers's conspicuous gallantry, extraordinary heroism, and supreme devotion to his men were well above and beyond the call of duty, follow the finest traditions of military service, and reflect the utmost credit on him and the United States Army.*[5]

AEF officials noticed that on numerous occasions the most successful way for a white soldier to openly disobey an order was to give a racial reason for doing so. White soldiers could walk by black guards without showing a pass, assault black troops, refuse to salute black officers, and even destroy army property or kill black soldiers with little fear of recrimination or punishment from white authorities. At first glance, the tendency of officers to look the other way when enlisted men committed these offenses seems to reveal little more than shared racial prejudice. There was a significant danger that allowing racial prejudice to serve as a legitimate reason for soldiers to disobey orders or ignore an officer's rank had the potential to undermine the entire basis for command authority. It simply wasn't feasible to allow the rank and file to choose which orders they wanted to obey.

In an attempt to counteract the situation, Washington-based General Staff tried to deal with the problem head-on by carefully orchestrating interaction between white and black troops. They witnessed explicit examples of how racial intolerance emanating from white soldiers was circumscribing the army's authority when it rejected a plan to assign black soldiers as cooks for white units. Advocates of this plan pointed out the importance of freeing up white men for infantry training, and claimed that having black men perform these menial duties within white units would both maintain the racial status quo and accelerate the pace of white infantry troops preparing for overseas deployment.

It was a delicate balance. The General Staff recognized that if the army embraced this plan it would subsequently be impossible to use kitchen duty as a punishment or legitimate assignment for white troops. One General Staff officer observed that "There is at present widespread objection in the service to the performance of duties of a menial nature, but to admit their menial quality by assigning such duties exclusively to an inferior race would make it well-nigh impossible to persuade white men to ever again resume these duties."

Despite the institutionalized prejudice that was rampant in America in 1917, thousands of African Americans made their way to the recruiting offices to join their country's fight. Most black Americans that served as part of the AEF France were confined to laboring tasks. Roughly 80 percent, or 160,000, of those who crossed the seas during World War I shouldered the shovel rather than the rifle, and one-third of all army laborers were black. The army intentionally consigned most African-American recruits to positions in which they would not only be forced to perform the most demanding and ignoble tasks, but also receive as little attention and praise as possible, justifying their blatant stereotype of blacks as inferior.

## JOHN JOSEPH BRENNAN, SPECIALIST, 102ND ENGINEER TRAIN, 27TH DIVISION

*The colored [soldiers] are very much afraid of the white people; they still are slaves. The [locals'] homes are built on stilts about two or three feet above the ground, and most of the houses have three large rooms. In the bedroom it is whoever gets in first, man, woman, daughter, son, or relative. It looks to me as though they are all relatives. In some of the bedrooms there is a large piece of cloth hanging from the ceiling down (call it a curtain), to separate the beds. Yet they are a happy, jolly crowd of people. They have very little education; in fact, none.*[6]

## Bruce G. Wright, Company L, 6th Regiment, Massachusetts National Guard

*April 2, 1918, was a very rough day. The old boat rocked from side to side; men were detailed to the mast, or "lookout boxes," as they called them. There were three of them [who] were supposed to look out for submarines. I was glad to escape this day up there. More boys got sick; most of them wanted to die. It was funny.*

*On April 3, storm quieted down; not so many in the mess line today. Lot of fun just the same. April 4, still nothing but water to look at; the sick boys were slowly coming back to life. Scraped some dry mud off my shoes and put [it] in a tin can, punched a little hole in each end, and went through the ship, letting fellows see land through my newly invented stereoscope, 5 cents a look. Made a lot of money and treated the bunch.*

*April 5th, fair day, games and plenty of fun, but submarine drill, pompous. April 6th, began clouding up; boat turned out of its course trying to duck a storm, but instead of ducking it, ran right into it. The boat was too slow; she was listing from side to side, the waves rolled over the deck. We stayed in the hatch most of the time to keep from being swept overboard. In the mess line the cooks would chase us all over the mess hall, trying to put a spoonful of food in our kits.*

*I was detailed to [the] lookout masts; the wind was so strong and the water splashed so much, it took fully a half an hour to climb to the box. When I got there I was wet as could be. I was supposed to stay there until they sent me relief. I got in the box and tied myself in and just began to get some real pleasure out of my trip. It was just like a swing and was fanning me back and forth through the air. I was dry in a short time. When I started up there it was 5:30 p.m. and now it was eleven, and no relief yet. It was storming too late now for anyone to get up to me, and I didn't intend to try to come down while the deck was being washed by the sea. At times the boat would rock so far that my little box would almost touch the water. I was hungry now and I went in my pocket to get a chunk of bread I had put there, but all I could find were a pocket full of crumbs mixed with tobacco. I ate it, tobacco and all, then I was real dizzy and felt right foolish. Couldn't have seen a submarine if one should have come in sight.*

*Day began to break, and now it seemed as though the storm was quieting down a bit. I wasn't swinging so near the water. I loosened the rope which I had tied myself by a little so as I could look around at the other lookout boxes. The middle one seemed empty, and in the one at the other end of the ship I could see a face of a white man but he wasn't moving. Someone hollered up through the tube to stick it out a while longer, and just as soon as they could get across deck I'd be relieved. Along about six o'clock by my wristwatch a grayish-blue spot crept into the sky and the boat began to settle and the hole opened and I was relieved by one of my buddies. I was so stiff when my relief came that I could hardly get out of the box. Then I learned the boy in the next box had been lost, and Charlie in the rear box was found unconscious in his box. The boys were all glad to see me, but I was more glad to see them, I guess. I lived the life of a king the rest of the trip, even had my meals brought to me for the next two days.*

*April 7, laid on deck in sun all day, learning from the sailors how to tie knots and feeling like a real seaman. April 8, now in the danger zone; men were stationed along the sides of the ship to report every tin can, board, barrel, or any other object they might see on the water, as the submarines used to disguise their stereoscopes with such objects. April 9, still nothing to see but water outside of five other transports, which we had met during the night. We were now sailing the seas in battle formation with them. We could make out soldiers on these other boats as soldiers, but that's about all we could tell, as they were such a great distance from us.*

*April 10, one of the lookouts sighted a submarine. The ship crew turned loose their guns at it, and the ship shook and creaked. The submarine signal was sounded; some were putting on three or four life belts to make sure they wouldn't sink. Everyone thought the ship had been hit, and several boys did dirt in their pants. We weren't hit; the submarine had been sunk, and everything went on about the same except for those boys who had to retire to the washroom to get their underwear clean.*

*April 11, we met the little torpedo boats that were to guard us through the rest of the trip. There were several of them. They traveled so fast they could circle all around us and still keep up. It was fun to watch. April 12, the other four transports headed off in another direction. They were making Brest, and we kept straight on heading to Saint-Nazaire. April 13, went on deck and still after fourteen days could see no land. Just beginning to realize how large this world was. The sailors told us that we would see land today, and believe me, we were all very eager to get one more glimpse of land. Now and then we would pass parts of boats that had been shot to pieces, and along about 10:00 a.m., the guard from the crow's nest, where I had spent such a terrible night on April 5, hollered down the tube that he saw land. Of course him being higher up than us, he could see it before us.*

*We all strained our eyes from the side of the ship as she sailed on. In an hour's time, about eleven o'clock, we got our first glimpse of foreign soil. Yes, it was foreign, but was very much welcomed by us. We weren't in the harbor yet, but we entered the harbor about 4:00 that afternoon. As we entered the big harbor, guns saluted us by firing several times. When we heard all that booming we naturally thought that we were right at the front line, and that we'd have to fight our way into the land that we so longingly looked at and wanted to walk on. But afterwards we learned that the French were saluting us. Finally, we got close enough to see the people standing on hills waving towels and white things and dancing jigs, so happy to see more help coming. We went up the channel to Saint-Nazaire by pilot and got our first look at French villages. That night we had to stay on board; they threw cake, candy, fruit, and wine up on deck to us, and that night was a restless one, as we wanted to get on shore as quick as possible.*[7]

The commander of the American Expeditionary Forces, Gen. John Pershing, decided after consultation with the French marshal Philippe Pétain to merge all of his African-American regiments in the French Army. In contrast with the United States and many other countries, France had no problem sending these brave men to fight at the Front. The 92nd was the only all-black division that fought in World War I. The 93rd was never brought up to full strength, but its ranks were filled with a heavy majority of African Americans. The 93rd was the first division to be organized and deployed in France. It consisted primarily of black National Guard units plus some draftees. The latter formed the 371st Infantry Regiment, while the guardsmen constituted three other infantry regiments, namely the 369th, of New York; the 370th, of Illinois; and the 371st, of Maryland, Massachusetts, Ohio, and Washington, DC. The 370th had the distinction of being the only African-American regiment completely staffed with black officers.

The 92nd Division consisted almost entirely of African-American draftees. It contained four infantry regiments that included the 365th, of Texas and Oklahoma, the 366th, of Alabama, the 367th, of New York, and the 368th, of Tennessee, Pennsylvania, and Maryland. The 92nd also included several smaller regiments, such as three devoted to field artillery. More than thirty thousand black combat troops, from all over America, would see duty in France.

At the time W. E. B. Du Bois was one of the most important African-American activists during the first half of the twentieth century. Du Bois had made a calculated decision to support World War I as a quid pro quo for possible racial advancement. It was his assertion that if African-American troops trained and fought alongside white troops, there would be reasonable cause to hope that these same African Americans could be integrated into American society after the war. He was a respected intellectual, whose call for racial equality marked him as a radical thinker in his era. Although he strongly supported the war effort, he noticed that the patriotism of African-American soldiers was not recognized or rewarded by white military commanders, as they obviously deserved. He managed to obtain some highly classified documents regarding the treatment of African-American soldiers in World War I and ultimately proved their authenticity. The French Committee dispatched the first document at the request of the US Army. It represented American and not French opinion, and Du Bois was reliably informed that when the French Ministry heard of the distribution of this document among the prefects and sous-prefects of France, they ordered such copies to be collected and burned.

## FRENCH MILITARY MISSION

### Stationed with the American Army, August 7, 1918

## SECRET INFORMATION CONCERNING BLACK AMERICAN TROOPS

*1. It is important for French officers who have been called upon to exercise command over black American troops, or to live in close contact with them, to have an exact idea of the position occupied by Negroes in the United States. The information set forth in the following communication ought to be given to these officers, and it is to their interest to have these matters known and widely disseminated. It will devolve likewise on the French Military Authorities, through the medium of the Civil Authorities, to give information on this subject to the French population residing in the cantonments occupied by American colored troops.*

*2. The American attitude upon the Negro question may seem a matter for discussion to many French minds. But we French are not in our province if we undertake to discuss what some call "prejudice." American opinion is unanimous on the "color question" and does not admit of any discussion. The increasing number of Negroes in the United States (about 15,000,000) would create for the white race in the Republic menace of degeneracy were it not that an impassable gulf has been made between them. As this danger does not exist for the French race, the French public has become accustomed to treating the Negro with familiarity and indulgence. This indulgence and this familiarity are matters of grievous concern to the Americans. They consider them an affront to their national policy. They are afraid that contact with the French will inspire in black Americans aspirations, which to them [the whites] appear intolerable. It is of the utmost importance that every effort be made to avoid profoundly estranging American opinion. Although a citizen of the United States, the black man is regarded by the white American as an inferior being with whom relation of business or service only are possible. The black is constantly being censured for his want of intelligence and discretion, his lack of civic and professional conscience, and for his tendency toward undue familiarity.*

*The vices of the Negro are a constant menace to the American who has to repress them sternly. For instance, the black American troops in France have, by themselves, given rise to as many complaints for attempted rape as all the rest of the army. And yet the [black American] soldiers sent us have been the choicest with respect to physique and morale, for the number disqualified at the time of mobilization was enormous.*

*CONCLUSION*

*1. We must prevent the rise of any pronounced degree of intimacy between French officers and black officers. We may be courteous and amiable with these last, but we cannot deal with them on the same plane as with the white American officers without deeply wounding the latter. We must not eat with them, must not shake hands, or seek to talk or meet with them outside of the requirements of military service.*

*2. We must not commend too highly the black American troops, particularly in the presence of [white] Americans. It is all right to recognize their good qualities and their services, but only in moderate terms, strictly in keeping with the truth.*

*3. Make a point of keeping the native cantonment population from "spoiling" the Negroes. [White] Americans become greatly incensed at any public expression of intimacy between white women and black men. They have recently uttered violent protest against a picture in the "Vie Parisienne" entitled The Child of the Desert, which shows a [white] woman in a "cabinet particulier" with a Negro. Familiarity on the part of white women with black men is furthermore a source of profound regret to our experienced colonials who see in it an overweaning menace to the prestige of the white race. Military authority cannot intervene directly in this question, but it can through the civil authorities exercise some influence on the population.*

*(Signed) LINARD.*[8]

The French Army may have garnered a reputation for being particularly punitive where colonial regiments were concerned, but they found the American attitude toward African-American soldiers particularly repugnant. Throughout the course of the Great War roughly between 81,000 and 97,000 men from the French colonies were killed in action, including 26,000 Algerians. French colonial troops had been among the first unfortunate recipients of the very first gas attack at Ypres in 1915. At around 5:00 p.m. on April 22, 1915, the German Army released around 168 tons of chlorine gas over a four-mile front on the part of the line held by French territorial and colonial Moroccan and Algerian troops of the French 45th and 78th divisions.

When they arrived in France, many African-American soldiers interacted with African soldiers and laborers from the French colonies in North and West Africa that were fighting in the French Army. They established ties and formed enduring friendships; moreover, these African-American soldiers became cultural ambassadors, introducing France and the world to jazz through the various regimental bands that eventually took the country by storm.

## HARLEM HELLFIGHTERS

The 369th Regiment consisted entirely of African Americans and Puerto Ricans hailing mainly from the New York district of Harlem. After having been treated as second-class citizens, this unit had every aspiration to prove themselves as first-class soldiers. When the men of the 369th first arrived in France, they were reminded of the War Department's segregation policy that prevented colored regiments from being placed in the same military division as white regiments, and there weren't enough colored regiments to form a division of their own. General Pershing was extremely reluctant to commit these troops to combat, and none of the other US divisions wanted this black regiment in their ranks. Many gave the excuse that these soldiers were untrustworthy, inferior to their white counterparts, and completely unmotivated. These African-American soldiers were regarded as poorly trained and only capable of the most menial labor, such as unloading ships and digging latrines.

French officers were unencumbered by the prejudices that African Americans faced in the US Army. Some of them had previously commanded and fought alongside African troops in the French colonies. By

April 1918 the French Army's strength had been significantly depleted, and according to some military officials, they were on the verge of collapse. The "Harlem Hellfighters" won their laurels using French weapons and wearing mostly US uniforms, although some were issued French uniforms, and many wore the famous French Adrian steel helmet.

The African Americans quickly learned how to operate French weaponry, use French battle tactics, and, in many cases, even learn the French language. The French were considerably less preoccupied with race than the AEF, and were quite content to welcome these men into their ranks. It's well documented that many French soldiers preferred the African-American soldiers above their white counterparts because they regarded them as being better-behaved; this was probably because of the stricter discipline to which their officers subjected them. Col. Edouard Renquin of the French Military Commission to the United States prepared the following statement concerning the participation of black French Army troops in the Great War:

*France has had colored troops ever since it has had colonies. These troops have participated in all our expeditions overseas; they have been the best instrument of our colonial expansion. Algerian troops (Arabs and Kabyles) fought in France in 1870–71 against Germany. But it was for the first time, in 1914, that black troops (Senegalese and Sudanese) took part in the European war against an enemy as redoubtable as Germany. If it is asked what have been the results of this experience, there is only one answer: They have been excellent. The black troops of Africa are grouped either by battalions or by regiments with our colonial French troops. The reason is that the colonial officers understand them thoroughly, and that the men themselves, in fighting together in the colonies, have acquired a mutual confidence in each other.*[9]

This expression of regard from the French Army for French colonial troops was alien to African Americans, who were often made to feel as if they were fighting two wars—one against the Germans, and the other against their white officers.

The 369th Infantry Regiment (15th New York) established the best World War I record of any US Army infantry regiment, and served for 191 consecutive days in the trenches, earning the further attribute of never having lost a foot of ground to the Germans. The extraordinary valor of the 369th earned them fame in both Europe and America, 171 of the 369th's officers and men receiving individual medals, and the unit receiving a Croix de Guerre for taking the strategically important city of Séchault.

During the Second Battle of the Marne, the 369th soon proved themselves to be a tough, reliable fighting machine. Their attack on Séchault went so well that they advanced ten miles deep, well ahead of the French troops on their flanks. The Germans who were notoriously reluctant to show any respect for their black adversaries nicknamed this unit the *Blutlustige Schwartzmanner* ("bloodthirsty black men"), and, more famously, *Die Männer aus die Hölle* ("the men from hell"; hence, the nickname "Hellfighters"). When the war finally ended, the highly decorated 369th Hellfighters were given the honor of serving as the Allied Forces' advance guard, and becoming the first Allied unit to reach the Rhine River.

One of these soldiers was Sgt. Henry Johnson. Born in Winston-Salem, North Carolina, Johnson moved to New York as a teenager. He had done various jobs, working as a chauffeur, soda mixer, laborer in a coal yard, and redcap porter at Albany's Union Station. He enlisted in the US Army on June 5, 1917, and was assigned to Company C, 15th New York (Colored) Infantry Regiment, an all-black National Guard unit that would later become the 369th Infantry Regiment. The 369th was ordered into battle in 1918, and Johnson and his unit were brigaded with a French Army colonial unit in frontline combat. Johnson served one tour of duty at the western edge of the Argonne Forest in France's Champagne region, from 1918 to 1919.

Equipped with a French military uniform, Johnson and another private, Needham Roberts of New Jersey, were serving sentry duty on the night of May 4, 1918, when German snipers began firing on them. Johnson began throwing grenades at the approaching Germans; hit by a German grenade, Roberts could only pass more of the small bombs to Johnson to lob at the enemy. When he exhausted his supply of grenades, Johnson began firing his rifle, but it soon jammed when he tried to insert another cartridge. By then the Germans had surrounded the two privates, and Johnson used his rifle as a club until the butt splintered. He saw the Germans attempting to take Roberts prisoner, and charged at them with his only remaining weapon, a bolo knife. (Produced from 1897 through 1918, the US Army bolo knife remained in service well into World War II.)

With this lethal weapon in hand, Johnson stabbed one soldier in the stomach and another in the ribs, and was still fighting when more French and American troops arrived on the scene, causing the Germans to retreat. When the reinforcements got there, Johnson fainted from the twenty-one wounds he had sustained in the one-hour battle. In total he had killed four Germans and wounded some ten to twenty more, and prevented them from breaking the French line. The French awarded both Johnson and Roberts the Croix de Guerre; Johnson's included the coveted Gold Palm for extraordinary valor. On his return to the United States he was given the nickname "Black Death."

Sadly, his fame would be short-lived. Henry Johnson's postwar years were desperate, to say the least. His discharge records erroneously made no mention of his many injuries; consequently, Johnson was denied not only a Purple Heart, but a disability allowance as well. Uneducated and illiterate, he was unable to dispute this grave clerical error. He resumed his job as a porter with the railways, but due to his disabilities, he wasn't able to perform this work adequately. With no other prospects in sight, Henry became a chronic alcoholic. His wife and two children left him, and in 1929, at the young age of thirty-two, this war hero died in poverty. Nearly a century after his service, in June 2015, Johnson received America's highest military award, the Medal of Honor, in a ceremony at the White House. The medal is currently housed in the New York State Capitol building.

### OFFICIAL CITATION

*The President of the United States of America, authorized by an Act of Congress, March 3, 1863, has awarded in the name of Congress the Medal of Honor to*

## PRIVATE HENRY JOHNSON
## UNITED STATES ARMY

*For conspicuous gallantry and intrepidity at the risk of his life
above and beyond the call of duty:*

*Private Johnson distinguished himself by acts of gallantry and
intrepidity above and beyond the call of duty while serving as a
member of Company C, 369th Infantry Regiment, 93rd Division,
American Expeditionary Forces, during combat operations against
the enemy on the front lines of the Western Front in France on May
15, 1918. Private Johnson and another soldier were on sentry duty at
a forward outpost when they received a surprise attack from a German raiding party consisting of at least twelve soldiers. While under
intense enemy fire, and despite receiving significant wounds, Private
Johnson mounted a brave retaliation, resulting in several enemy casualties. When his fellow soldier was badly wounded, Private Johnson
prevented him from being taken prisoner by German forces. Private
Johnson exposed himself to grave danger by advancing from his position to engage an enemy soldier in hand-to-hand combat. Wielding
only a knife and gravely wounded himself, Private Johnson continued
fighting and took his bolo knife and stabbed it through an enemy soldier's head. Displaying great courage, Private Johnson held back the
enemy force until they retreated. Private Johnson's extraordinary heroism and selflessness above and beyond the call of duty are in keeping
with the highest traditions of military service and reflect great credit
upon himself, his unit, and the United States Army.*[10]

For his battlefield valor, Johnson became one of the first Americans
to be awarded the French Croix de Guerre with Gold Palm, France's
highest award for valor. He is buried in Arlington National Cemetery
in Arlington, Virginia. Johnson was posthumously awarded the Purple
Heart in 1996 and the Distinguished Service Cross in 2002.

As the war entered its closing months, the men of the 369th executed
a string of audacious battlefield exploits. At the battle of Belleau Wood,
Colonel Hayward dismissed the advice by French soldiers to retreat and
led his troops through a German artillery barrage, declaring, "My men

never retire. They go forward, or they die!" Captain Fillmore, the man who initially sponsored the regiment in New York, received the Croix de Guerre for conspicuous bravery in an offensive against the German stronghold of Butte de Mesnil.

The Harlem Hellfighters can also claim the accolade of having helped introduce the French public to jazz. The French people pitied the racist oppression of African Americans, and immediately fell in love with this core product of African-American culture, regarded as the classical music of black America. It became widely accepted and played a key role in the life of Paris's community during the twentieth century. Right from the beginning of its history in New York, the 369th Infantry Regiment included an excellent forty-four-piece jazz band, led by bandmaster James Reese Europe and the drum major Noble Sissle, two of Harlem's finest musicians. James Reese Europe was born in Mobile, Alabama, on February 22, 1881. Both of his parents were musicians, and when Europe was about ten, his family moved to Washington, DC, where he studied violin with Enrico Hurlei, the assistant director of the Marine Corps Band. Europe enlisted as a private in the army. After passing the officers' exam, he was asked by his commander, Col. William Hayward, to form a military band as part of the combat unit. Europe felt that it would be hard to convince New York City musicians to leave their highly paid jobs to go to war, but Colonel Hayward instructed Europe to get the musicians wherever he could. He did just that, even traveling all the way to Puerto Rico to recruit his reed players. When the unit arrived in France on New Year's Day 1918, it was the first African-American combat unit to set foot on French soil. Europe's band entertained troops and citizens in every city they visited, and was received with great enthusiasm. Noble Sissle said at the time that the "jazz germ" hit France, and it spread everywhere they went.

In August 1918 Europe's jazz orchestra achieved further notoriety and acclaim when it played the Théâtre des Champs-Élysees in Paris in the presence of French president Raymond Poincaré and many other notables who were in attendance.

The Hellfighters Band signed a major recording contract with the Pathé Record Company, and was making plans for a tour across the

United States. Regiment and band alike were welcomed back to New York City with a grand parade viewed by almost one million people. It looked very much like a bright and successful future lay ahead. But then tragedy struck. Only a few weeks later in Boston, on the final leg of the band's first tour, James Reese Europe was killed. The final concert on the tour was at Mechanics Hall in Boston on May 9, 1919. That evening another band member, Herbert Wright, became angered by Europe's strict direction, and attacked the bandleader with a knife during intermission. Noble Sissle recalled: "Jim wrestled Herbert to the ground; I shook Herbert, and he seemed like a crazed child, trembling with excitement. Although Jim's wound seemed superficial, they couldn't stop the bleeding, and as he was being rushed to the hospital he said to me: 'Sissle, don't forget to have the band down at the State House at nine in the morning. I am going to the hospital and I will have my wound dressed. I leave everything for you to carry on.'"[11]

Jim Europe's jugular vein had been severed, and within a few hours he passed away. The following day the papers carried the headline "The Jazz King Is Dead." James Reese Europe was buried with military honors at Arlington National Cemetery.

Another former Harlem Hellfighter, Horace Pippin, was born on February 22, 1888, in West Chester, Pennsylvania, moving to Goshen, New York as a small child. Although he faced some initial challenges from school authorities, Pippin developed a love for creating art, winning accolades and developing a reputation in his neighborhood for his craft, even with the limited tools at his disposal.

With his mother in poor health, he left school in his early teens to earn an income, working for years at a hotel and subsequently holding other jobs. Upon joining the army, he was sent overseas to France to fight in World War I as part of Harlem's Hellfighters, in the African-American 369th Infantry. While serving with the French, Pippin's life revolved around the routine of twenty days in the trenches followed by ten days in the rear. Before long he became a seasoned veteran who had witnessed all the horrors that the Western Front could reveal. His war was terminated in late September 1918 during the assault by the 369th on Séchault. On the second day of the advance, Pippin was hit in the shoulder by a

German sniper's bullet while diving into a shell hole for cover. He was badly hurt. Because of the wound he lost the use of his right arm. A fellow soldier tended his wound before leaving Pippin alone to fend for himself. Pippin tried several times to return to his lines and head for the rear, but each time he attempted to leave the shell hole, a German sniper kept him pinned down. Finally, he decided to huddle down deep in the shell hole, too weak to do anything but wait for help.

The first sign of hope came later in the day when a passing French sniper discovered the wounded American. Before Pippin could warn him to stay down, a German sniper shot the French soldier clean through the head without even knocking off his helmet. Pippin recalled: "He stood there for at least ten seconds before he slipped down, and when he did, [he] slid down on top of me. I had lost so much blood by this time I couldn't even move him." Pippin lay completely sedentary with the dead French soldier laying on top of him for several hours. He was thankful for the water and bread that the man carried. Finally, a rescue party arrived and put him on a stretcher by the side of the road. Pippin waited in a steady, cold rain for another twelve hours before an ambulance transported him to a field hospital.

Horace Pippin was deeply affected by his experiences as a soldier in France in a segregated troop during World War I. The experiences left him bitter and suspicious of white people. He never forgot how poorly African-American soldiers were treated after they returned home.

After the war Pippin's family survived on his $22.50 per month disability allowance and his wife's work as a laundress. Pippin took an active interest in his community and served as commander of his local black American Legion post in West Chester, Pennsylvania, for several years. Yet despite his normal outward appearance, he experienced severe bouts of depression, and was haunted by his memories of combat. He tried writing about and making sketches of his experiences, but was initially unhappy with the results. He finally decided to try painting, laboriously using his left hand to guide his right for each stroke of the brush.

His artwork provides an insightful perspective into the horrific and often disturbingly poetic aspects of industrial warfare. Among other things, he depicted the terrifying experience of encountering mustard gas as it descended on troops scrambling for their gas masks, the desolate terrain ravaged beyond recognition by constant artillery bombardments, the fearless exploits of aerial pilots engaged in a dogfight, and the utter desolation that each man privately experienced, even while surrounded by his comrades. He even painted the final moment when German soldiers emerged from their cover to surrender. He was awarded the Croix de Guerre. For Pippin, combat in the First World War provided many personal epiphanies that were movingly and starkly depicted in his often simplistic but always incredibly profound works of art. For all the pain and tragedy he experienced, Horace Pippin discovered that art provided a much-needed catharsis that helped him to process and learn to understand what he'd endured.

In 1937 Pippin was discovered by the Philadelphia art community, and soon received national recognition as a true primitive artist, much like his better-known contemporaries, Jacob Lawrence and Grandma Moses. Pippin went on to become the best-known African-American visual artist of the 1930s and early 1940s. He also wrote several unfinished recollections of the war, and a four-page autobiography. Pippin's story should have culminated in a happy ending, but unfortunately, his physical pain, increasing taste for alcohol, and mounting family problems made his success bittersweet. In 1946, Pippin died suddenly of a stroke.

In Emmett J. Scott's *Official History of the American Negro in the World War*, he wrote:

*The Negro, in the great World War for Freedom and Democracy, has proved to be a notable and inspiring figure. The record and achievements of this racial group, as brave soldiers and loyal citizens, furnish one of the brightest chapters in American history. The ready response of Negro draftees to the Selective Service calls—together with the numerous patriotic activities of Negroes generally—gave ample evidence of their whole-souled support and their 100 percent Americanism. It is difficult to indicate which rendered the greater service to their Country—the 400,000 or more of them who entered active military service (many of whom fearlessly and victoriously fought upon the battlefields of France), or the millions of other loyal members of this race whose useful industry in fields, factories, forests, mines, together with many other indispensable civilian activities, so vitally helped the Federal authorities in carrying the war to a successful conclusion.*[12]

## CHAPTER FIVE

# Playing Safe

By June 1917, fourteen thousand US soldiers had already arrived in France, and by May 1918, over one million US troops were stationed there. Half of them had been allocated to the front lines, mainly to quiet sectors. Pershing may have made a brief exception to his own rule regarding the autonomy of US divisions during the German "Spring Offensive," but he continued to insist that American forces would not be used merely to fill gaps in the French and British armies. He ardently resisted European efforts to have US troops deployed as individual replacements in decimated Allied units.

During early 1918, four battle-ready US divisions were deployed alongside French and British units to gain combat experience. They were alongside but maintained autonomous command from these Allied units. Slowly but surely American troops began pouring into French and British ports. Plans had been devised to considerably increase the strength of American infantry and machine-gun units to be transported to Europe in the near future. To allow the release of veteran French divisions for more-active employment elsewhere, the American 1st, 2nd, 28th, and 42nd Divisions were allocated to various "quiet" sectors. Other American divisions were swarming into training areas behind the French and British lines.

## GEORGE B. DEMPSEY, MEDICAL OFFICER

*January 28, 1918: Arrived at [Le] Havre at 4:00 a.m. and left boat at 9:00 a.m. and hiked six miles through [Le] Havre and to British rest camp No.*

*1, north of the city. Quartered in tents, we officers are getting our meals at a French house nearby. France seems to be much better supplied with food than England. There are also more men working among the civilians. The weather is quite like that we have at home in April.*

*January 29, 1918: Had fine night's sleep and got busy this morning making things comfortable for the men. Had some drill in the morning and a hike in the evening. A beautiful view of the English Channel can be had from some high ground near the camp. Saw airplanes and a dirigible balloon hunting U-boats over the Channel. Preparing to make another move probably early in the morning.*

*January 30, 1918: Up at 1:00 a.m. and at 2:30 a.m., ready to start for train. Men loaded on boxcars and officers on third-class cars at 4:00 a.m. Everyone provided with rations of hardtack and bully beef for four days. We must be going a long ways. Train left station at 6:00 a.m. and we traveled all day through pretty French villages. Train very cold, no provision being made for heating.*

*January 31, 1918: Had a miserable night, train too cold to sleep in, and didn't try to sleep until after the air raid. This morning we crossed the Marne River and passed the scene of the Battle of the Marne. Many evidences of the battle could be seen. Have been anything but comfortable all day; tried to play cards but it was too cold. Hope to arrive at our destination tonight.*

*Night of January 30–31, 1918: Arrived in the railroad yards northeast of Paris at 11:00 p.m. A clear moonlit night with the sky full of stars. Sat in our compartment of train trying to keep warm and to sleep a little. At about 11:30 p.m. the booming of guns in the distance could be heard, so we left the car to see what was going on. In a few minutes a whirring noise could be heard, and lights began to appear in the sky. Then we realized we were about to witness an air raid. Soon light rockets were shot up and the sky was illuminated by large balls of light. Occasionally the frames of airplanes could be seen passing between us and the light stars. The sky seemed to be full of airplanes, some with white and others with red and green lights. These lights moved to and fro in circles, spirals, loops, etc. Now and then loud thundering explosions could be heard as bombs were dropped on the city. Here and there signals could be seen from the French airplanes, and these were followed by the flash and sharp crack of shrapnel from the antiaircraft guns.*

*All at once a deafening explosion was heard of a bomb dropped about 300 yards from us. Our engine pulled away from the train so that the light of the engine would not attract attention to our troop train. The trainmen running to and fro carried their lanterns under their coats so that they wouldn't show any light.*

*At times the sky seemed to be full of airplanes and the whirr of their motors filled the air. This whirr was much accentuated at times by the fire of the machine guns on the airplanes. The raid seemed to last for almost an hour and a half, for after 1:00 a.m. no bomb explosions or bursting shrapnel could be heard. Many airplanes continued to circle in the sky and were still doing so when we left the railroad yards at 3:00 a.m., and continued the journey. The whole engagement was a thrilling night and would have been witnessed with pleasure if we had not realized the bombs were carrying death for many innocent women and children.*

*February 1, 1918: Passed another night in the cold car without sleep. Train stayed all night in the freight yards of a village not far from our destination. Got under way again about 5:00 a.m. and arrived at Bazoilles at 12:00 p.m. Left train and went immediately to camp. Now only about twenty miles from the trenches. Could hear the roar of the big guns tonight. After about two weeks we will probably move near the Front.*

*February 2, 1918: Casualties of air-raid, deaths, 45; wounded, 207. Much material damage to buildings in and about Paris. Up this morning at 7:00 a.m. and my, how cold and damp the barracks [are], almost as cold as Fort B. H., and no stoves to be had. During the day the sun came out brightly, and about noon the air was warm and everything was mud. Still living on bully beef and hardtack, but hot coffee makes it a good meal. Busy all day unloading hospital parts from trains.*

*February 3, 1918: Worked in morning unloading lumber. This evening walked to Neufchâteau to get pictures taken for identity cards. Between Bazoilles and Neufchâteau is a high hill which is crossed by the rue Nationale. A beautiful view can be had from this hill of Bazoilles, Neufchâteau, and other surrounding villages. The ——th division is being moved to the Front. A German offensive is anticipated.*

*February 4, 1918: Received two letters from Nan this evening, the first mail I have had from the USA. The "Base Hospital"–John Hopkins unit is located near us, and also a regiment of engineers, the ——th regulars. Airplanes can be seen in the sky at most any time during the day, sometimes eight or ten at once.*

*February 5, 1918: Have heard that our hospital is to be increased to one thousand beds. That will mean many more officers and enlisted men. All around us the infantry and artillery are at target practice. The machine guns, cannons, and rifles make quite a racket. Had a bath today at the community bathhouse. Allowed four minutes of hot water; quite a relief to wash up and get on some clean clothes.*

*February 6, 1918: Walked down to Neufchâteau today to get a pair of heavy shoes. Alas, none were to be had in the whole town. Sat around the barracks all afternoon but couldn't get comfortable, as the place is cold and damp without a stove. Go to bed every night now between 7:00 and 8:00 p.m. The barracks are very cold at night and we have nothing but candlelight, so cannot read with any comfort. Am looking forward to the warm summer days.*

*February 7, 1918: Having beautiful spring weather. The ground is settling and the days are warm and sunny. Am enjoying the rest here, or at least the opportunity to straighten things out. Enjoy reading the N.Y. edition of the* Herald, *[which] we get one day late.*

*February 10, 1918: The calendar says this is Sunday; otherwise, it could never be guessed. Inspection of equipment in the morning and work at lumber pile in afternoon. The only encouraging feature is the beautiful weather.*

*The sooner it's over the sooner to sleep*
*For there's little to earn and many to keep.*

*February 11, 1918: Several companies of Negro engineers have arrived. They will help out in the heavy work. This afternoon a squad of Negroes were digging a ditch out in the field out about 100 yards from camp. About the middle of the afternoon a couple of airplanes flew overhead. They, [the] Negroes, thought they were Germans and became highly excited. Some of them ran at full speed for camp. Others threw themselves down and covered their heads. I supposed they were playing safe.*[1]

## C. HAROLD FLOYD, 107TH INFANTRY REGIMENT, 27TH DIVISION

*On Memorial Day, the old veterans of 1870, looking much like our G.A.R.s [Grand Army of the Republic], marched with our own doughboys to the little cemetery on the hill at Saint-Aignan and decorated the graves of our dead, while the town officials made long and, judging by the gestures, very eloquent speeches, which were replied to by our high-ranking officers. It was the most impressive Memorial Day ceremony I ever witnessed. On the Fourth of July, very early in the morning, Madame came to my room before I was up with a large bunch of flowers, which she explained were in honor of the great fete day of my country. I went out to find the houses all decorated with flags and the people in gala attire. In the afternoon, the officers were invited to the mairie, or town hall, where we were greeted by the mayor and principal inhabitants, presented with more flowers, and some very choice wine. We tried to return the compliment, ten days later on the great French holiday, with parades, band concerts, and a ball game.*[2]

# CHAPTER SIX

# The Fighting Irish

FOR ALL INTENTS AND PURPOSES, THE STORY OF THE 69TH NEW YORK State Militia begins in 1851 when it was officially designated by the state of New York as their 2nd Regiment of Irish Volunteers. The reputation of this unit was forged in blood and steel long before the outbreak of World War I. They were apparently nicknamed "the Fighting 69th" by Confederate general Robert E. Lee, who fought against them in the Civil War and was impressed by their remarkable tenacity. When President John F. Kennedy addressed the Irish Parliament in 1963, he said,

> *At Fredericksburg thousands of men fought and died on one of the bloodiest battlefields of the American Civil War. One of the most brilliant stories of that day was written by a band of 1,200 men who went into battle wearing a green sprig in their hats. They bore a proud heritage and a special courage, given to those who had long fought for the cause of freedom. I am referring, of course, to the Irish Brigade. General Robert E. Lee, the great military leader of the Southern Confederate Forces, said of this group of men after the battle, "The gallant stand which this bold brigade made on the heights of Fredericksburg is well known. Never were men so brave. They ennobled their race by their splendid gallantry on that desperate occasion. Their brilliant though hopeless assaults on our lines excited the hearty applause of our officers and soldiers."*

In the twentieth century, the Army Center of Military History currently located at Fort Lesley J. McNair, Greenleaf Point, Washington, DC, altered the historically accepted lineage of some of the New York regiments, and attributed an earlier inception date to the 69th. This change implied that the regiment had stronger ties to the Irish revolutionary movement that was organized by refugees of the failed "Young Ireland" insurrection of 1848 in New York City. This was a significant change that subsequently obliterated all previous existing histories of the "Fighting Irish."

All previous National Guard regiments received new regimental numbers in 1917, and in accordance with new War Department regulations, they were doubled in size. On July 25, 1917, the 69th was renumbered the 165th Infantry Regiment, and ordered to active duty as part of the freshly inaugurated 42nd "Rainbow" Infantry Division. One of the commanders appointed to the Rainbow Division was General Douglas MacArthur. The rank and file of the 165th was composed primarily of Irish Americans and New Yorkers assigned from other regiments, and it clung fiercely to its Irish heritage by retaining its Irish symbolism and spirit. Everyone who served with the unit can claim the title of "honorary Irishman" by default. The most celebrated US Army chaplain in the Great War, Father Francis Patrick Duffy, a Roman Catholic priest, pronounced those of non-Irish ancestry who joined the regiment in the following terms: "Irish by adoption, Irish by association, or Irish by conviction."[1]

## FRANCIS P. DUFFY, CHAPLAIN, 165TH INFANTRY

### CAMP MILLS 1917

*We are tenting tonight on the Hempstead Plains, where Colonel Duffy and the Old 69th encamped in 1898 when getting ready for service in the Spanish War. It is a huge regiment, now bigger, I think, than the whole Irish Brigade ever was in the Civil War. We have received our new men transferred from the 12th, 14th, 23rd, and 71st National Guard New York (NGNY). Our band played them into camp with the regimental air of "Garry Owen," mingled with the good-fellow strains of "Hail! Hail! The Gang's All Here." All in all, the newcomers are a fine lot. A couple of our sister organizations have flipped the cards from the bottom of the pack in some instances and worked off on us some of their least desirables. On the other hand, all the regiments have made up for that by allowing men anxious to come to us to change places with those who prefer to stick where they are. This gives us a large number of the men we want—those that feel their feet on their native heath in the 69th, and those that like its recruiting slogan, "If you don't want to be amongst the first to go to France, don't join the 69th."*

*For the rest, the company commanders and surgeons know "thirty-five distinct damnations," or almost that many, by which an undesirable can be returned to civilian life to take his chances in the draft. Our recruiting office has been reestablished at the Armory. We can get all the good men we want. As he had put the matter in my hands, Kilmer did not come over with the men from the 7th, but I had the matter of his transfer arranged after a short delay. We will soon be off to the war and I have been looking over the regiment, studying its possibilities. About the enlisted men I have not a single doubt. If this collection of handpicked volunteers cannot give a good account of themselves in battle, America should keep out of war. The men will fight no matter who leads them. But fighting and winning are not always the same thing, and the winning depends much on the officers, their military knowledge, ability as instructors, and powers of leadership.*

*The non-coms are a fine lot. Maj. William J. Donovan, who commands the First Battalion, was transferred to us from the Brigade Staff, but he is no stranger to us. On the border when he was captain of Troop I of the 1st Cavalry, he was the best-known man of his rank in the New York Division. It was almost certain that Donovan would be appointed our colonel after the efforts to get Colonel Haskell had failed, as he was our next choice, and General O'Ryan knew that there were no politics about it, but a sincere desire to find the best military leader. General O'Ryan esteems Donovan as highly as we do.*[2]

Present-day visitors to Times Square seldom pay homage to the statue of Father Duffy that stands nearby in Duffy Square, on Broadway between 46th and 47th Streets. There's another statue of him outside the Post Chapel at Camp Smith, the New York Army National Guard base in Cortlandt Manor, near Peekskill, New York, about thirty miles north of New York City.

One of the regiment's most popular NCOs at the time was Sgt. Joyce Kilmer, who was also part of the regimental intelligence section, and already a nationally renowned poet and a veteran of the border before he joined the Fighting Irish. He is more famous for writing the inimitable poem "Trees" than for his Great War exploits, and eventual sacrifice. Kilmer was a family man with a wife and children, and normally would have been exempt from fighting, but when the United States declared war on Germany in 1917, he enlisted as a private in the 7th Regiment, New York National Guard. At his request, and with the assistance of Father Duffy, he transferred to the 165th Infantry. While the regiment was at Camp Mills, he was transferred to Company H, Headquarters Company, and assumed the position of senior regimental statistician.

Once in France, Kilmer quickly attained the rank of sergeant, and was attached to the newly organized regimental intelligence staff as an observer. He spent many nights on patrol in No Man's Land, gathering tactically important information. As a member of the regiment's intelligence staff, Kilmer wasn't obliged to spend time on the front lines, but he repeatedly refused to be detained from participating in the action with his comrades. On July 30, 1918, during the Battle of the Ourcq, he attached himself as adjutant to Maj. William Donovan, commanding the First Battalion. Donovan's adjutant, Lt. Oliver Ames, had been killed in combat the day before. A sniper's bullet ended Kilmer's life. The soldier-poet died at thirty-one years of age, facing the enemy.

The regiment's principal objective on that day had been the high ground of Meurcy Farm. Lieutenant Ames and Sergeant Kilmer were buried side by side in a creek bed on that farm. Joyce Kilmer was awarded the French Croix de Guerre for bravery. Camp Kilmer in New Jersey is named after him. According to his correspondent and friend, Father Daly, he was "the most distinguished and widely regretted American to fall in battle during the Great War." His mortal remains are buried in the Oise-Aisne American Cemetery in France, and his poem, "Rouge Bouquet," written during the war, was read at funeral services for all members of the 69th.

## Francis P. Duffy, Chaplain, 165th Infantry, The Fighting Irish

*Major Donovan's post of command was a hole at the southern edge of Bois Colas. Lieutenant Ames's body had been brought in during the night and buried nearby. Ames's place as battalion adjutant was filled by Sgt. Joyce Kilmer, whose position as sergeant of the intelligence section would naturally have entitled him to a place nearer regimental headquarters. But he had preferred to be with a battalion in the field, and had chosen Donovan's. The major placed great reliance on his coolness and intelligence, and kept him by his side. That suited Joyce, for to be at Major Donovan's side in a battle is to be in the center of activity and in the post of danger. To be in a battle, a battle for a cause that had his full devotion, with the regiment he loved, under a leader he admired—that was living at the top of his being. On the morning of the 30th Major Donovan went forward through the woods to look over the position. Kilmer followed, unbidden. He lay at the north edge of the woods looking out towards the enemy. The major went ahead, but Kilmer did not follow. Donovan returned and found him dead. A bullet had pierced his brain. His body was carried in and buried by the side of Ames. God rest his dear and gallant soul.[3]*

Another Fighting Irish notable during World War I and beyond was Col. William "Wild Bill" Donovan, who commanded the 1st Battalion and later on the Regiment. According to one particular story when the unit arrived in France Donovan ordered them to do a five-mile run loaded with fifty-pound packs. When one soldier complained, Donovan allegedly countered by saying, "What's the matter with you guys? I've got the same fifty pounds on my back as you men, and I'm ten years older." He was thirty-five at the time. To which one anonymous soldier replied, "But we ain't as wild as you, Bill." He was referred to as "Wild Bill" for the rest of his life.

Donovan was born in 1883, the son of an impoverished Irish-American family living on the waterfront of Buffalo, New York. He greatly admired Theodore Roosevelt, and grew up reading about the exploits of his hero. He badly wanted to emulate Roosevelt by becoming the same kind of rugged, tough-speaking, maverick adventurer, but it would take a while before he could match the former president's aristocratic heritage. Donovan wasn't a professional soldier; he was a qualified lawyer, but he became a member of the Organized Reserve Corps, and assisted in creating the first cavalry troop in his hometown. This was Donovan's first real attempt to emulate his Rough Riders hero. His contemporaries quickly acknowledged Donovan's natural organizational and leadership abilities, and soon elected him to become sergeant of the company. Shortly after that, he became their commander.

Donovan was asked to command the 1st Battalion of the 69th "Fighting Irish" Regiment after participating in the attempt to capture Pancho Villa. In August 1917, the 69th was selected from all of the National Guard Regiments of New York to represent the state in the newly formed 42nd Rainbow Division. The name of this division was attributed to a relatively unknown colonel by the name of Douglas MacArthur. Although the regiment was renamed the 165th infantry in the Regular Army, throughout the Great War it continued to call itself the "Old 69th."

Donovan was a studious commander who analyzed all the aspects of trench warfare at the Field Officers' School, and read numerous works of military science. Donovan and the 69th were collectively responsible for many tremendous exploits during the Great War. For his bravery he was awarded the Distinguished Service Medal, as well as the Medal of Honor, for heroism and sustaining serious wounds during the Meuse-Argonne Offensive. General Pershing awarded Donovan the Distinguished Service Cross on September 7, 1918, citing him for "being in advance of the division for four days all the while under shell and machine gunfire from the enemy, who were on three sides of him, and he was repeatedly and persistently counterattacked, being wounded twice."

### Donovan Citation in the Congressional Records

*Before Landres and St. Georges in the Argonne on October 14 and 15 the positions were known to be strong. The artillery preparation was brief. It was evident that the attack could be carried through only by desperate resolution. This resolution Lieutenant Colonel Donovan determined to reinforce by his own example. When the Third Battalion moved out to the assault, he went forward in the rear of the first wave, deliberately wearing the marks of his rank so as to be easily recognized by his men, though it also rendered him conspicuous to the enemy.*

*The assaulting battalion met with a terrible reception as it crossed the open ground and moved up the slopes toward the trenches. Machine guns and artillery ravaged it from the front and flanks. Officers and many of the best non-commissioned officers were hit and some platoons began to be disorganized. Then Colonel Donovan, moving erect from place to place in full view of the enemy, reorganized and heartened his men. As spurts of dust went up around him and shells broke in the vicinity, "See," he said, "they can't hit me and they won't hit you."*

*Officers and men of this battalion say that it would have been impossible for them to have made the advance they did had it not been for the cool resolution, indifference to danger, and personal leadership of Colonel Donovan. It is the general opinion that his conduct on this occasion was of the highest type of courage witnessed by anybody in this regiment during the four major actions in which it has been engaged.*[4]

Donovan's heart must have swelled with Irish pride when his boyhood hero Roosevelt wrote him a personal letter in 1918, which he valued as much as any award. The letter stated that Roosevelt's son, who was at that time also serving in Europe, near Donovan, had written to the former president, saying, "He would give anything if only he could be made a Lieutenant Colonel in a regiment under you as Colonel, and Frank McCoy as Brigadier General. My boys regard you as about the finest example of the American fighting gentleman."

Other members of the Fighting Irish also received the Medal of Honor:

### Sgt. Michael Aloysius Donaldson, Medal of Honor Citation

*The President of the United States of America, in the name of Congress, takes pleasure in presenting the Medal of Honor to Sgt.*

*Michael Aloysius Donaldson (ASN: 89868), United States Army, for extraordinary heroism on 14 October 1918, while serving with Company I, 165th Infantry, 42nd Division, in action at Sommerance and Landres-et-Saint-Georges Road, France. The advance of his regiment having been checked by intense machine-gun fire of the enemy, who were entrenched on the crest of a hill before Landres-et-Saint-Georges, his company retired to a sunken road to reorganize their position, leaving several of their number wounded near the enemy lines. Of his own volition, in broad daylight and under direct observation of the enemy, and with utter disregard for his own safety, he advanced to the crest of the hill, rescued one of his wounded comrades, and returned under withering fire to his own lines, repeating his splendidly heroic act until he had brought in all the men, six in number.*[5]

### Sgt. Richard O'Neill, Medal of Honor Citation

*In advance of an assaulting line, Sgt. Richard O'Neill attacked a detachment of about twenty-five of the enemy. In the ensuing hand-to-hand encounter he sustained pistol wounds, but heroically continued in the advance, during which he received additional wounds, but, with great physical effort, he remained in active command of his detachment.*

*Being again wounded, he was forced by weakness and loss of blood to be evacuated, but insisted upon being taken first to the battalion commander in order to transmit to him valuable information relative to enemy positions and the disposition of our men.*[6]

After his discharge from the hospital, Sergeant O'Neill rejoined his regiment for the Argonne campaign, and was wounded again. He was actually wounded eleven times.

Sgt. Tom Fitzsimmons, another of the Fighting Irish, and the acting Stokes mortar platoon leader, stopped a German counterattack on October 15, 1918, with fire from his mortars and two machine guns. For fearlessly exposing himself to enemy fire while directing the mortars, he earned the Distinguished Service Cross. Such was the caliber of those Fighting Irish.

In World War II, Wild Bill Donovan founded the Office of Strategic Services (OSS), which became the predecessor of the Central Intelligence Agency (CIA).

CHAPTER SEVEN

# An Acceptable Standard

GENERAL PERSHING ARRIVED IN FRANCE IN 1917 WITH TWO SPECIFIC orders from Newton Diehl Baker, US President Woodrow Wilson's secretary of war. The first order was "Go to France," and the second order was "Come home." Shortly after arriving there he established his own General Staff that mirrored the French chain-of-command system. His AEF staff ultimately included a chief of staff, a deputy chief, and five assistant chiefs supervising five sections: G-1 (Personnel), G-2 (Intelligence), G-3 (Operations), G-4 (Supply), and G-5 (Training). As the war progressed, the staff officers could—and did—increasingly act and speak for Pershing, without waiting for his personal approval. This practice occasionally incurred the displeasure of subordinate commanders, who were more accustomed to direct contact with their commanding officer as opposed to receiving directives and guidance through staff officers.

On June 26, 1917, the advance elements of the 1st Division joined Pershing and his staff in France. The 1st Division was destined to be the first in and the last one out. The 1st is sometimes nicknamed the "Fighting First," and often simply referred to as "The First." Since World War II, it has been known as "The Big Red One." From Saint-Nazaire, the port of debarkation, the division traveled to the Gondrecourt area in Lorraine, approximately 120 miles southwest of Paris. At this location the division would undergo badly needed training. The War Department had brought many regiments up to strength with new recruits, along with requisitioning numerous well-trained veterans to provide the nucleus for the new divisions forming in the United States. The trickle of American forces arriving in France needed to become a tsunami in order to tackle the problems the Allied armies were now experiencing on the Western Front.

As the bulk of the 1st Division settled in to learn the basics of soldiering, on July 4, the French authorities persuaded Pershing to allow a battalion of the 16th Infantry to march through Paris in the hope that the appearance of these new American troops would reinvigorate the war-weary French public. The parade culminated at Picpus Cemetery, the final resting place of American Revolutionary hero, the Marquis de Lafayette, after whom the Flying Corps had been named. Standing beside this tomb, Col. Charles E. Stanton, a quartermaster officer, delivered a stirring speech on behalf of Pershing. Stanton spoke almost word-perfect French, and finished his oratory with the words, "Lafayette, we are here!" This speech has often been mistakenly attributed to Pershing himself.

### BEN ALLENDER, COMPANY G, 168TH INFANTRY DIVISION

*We left the boat about 7:30, marching to another rest camp about three miles from the dock. Not a very encouraging sight greeted us when we landed there. Trainloads of wounded soldiers pulled in from the Front. This camp was very crowded, twelve men in a tent barely enough for four men. We were given tickets with three parts, each part numbered and marked breakfast, dinner, and tea. As we are still on English rations, the meals were still quite small.*

*We left this camp on December 13, 1917, about 9:00 p.m., and again boarded a train. And it sure was some train. Barely room enough to turn around. On this trip we passed through many principal cities of France, among them Versailles, where coffee was served us.*

*December 15, 1917: We arrived at Langres this morning and immediately unloaded. Our company separated from the rest of our battalion, and we were sent to an old [French] fort called Fort de Pugny, which is situated on the top of a hill. It is a very old fort, having all the old-fashioned tunnels and old-fashioned moats.*

*December 16, 1917: We are comfortably situated in the fort, and I finally got a chance to wash my clothes. I sure did work on them. We are on detached service under command of Colonel Parker, and he sure is a prince of a man.*

*December 17, 1917: Made a trip to town with Captain Stiller to get a load of wood. I don't think much of the place. It is snowing here, the first time since we left Halifax. Just remember, we left Ottumwa just four months ago today. But it seems to me like four years.*

*December 19, 1917: Today we received a bunch of back mail and it sure did put "pip" in the boys. I got six letters.*

*December 23, 1917: Still been just a week since we arrived here, and we all like it fine so far. I am working in the kitchen the last few nights, baking biscuits for breakfast, as we haven't [any] way of getting bread at the present.*

*December 25, 1917: Well, this is Christmas Day, and many miles from home. I never will forget this Christmas Eve, for instead of being out having a fine time, I helped getting our dinner ready for tomorrow. But we can honestly say, that considering how far we are from home and friends, that it was a very Merry Christmas. No work was done all day. We had a very nice X-Mas dinner, including turkey, and after the meal we were given nuts. In the evening we were given a very interesting entertainment, and after this we were presented with some smoking tobacco, which was presented by the* New York Sun. *We had the pleasure of having Colonel Parker, Major Shorts, Major Brown, and Major Scotts as our guests. Altogether we had a very good time, even though we were so far away from home, and we went to our bunks in good spirits.*

*December 28, 1917: We held a large maneuver, advancing under a barrage of machine-gun and mortar trench gunfire. We had a small platoon of every branch used in the modern warfare and all the new guns that America expects to make a big drive with. There was a hundred of our company used in this maneuver. I acted as a scout for an automatic rifle team, Lieutenant Mills being the gunner in our team. This is my greatest experience since I joined the army. Everything went along fine, nobody hurt.*

*January 1, 1918: We were supposed to have moved today, but received different orders. We would have had a New Year's celebration, but expecting to move New Year's Day spoiled it. We were given some tobacco and cigarettes, from the Ladies' Suffragettes Association of Wapello County and a friend, and Lieutenant Mills of New York City.*

*January 17, 1918: Moving again; the company hiked to another town, about fifteen miles. As I was working in the kitchen, I got to ride on the auto with the supplies; pretty soft for me, I landed in the town about 5:00 p.m.*

*January 18, 1918: I woke up this morning and found myself in a barn where I was sent last night. The whole company is in barns; some barns better than others, none of them good. The barn I am in has three floors; a French family and stock on the first floor, and on the second floor is our home and about ten tons of hay, and the attic is full of hay. But one good thing about this barn—we have our bed ticks just as full as we can possibly get them. We climb up over a wagon. If the man moves his wagon, we will lose our home.*

*This town is very small, about a hundred [in] population, and all of them are real old people and schoolchildren, and the town is just as dirty as it is small, but if G Co. is here very long, we will have it clean for once in its history, for we are getting to be pretty good [at] cleaning up places, as we did old Fort de Pugny. There are several small towns near here, but they all are about twenty families' population.*

*January 20, 1918: We are having spring weather here. It was so warm, we have been playing ball. I have been orderly for Lieutenant Mills—the first time I have been dressed up since we left the United States. Lieutenant Mills is now acting commander of the company, and Lieutenant Milligan is mayor of the town. All our officers but these two lieutenants have gone away to officer training school. They have been gone since the first of the year.*

*January 21, 1918: I have used all the writing paper I have and no chance of getting any soon, for there isn't a YMCA close by. I haven't seen but one since we landed in this country. As we haven't drawn any pay since we left the USA, hard telling when I will be able to write again.*

*January 22, 1918: Squad splitting again; I am now in the infantry rifle squad, first squad of third platoon.*

*January 25, 1918: Drilled all day in our short sleeves, just as warm as middle of summer at home. Take up new trench war drill formation. I am assigned to an automatic rifle team, three men in a team. Pay day has been allowed and we will get paid sometime this afternoon, the first pay day since November 7, 1917, and we sure can make good use of it. We are not drilling today; we are drilling five and a half hours a day.*

*January 31, 1918: Worked all day on trench detail. For dinner we had two pieces of dry bread and one piece of bacon. We stood muster of pay tonight in the dark after supper.*

*February 1, 1918: Throwing defensive grenades that have the powder taken out of them. We have our steel helmets, and gas masks. We have orders to wear these new tin hats all the time.*

*February 2, 1918: Instead of having inspection, as we usually do on Saturday, we have to go out and dig trenches all day—the first day we have [had to] work on Saturday [since] we have been in France.*

*February 3, 1918: We were invited over to the YMCA by E and F Cos. of our battalion; we marched over, led by our jazz band. They are located about a mile from here in another small town. We had the pleasure of hearing our regimental chaplain Robb, the first we heard him since we left Camp Mills. He sure gave a fine talk, and I do believe that every man in the regiment enjoys hearing him talk.*

*February 4, 1918: We are being taught to put our gas masks on in a very short time. We are supposed to be able to put them on in six seconds. This afternoon we were on the rifle range. I got to shoot my rifle twenty times, the first time I have shot it since I joined. I claim this is going some just a few miles from the Front, and also just a few weeks, and never shot again yet. But believe me, we sure are getting enough of every kind of French warfare training that we could possibly get, for we are drilling eight hours a day. We are out as soon as we can get out after daylight and drill to nearly dark, with only an hour for dinner.*

*February 5, 1918: We had automatic school for all automatic rifle teams, and went out to the range and shot two clips apiece.*

*February 7, 1918: The company had their first practice throwing live grenades. The major and our company done better than any of the other companies.*

*February 8, 1918: We went out for Springfield rifle practice; [we] all shot very good. I shot very good, really surprised myself, making a score of forty-seven out of a possible fifty. One of the highest of the day.*

*February 10, 1918: All of our officers returned after being at a training school for about six weeks. Our regimental band came through here and played a few pieces on their way. The music sounded so good, and being in the habit of following a band, we followed them and heard a fine concert.*

*February 11, 1918: We had a regimental maneuver . . . about seven miles from here. We had call at 4:15 a.m. We were furnished with one sandwich for our dinner. In the morning we were to take and hold a town that was fortified by the Alabama regiment, but we failed. In the afternoon they tried to take it from us and they also failed. We got back home again at 6:30 p.m.*

*February 12, 1918: Automatic rifle practice in the morning and another review in the afternoon at a small town about five miles from here. We got another small bunch of mail.*

*February 13, 1918: Today we had another all-day maneuver at the same town about five miles from here. And after the day of marching we got home at 7:00 p.m. and received a large bunch of mail, and also got paid, so the thirteenth is not so bad after all.*

*February 14, 1918: Well, this is Valentine's Day, and we are having our all-day maneuver as usual on our one sandwich for dinner.*

*February 16, 1918: This morning we have been out playing games—that is, the most important exercise we get over here. This afternoon we get to take a bath, the first time [we've] had this opportunity since we left the United States, without taking it out in the cold, with cold water, which won't be very pleasant over here right now. We only have to walk two and a half miles for our bath.*[1]

The American troops had arrived in France brimming with enthusiasm and galvanized by training-camp lectures on how the American initiative would reintroduce a war of movement, to redress the trench warfare stalemate that had existed for over three years on the Western Front. The theory was sound, but putting it into practice would be another matter entirely. The first American division to arrive in 1917, seven months after the declaration of war, was regarded as more of a gesture to boost the morale of the Allied armies than a force that would tip the balance in favor of the Allies.

The Allied propaganda had worked well, and these fresh-faced young Americans were welcomed with open arms by both British and French civilians and military, but the initial ardor would soon dissipate. By October 31, 1917, the Americans had 6,064 officers and 80,969 men in France. The first Americans were deployed on October 21, 1917, to what was regarded by the Allies as a quiet sector. The American tactical doctrine at the time was still based erroneously on large maneuvers in open country. This contrasted sharply with what the Allied armies had developed after three hard years of bloody trench warfare, and after incurring innumerable casualties. By December 31, 1917, the number of American soldiers in Europe had risen to 174,884.

The British and French military authorities remained insistent that the appearance of American troops in the line would inevitably have a favorable effect on the morale of their own weathered troops. Such was the eagerness to deploy these men that the Allies advised that prior training be limited to the absolute minimum necessary required for trench warfare. They repeatedly emphasized the shortage of Allied troops in the line, and further requested that American troops be immediately assigned to compensate for this deficiency. The Allies also emphasized that among other things, the current vulnerability of the situation was due to Russia being eliminated, together with consecutive defeats on the Italian front.

In late October 1917 the Germans had already earmarked troops released from their commitment on the Eastern Front to spearhead a powerful Austro-German offensive against the Italians along the Isonzo River. Less than one month later the Italian forces had been resoundingly defeated and forced to retreat more than sixty miles, in some disarray. What had up until that time essentially been regarded as a three-front war for the Germans was now fusing into a single front.

The American commander in chief agreed that every combat unit in France should indeed be made available for frontline service, but remained intransigent in his determination that all Americans must remain independent of any form of protracted amalgamation with the Allied armies. He was, as previously mentioned, prepared to make a notable concession regarding the African-American units when he wholeheartedly agreed to transfer the 93rd Division's four African-American infantry regiments to the French Army, where they could be incorporated into French divisions. Pershing wasn't unsympathetic to the Allied need for fresh troops, but he didn't share their pessimism. His General Staff had informed him that it was their considered opinion that reports of a possible Allied collapse were greatly exaggerated, and that despite the deficiencies, neither the British nor the French forces were on the verge of disintegration, and still more than capable of sustaining and maybe even repelling a concerted German offensive.

By January 26, 1918, the 1st Division relieved a French division in an active sector north of Toul. It was unanimously agreed that the 1st

Division had trained to an acceptable standard that allowed them to be deployed in these frontline positions.

## Theodore Kohls, Company A, 26th Infantry Regiment, 1st Division

*I enlisted at Jefferson Barracks. Was sent to the border to the 26th, which was one of the regiments picked to go to France with the first troops. We sailed from Hoboken on June 10, 1917; our trip lasted fourteen days. We landed in France on June 27, 1917, at the harbor of Saint-Nazaire. We stayed at Saint-Nazaire for about two weeks, then we were sent to Demange in Meuse county, where we found out for the first time how heavy seventy pounds was. Oh, my poor back. We went up a hill every day to our drill grounds where we learned modern warfare from the 54th Regiment of the French Blue Devils.*

*From there we went to Boviolles, a little village not far from Demange, but over some very big hills which we had to hike over. We started maneuvering; oh how I wished I was home, the soles worn off my shoes, my clothing all torn, and I was wet all through. This is what we got while in training in France.*

*On October 29, 1917, we went into the trenches for the first time. My company stayed in reserve for ten days, then we went to relieve a company of my battalion. It snowed that night; it was the first snow I experienced in France. We waded through trenches with mud and water and stood in rain all night while experiencing my first time in the trenches. When I was relieved the next morning, I was wet through and through.*

*We stayed in these mud holes for five days without even seeing a German. We were relieved by the second battalion of my regiment. We went back to our old billets where we spent a week getting our clothing in halfway decent shape again. After that maneuvering started in the cold, we spent nights out in the open field and nothing to eat; these maneuvers lasted as long as fourteen days. Such was our life in France the first few months.*

*Until we went into the Toul front, my division held trenches at Toul for three months. This front wasn't as bad as the others. The Germans would throw a barrage on us every now and then. Here I was sent on my first patrol, seen the first one of us to be killed or wounded. I went on my first wiring detail, which was done under cover of night. So went by our three months. On this front we also didn't get much to eat. From this front we [were] relieved by the*

*26th Division, and we took to hiking with full packs on our back. We kept this up till we got close to the Montdidier front.*[2]

In a letter prepared by the prime ministers of Great Britain, France, and Italy, at Versailles on June 2, 1918, the leaders expressed their growing concerns:

> *We desire to express our warmest thanks to President Wilson for the remarkable promptness with which American aid, in excess of what at one time seemed practicable, has been rendered to the Allies during the past month to meet a great emergency. The crisis, however, still continues. Marshal Foch has presented to us a statement of the utmost gravity, which points out that the numerical superiority of the enemy in France, where 162 Allied divisions now oppose 200 German divisions, is very heavy, and that, as there is no possibility of the British and French increasing the number of their divisions (on the contrary, they are put to extreme straits to keep them up), here is a great danger of the war being lost unless the numerical inferiority of the Allies can be remedied as rapidly as possible by the advent of American troops.*
>
> *He, therefore, urges with the utmost insistence that the maximum possible number of infantry and machine gunners, in which respect the shortage of men on the side of the Allies most marked, should continue to be shipped from America in the months of June and July to avert the immediate danger of an Allied defeat in the present campaign wing to the Allied reserves being exhausted before those of the enemy.*
>
> *In addition to this, and looking to the future, he represents that it is impossible to foresee ultimate victory in the war unless America is able to provide such an army as will enable the Allies ultimately to establish numerical superiority. He places the total American force required for this at no less than 100 divisions, and urges the continuous raising of fresh American levies, which, in his opinion, should not be less than 300,000 a month, with a view to establishing a total American force of 100 divisions at as early a date as this can possibly be done.*

*We are satisfied that Marshal Foch, who is conducting the present campaign with consummate ability, and on whose military judgment we continue to place the most absolute reliance, is not overestimating the needs of the case, and we feel confident that the Government of the United States will do everything that can be done, both to meet the needs of the immediate situation, and to proceed with the continuous raising of fresh levies, calculated to provide, as soon as possible, the numerical superiority which the Commander in Chief of the Allied Armies regards as essential to ultimate victory.*

*A separate telegram contains the arrangements, which Marshal Foch, General Pershing, and Lord Milner have agreed to recommend to the United States Government with regard to the dispatch of American troops for the months of June and July.*

*Signed,*
*CLÉMENCEAU*
*D. LLOYD GEORGE*
*ORLANDO*[3]

This letter was probably incited by the German Spring Offensive that had occurred a few months earlier, when Allied troops sustained the full force and suffered greatly. It occurred March 21, 1918, as the German Army amassed its troops and launched an offensive on a front south of Arras in the Saint-Quentin sector. At this time, there were approximately 300,000 American troops already in France. The 1st, 2nd, and 42nd Divisions had occupied trenches, and the 26th was regarded as being "battle-ready." Two divisions were designated as replacements, the 32nd and the 41st Divisions. The 32nd was ordered to a training area with headquarters in Haute-Marne, while the 41st, which had been the fifth US division to arrive in France, in 1917, never saw combat as a complete division. Soon after arriving it was broken up and its men used as replacements for other divisions.

For the first time since the beginning of the war, German transference of its divisions from the east to the west gave the Central Powers numerical superiority over the Allies. Despite this, Gen. Erich Ludendorff, chief of staff of the German armies, didn't expect to win the war, but by launching as many offensive actions as possible, the German high command aimed to lure the Allies to the negotiating table. They wanted to place themselves in a strong position to be able to negotiate a more-favorable peace settlement, and place Germany on a more-equal footing with the Allied countries. Both Hindenburg and Ludendorff expected these newly arrived German divisions to tip the balance and drive the Allies back to the Channel. They almost succeeded with what became known as the Spring Offensive. The purpose was to inflict as much damage as possible on the Allied armies before the Americans could be deployed along the Western Front in any significant numbers. It was a desperate race against time that would see the AEF finally committed for the first time.

Shortly after 4:00 a.m. on March 21, 1918, more than 6,500 German heavy guns and 3,500 mortars unleashed one of the most devastating artillery bombardments in the history of modern warfare. In less than five hours, nearly 3.5 million shells had shattered British command posts and gun batteries, while salvo after salvo of deadly chlorine and mustard gas rained down on the trenches.

Sixty-three German divisions launched a coordinated, withering attack along a sixty-mile front held by twenty-six British divisions. The attacking soldiers were not of the usual caliber; these were the Kaiser's elite *Sturmtruppen*, or storm troopers—handpicked men, specially trained and armed to the teeth. They were using techniques hitherto unseen on the Western Front that almost completely subdued British and French defenses and caused the Allies to retreat in disarray to the west. The British had expected the attack would be widely dispersed in an attempt to outflank them in the Somme woods and valleys, but the Germans concentrated on infiltrating strongly in one central area. The British 3rd Army and 5th Army were completely taken by surprise, divided, and forced to retreat. German troops then rapidly advanced across the Somme battlefield toward Amiens. In five days, they had recaptured all the land they had lost around the Somme in the previous two years. After nearly four years of war, victory for the Kaiser seemed tantalizingly within reach.

Pershing understood the gravity of the current crisis that was unfolding and was eager to provide troops for the Allies, even at the expense of temporarily relinquishing his primary aim of keeping US divisions under AEF command. He approached Marshal Foch in an uncharacteristically conciliatory mood and said, "I have come to tell you that the American people would consider it a great honor for our troops to be engaged in the present battle. I ask you for this in their name, and my own. At this moment there are no other questions but of fighting. Infantry, artillery, aviation, all that we have are yours: use them as you wish. More will come, in numbers equal to requirements. I have come especially to tell you that the American people will be proud to take part in the greatest battle of history."

## Bruce G. Wright, 372nd Infantry Regiment, 93rd Infantry Division

*The next morning, April 14, 1918, we landed at Saint-Nazaire, France. Camp was about three miles from the dock, but as we walked through the streets looking at the strange-looking people, funny houses, and other odd sights, [we] were in camp before we realized it. Now it was after noon and we were very hungry, as we hadn't eaten since early morning; there was no food in camp, as our regimental supplies hadn't been brought up from the ship as yet.*

*The camp known as Camp No. I was a large one, and had many soldiers there, most of whom were "stevedores." Each company had one barrack which was about 100 yards long and 10 yards wide, and had enough boards on the side to keep some of the wind out, but the roof—well, there practically wasn't any roof at all. Beds were made of trees, very strong but crude. The mud on the floor was no more than a foot deep. However, we were so glad to be on land once more [that] this hole, as it was, seemed like a palace to us.*

*The boys got their French books out and began studying. But I and a few of the other boys knew how to say "Avez vous de vin?" which means "Have you some wine?" and "Je suis faim," which means "I am hungry." That covered the whole French vocabulary for us, and we set out to find either one or the other, or both, which we did, and in so doing looked up several new words, and when we got back to the barracks we felt like regular French men. Here I picked up a new "buddy" in Ed Taylor, and he and I proceeded to light up Saint-Nazaire. We took nothing serious and perhaps it was just as well.*

*The following two weeks were spent in being detailed to work on railroad tracks. But there was much work done by our boys, as we couldn't see wherein we should handle a pick and shovel, as we as infantry came to France to fight. So when they found [we] refused to be made to do stevedores' work, [they] gave us orders to be shipped to the Front.*

*Somewhere about the last of April we boarded trains in Saint-Nazaire, and trains they were, too. The cars measured thirty feet by five feet, built like cattle cars. They packed about fifty men to a car and here we rode, half standing up and half laying down, for three days and nights in the rain. Now on this train we got our first sound from the front line, the booming of the big guns. It made us shudder. [We were] still thirty kilometers from the lines, but on hearing this, most of us must have felt inwardly like turning back to good old Saint-Nazaire and grabbing the longest pick and the biggest shovel in that city. We got out of that train about 6:00 p.m. on the 1st of May 1918. It was raining hard, but we had a walk of about eighteen kilometers before we reached our next camp.*

*Walked until early the next morning, and then we all but fell into a little town known as Conde en Barrois, wet to the skin and no shelter to be found, and food that was well out of the question. [We heard] the command of "Fall out," and right there we made our first attempts to sleep outdoors in the rain. Of course, we covered with our shelter-halfs as much as possible, and found no trouble in sleeping, we [were] so tired. The first faint wave of odor coming from the cook shack reached our sleeping noses early that afternoon, and it seemed that the whole outfit awoke at once as if by bugle call, and all started one grand stampede for the cook shack. The food wasn't finished cooking, and what little there was, was about half done, but it tasted like a ten-course Christmas dinner to our unconscious stomachs.*

*At once our regiment was ordered for general cleanup, as we were to be inspected by General Pershing and his staff on the following day. Then such cleaning of rifles and equipment, all getting ready for inspection by the general before we were let out by the Federal Government of the United States.*

*The following day, spick-and-span, looking just as if we had stepped out of a bandbox (instead of a freight train), the general came. A grand parade followed, then the equipment. After the inspection we were passed and now put in full control of the French government to do our six weeks' training for the battle lines The first [letter] from the States reached me in this camp on May 4th, addressed to me at Newport News, Virginia, and forwarded to me at Conde. The sender—then a very dear friend but now a sweetheart, and later, I hope, my wife—Miss Lovette L. Harvey, 145 Washington Street, Cambridge, Massachusetts. The time passed on, and many funny incidents happened, such as to find out that our meats were [veal] and horse meat, and our bread was made up of sawdust of some compound or other.*

*We all got sick at the start of the peculiar diet, and all of us were as good as dead for a few days, but come out of it good. Then this queer food began to taste as good to us poor suckers as anything else. The French population grew very fond of us, as well as our French instructors. The* polius [poilu], *or Frog soldiers, who were tickled to death at how fast we were and how quick we learnt the different things, such as hand grenade throwing, shooting with French guns, French style of bayonet fighting, and their idea of going into battle in two waves.*

*We watched air battles day in and day out while about our different drills: had two hours a day at target practice, and all of us were getting fat and wise. Could hear the big guns very plain, and when there would be a barrage up at the line. It would make us fellows sit down and think what we would be up against in the near future. We got onto the game so speedily that the French thought that they had better take us up to the Front and try us out, so the 25th of May, 1918, our mixed officers and few sergeants went up to the line to reconnoiter our places. They came back the 27th a sad and sick-looking bunch. One had been killed and two were wounded. Lieutenant Berkley, our platoon commander, didn't look the same. He was a scared man, as he had had a close shave [with] death. There was no change in Captain Pryor, our company commander, however. He proceeded to tell us as best he could just what we were up against, and how we must use all of the tactics of trickery that the Frenchmen had shown us, as well as our own mothers' wit. There was a solemn crowd of boys in camp, but we were paid on the 28th of May, and that did break the monotony. The townspeople opened their wine cellars and beer gardens, dance halls, and the bronze doughboys ran amuck with 200 francs apiece as pay.*

*The next day, the 29th, we were supposed to move, and were ordered to pack our barrack bags and take them on the supply truck, so as we wouldn't have to carry them. But when my buddy Ed Taylor and I got paid, the [town] wasn't big enough for us, so we jumped a train and went to a city about twenty kilometers from Conde and spread joy the day of the 29th and night also. But toward midnight as we sobered up a bit, we remembered that we were supposed to leave for the Front the next morning from our camp, which was about twenty miles away, so we grabbed a train out of this city, Bar-le-Duc, as we bid our newly made friends good-bye en route to our camp. But the cussed train fooled us and only went two stations farther, and that left us eight miles to walk. It was about 1:00 a.m. as we fell off the platform of this little one-horse station into the road, which had the eight miles between us and Conde. Here we were walking like two jockey hounds with a quart of champagne in each hand and a pint of two-in-one whiskey in each pocket; [we'd] sit by the side of the road and drink, then walk until sober.*

*My, what a long eight miles. We reached Conde about 4:30 a.m. and paid off the guards in drink to let us in camp, and had just hit our sleeping quarters when the bugler sounded reveille. Everyone was hollering rifles and waste belts and all out. The barrack bags had all gone except for Ed's and mine, and us two didn't even have them packed. We decided to go along without them, but just as we were making our getaway, Sergeant Conevi sang out that there were two barrack bags left behind, and of course our names on the things inside showed the rightful but unwilling owners.*

*The next town we entered was the town Bellefontaine, which was torn to pieces by shells. Not a whole house remained in a couple of miles behind the line. We stayed there from the 29th [of May] until the evening of the 2nd of June. There we did guard duty, shot craps, played cards, and had good times as long as we stayed out of sight of the German airplanes.*

*On June 2 at 4:00 p.m. the order came to pack, and at 4:30 we were marching out of Bellefontaine, on our way to the trenches. The Germans must have got wind of our presence on the road, as they began to throw shells, and the first shell that we ever heard whistle broke on the side of the road, but didn't harm any of us, as we used the French idea and made use of the ditches that had been dug at the side of the road. Several shells fell near[by], and only two men were killed, and one mule. When the signal came for forward march, I had to drink nearly a pint of wine before I could get up enough courage to get up out of that ditch. I was scared stiff, and so was everyone else. Of course, many of them wouldn't admit that they were scared after things quieted down, but they didn't have to admit it, as they were so pale they looked like white soldiers. We went into holes in the ground about 9:00 p.m. that night, and so many shells fell around there that it seemed as if the earth shook all around us. Big rats walked over us all night long, and we awoke next morning, those of us who slept, with an awful itch, not knowing then that we had lice, or "cooties."*

*Most of us were over our scare of the night before, and we enjoyed ourselves by sitting up in the trees at the top of the hill, watching the maneuvers of the Germans, less than a mile away. That evening, June 3, we started on our last lap. We walked in single file, one man about ten yards behind the other, so if a shell broke, it would only get one or two, but everything was quiet. We reached News Cottage after dark, [and] formed our squads.*

*The 1st platoon was given Sector 34, and the 2nd platoon, my platoon, was ordered through these winding trenches to Sector 32, with orders to hold ground at all costs. We relieved a French regiment, and naturally, they had to transmit their orders to us and they couldn't talk English, so here's how they did it. "Shhh, shhh—Boche, là" ("Germans, there," pointing in a direction); "Shhh, shhh—Boche, là" ("Germans, there," pointing in another direction); "Fusi metraleues [sic], là," ("Machine guns, there," pointing), meaning just about the direction the Germans had their machine guns. Bizz, bizz, and a few sharp reports from German rifles told us the rest, and the French men departed as polite as could be, even saying* Au revoir.[4]

The German Spring Offensive had been nigh on disastrous for the Allies. They lost nearly all the territory taken during the previous two years that thousands of men had died trying to capture, and less than ten days after launching the offensive, German troops were almost at the gates of Amiens. Capture of this town would have meant acquiring a pivotal link in the supply chain for both the British and French armies on the Western Front. Fortunately, the Germans were prevented from capturing the strategically important town of Amiens. Its loss would have effectively severed the French Army from the British Army, enabling the Germans to operate against each of them piecemeal. The Germans did, however, succeed in cutting one railroad into Amiens from the south and seriously impeding traffic on some of the others. They also increased the frontage, which the Allies were forced to hold with diminished numbers.

More worryingly, the Germans had conclusively proven that their forces could penetrate and neutralize highly organized defenses of the Western Front. On March 25, the 3rd and 4th Australian divisions were hastily instructed to get up to the Front and plug the gaps in the Allied line. Although the German offensive eventually dissipated and failed in its objective, it had seriously unnerved British and French forces. In response to this attack, on March 26, Marshal Foch was appointed Allied commander, tasked with coordinating the French and British armies, and shortly thereafter, on April 3, he was given tactical command of the French, British, and American armies on the Western Front.

The AEF's entry into battle during the German Spring Offensive in March 1918 contributed significantly to restoring Allied morale. Without this assistance, there was every possibility that the Allied armies might have disintegrated under the pressure. Although German attempts to eliminate the British Army had failed, and the German offensive had fallen marginally short of its goal, the British had paid a heavy price. Ludendorff's effort to divide the British from the French and destroy each army piecemeal didn't achieve the expected results, but that didn't dissuade or deter German high command from launching another offensive later that spring. This one would directly involve soldiers from the AEF.

Due to the crisis caused by the German Spring Offensive in 1918, Allied shipping increased, facilitating the remarkable increase of American arrivals that peaked with the efficacious transportation of more than 300,000 officers and men in one month.

The second German offensive, known as the Georgette Offensive, began when forty-six divisions of the German 6th Army attacked the British 2nd Army around Ypres. On April 9, the Germans broke through the British lines in Flanders on a twelve-mile front along the Lys-Cantigny River, south of the destroyed city of Ypres. The area we now associate with the location of Flanders Fields is relatively flat, apart from a few gradual slopes and inclines. The one geographic feature that still protrudes from the landscape there is the hill known as Mont Kemmel. On April 25, the German troops succeeded in capturing this strategically advantageous location. During the night of Wednesday, April 24, 1918, they had begun to bomb the position with noxious gas shells, and were already across the little River Douve, just to the south of the height, while simultaneously hitting the village of Dranouter, to the southwest. By 9:00 a.m. on Thursday, April 25, the French garrison had withdrawn from the summit, and late on the Friday evening, the Allies acknowledged that the famous hill had passed into enemy hands. It was later claimed that the Kaiser himself had watched the assault on Mont Kemmel from an advanced field position, but these reports were never substantiated.

A number of American medical, engineering, and air service units with the British Army participated in the operations near Amiens and along the Lys River. The Germans succeeded in pushing the British back three miles to the outskirts of the devastated town of Ypres; this included the retaking of the hard-won Passchendaele Ridge. Under normal circumstances, a spring offensive in the valley of the Lys would have been nigh-on impossible. The whole country was usually submerged in this season, but in the spring of 1918, the ground was exceptionally dry. The AEF didn't contribute any significant numbers to the active inter-Allied defense against the first two German offensives of 1918, because in March on the infamous Somme River, and in April on the Lys River, there simply hadn't been sufficient AEF troops in place to make any substantial difference to the eventual outcome.

The German Sixth Army directed the main attack between Armentières and the La Bassée Canal with seventeen divisions, the main thrust being directed toward Hazebrouck. The German Fourth Army with eight divisions was to take the heights of Messines, and then connect with the German Sixth Army to exploit the intended gains. In this, their second offensive of 1918, the Germans again missed achieving a stunning victory by a very narrow margin. Both Hindenburg and Ludendorff expressed their conviction that success in the Lys operation would have dealt the Allies a shattering blow. American troops played a small part in the Lys defensive. The American 30th Engineers, the 16th Railway Engineer Regiment, and the 28th Air Squadron were attached to and served with British units.

## ROY SCOW, COMPANY D, 163RD INFANTRY REGIMENT

*It was an exploding German shell. Those Germans were shooting at us all the time out there. Bang bang bang bang bang, and the big old shell busted right in front of me and knocked me on my, gunnywhacker, you know. Whatever that is, you know, your, you heard about them, well, then, I was down there, that the explosion knocked my ears out. I had a good job on the railroad. I was going right, and I had brains enough to be an engineer, you know. Shoveling, shoveling coal in the locomotives. Afore you's a fireman, see. And I never got that far up.*[5]

In a meeting of the Supreme War Council convened at Abbeville on May 1 and 2, 1918, Allied commanders discussed the way forward. The gravity of this conference could not be underestimated. French prime minister Georges Clémenceau opened the conference with a powerful statement: The first subject for discussion was the immediate allocation of American troops to the Allied forces. British prime minister David Lloyd George told the assembled party that ten British divisions had been almost completely eradicated, and providing British replacements wasn't an option at this time; hence, the necessity for American battalions to reinforce their depleted ranks. Marshal Foch agreed that the British had indeed suffered the greatest losses recently, but maintained that this didn't set a precedent for future assistance.

Lloyd George interjected that the new recruits wouldn't be available until August 1918, and that both the French and British armies required concerted aid. The fiery Welshman turned to General Pershing and urged him to provide assistance until that time by allowing American units to serve in the British and French armies. Pershing got to his feet and replied, "I do not understand that the American Army is available for allocation as recruits to either Great Britain or France, nor for any indefinite period. We must have an American Army. I shall insist on this principle, that no parceling out of the American Army shall prevail. I want this principle taken up and agreed to now by this Council." The French, Italian, and British authorities accepted the policy of the ultimate formation of an American army, but ascertained that its organization should not be attempted until the outcome of the current military operations could be determined. Further efforts and heated arguments were used to impress this idea upon the American representatives. General Pershing finally drew the meeting to a close with his typical candor when he said, "Gentlemen, I have thought this program over very deliberately, and will not be coerced."

The arrangement finally achieved at this conference between all present became known as the Abbeville Agreement:

> *It is the opinion of the Supreme War Council that, in order to carry the war to a successful conclusion, an American Army should be formed as early as possible under its own commander and under its own flag. In order to meet the present emergency, it is agreed that American troops should be brought to France as rapidly as Allied transportation facilities will permit, and that as far as consistent with the necessity of building up an American Army, preference be given to infantry and machine-gun units for training and service with French and British armies, with the understanding that such infantry and machine-gun units are to be withdrawn and united, with their men, artillery, and auxiliary troops, into divisions and corps at the discretion of the American commander in chief after consultation with the commander in chief of the Allied armies in France.*

The decision reached at the Abbeville Conference, which covered the shipment of American troops through June, leaving July for later review and determination, appeased all participants, and General Pershing felt that the matter had been conclusively resolved.

## C. Harold Floyd, 107th Infantry Regiment, 27th Division

*Altogether, our relations with the French people were very happy, especially in the case of the enlisted men, who lived in the French families and might be seen at all hours, sitting on the doorsteps, chatting with the little dark-eyed mademoiselles and playing with the French children. They formed fast friendships, often without knowing a word of each other's language. The days dragged wearily on in the camp, and we began to believe that we were going to get through the war without seeing any actual service. Many of the other officers were as anxious to get away as we, especially when we heard that there were numbers of wounded officers and officers unfit for frontline service, waiting at Blois, a few miles away, for something to do. However, we did our best, and during the fighting at Château-Thierry, when our particular kind of supplies were much in demand, both night and day forces worked continuously.*

*Finally, about the 5th day of August, rumors began to fly about that Burtis, Brundage, and I were to leave Saint-Aignan. We tried to run them down, but without success. They persisted, however, and I asked the captain once more when we were going. "Today," he replied. There was joy in our little circle immediately, though our orders did not come until the 8th, and we left on the 9th. The intervening time was devoted to a hasty gathering of necessary equipment, attending a lecture on gas attacks, going through the gas chamber, etc.*

*Our orders took us to the II Corps, Reinforcement Camp at Hesdigneul on the Channel, and required some study of the maps before we knew which direction to take. We spent the first night of freedom at Tours, and proceeded by the early train next morning to Paris. This city was the same old attractive place that it was before the war, and yet in many ways it was different. The base of the Vendôme Column was protected from air bombs by [a] thick cement casing, while about two blocks away we saw a small hotel with a big hole in the front wall made the day before by Big Bertha, the German long distance gun. At intervals, along the avenues at the entrance to a building, was a sign marked "Abri," followed by the number of people that could be sheltered there in case of raid. At night, the city was absolutely dark. Crowds stumbled about, people ran into each other, lost their friends and themselves and nearly got killed by taxis. But for a few pale blue lights hidden from above by protecting shades, we never could have found our hotel.*

*Soldiers were everywhere. The boulevards were thronged with them, and they represented all the Allied countries. Most of them were back from the Front for a few days. They had been through the most terrible slaughter and had escaped themselves by what they considered a miracle, for the fighting at that time was intense. Ahead was discomfort, privation, and perils of many kinds. It seemed only a question of time before they would be killed or wounded. Hence, they were making the best of their few days in Paris, and a grand and glorious time most of them were having. We stayed at the Meurice and had most of our meals at the Richmond, the American Officers' Club run by the YMCA. At the latter place, you met every officer in the army that you knew, provided you stayed long enough. Two days were spent in Paris, seeing the sights, going to the theater every night, and enjoying the freedom from work and discipline.*

*On the evening of the 12th, we took the train for Hesdigneul—that is, Brundage and I did. Burtis had gone to see a friend stationed near Paris and lost the train in consequence. It was an all-night trip in a small compartment with two British naval officers and several French people, who woke us up at every station, rushing from side to side in a wild endeavor to find out if it was the place they were going to. The train was kept dark because of the danger of air raids, and these people fell over everybody three or four times at each station.*

*At dawn, we pulled into Hesdigneul, went to the camp and reported, and had lunch. Shortly after noon, we were on our way again, but Brundage had in the meantime acquired a company of replacements to take from that camp to the 27th Division Reception Camp at Esquelbecq. We had no idea where Esquelbecq was, or how [we] were to get there, except that we were given boxcars for the men and a passenger car for ourselves, and knew that we would be shipped through somehow, like so much freight. The train stopped at Étaples, and the RTO [railway transportation officer] ordered us to detrain and proceed to the British rest camp on a hill, just above the station. It was an enormous camp with row on row of wooden shacks and myriads of tents. A British sergeant received the men and gave them a short lecture regarding their quarters and meal hours, and ended by telling them the signal for an air raid and the location of certain trenches where they were to go in case the signal was given.*

*Brundage and I spent the evening at the officers' mess, a very comfortably furnished building like all places for the entertainment of British officers, and then retired to our tent, passing on the way the entrance to a dugout in which the officers took cover during raids. Aft about midnight, the signal for a raid sounded. Brundage called to me as he went out into the darkness. Whistles were blown all over camp. I had been told that the tent, having a floor sunk below level of the surrounding ground, was perfectly safe unless a direct hit was made on it. I decided to stay for a while. Then I heard the engine of a Boche plane overhead and changed my mind very quickly, and made tracks for the dugout. At the entrance were several British officers telling stories of past experiences with air raids; and there we stayed. When Jerry came directly over us, we would step inside until he passed and then come out and watch the sights. "Jerry" was the British name for a German.*

*All around, the archies [British military slang for German antiaircraft fire] were giving their dull thuds, followed by a burst of shrapnel up in the* sky. Then came a loud crash as the bombs from the planes exploded, all at some distance from where we were standing. The rumble of the guns and the flashes of explosions made it all seem like a terrible thunderstorm on a dark night. Finally, the "all safe" sounded and we returned to our bunks, only to be called out a few hours later for a repetition of the experience. It was hardly what could be called a restful night.

Early in the morning, we assembled our little company, once more entrained, and reached Esquelbecq without further adventures. Here, we were relieved of the men and spent the night on the ground in a tent, somewhat annoyed by Jerry planes, which, however, passed over in search of bigger game. The next day we got orders taking us direct to the 27th Division, and after a trip on a toy railroad which went little faster than a man could walk, we reached the little Flemish village of Winnezeele, from which a walk of a few miles brought us to Oudezeele, and Division Headquarters. From here, we were ordered to Regimental Headquarters at Saint-Laurent, and after waiting several hours, managed to get a car to take us and our luggage the few miles necessary to get us "home."

Regimental Headquarters impressed me right away as being utterly insignificant as compared with the very dignified and rather elaborate headquarters at home. All the officers seemed to be compressed into a small Nissen hut, while a few tents scattered about and a little Flemish house quartered the officers. There may have been more of it out of sight, but I did not wait to find out. The adjutant told me that I was now in K Company and that my company went into the front line that night for the first time. All we had missed was the training period and a tour in the reserve line. Colonel Debevoise came in while we were talking, a perfect example of the best type of American soldier. I had seen him as a cavalryman on the border, but he had come to the 107th while we were away. He received us very pleasantly and cordially. We also found that we had left Saint-Aignan so suddenly, not because of any belated desire on the part of authorities there to live up to our orders, but because of a demand from the regiment.

I had hardly been at Saint-Laurent more than an hour or so when a messenger from the 3rd Battalion Transport rode into camp and I went back with him, riding his horse part of the way and walking the rest. We were approaching the Front and civilians became less and less in evidence, while *everything relating to the military became more and more common. We reached the Transport, as the wagons and animals are called, just as it was about the start for the Front, and I went along with it. Lieutenant Rambo of K, just back from school, was going up too, so [we] went together.*

*We followed a long line of British limbers [carriages], carrying food and other supplies. Some of these limbers belonged to British units, and some had been issued to our own. A little way out we passed through a village which had recently been shelled. It was absolutely deserted, except for an MP [military policeman] on the corner where the two main streets came together. A few ruined houses, and many with the tiles lifted from their roof by the concussion, bore witness to the destructiveness of the Boche shells. We passed along several roads with great, camouflage screens made of high wire fences, hung with parti-colored burlap, hiding our movements from the enemy who looked down on us from nearby Mont Kemmel. The sun set as we plodded along, and it began to grow dark. Then came a noise between a hiss and a whistle, which started with a high note and rapidly descended the scale, ending with a crash in a field on our left, a Boche shell, then another and another. The British Tommies, following their limbers, began to curse. The Americans jogged along quietly. The drivers sped up a little and we on foot got left behind temporarily. Meanwhile, the Transport began to split up and turn down different roads according to its different destinations.*

*When we caught up, we found we had followed the wrong limber. We were now on a narrow trail in the middle of a flat, low country covered with several years' growth of weeds. The Boche shells were passing over us in a steady stream, many of them shrapnel. In the opposite directions, our own shells were screeching by in even greater numbers. A little distance ahead, the darkness was pierced by what looked like Roman candles, except that most of them were white and remained up much longer. These were the "Very lights" sent up to illuminate No Man's Land and enable those using them to see if the enemy was up to any tricks. A British sergeant in charge of the Transport ahead of us, learning that we had followed the wrong limber and did not know which way to turn, advised us to wait until he returned, when he would guide us to Battalion Headquarters. So we sat down in an inferno of noise and listened to the screech of the shells and watched flashes of the explosions all about us. It was about an hour since we first came under fire and I was already wondering if the war would ever end.*

*Before long the sergeant returned and led us to Battalion Headquarters in an old farm. But it was a British battalion and not ours. Fortunately, a British officer was leaving on a visit to the Americans and invited us to accompany him. As we picked our way over and around shell holes and wreckage, sometimes nearly falling into some hole obscured by the darkness, shells began to fall closer and closer, the fragments occasionally flying by us with a swish. We reached another farm, a group of brick buildings, and took cover behind the wall of a wrecked house. A shell burst just in front and shrapnel tore the air all around and rattled against the building. Then it let up a bit and we went on. At a crossroads, we hesitated while our guide decided on a proper road. Then on again for fifty yards, when two shells landed exactly where we had just stood.*

*Finally, we reached our headquarters and I found Captain Egan, standing outside our little group of farm buildings, directing the distribution of supplies just arrived. I wondered at the time how he could be so cool with the air so full of shrieking explosives. A few days later in the same place and under the same circumstances, I was much amused at the apparent nervousness of a man who had come up to the line for the first time. One soon gets used to anything.*

*Captain Egan, my old company commander, was now in command of the battalion. He greeted me very cordially, said my company had just gone into the line, and as he was going down to the support line in a few minutes, we could go as far as that together. We were soon on the way, crossing a field which had once been part of a well cultivated Flemish farm, but was now overgrown with four years' growth of rank weeds and dotted with shell holes, some fresh, others half hidden by the high vegetation. Here and there, we passed the ruins of a little farmhouse, nothing left but the cellar and a heap of rubbish. Ahead and on both sides, the sky was lit up with star shells sent up from the front lines. We were holding a salient with Boche on three sides of us. Just north was the ruined city of Ypres, scene of some of the bloodiest fighting of the war.*

*To the south was Mont Kemmel, from which the Boche could overlook all of our lines, and as a consequence, made it necessary for us to keep still in the daytime and limit our movements to the hours of darkness. Ahead were the ridges of Wytschaete and Messines, which the Allies had held until the German drives, earlier in the year, had forced them back. Another drive was expected at Ypres, and we had been sent up there to help stem it if it came. But the Allied successes further south had depleted the German reserves opposite us, and just now we were waiting for plans to be perfected for an assault which would give us back Mont Kemmel and save us from the inconvenience of having our every move watched by the Germans on the top.*

*At the end of the long desolate field, the captain and I came along in the shelter of the Bund until we reached the far end, by a ruined house, where the guide halted the column and told the men to rest. "Take all the rest you need," he told them, "for you won't be able to rest again until we get through the woods. If Jerry starts shelling after you leave this place, God help you." Leaving this shelter, we followed a little footpath across a marsh. About halfway across, Jerry started shelling. The high explosives came shrieking through the darkness. Every one of them seemed to be coming right toward our little party. They landed all around, exploding with a deafening crash and a flash of light, and sending up fountains of black earth. The doughboys bent under their heavy loads and struggled on. The flashes of light made the intervening darkness seem more intense. Now and then some boy would fall into a shell hole, unseen in the dark, would pick himself up, recover his water cans or ration bags, and stumble along into his place in line. I thought of Saint-Aignan and how hard I had worked to get away and tried to believe I hadn't been a fool.*

*At the end of the marsh, we came to a wood and the column halted. The shelling was intense and I pushed up to the front to see what was causing the delay. The guide had disappeared, had vanished ahead in the darkness, running at full speed, and the doughboys with their heavy loads could not keep up. Another path crossed ours at this point, and all around us were heaps of corrugated iron, torn and twisted by shellfire, the remains of a British rest camp, which had once been far in the rear, but had been brought by the German advance, almost into the front lines. The place where two roads or paths cross is a favorite target for shellfire, as you can thereby block two roads or paths instead of one, and there is more traffic at that point. Then, the ruined huts might also attract attention. Altogether, it was no place to wait. But I didn't know which path to take, and the men up in the line for the first night didn't either. One or more of the paths very possibly led into the Boche lines. There was* nothing to do but to return to the shelter we had left, so I started the men back. Just then, the shelling ended as suddenly as it had begun; we halted, the guide reappeared, and we started once more on our way.

It was the first time I had seen the American doughboy under fire, and although we had not lost a man, it had been a pretty hot experience. I guess we were all pretty well scared, but the lads of K Company didn't show it. Weighted down with all they could carry, they marched on quietly and in good order. Only one man stopped, and that was because the bundle he was carrying had come apart. He might have been justified in abandoning it, but instead he coolly fixed it and regained his place in line, at the halt. We continued on through what was known as Scottish Wood. It had been a little forest of big trees, but was now a jungle of wreckage; tall shattered stumps, uprooted trees, torn and twisted by the explosives. We picked our way around and over these, walked around shell holes, which were pools of slime and green water. The air was thick with the smell of explosives and that worse odor of human bodies which had lain unburied for weeks.

The rattle of machine guns, which we had heard for some time at a distance, was now close by—sometimes the quick whirr of our guns, then the more deliberate putt-putt of the German as he would sweep some portion of the path we were walking on. Finally we came to a ruin, a few walls standing, but not enough to tell what kind of building it had been. On the side away from the enemy was a door opening on a long flight of steps which led down into the earth. At the bottom, I found a little room with bunks around the wall and occupied by a group of officers, English and American. I reported to Lieutenant Bradish, in command of K Company, and was held for a while until he decided what to do with me.

The company had been broken up and scattered through an English company for training purposes. A squad of Americans would hold one post and a squad of English the next, and so on down the line, except that there were more American squads owing to the larger size of our companies. K Company had just relieved I Company, and a platoon of the latter was waiting in the shelter of the ruins on its way out, while its lieutenant, Percy Hall, had a final word with Bradish. Percy was always a good deal of a humorist, and now, with the trip ahead of him which we had just experienced, he was particularly witty, and left the dugout in an uproar of merriment as he disappeared up the stairs.

*He had fourteen casualties in his platoon, a few minutes later, crossing the marsh where we had been shelled.*

*I was sent from this dugout on another trip through the woods to "Advance Company Headquarters," and, as that was already crowded to capacity, was sent ahead to the front line, under the chaperonage of an English officer. The first signs of dawn were appearing as we left the woods and walked across a short stretch of open country to a shallow irregular trench, which extended indefinitely in both directions. It was not at all the deep, well-ordered trench I had read about; in fact, it was hardly a trench at all. The wet marsh ground did not permit digging much below the surface. Shell holes had been connected together by a shallow ditch, in front of which was rough breastwork. There were short stretches here and there where you could stand up and walk around, sheltered by the breastwork. Between these stretches were others where the parapet top was level with your waist or knees, and still others where there was no protection at all. There were no trenches leading to the rear. You had to enter your particular post by walking boldly over the top under cover of darkness, and once it got light you had to stay there until night came again. It was as impossible to move along the trench in the daytime as it was to go to the rear.*

*Daylight was fast approaching when we entered the trench. I looked out over the flat waste of No Man's Land and tried to make out some object in the gloom that had the appearance of a German trench. Everything looked as quiet and peaceful as an abandoned farm at home. Now and then a rifle spoke or a machine gun rattled for a few seconds, but, otherwise, nothing was happening. In the foreground, the land was rough and shell marked, and scattered about were bits of equipment, broken rifles, and bloody fragments of clothing, souvenirs of all the armies that had fought in the Ypres sector. It was hard to realize that this was the line, that somewhere out in front was the German line, which we were to hold in place and eventually push back.*

*We came to a little group of men standing, rifles in hand, looking over the top, for this was the hour of dawn when attacks were made and everyone was at "stand-to" and alert. Then we went on for some distance without seeing anyone, then around a bend in the trench and upon another group. It hardly seemed possible that these groups so far apart could be expected to hold this line. In fact, as against an attack in force, the stand would be made farther back and we, out in front, would have to be sacrificed.*

*My English officer guide led me up and down the line, pointing out this and that position until I felt like a Cook tourist. He seemed to be utterly fearless. In spite of the fact that it was getting so light that objects could be made out at a considerable distance, he walked on top as if there were no Germans within miles. I was quite certain that he was trying to stump me, which made it much easier to follow him. At the far end of our walk, he took the rifle from an English Tommy and tried a few shots at the opposite trench, wanted to stir them up a bit, apparently, so that we would have an interesting return trip. He did not succeed, however, for which I was duly thankful. Finally, our tour of inspection was completed and we parted great friends, he to take charge of his post and I of mine.*

*It was now nearly broad daylight. There was nothing to do, as the enemy would not be likely to come over in the daytime. The men were sitting around cooking breakfast, washing mess kits in a shell-hole pool or smoking, while one man from each squad looked through the grass on the parapet toward the enemy trench. I searched the landscape again with the greatest care but could see nothing but a weed-covered waste as devoid of human life, apparently, as the Texas desert. Off to the left, in the middle of No Man's Land, stood two large brick gateposts with ornamental tops, evidently the entrance to some estate. Near them were two French army wagons, caught in the advance and showing, at that distance, no sign of damage.*

*I had now been on the jump for twenty-four hours and had been kept awake by air raids a good part of the two preceding nights, so retired to my headquarters for a little sleep. This headquarters consisted of a slit cut in the bank in front of the trench, covered by a piece of corrugated iron, with another sheet of the same material for a floor. Lying on this somewhat uncomfortable floor, you could look out in the open and watch enormous rats chasing each other up and down the trench. Overhead, airplanes soared about, while archies and machine guns tried to bring them down. Occasionally, a shell would shriek past, but they were intended for the areas back of us.*

*I slept all the morning and sat around and did nothing all the afternoon. For a while, we watched the Germans shell a trench mortar position in a clump of bushes a hundred yards back of us. The shells would fly over our heads with a roar like an express train and land in the bushes with a great splash of black earth and twigs. Whether any of them took effect or not, it was impossible to tell. Our trench mortars had a habit of taking up a position, firing for a while, and then moving to another part of the line before the Germany artillery located them. The Boche would then shell the place where the trench mortar had been and the infantry in the vicinity were the only ones to suffer. The trench mortar men were not popular with the infantry.*

*At dusk, there was great activity among the airplanes. A whole squadron of our planes passed over the Boche lines with all the enemy antiaircraft guns firing at them. Later, some Boche planes appeared and fired tracer bullets at our trenches, luminous bullets which made a streak of light as they sped toward us. Then more of our planes appeared and the Boche went scurrying away. As soon as it was dark enough, I returned to Company Headquarters and after three trips through the Scottish Woods and the adjoining marsh on various errands and without particular adventure, I was assigned to the command of a support platoon, with headquarters in a Bund dugout. I felt keenly the loss of the training period which the others had had while I was detained at Saint-Aignan; but with English advisers all around, it was not possible to go very far wrong, and I had hopes of picking up the necessary knowledge before our instructors were withdrawn.*

*It was not necessary, however, for on the following day, late in the afternoon, a messenger appeared with orders for me to report at once at Battalion Headquarters with all equipment. On arrival Captain Egan told me I was to act as his adjutant, doing for the battalion the same work that, as first sergeant, I had so long done for Company I, and with the same commanding officer.*[6]

As US servicemen were arriving and settling into life in Europe, nurse Alice Duffield was busy with everyday nursing at Fort Pike, Arkansas.

## ALICE L. MIKEL DUFFIELD, US ARMY NURSE CORPS

*Giving baths to the boys, took their temperatures . . . I don't remember giving any medicines. You see, the office . . . there were so many nurses there . . . they gave those girls the medicines, to the older nurses, they gave the medicines. And, we took their temperatures. And we were told . . . they didn't put the thermometers in their mouths because they ran high temperatures, and people with high temperatures would bite the thermometers, so we put them under their arms, and held their arms down.*[7]

Harlem Hellfighters: Members of the 369th Infantry Regiment, known as the "Harlem Hellfighters," pose wearing their Croix de Guerre medals while sailing back to the United States in 1919. (COURTESY NATIONAL ARCHIVES)

Germans, Turn in Your Arms: The day after war was declared on Germany, President Wilson announced that all German "subjects" must turn in any weapon in their possession to the police within twenty-four hours, or else they would be arrested and their weapons removed. (COURTESY BERKSHIRE ATHENAEUM)

## GERMAN SUBJECTS MUST TURN IN THEIR ARMS

**Local Police Will Act, if Firearms Are Not Surrendered Inside of 24 Hours.**

German subjects in this city must turn over to the police inside of 24 hours all their firearms, weapons or implements of war, ammunition or explosives or else the police will take action to see that those articles are turned over to the authorities. Chief of Police John L. Sullivan issued a notice today to that effect. Any alien enemy found with such articles in his possession after 24 hours have expired from the time of the issuance of the notice will be subject to arrest and the articles will be forfeited to the federal authorities.

The notice of the police chief is in compliance with a proclamation of President Wilson and is being given in the various cities and towns throughout the United States. It is a notice from United States Attorney General T. W. Gregory and reads as follows:

"Under the proclamation of the president, dated April 6, 1917, it is unlawful for alien enemies to have in their possession the following articles:

"Any firearms, weapons or implements of war, or component parts thereof, ammunition, maxim or other silencer, bomb or explosives; any aircraft or wireless aircraft or wireless apparatus, or any form of signaling device, or any form of cipher code, or any paper, document or book written or printed in cipher or in which there may be invisible writing.

"Your cooperation in enforcing this proclamation is earnestly desired; and you are required, if possible, to post notices or otherwise notify all alien enemies within your locality to bring to police headquarters and surrender any and all articles which it is unlawful to have in their possession. A detailed receipt should be given for all articles so surrendered, and at the close of the war such articles should be returned.

"Any alien enemy who fails to surrender such articles within 24 hours after public notice given by you, will be subject to summary arrest if such articles shall be found in his possession; and the article will be seized and forfeited to the use of the United States."

Sgt. Alvin York: Although he was a conscientious objector, York was drafted into the army and fought with Company G, 328th Infantry Regiment, 82nd Division. He received the Medal of Honor for his role in the capture of 132 Germans and for silencing several machine-gun nests. (COURTESY NATIONAL ARCHIVES)

Henry Johnson: Born in North Carolina, posthumous Medal of Honor recipient Henry Johnson fought in France with the famed Harlem Hellfighters (the 369th Infantry Regiment). He fought off a large group of Germans with just his bolo knife after a comrade was seriously wounded. For this action he became the first American to receive the French Croix de Guerre with Gold Palm, France's highest award for valor. (COURTESY NATIONAL ARCHIVES)

THE BATTLE OF HENRY JOHNSON
MEDAL OF HONOR
AWARDED POSTHUMOUSLY
JUNE 2, 2015

FIRST AMERICAN AWARDED
CROIX DE GUERRE
WITH
GOLD PALM
FOR
VALOR

Henry Johnson Memorial: The Henry Johnson Memorial is located in Albany, New York, on Henry Johnson Boulevard, outside of Washington Park. Albany resident Johnson was honored with the memorial in 1991; it has since been updated to reflect his posthumous awarding of the Congressional Medal of Honor.
(COURTESY MICHAEL COLLINS)

Fr. Duffy: Canadian-American priest Father Francis Duffy was the military chaplain for the famous "Fighting 69th" New York National Guard Unit, which became the 165th Infantry Regiment during World War I. He served on the front lines with litter bearers, recovering the wounded and providing counsel for soldiers throughout the war.
(COURTESY NATIONAL ARCHIVES)

O'Neil Bilodeau: Michigan-born O'Neil Bilodeau volunteered to fight with the French Army at the beginning of the war; later he joined the US Army's 78th Division and fought in the Saint-Mihiel and Meuse-Argonne campaigns. His mental breakdown due to shell shock would be the sad fate of many returning US service members.
(COURTESY BERKSHIRE ATHENAEUM)

Longshaw Kraus Porritt: Connecticut native Longshaw Kraus Porritt served first in the US Navy and later in the American Ambulance Field Service, in France and in Italy. He wrote extensively and took hundreds of photographs of his time in Italy, to illustrate what the Great War was like there. (COURTESY LIBRARY OF CONGRESS)

John "Black Jack" Pershing: A West Point Graduate, Gen. John "Black Jack" Pershing fought during the Spanish-American War and served on the Mexican border, fighting against Pancho Villa's revolutionaries. He was appointed the commander of the American Expeditionary Force throughout World War I, and because of his leadership, he became a national hero. (COURTESY NATIONAL ARCHIVES)

Marino Ballardini: Italian-born Marino Ballardini joined the US Army and fought in several major campaigns. After returning home, he suffered from shell shock, known as PTSD today, and committed suicide via natural gas poisoning. (COURTESY BERKSHIRE ATHENAEUM)

Hillie John Franz: Born in Texas, Hillie John Franz fought with Company L, 34th Regiment, 7th Division. He described in his diary what life was like in the trenches for the ordinary soldier in France. (COURTESY LIBRARY OF CONGRESS)

Richard W. O'Neill: Born in New York, Richard O'Neill was an army infantryman who fought with the 42nd "Rainbow" Division. He was awarded the Medal of Honor for his leadership on an attack against a German machine-gun position on the Ourcq River in France. (COURTESY NATIONAL ARCHIVES)

Sergeant Stubby: The official canine mascot of the 102nd Regiment, 26th Yankee Division, Sergeant Stubby was appointed a sergeant by alerting soldiers to gas attacks, and even prevented a German from mapping out their trench positions. (COURTESY NATIONAL ARCHIVES)

Waldo Heinrichs: Waldo Heinrichs was a decorated member of the 95th Aero Squadron, which was the first all-American squadron to fight in Europe during World War I. He was shot down in 1918 and captured as a prisoner of war, where he remained until the end of the war. (COURTESY UNIVERSITY OF MASSACHUSETTS)

Alice Mikel Duffield: Alice Mikel Duffield served as an army nurse at Camp Pike, Arkansas, during World War I, treating primarily black troops who were dealing with the Spanish flu epidemic of 1918. (COURTESY LIBRARY OF CONGRESS)

Charles Whittlesey: Wisconsin native Charles Whittlesey was a practicing lawyer when war broke out, and he ended up commanding the 1st Battalion of the 77th Division (the "Lost Battalion"), which was surrounded in the Argonne Forest from October 2–8, 1918. He was awarded the Medal of Honor for his leadership and fortitude during this period. (COURTESY BERKSHIRE ATHENAEUM)

William "Wild Bill" Donovan: William "Wild Bill" Donovan fought with the Fighting 69th and received the Medal of Honor, along with the Distinguished Service Cross. Later on in life he established the Office of Strategic Services (OSS) during World War II, which is now the CIA. (COURTESY NATIONAL ARCHIVES)

Fifth Avenue WWI: Triumphant US Army soldiers march down Fifth Avenue in New York City in celebration of the end of the war. (COURTESY NATIONAL ARCHIVES)

# PART III
# TO BATTLE!

# CHAPTER EIGHT

# Cantigny

ALMOST IMMEDIATELY FOLLOWING THE BATTLE IN FLANDERS, THE American 1st Division had been holding what was deemed by the French to be a quiet sector near Seicheprey, in the Saint-Mihiel region. The other AEF division in the area was the 26th, known as the Yankee Division. The name was attributed to to its formation in Boston and its component units hailing mostly from the New England area. They were comprised of two brigades and four regiments, the 101st, 102nd, 103rd, and 104th respectively. The whole point of allocating these untried men to the Saint-Mihiel area was to provide them with an opportunity to gradually acclimatize to modern warfare. In an attempt to test the mettle of these new arrivals, well before dawn on April 20, the Germans unexpectedly hit the area with storm troopers.

In the frontline "Sybil trench" at Seicheprey stood 350 Connecticut boys, seven platoons of the 102nd Regiment with members of the 102nd Machine-Gun Battalion. The reserves had been placed a mile and a quarter behind, and at that time had no orders to provide support. It was a miserable, filthy night as incessant squally rain drenched the men and their equipment. Voracious rats, bloated by human remains, swam in the putrid calf-deep water of the waterlogged trenches, while out in No Man's Land, visibility was hampered by dense fog. Doughboys thousands of miles from home huddled in alcoves tilled out of the trench walls. Some tried to sleep while others only visible by the lighted ends of their cigarettes talked in whispers. Every man except the sentries had been stood down.

At 2:00 a.m. the roar of German artillery emanating from the north suddenly pierced the silence and the gloom, and in an instant the space between the Sybil trench and the rear areas behind the town of Seicheprey erupted into an explosive inferno. German artillery was so accurate that scarcely a foot of the mile-and-a-quarter stretch to the second-line trench was undamaged. High explosive shells, shrapnel, and gas shells fell at regular intervals, while above the inferno a menacing cloud of mustard gas permeated the dank air. Those seven platoons in the Sybil trench were completely isolated. From the northwest around 1,800 German storm troopers in organized small groups began to expertly maneuver around the shell holes in No Man's Land, with one purpose: to really show these green doughboys what fighting in this war entailed. To the northeast, through Remieres Wood, the storm troopers pressed confidently on as a further 1,500 Germans deployed to cauterize each end of the Sybil trench.

## GEN. CLARENCE R. EDWARDS, 26TH DIVISION

*They intended to crucify us. They wanted to put the iron into our souls and show us that we couldn't fight in this war in which they had been so long triumphant. And I want to say right now—and I want the people of Connecticut to appreciate it, for I am mighty glad that they are interested in their boys—that no regiment in the American Expeditionary Force in France has a better record than the 102nd Regiment, which was made up of the old Connecticut National Guard.*[1]

The sheer magnitude and force of the German attack caused the Americans to fall back in disarray, taking heavy casualties. As the day wore on, desperate hand-to-hand fighting ensued. Only 30 men of the original 350 made it out of the Sybil trench alive. Practically every man of the 102nd became embroiled in this bitter struggle; even the cooks and the marching band were seen attempting to repel these seasoned German veterans. According to one firsthand account, one of the advancing Germans was armed with a flamethrower, and he'd projected his flame into the cook's kitchen where the cook was preparing breakfast. The breakfast menu would have to wait as the cook grabbed a meat cleaver from his block, rushed into the street, and, yelling furiously, dived into the ensuing hand-to-hand melee and allegedly killed two of the storm troopers with his erstwhile weapon.

Seicheprey was eventually retaken, thanks to a hurriedly organized counterattack, but the toll of over 650 Americans dead or wounded had been a stark wake-up call for the AEF. The battle was hailed as a resounding victory by the American press, but the darker truth was later revealed: It had been the Germans who had carried the day, and in the process, given these green soldiers a serious beating that they wouldn't forget in a hurry.

## GEN. CLARENCE R. EDWARDS, 26TH DIVISION

*My division front extended between eleven and twelve miles. That means that of the entire division there [were] less than 2,500 men to a mile, and as only about a seventh of the men were in the frontline trenches, it would mean that 350 men were called upon the frontline trench to cover a distance of nearly a mile. That gives some idea of the thinness of the line, which the Germans struck on that morning of April 20. The topographical layout of the ground in front of Seicheprey and Richecourt, which was to the northwest of Seicheprey and of the American trench, was the first town beyond the American line held by the Germans. That was the town from which half of the German troops advanced on the morning of April 20.*

*On the right, to the northeast, was Remieres Wood, and on the left of that and to the north was the famous Apremont, or Bois Breuilles, which was later made famous in the advance along the Meuse. Between Apremont and the Bois Breuilles is the valley of the Vir, which is nothing but a marsh. It was through the ravine bordering that marsh that the Germans troops came from Remieres Wood when they turned the flank of the Sybil trench. Across No Man's Land, directly in front of the Sybil trench, was open ground with the German wire, the German first-line trench, and the system of supporting trenches. Richecourt had been badly battered in the many attacks in that sector.*

*If I were put on oath as to which was the first and best of my regiments, I could not say, because each had its own special line of endeavor and achievement, which was not equaled by the work of another in that particular line. The record in the war has been such that all of them did gloriously. But I will say this, and I say it without fear of contradiction—that no regiment in the whole American Expeditionary Force had a better record than the 102nd. In the battle of Seicheprey these young lads were led by platoons, by their lieutenants. The captains were in the rear of their companies, and in that battle in which they received their introduction to the World War, and in all the other battles in which they took part, not a man quailed, no matter what the situation was. They stood up to their duty and even in the thickest of the fight, when the odds seemed to be death or capture, not one of them asked to be relieved, and none of them would be relieved, until the order came from the commanding officers.[2]*

Meanwhile, the 1st Division had been redeployed to occupy an active portion of the line west of the town of Montdidier, in the French sector. Eager to prove the fighting spirit of his unit, the commander of 1st Division, Maj. Gen. Robert L. Bullard, a longtime friend of Pershing, requested permission to attack without the assistance of French infantry. His request was approved on May 15, 1918. The 1st Infantry Division, which was at that point tactically a part of the X Corps of General Debeney's French First Army, methodically prepared an operation to capture the heights of Cantigny. Col. Hanson Ely's 28th Infantry Regiment meticulously rehearsed their modus operandi for the attack behind the lines. Present at the forthcoming battle would be Theodore Roosevelt's son, Lt. Col. Theodore Roosevelt Jr., who commanded the 26th Regiment, 1st Division, and Col. Robert McCormick. Upon America's entry into World War I, McCormick joined General Pershing's staff in France. He was granted a combat assignment with the 1st Division's 5th Field Artillery. As the commander of 1st Battalion of the 5th Field Artillery, he led the unit in providing crucial artillery support to 1st Division troops in their attack. He was so impressed by the American soldiers' performance at this battle that he changed the name of his personal estate from Red Oaks to Cantigny.

## BRUCE G. WRIGHT, 372ND INFANTRY REGIMENT, 93RD INFANTRY DIVISION

*Then we found ourselves all alone. The fellows were nervous and kept shooting at what they thought were Germans on No Man's Land. Of course, the Ger-*

mans thought that we were getting ready to attack, and from then until morning there was a continuous roar of rifles on both sides, neither side advancing, but just one holding the other.

Finally, the day broke and everyone there welcomed the dawn of that first day in the Argonne Forest, and we got our very first look onto "No Man's Land" that we had heard and read so much about. Masses of barbed wire, skeletons of men, tin cans, rotted clothes, and an awful smell greeted our eyes and noses. We were so anxious to get a real pot shot at a Dutchman that we had a tendency to get our heads too high up and the crack of a rifle from the Boche would bring it down with a jerk. We used to hold our helmets up on sticks and get it shot full of holes. Found lice on us, funny-looking things, says one fellow. And introduced to Josi. We stayed there twenty hard days and nights. Probably some nights would be very quiet, not more than fifty shots sounded, and then other nights would sound like an old-fashioned Fourth of July. In our twenty days' stay there we captured forty-two Germans, went out on patrol, and learned how to detect German patrols, saw how they fought, learned the correct way to crawl. Lots of our men couldn't crawl before they went into the trenches, but before long those same men could crawl along on their stomachs without using their hands or even lifting their heads or feet, one better than a snake.

On the 24th we moved back to the second line of trenches and let the other battalion take the front. They weren't so lucky, as they lost several men and got sixteen prisoners. The French decided that we were all right, but wanted to give us one more tryout in a different front line, so about the 29th of May we hiked to the Vaquah Sector, where your life was in your hands all the time. From the first to the third of June, our main trouble was keeping out of the way of big shells that were always landing through the trees.

On the night of the third of July, the night before the Fourth, the whole place started shooting, and that continued throughout the night. We were celebrating the Fourth of July 1918. On the Fourth, along about evening, word came that there would be an attack on the Germans by the French regiment on our left, and for us to hold our ground and not let them through an open and treeless space, which was in front of us, so at dark we crawled out there on our bellies with pick and shovel. At midnight, when the attack started, every man had dug himself a home in this field and was well protected in case they started through this open space. There was plenty of excitement that night, however, *and between the gas shells, whiz bangs, and bullets, we had our hands full. Two men were wounded, then we were all full-fledged trench men, and ready for battle. But as our division, which consisted of the 15th NY, 8th Ill, 371st USA, and 372nd USA 93rd Infantry regiments had no artillery, they decided to keep us with French divisions and use us as shock troops.*

*The duty of shock troops is attack the enemy and be followed up by the French. Our regiment, the 372nd, went under the command of Colonel Tupes, a regular army colonel, and the 372nd and 371st were mustered into the 157 French divisions otherwise known as the red band division.*

*July 7, 1918, in the rear of Vaquah. The 15th NY (or 369th) and the 8th Ill (or 370th) regiments went into 161st French divisions. Now we were ready for the real stuff. Off for Verdun front, which was quite some distance away. We walked three nights, as we traveled nights and slept days, and we reached a Camp Normandy where we made our final preparations and wrote out last letters home to our folks. Entered the Verdun front lines at the point known as Dead Man's Woods and Dead Girl's Valley, about the middle of July, and lived in that living hell until late in August, when we were relieved by American troops. Took many prisoners here, lost several men and many wounded. Cliff [illegible] killed in Camp Normandy. Maceo Harris, Fish Davidson, Curtis Wash, Jonie McLain wounded. Took in new men to fill the old men's places, and were so ragged and worn-out that we looked like we were after Robinson Crusoe's record, and as hungry as could be, as we only could get one meal every twenty-four hours. We were so skinny that you could have packed our whole regiment in one good-size freight car and we wouldn't have been crowded at all.*

*Captain Pryor dismissed several other colored officers, and white officers took their places. Then we were walked for the two nights following far enough to get aboard trucks, which drove us for the next couple of days and nights. We thought we were going way back to the rear for a rest, but instead they were carting us as near to another front as possible. Got off trucks, and pitched camp near a railroad (when I say near, I mean about seven miles or so). The next morning we got up early [and were] given our emergency rations, which consisted of two cans of "corned-willie" (or horsemeat) and ten [pieces of] hardtack, and now started on our way again.*

*Walked to the railroad, got on a train, rode about ten miles, and got off and walked the following [distance], pitching camp once every other eight hours. It was raining. As usual we were wet, [and] we stayed wet, and if we did pitch our tents in a dry place it was an unlooked-for surprise, and at that, when we woke up all we had to do was to turn over and stick our heads out of the cover and let the rain wash our faces.*

*It was now somewhere about the middle of September, and the big drive was to begin about the 26th of September, 1918. However, with hardships untold, we reached the line of advance. Here there were about fifteen French divisions. Included in these divisions were five or six regiments of Senegalese, the Negro troopers from the French islands, and known by all to be the best and most reliable and hardest-fighting soldiers in history. Four regiments of Moroccans. Our four regiments of American Negro soldiers. The rest were white French. The fortress of trenches that these troops were set apart to take were the best fortified by the Germans than at any other section on the long battle line. Twice before had the Allies tried to take this section, known as the Champagne, but were repulsed in each attack.*

*But now it was our lot, and even though we heard of our own race of people being lynched every day back in the United States, we all wanted to do our best in hopes that sooner it would be made easier for those at home. We kept saying to ourselves we're fighting for "democracy."*

*The night of the 25th of September we spent in leaving everything behind but one blanket, our guns, ammunition, and emergency food. Sent what would perhaps be our last letters home, and left messages with other fellows in case they got back home and you didn't. Most of the boys got quiet, but my special little gang of about eight of us raised more Cain than ever, trying to make the others throw their blues away. And when the captain came through our barn about 11:00 p.m., we were playing poker. The captain said in a gloomy voice, "Fellows, here you are, just about to go into battle, and sitting down here with a deck of cards, gambling; why, you all should be on your knees." So the card game ceased and before we knew it, we were all on our knees, shooting dice.*

*The next two days, September 26th and 27th, were spent in lolling around, collecting all our strength for the words "Over the top." We took our abode in trench of attack at midnight and were anxiously awaiting the words to go and get 'em, as all the boys were very uncomfortable. Packed with dirt and "cooties," which were little bugs that infested our body. It was raining, but not hard, and some of us, I guess, would be almost tempted to pray for a quick death to end it all. At 5:00 a.m., the time we supposed that we were going to attack, came and went. Now it was broad daylight and no order as yet. Gas shells were thrown in and around our trench, but our well-trained men were too quick at protecting themselves for gas to get them then.*

*At 11:00 a.m., in broad daylight, the command came: "Over, boys, over!" and that first wave made up of colored boys with bayonets fixed dashed through No Man's Land in a perfect formation. It was three or four minutes before the buglers sounded the call to start firing. The Germans leaped out of their first trench and started falling back, so after they abandoned that first trench, we fell in it headfirst, but no sooner had we got to our feet [that] the world came like lightning. "Up boys, and at 'em!" That was the beginning of the most fierce struggle that I ever was in. It lasted until October 9. But at the command, those black boys seemed to all come out of the trench at once, all shouting at the top of their voices in a sort of a weird "Eh joa." The Dutchmen were fighting hard to hold their second-line trenches, but 'twas of no use as they soon found out.*

*Sergeant Cristfield fell with blood gushing from his head. Morell went down. Perry was blown up in the air and came down dead. Turner [was] killed. Several more of my company went down, wounded. Robart and Yancy and two more went to capture a German who was standing upright, waving a handkerchief, and when they got about ten yards from him, he started patting his foot on a machine gun and mowed them all down. Yancy and the other two boys were killed, but although Robert [was] badly wounded, his life was spared.*

*My squad was still intact, and after seeing this, [we] decided that we would try to take no prisoners, which we didn't. Still we pushed on. It was getting dark. The way became harder now. We were advancing about five yards at a time. The wounded were in so much pain that they were begging to be put out of the way. Now night is on us. Have come to a big hill. The Germans were shooting down on us. We tried to rush the hill. As we would get halfway up, a barrage would force us down to the foot again. The French had caught up to us by this time, and all night long and the next day and night, we fought up* and down this hill, to no advantage. Our men were getting fewer and fewer, but on the third day, September 30, 1918, we hit the top of this hill, tired and worn-out. But that was just the time we couldn't stop, as we had to hold this hill at all costs. The other side of this hill was a bare stretch of about two hundred yards, at the edge of which were dense woods, and now we set about to the task of getting them out of these woods. The boys had all thrown away their French guns and opted for the Germans guns and ammunition that had been left behind.

Then came the charge on the woods which lasted for about four hours. Now in the woods we found cows, pigs, chickens, horses, beer, and wine, and right here we proceeded to put on the feed bag: fresh-killed cows (which we killed ourselves), the meat still warm, cut-off chunks of beefsteak (top of the round, bottom of the round, and everything else), cured and cooked inside of a half an hour; we drank beer and were soon on our way again. Our objective was Monthois, which was now only about four miles away.

Now we hit the other edge of these woods, and coming out of them seems just as hard as going in them. But at this hour the [Moroccan Cavalry], who are little brown men with long hair riding without saddles, dashed out ahead of us, riding and fighting like madmen. Different places we found Germans tied to their guns. Still raining hard, we are drenched. Now only about three miles to go, but seemed to have come to a standstill, firing fiercely at this point, but not able to gain any more ground. Had a chance to get a fairly good rest, but no sleep yet.

Now about October 2, 1918, still fighting hard. The "Prussian Guards" had come up, and now we were up against real fighters. From October 2 to October 7 we had all we could do to hold our position. We had dug ourselves halfway in for protection, and in between this time we managed to get a wink or two. That is, we slept in turns, but not for long; twenty minutes' sleep was as good to us as eight hours then. Then on October 7, late in the afternoon, came the final break, and [we] threw ourselves across the river into the ruined little town of Monthois, half dead as we were. October 8, 1918, our object reached, to be relieved the next day by fresh divisions. (Happy Day!)[3]

This would be the first real American offensive of the Great War. The village of Cantigny is located about three miles northwest of Montdidier in a hilly area surrounded by forests. It was the apex of the area that the Germans had taken during their previous offensive, and the village provided a good view to the west. It was the only prominent feature in the sector. Constantly bombarded and on fire since its capture, the village was said to be almost uninhabited, as it had been partially evacuated. As the 1st Division arrived, only its church tower still remained intact, and since it was believed to be an enemy observation post (OP), division artillery reduced it to rubble within two weeks.

The mission assigned to the 1st Division was to organize the sector by installing successive lines of resistance and to hold its position on the Front. Allied High Command regarded this as a vitally important sector because they expected the enemy to make another drive in the direction of Amiens. Previous French Army occupants of the position had found it nigh-on impossible to construct trenches due to the constant pounding from more than ninety German batteries. The 1st Division partially avoided this problem by working at night to complete a 6,000-meter communication trench between the front line and the Bois-de-Villers, which was completed during the night of May 13.

German artillery fire rained an average of 2,000 shells a day on that section. Gas was also included in the heavy shelling, and during the afternoon of April 30, approximately 700 gas shells, including 50 marked with a yellow cross, fell on a group of 1st Division 75mm artillery pieces. All the combatants used color-coded markings on their shells, and the Germans used this system to simplify the complex varieties of chemical fillings according to their function. A yellow cross usually indicated mustard gas, based on a noxious sulfur-mustard mix. Diphosgene shells and others containing lethal lung irritant gas, which might dissipate in a few hours, were marked with a green cross. During the 1st Division's seventy-two-day occupation of this position, roughly half of the casualties incurred were due to gas.

Precisely one hour before the expected launch of the attack, the heavens suddenly erupted as a preliminary barrage delivered by all guns supporting the 1st Division front opened up simultaneously. They hammered the German positions with every caliber, including gas shells. The low, slate-gray clouds in the distance reflected yellow, orange, and white as the shells impacted their targets.

During the previous night, the 28th Infantry had taken up positions for the attack on Cantigny. The 3rd Battalion was placed northeast of Bois St. Eloi, the 2nd Battalion, directly west of Cantigny, and the 1st Battalion, at the western edge of the Bois de Cantigny. A company of the 26th Infantry under the command of Maj. Theodore Roosevelt Jr. was in regimental reserve behind the 28th, with two further companies of the 18th Infantry also in reserve north of Villers-Tournelle. As the troops assembled, twelve French Schneider CA1 tanks and a detachment of flamethrowers and French air cover joined them for the assault. At 6:45 a.m. on May 28, supported by 173 pieces of French artillery, the 28th Infantry jumped off from their positions and advanced in three successive waves, approximately one hundred meters every two minutes, behind a carefully timed rolling barrage.

They overran the opposing German front machine-gun nests within forty-five minutes, reaching their objectives at 7:25 a.m. without sustaining major casualties by Great War standards. Once the positions had been reached, patrols were sent forward and automatic rifle posts were established in shell holes on the line of surveillance to cover the consolidation. The whole assault had been expertly prepared to the last detail, and it was one of the extremely rare occasions when everything went according to plan. A company of the 1st Engineers supervised the consolidation of the captured strongpoints and the lines of surveillance and resistance. The attack had progressed with only slight German resistance, and with practically no reaction on the part of the enemy artillery. The section of French flamethrowers proved invaluable in cleaning up the town and driving the enemy out of dugouts. During the cleaning up, 1st Division troops encountered some minor skirmishes, but on the whole the objective was gained with rapidity and with considerable ease. In the process they captured around 240 prisoners.

## SGT. BOLESLAW SUCHOCKI, 28TH INFANTRY, 1ST DIVISION

*Into the village of Cantigny we go. There remained nothing but ruins. We passed on through to the other side of the village. Here we encountered barbed-*

*wire entanglements, but it was our good fortune to get through these without any mishap. But once across I noticed that the boys were falling down fast. A shell burst about ten yards in front of me and the dirt from the explosion knocked me flat on my back. I got up again but could not see further than one hundred feet.*

*I heard someone yell "Lay down." I knelt on one knee and wondered what would come next . . . We laid down and started to shoot, and it was our good fortune that the second wave reached the place at this time. About twenty Dutchmen came out of the holes, threw down their rifles, and stood with their hands up. The doughboys didn't pay any attention to this, but started in to butcher and shoot them. One of the doughboys on the run stabbed a Dutchman and his bayonet went clear through him.*

*The German artillery was in action all the time. . . . I stopped at a strong-point and asked the boy in the trench if there was room for me to get in. "Don't ask for room, but get in before you get your [!#%&] shot off," a doughboy said.*

*We stayed there all that night and the next day, being relieved at two o'clock the following morning, taking position in the first line of reserve trenches. We ate a cooked dinner at eleven o'clock, that being the first meal we'd had in three days.*[4]

## THEODORE KOHLS, COMPANY A, 26TH INFANTRY REGIMENT, 1ST DIVISION

*Our division went into this front on the first of May. Here is where we experienced real war for the first time. It was continuous shellfire on us all the time. Many times our chow details were shot to pieces and we were held without something to eat. This close fighting was kept up till the morning of May 27, when a hundred and fifty Germans made a raid on my company. We immediately started killing Germans. The Germans had thrown a four-hour barrage on us and about leveled the woods with the ground that we were in, such was the effect of the barrage. We fought for about thirty minutes, when the Germans retreated and left two-thirds of their men dead behind them. That day there was continual bombarding on all sides.*

*On the following day, early in the morning, our artillery started a barrage on the German trenches. Such was the fighting begun that day. Our men went over the top at 6:15 a.m., the designated hour. We took our objective, but that was when the fun began. The Germans started counterattacking, six counterattacks did they launch, but each time without success. This was kept up the following day, but again, each time without success, so were the Germans defeated the first time in the one by Americans, whom they called tin soldiers.*

*We kept up the fighting for a whole week after. One night when my platoon was on a wiring detail, the Germans started a gas bombardment. It was my first time in real gas; we immediately put on our gas masks. Early in the morning we went back to our trenches. We laid around for the day; we couldn't stick our heads above the trenches, some German would take a potshot at us. Toward evening I thought I was getting a cold, for my voice started getting rougher. We stayed in these trenches for six more days. My cold was getting worse—or what I thought was a cold.*

*We were relieved by the French on this front. Shortly after we were relieved I got so that I could only whisper. I then went on sick report and was told by the doctor that I was gassed. I was sent to a hospital where I stayed for three weeks without my voice improving a bit, so I went downtown one night and drank all the cognac in sight, came back a drunken fool. But, the next morning I could whisper; after that I was getting better every day.*

*I was then sent back to my outfit. We went into the trenches again and stayed ten days. I was in the trenches on the 4th of July 1918; we were relieved by the French again. We then went back for a rest, while in a little village a good distance behind the lines, the major came around and picked me to parade in Paris on the 14th of July, the French Independence Day. We at once got ready and dolled up the best we could. This was the first time I wore my service stripes since I was in France.*

*On the 13th of July we left our company to parade in Paris. We got to Paris that night. On the morning following, we got ready for the parade, which was to start at nine o'clock. This was the first time I'd seen Paris. After parading down some of the most important streets in Paris, we stopped at some park or square not far from the subways. Here we got to see all the Allied troops that had paraded, there was a battalion of each. I am sure that that parade will live [on] in the history of the world.*

*After that we were turned loose for thirty-eight hours, and then I got to see some of the important buildings of Paris. After that we got ready to join our outfit. We didn't know where they [were] at. While in Paris that long-range gun of the Germans started to bombard the place and caused quite a bit of damage. We left on a train but didn't know where it was going. After spending a whole night on train cattle cars, we got to a place near the Front.*[5]

Although Cantigny had been captured with relative ease, holding on to the position was going to prove to be another matter entirely. Once the supporting French guns had withdrawn to deal with another German offensive, the 1st Division would have to rely on their own artillery for support. Around noon on May 28, the Germans began a series of heavy bombardments and powerful counterattacks that continued almost unabated for two and a half days. The American gunners proved themselves extremely capable in replacing the French guns and stunting several German attempts to retake the position.

Between May 28 and May 31, the 28th Infantry Regiment incurred almost 1,400 casualties, but reinforced by a battalion from the 18th Infantry and a battalion from the 26th Infantry, it held the ground that had been won. The attack of the 1st Division at Cantigny was the first time in the war that an American division had fought as a unit in an offensive operation. The Germans respectfully described their new adversary as "brave and stubborn." News of the American 1st Division's success at Cantigny buoyed both the French and British armies, but the significance of their fight was far greater than providing a mere boost to morale. With this action the AEF had done more than proven their worth. The 1st Division had been the first US Division to set foot on French soil; they had been eagerly awaiting this chance to display their talents to the other Allied armies and show them what they could do. French and British observers of this American attack were surprised and amazed by the almost suicidal zeal that these young men displayed as they moved out to confront the enemy. They weren't tainted and cynical like many of the other British and French soldiers who had endured three long, punishing years of attrition. These AEF soldiers were fresh, eager, and competent. Needless to say, General Pershing was satisfied with the result.

CHAPTER NINE

# The Aisne-Marne / Belleau Wood

ON MARCH 23, 1918, THE CITY OF PARIS BECAME THE RELUCTANT recipient of massive 234-pound shells launched by German artillery pieces known as the "Paris guns," positioned seventy-five miles away in the Coucy forest, near the Aisne River valley. Somnambulant Parisians were abruptly shaken from their slumber by the dull stomach-churning thuds of these massive shells, impacting buildings in their age-old city. It was a clear indication that trouble was brewing yet again on the Western Front.

Four days later, on May 27, 1918, the day before the 1st Division took Cantigny, general in chief of the German armies, Erich Friedrich Wilhelm Ludendorff, launched an offensive from his position on the high ground at Chemin des Dames in the Champagne region of France. Like all previous offensives, an intense and precise artillery barrage also preceded this one. German troops advanced eleven miles on the first day and forced the French out of the Aisne valley. The initial accomplishment of this latest German offensive caused a lot of concern and furrowed many brows at Allied HQ. They knew that a German attack was coming, but had little idea where it would hit. A certain unknown corporal by the name of Adolf Hitler participated in this offensive as a soldier in the 16th Royal Bavarian Regiment of Reserve Infantry.

This latest German offensive was the reason why the French had hurriedly withdrawn their artillery from the Cantigny sector. It was considered implausible that an enemy attack would occur along the Aisne front; consequently, many French troops had been redeployed from there to the area controlled by the British Army. Without much prior warning, forty-one divisions of the German 1st and 7th Armies successfully attacked the French 6th Army along a twenty-five-mile front east of the Aisne River. After a highly effective artillery barrage, German storm troopers steamrollered the French 6th Army.

The startling success of this latest German offensive inspired Ludendorff to reassess his general strategy. Being the impetuous man that he was, he decided to abandon caution and make a charge toward Paris, in hopes that this move would draw the Allies into a final decisive, climactic battle that would ultimately bring the war to a favorable conclusion. Within two days the Germans had crossed the Aisne River and were rapidly advancing westward, until they were just fifty miles from the French capital city.

By now 650,000 American soldiers had arrived in France, and their number was growing by 10,000 per day. Despite the growing numerical superiority for the Allies, however, ultimate victory remained elusive as the Germans continued to launch further punishing offensives. By May 31 the American 2nd and 3rd Divisions that Pershing had reluctantly, but temporarily, handed over to French control were returned to AEF command and hurriedly sent toward Château-Thierry to reinforce the line. The 3rd Division's motorized machine-gun battalion arrived first, in time to assist in repelling a German attack, preventing them from crossing the Marne River. Every available means was employed to get these badly needed American troops up to the Front. The rest of the 3rd Division assisted in reinforcing the 10th French Colonial Division that held the south bank of the Marne as far eastward as Courthiézy, just eight short miles from Château-Thierry.

As the Third Battle of the Aisne, which lasted from May 27 until June 3, 1918, drew to a close, leading elements of the German Army hadn't succeeded in their objective of getting to Paris, but were dangerously close to the road to Rheims. At that time Allied intelligence reported that there were four German divisions located in an overgrown old hunting preserve covering only one square mile, known as Belleau Wood. This was a picturesque area with dense undergrowth that limited visibility, five miles northwest of Château-Thierry.

The 2nd Division was there by June 2, whereupon they immediately de-trucked and took up positions northwest of Château-Thierry. The speed with which these soldiers mobilized and deployed was almost unprecedented in the Great War. The 2nd Division managed to field two battalions, along with one marine battalion from the 4th Marine Brigade, each unit numbering between 6,000 and 7,000 men, all trained and ready to help check the German advance at Château-Thierry. Gen. James Harbord, commanding the Marine Brigade, received an urgent order from Gen. Denis Auguste Duchêne, commander of the French 6th Army, to the effect of: "Have your men prepare entrenchments some hundreds of yards to rearward in case of need." Harbord briefly studied the message and promptly replied, "We dig no trenches to fall back on. The Marines will hold where they stand." Although he knew his men weren't lacking in courage, hardly any of them had experienced action before. They would be spending the next month trying to dislodge four seasoned German divisions from superb defensive positions in Belleau Wood.

On that same day marines were dispatched to support the French Army at Belleau Wood. As the marines arrived at the scene, they found French troops retreating through their lines. A French colonel, attempting to acquaint the Americans with the realities of the situation, and struggling with poor English-language skills, scribbled a note to Capt. Lloyd W. Williams, commanding the 51st Company, 2nd Battalion, 5th Marine Regiment. Williams gave a steely-eyed glare at the Frenchman as he coldly retorted, "Retreat, hell! We just got here." Nine days later Williams would be dead, but his sturdy riposte is still hallowed among the ranks of the United States Marine Corps.

## Pvt. William Kizer, 55th Company, 5th Marine Regiment

*It was on the 7th of June that we saw the harbor of Bordeaux, and a few hours later left the ship for what we thought was a good rest and more training. Imagine our feelings when, four days later, we were in the frontline trenches and took our stand alongside hardened veterans at Château-Thierry. The next day we had our first chance to go "over the top," and over we went. My buddy, Pvt. Ford Erdman, who enlisted at the same time that I did, was wounded in the ankle and refused to go back for aid to the nearest dressing station. He and*

*I were fighting shoulder to shoulder when he was hit again. This time he went down and I carried him to our trench. He died on the way. I vowed then that I would never go home until I had avenged his death, and I know that there are more widows in Germany now than there would have been had he lived.*

*We were split up into different companies after that skirmish, and I was attached to the famous 5th Regiment, 55th Company. Only a few of the fellows who came over with me were kept in the front line during the thirty-three days of continuous fighting that followed. Believe me, it was there that I lost all hope of ever seeing my home again. Man after man fell beside or around me, and I sure thought that every minute was going to be my last.*

*We were moved to rest billets on the 14th of July and only rested three days before we were sent to replace casualties in our former position. I think that it was our thirty-three-day fight that saved Paris. It was during the months of August, September, and October that we had little to do except hold the lines and enjoy life. There wasn't a fellow in the regiment who didn't carry a Bible, and [we] almost knew it by heart. My little Bible was given to me by a Salvation Army lass, and did much to console me during the weary hours in the trenches.*

*On October 26th we were moved from Soissons to the Argonne Forest, and on November 1, while two doughboys and myself were exchanging lead with the Fritzies from a shell hole, one with my name on it buried itself just above my right temple, and I woke up in the hospital. The first thing I asked for was my Bible, and when it was brought to me it seemed that I had a new lease on life. The next few days nearly finished me, but they say that the good die young, so I got through all right and was sent home on a stretcher. When the Statue of Liberty was sighted I felt amply repaid for all I had been through. When asked if I would be willing to go through it again if necessary, I said, Can a duck swim?*

The importance of Belleau Wood cannot be underestimated. The most recent German offensive had taken them to within thirty-seven miles of Paris and made a significant dent in the Allied line. It was dented but not entirely broken. The offensive had made this line vulnerable, and despite everything that Ludendorff's forces threw at the Allies, they somehow managed to retain control of their lines. It was at this critical juncture that the potential conclusion of the war was hanging in the balance. It was a race against time as the Allies regrouped and began to organize new countermeasures to deal with the latest German threat. Belleau Wood marked the apex of the German advance to Paris. While the Germans controlled it, they had a key strategic position from which they could further continue their move on the French capital city. To ensure that this was ultimately prevented, it was imperative that Belleau Wood be cleared.

It was to be the battle where legends were made. June 6, 1918, was arguably the most significant day in the history of the US Marine Corps. The arduous task of taking out these seasoned German veterans was not going to be easy. As the sun beat down mercilessly, waves of men from the 4th Marine Brigade prepared to advance across open ground in a style that had cost the Allies dearly during the previous years. This would be the first time that American troops would mount a concerted offensive alone since the declaration of war, precisely fourteen months before. There were murmurs among Allied commanders that the AEF wasn't up to the task, and that their troops weren't well trained enough for a task of such vital importance. Supported by American artillery, they jumped off and advanced in formation, each line keeping five yards apart abreast and twenty yards ahead or behind each line of men. As they coursed through the open wheat field and closed on their objective, withering German machine-gun fire emitting from well-covered interlocking fields of fire began to mow them down. They encountered bitter resistance from the German positions as they attempted to penetrate the southern edge of Belleau Wood.

Some marines managed to reach the perimeter of the woods, but at a terrible cost in dead and wounded. The most disabling problem for the marines in Belleau Wood was that they were never entirely sure where the Front was. They would advance cautiously through the dense undergrowth to where they assumed the German fire was coming from, only to discover that the shooting was coming from behind or from their flank. On five successive occasions the marines made ground and five times they were forced to pull back. It was only on the sixth attempt that they managed to laboriously eject the defending Germans from their positions in the wood. Most of Belleau Wood was captured between June 8 and June 11, and despite desperate German counterattacks, by June 21 it was completely in American hands—but at a terrible cost. The marines incurred over 10,000 casualties in their first Great War battle.

AEF command praised Marine Corps marksmen who had indeed done a superb job of taking out German machine gunners, while the infantry did its part by continuing to advance in the face of withering fire, and regardless of the terrible casualties incurred. In less than a month, the Germans were compelled to relinquish a strategically important position. The Battle of Belleau Wood further asserted the notion that the AEF could and would contribute significantly to any eventual Allied victory. It was said that if General Pershing's men hadn't arrived in Belleau Wood when they did, the German forces would have driven through the war-wearied and demoralized French troops, and may have even made it all the way to Paris. It's possible that they would have compromised the French Army entirely, which would have effectively taken France out of the war.

Stateside press soon pounced on the victory and was effusive in their praise of the AEF. The *New York Times* reported one incident with great patriotic zeal, as it lauded the accomplishments of certain individuals such as Pvt. Frank P. Lenert, who was surrounded by eighty-five German soldiers who "showed great interest in knowing how many were in the attacking party." Lenert lied and told the German soldiers that "Eight regiments had attacked and many more were coming after them." The German soldiers told Lenert that since so many Americans were coming, it would have been useless for them to fight any longer, and they craved the honor of surrendering to Lenert. The account concluded with Private Lenert hauling in no less than eighty-five German prisoners. The Silver Star was awarded to a certain marine by the name of Henry P. Leonard (*sic*, Lenert) for capturing seventy-eight German soldiers. It is noted though that the AEF HQ ridiculed this story, and although this soldier was awarded a Silver Star, after a four-day furlough in Paris, he went AWOL.

Although the veracity of the story remains questionable, its impact and propaganda value at the time was significant in convincing the

American public that "they" were winning the war. There were doubtless many heroic deeds performed at the Battle of Belleau Wood by these eager, courageous young men, and some stories were substantiated, such as this one by Corp. Elton E. Mackin. After the war, he wrote an account of the grim struggle for Belleau as part of a book-length manuscript he titled *Flashes and Fragments*, in which he refers to himself as the character "Slim."

## CORP. ELTON E. MACKIN, 1ST BATTALION, 5TH MARINE REGIMENT, 2ND MARINE DIVISION

*Zero hour. Dawn of June 6, 1918. Undertone commands brought the chilled, sleepy men to their feet. A skirmish line formed along the edge of the woods. There were last-minute instructions, and bits of advice flung here and there. Careless of cover, the first wave stood about in the wheat, adjusting belts and hitching combat packs to easier positions. The mist of early morning thinned before a red-balled sun. There were half-heard murmurs of conversation among the men and, at times, a spurt of nervous laughter, quickly stilled. The entire front was quiet where we were. There was only the distant background of way-off guns warning the lines to come awake.*

*First sergeant "Pop" Hunter, top-cutter of the 67th Company, strode out into the field and threw a competent glance to right and left, noting the dress of his company line. Pop was an old man, not only of portly figure and graying hair, but in actual years, for more than thirty years of service lay behind him. No bugles. No wild yells. His whistle sounded shrilly, once. His cane swung overhead and forward, pointing toward the first objective, a thousand yards of wheat away, where the tensely quiet edge of Belleau Wood was German-held. The spell was broken. A single burst of shrapnel came to greet the moving line of men. There was a scream of pain. A soldier yelled, "Hey, Pop, there's a man hit over here!" Reply was terse and pungent. "Gawdammit, c'mon. He ain't the last man who's gonna be hit today."*

### We Were Young

*We met the war at a crossroad. We were young. Europe had been aflame for more than three years, and we had come a goodly way to smell the smoke. Full of wonderings and wanderings, full of restlessness and spice, we heard it scream and writhe and crash among the distant trees. The guns around us added to the din and suddenly we didn't want to die. The fellows walked with disciplined eyes that stared in fascination. They walked in fear, and pride. They shot quick glances here and there at other men to gather strength to imitate their still-faced calm and to match their stride. It was difficult to still that awful growing dread. Dark of night would have been welcome then so that a man might hide the terror in his eyes. The war met us at a crossroad near Marigny Château. Because the long-range German guns over Torcy way were spewing high explosives, we were put into partial shelter of the roadside hedge, allowing time to pass.*

*The war had come down our road to meet us. We took the time to study it, to note its greeting. We had an hour or more of sunny June-time afternoon through which to wait and watch, and gather swift impressions. Somewhere off to [the] north of us, a German battery was zeroed in, firing from the depths of Belleau Wood. The shells came down in perfect flights of four, always of four, and four and four, just spaced enough between the blasts to serve the guns. Methodical, precise, deadly, the gunfire swept the crossing. Men and horses died. Huge old army camions and Thomas trucks crashed and smashed and burned, while engineers died recklessly, moving wrecks to keep the roadway clear. Have you ever watched a gut-shot horse, screaming, drag his shell-killed mate, his dead driver, and his wagon down a bit of road until he dies? Horses die more noisily than men, as a rule. Most men die quietly if death comes soon. They seldom make a lot of fuss unless the first dulling shock has worn away. The strongest weaken and scream, given enough of burning pain.*

*The business of war is a pressing one and movement must go on in spite of anything. We were enthralled. We were privileged men to lie out there, short rifle range from carnage, learning, watching how things went. Traffic scarcely slowed. Horse teams went their way, their heads held high, snorting as they passed insensate things. A figure came among us along the right-of-way, seeking our lieutenant. Word spread that a runner had come down to guide us in. We would be needed on the firing line that night. We had been hearing tales about the runners, the risks they dared, the prices they paid. Not without reason were they included among the elite details known as the "suicide squad." We understood that the work, except in an emergency, was voluntary, and that no man need accept the job as regular assignment if he preferred otherwise. Of all the risks we had heard about along the Front, we were of one mind concerning the job those fellows did. "No runner job for us; too dangerous."*

*A wounded fellow, walking, came our way and was hailed with a shower of eager questions by us toots. He didn't even take the time to talk to us, just passed us by, stony-faced, looking holes through us in some contempt, as though he missed a quality we lacked and didn't think us much. We heard him call the runner Jack, saw him stop to chat awhile, and later, answer our lieutenant civilly enough. As he left us, drifting back to find an ambulance, he shouted, "Hey, Jack, has the outfit got to hold the woods with them goddamn replacements?"*

## Signpost

*The path out of Lucy-le-Bocage skirted a trampled garden, passed a dead cow, followed the road to a gap in the hedge, and dropped into a drainage ditch. It cornered a bit of the field, and was covered by a copse of saplings across some open ground. At the copse the path divided, one way going forward toward the ravine, the other turning half-left through the underbrush to Hill 142. In the fork of the path, a German soldier had died, grotesquely and in pain. One up-flung arm, spread-fingered and beseeching, was caught among the branches of a scrubby bush. For the guidance of travelers, some humorous soul had laced a cardboard sign between the dead man's fingers. Rough lettering bore the legend "Battalion P.C." above an arrow pointing west.*

## Initiation

*The garish flare of a star-shell, blasting the deep gloom, brought into relief a file of replacements cautiously groping their way along the Front opposite Torcy, and gave to each his first view of No Man's Land at night. In the blinding light every man froze in his tracks. Rigid, their figures merged with the shadows of the wood that no enemy eye might detect movement among them. Since early dark these green troops had been making their way toward the firing line. Now, with night half gone, they were filtering through the trees along the crest of a ridge to take position in that thin line of shallow trenches and foxholes, which constituted the only barrier between Paris and the German drive. "Come on, close up! Close up!" came the hoarse whisper of a guide. The ghastly light waned and suddenly went out. There was muted sound of movement from the head of the column. Men dared to breathe freely again. Stiffened fingers relaxed their startled grip on rifle stocks, and again they groped forward.*

*After a few hundred yards came a command: "Pass the word to halt!" Each received the whispered message as he bumped into the man ahead, and soon the diminishing sound of rasping branches and stumbling feet ceased. Shortly there came a vague activity from the rear of the line and a gradual shuffling forward a few steps at a time, interspersed with undertone remarks to: "Step out a little!" "Hold it!" Shadowy forms came working from man to man. A quiet voice of authority bade each: "Take a five-pace interval, and lie down!" One felt an oppressive loneliness at losing contact with the next in line, a feeling soon replaced by relief as tired bodies relaxed on cool earth. The occasional boom of a heavy gun gave background to the eerie, brooding gloom. Somewhere a machine gun rapped into the darkness. At times, the sharp crack of a rifle, in the hands of a nervous watcher, punctuated the stillness.*

*The damned replacements had arrived [at dawn]. A distant gun barked and immediately after came a screaming roar followed by a flash, an explosion. There was a spatter of falling fragments among the trees, and somewhere near at hand, an anguished voice cried out in pain. As though by signal, entire batteries took up the chorus, the clatter of a machine gun, another, and the rising tide of sound merged into a crescendo that stifled thought and, for a moment, paralyzed all motion. Shrapnel rained upon the ridge. A running figure dashed along the line with a yell to take cover. Men sought shelter behind half-finished mounds of earth and hugged the ground. Whole trees crashed down as heavy shells shook and jarred the earth. The fumes of H. E. powder became a blanket, which crept over the forest floor. There were cries for "First aid, first aid," and other cries, wordless, terrible cries of men in agony. Figures moved between the inexperienced men.*

*Someone crouched at Slim's side and the voice of Sergeant McCabe came yelling at his ear, "Fix bayonets! fix bayonets! an' watch that goddamn wheat!" "Are they coming?" Slim managed to make himself heard, from a throat which seemed to choke the words in his breast. "Yeah, when this barrage lifts, they'll come, and in numbers, Bud. Shoot low, and be ready to go meet them if they get too close." His words penetrated Slim's consciousness like a sentence of doom. Further speech was beyond him. His pet horror, the prospect of using a bayonet, of facing enemy bayonets in action, appalled him. The very thought, the threat, left him weak. "Don't turn yellow and try to run, because if you do and the Germans don't kill you, I will." With that the sergeant left him. Fascinated, Slim watched the sergeant's progress down the line. He marveled that anyone could walk through such a hail of steel. He expected to see the man go down with every step.*

*As McCabe passed from sight among the trees, the meaning of his last words suddenly came to Slim. A flush of shame relieved the scared whiteness of his face and for a moment he lay his head upon his arm. It robbed him of what little strength remained. To be thought a coward on his first day of battle, in his first hour of action, threatened to place him beyond the regard of these men he strove to copy. The taunt had reached him and hurt his pride. At that moment, boyhood lay behind forever—a page of life's story turned—and back of a small mound of earth, a disciplined, determined soldier faced the long slope ahead.*

*The shellfire slackened. There were bursts falling behind the ridge now, centered on support positions, sweeping favored paths and roads over which reserves might come. How well the old Boche knew this bit of front! Just two days back he had consolidated here and now his dead and the debris of battle lay about. This ridge had been a strong point of his stubborn defense, the main objective of the marine attack of—"Was it only yesterday?" It was time for the assault.*

*Over to the right of the hill on which Slim lay arose the clatter and clash of a pitched battle. Officers hurried toward that part of the battalion position, the better to observe the result of what was evidently a flanking attack. The first assault had been aimed at a hollow off there to the right, out of sight among the trees, and its outcome might easily prove whether or not their hill was to be held. Someone near at hand cried "Here they come," and Slim's attention went to his immediate front. Out there beyond mid-field, figures took shape—a long double line of fighting men formed a wave of advancing infantry. Behind, at the far edge, another took shape, and even as he watched, a third wave debouched from a distant line of wood to join the advance. Three massed lines of bayonets reflected the first rays of a red sun peeping over the horizon.*

*Somehow the excitement which Slim had imagined would mark a battle scene was lacking. His own line was quiet now—too quiet; one could feel a mounting strain, a tension. The entire scene reminded him more of a maneuver, a sham battle, than the actual beginning of a fight. Word had passed: "Hold* your fire!" *The distant waves came nearer. Out in front, khaki-clad figures emerged from a low thicket and fell back with unhurried steps, the men glancing over their shoulders. Someone shouted: "The outpost is in!" Came a rapping burst of fire from a Hotchkiss gun close by. A gap opened in a gray-clad wave. Rifles began to crack, and, as the gap closed and the attack came on, the volume of fire increased to a pulsing roar. Slim lay spellbound. His emotions were a mixture of fear, horror, and appreciation of a spectacle undreamed of in all his little experience. The merging roar of rifle and machine-gun fire gave rise to a feeling of elation—a thrill—a mounting hysteria, which drew him higher and higher from behind his protecting pile of earth to better see the panorama of courage and death depicted on that awful field before him.*

*Unheeded, shells burst nearby, their splinters keening around like angry hornets. Bits of bark spun off the trees and twigs and leaves came drifting down, but these were sensed, almost unnoticed. Rapt vision could not leave that scene in front. Experimentally, his rifle raised to cover one of those forms. They were so like the silhouette targets of the rifle range at, say, six hundred yards. When glimpsed through the small aperture of a peep-sight they were nearly identical in outline, the breast-high figures of men, head and shoulders rising above the flood of waving grain through which they came. The difference was that these targets bobbed and swung along with the rise and fall of the terrain and were, or so it seemed, in never-ending numbers.*

*In fancy, all the German Army was coming there. Here was a pageant of men at war, but with actors who did not behave like the story men of the older wars. Nothing was to be seen of the brave clash of bold spirits. No waving flags or battle cries. Just a trudging mass of modern soldiery, closing in on another group of fellows who, for the most part, waited patiently to test in each the teaching of their trade—"Kill or be killed!" Somehow the three enemy waves had merged into one, and yet it was no stronger than the one had been before. Gaps opened in the surging rank and closed again, but not so rapidly as at first. The line thinned, and thinned again, while the air was wild with the sound of gunfire.*

*A fear that was almost panic gripped Slim's throat. The range was shorter now—too short. With its lessening panic, his fear fought for mastery over reason. The urge was to flee, to get away. This was impossible—unreal. That thin line must go back. "Damn it, why wouldn't it go back?" A cold bleak anger* rose. It would go back! "Kill or be killed!" And here was the tool of his trade, a fitting of wood and metal. It came up, to snug in comfort like the arm of a pal. Its smooth stock caressed from shoulder to cheekbone. Habit? Training! Target—the half-drawn breath—a finger pressure—recoil. Target? No. A man, a breast-high silhouette in dirty gray, under a dome of hat. He staggered and seemed to sag, suddenly, wearily, so close that one could see the shock of dumb surprise. A hand flung out, instinctive, to ease the fall; then, the figure settled, limp, at rest, pillowed in broken grain.

What had been a wave of fighting Germans became a broken outline, groups—individuals. Some still fell, some fled, while others dropped their arms to plead in fearsome stricken voices. Most firing fell away, though here and there the most hardened killers shot men as they ran. Victors rose. There were readjustments, shouts, commands. Stretchers passed, carried by willing prisoners. "Dig in! You—and you. Get ammunition, quickly now!" "They'll be back again." "Back?" "Sure! They want this hill. Lucky we broke up that flank attack early."

An elated comrade, drunk with excitement, dropped down beside Slim. A cigarette changed hands. "Light? Well, we sure stopped 'em that time, son, didn't we?" "Gee, I was scared at first. Did you see—?" Slow puffs, a nod, an empty word or two. The elated one passed on. The warm sun of a June morning poured on the now-quiet wood. Its heat soothed and rested. Slim turned a bit to let his glance sweep the field. His look paused to note a sodden bundle of gray, among others. His wandering eye was caught by the gleam of a single empty cartridge among the drying clods of his little breastwork. Its brazen shine peered back, unblinking, accusing, reflecting a bit of life-giving sun. Slim turned facedown, his head pillowed in the crook of his arm. He feigned sleep. One can always dream.

### Burial Detail

By the time the question of who was to hold Hill 142 had been hashed over a few times and seemingly settled in our favor, the Germans slacked off for a number of days while their spearhead swung to the east, toward Château-Thierry. Details, working at night, gathered the battalion dead into parkings just at the forest edge, opposite Lucy-le-Bocage. Some of the 67th's survivors of June 6 and 7 had guided members of the "damned replacements" with the *harvest, having vivid memories of the road the company had taken to get the bayonets into Belleau.*

*There were seventy-six dead Leathernecks at a corner of the wood, across that first wide field outside of Lucy, and the replacements had plenty to do. Most of them had been dead for a week, the majority having died in the wheat. The stretcher bearers wore their French gas masks while at work. During the night the Second Division Engineers, temporarily relieved from firing-line duty, had dug a long shallow trench for the burials. Someone had to work in the trench to receive the dead, and Lieutenant Long asked for a volunteer. "Tugboat" Wilson, an old-time marine with a corporal's chevrons, took the job, but found the work heavy. He was patient with our squeamishness (we had been at the Front only a week), and he asked repeatedly that some boot give him a hand with the laying out. We kept hurrying away for new burdens. It so happened that on one of his trips, Slim had passed his finals in wretchedness. In picking up a man who had been hit dead center above the eyes, he had noted that the fellow's chinstrap was still tightly in place. In swinging the corpse to the stretcher by his shoulders, the tin hat had flopped. The dead man's brains slopped messily across Slim's shoes. The gas mask was a handicap then, and by the time he reached the trench, burial work held no more terrors.*[1]

The victory at Belleau Wood had effectively denied Ludendorff's aspirations to take Paris. It was the first time ever that the German Army had taken on Americans in battle, and although it didn't win the war, it delivered a strong message to the Germans: Beating these doughboys was not going to be as easy as they had previously hoped. The victory delivered a punishing psychological blow to German morale, from which they would never entirely recover. Ludendorff had committed every available man that he had to those German spring offensives, and now he had to contend with a terrible truth: His army was overextended and demoralized. Despite all of his efforts, he hadn't managed to achieve his objectives and shatter the Allied line. The advantage now lay with the Allies, and thanks to American intervention, they were going to grab it with both hands and go on the offensive.

## CHAPTER TEN

# The Second Battle of the Marne

THIS WAS GOING TO BE THE FIRST MAJOR BATTLE OF MOVEMENT SINCE those first few months of the Great War, before both sides dug in to endure three long, terrifying years of attrition, stalemate, and misery. It was going to be the template for future battles in its use of infantry, artillery, tanks, and air support.

In March 1918 at the insistence of French prime minister Georges Clémenceau, Gen. Ferdinand Foch had been appointed Allied Supreme Commander, a role that frequently caused conflict between him and Pershing concerning the disposition of US forces along the Western Front. Despite this, Pershing reacted favorably to the appointment. France still fielded the largest army, and the AEF commander fully understood the need for cohesion and a unified Allied strategy in response to the critical situation that had transpired during the recent German spring offensives. He had already made some concessions when he decided to amalgamate AEF forces with other Allied units at the division level. What this meant in practice was that American soldiers would take their orders from American officers up to the level of major general, but overall strategic planning would be the purview of more-experienced French officers at the corps, army, and army group levels. This system was to prove highly effective at the watershed Second Battle of the Marne in July 1918.

On July 14, 1918, Kaiser Wilhelm personally visited German 1st Army positions as they prepared to cross the Marne River just northeast of Reims, to launch a surprise attack, in what would in effect be their last concerted offensive in World War I. They would launch along a fifty-mile-long front in one of the final all-out attempts to shatter the Allied resolve to continue the war. This time things were going to be remarkably different, thanks to a daring French raid across No Man's Land. Documents taken from German prisoners captured east of Reims revealed that the long-expected offensive would commence shortly after midnight. These intelligence documents were vital to the Allies; they stated times and places of impending German attacks, and ensured that the element of surprise would be obliterated. Details regarding the imminent attack were dispatched with great urgency along the whole of the Allied front line. The spearhead and most concentrated attack would be unleashed in the direction of the American 3rd Infantry Division and the French 125th Division section.

This time the Allies would have a serious advantage. At 11:45 p.m. a thunderous, bellicose roar pierced the night air as every single available Allied artillery piece in proximity released a devastating barrage. Shells of all calibers pounded the area where unsuspecting German troops were assembling in preparation for the planned attack, causing terrible damage. German forward positions and support trenches imploded as shrapnel reduced men to unrecognizable heaps of distended bloody flesh and bone. The shelling was so intense that some German units had to be replaced before the attack even got under way.

Despite this setback the attack would go ahead as planned on July 15, as twenty-three German divisions belonging to the 1st and 3rd Armies launched against positions held by the French 4th Army marginally to the east of Reims. A further seventeen divisions from the German 7th Army simultaneously attacked the French 6th Army in the west.

With this latest offensive the intransigent General Ludendorff planned to orchestrate a diversionary attack along the Marne River to draw out the British Expeditionary Force, while the main thrusts were intended to divide the French armies piecemeal. During the previous months, although they failed in their efforts to capture the city of Reims, the Germans had made a deep penetration into the west and southwest of that city, and its vitally important railway facilities. The forty German divisions holding this salient were in a potentially precarious situation because they relied heavily for their food and ammunition provisions on just one railroad that ran through the town of Soissons.

At that time the AEF effectively had sixteen divisions in the line, and in the event of a fresh German offensive, six of these were well situated to defend Château-Thierry. Under the command of Gen. Joseph Dickman, the men of the 30th and 38th Infantry Regiments, 3rd Division, would bear the brunt of the attacks, and as flanking units were driven back, these men would defiantly hold their positions at the Marne River. In recognition of this strategically important and heroic stand, the 3rd Division earned the nickname "Rock of the Marne." Activated at Camp Greene, North Carolina, in November 1917, just eight months later they went into action at midnight on July 14, 1918, for the first time.

Col. Ulysses Grant McAlexander was a West Point graduate who had seen action in Cuba during the Spanish-American War and later served in the Philippines. In July 1918 he commanded the 3rd Division's 38th Regiment. In 1907 he had been appointed commandant of cadets and professor of military science and tactics at Oregon Agricultural College. A stubborn, outspoken individual, he had arrived in France with the 1st Division shortly after he had been promoted to colonel. In one of his frequent altercations with other officers he was relieved of command after vehemently insisting that the French couldn't teach him anything about war. The 38th Regiment was located just west of where the Surmelin joins the Marne River and courses northwest either side of its valley, to a place where the two rivers converge. This was also where two navigable roads led south before joining the main Paris highway. These roads were intended to be the primary German route that would facilitate moving German artillery and supplies south to help exploit any potential breakthrough.

Initially, French commander General Montdésir wanted to divide up the available Americans among his troops, but McAlexander characteristically refused this request. McAlexander placed Maj. Guy Rowe's 2nd Battalion astride the Marne River, while the half-strength 1st remained further back in support, and the 3rd Battalion even deeper in reserve. Rowe's men fielded three companies each, with two platoons dug in down on the riverbank, and two more about 350 yards back, behind a nine-foot-high raised embankment that was part of the east-west Metz–Paris railroad. Fighting from behind this position would have been nigh-on impossible. When the German attack commenced just after midnight on July 15, the 38th Infantry caught the full force and was eventually compelled to confront assaults from the front and both flanks. In this hazardous position its men gallantly held their ground and brought the German storm troopers to a standstill.

The following is a lucid account of the action at the Marne written by Major Rowe. The (abridged) letter is dated August 4, 1919, and is assumed to be addressed to General McAlexander. After the war Rowe was promoted to brigadier general.

## Maj. Guy Ichabod Rowe, 38th Infantry Regiment, 3rd Division

*When the ball opened, I was on the left bank of the Surmelin at its junction with the Marne, making the round of the outpost. Herlihy, the two marines, my Adj., and S.M. were with me. That was my one big moment of fright. I was immediately reminded of Kipling's saying, "The dawn came up like thunder," and I still think it very apt.*

*It took no military genius to estimate the situation, and it seemed that my next job was to get back to my P.C. where I could be found, and where I could keep you informed of developments. This trip took just an hour and a half, through the gas, and trying to go where the shells weren't. Upon my return, I found Bresnahan in charge. He had moved everything into the dugout, and was standing by as if nothing was going on outside. About 2:30 a.m. I ordered Reid to occupy your trenches. I call them "your" trenches, because your mind conceived them, and they undoubtedly earned the day, for without them we would have been surrounded early in the morning, before daylight, and this would have been a different story. Reid was to take three platoons, leaving the other platoon under my direct command.*

*Thus, the long night wore on, with no news from the Front. No news is supposed to be good news, but at such a time one wonders if he hasn't forgotten some vital provision, and thoroughly longs for just a message that all is well. My intelligence section was busy, patrolling all along the Front, but reported that there was no attempt to cross. Thus, until well along into the middle of the fight, I had no intimation of what was going on.*

*As soon as it was light enough to see anything we moved up on the hill east of Moulin. On my way up there I received my first real report, and that was a damned lie. Here he came, seemingly direct from the Front, wild-eyed and followed by a few wild-eyed followers. Breathlessly he said, "You will have to get out of here right away, the Germans are across, and everything is lost." I asked him, "Is this all there is left of your company?" and he replied in the affirmative. There is where my justifiable homicide comes in, but, at the time, I wasn't sure but that his story was, at least, made out of whole cloth. Well, he did not buffalo me anyhow, and that is the main thing.*

*I ordered him and his gang into a trench nearby, and with the few men around we formed a thin line, covering the road where it rounded the curve just north of the town, thus forming a small point of resistance which would have to hold—in case D's story was correct—and would form the nucleus of a rear guard, after the others had pulled out. Soon the mist lifted, and we could see what the noise down by Messy was all about. First, a few scattering groups of men north of the R.R. bank, and which we couldn't at first tell whether they were Boche or our own men. Then, a little later, we could see that they were a mixture—Boche being collected by good American bayonets. Then Wooldridge's wheat field came in view, and at first the only thing that we remarked was its trampled and disheveled condition, and then from out of Messy came the result of Wooldridge's raid into the town, a mob of Boche, which in their formation filled that field from the river more than halfway to the R.R., and still they kept coming.*

*It was easy to see that the B were not having their own way all along the line, and so D was ordered first, to the trenches at cross road north of it, and then, when the big "kamerad" [used by German soldiers in World War I as a cry of surrender] started, back to his position on the R.R. Let me add right here, that on his way in, he fired into the backs of his own company, until stopped by Lieutenant Ross, who, at the risk of his own life, came out in the face of this fire, and gave D hell. This is authentic, though at the time I did not know much about what was going on at that point, because his report was all the information I had about E Company. Then, in the wheat field things began to happen. The B were dropping quite regularly, and, all of a sudden, they all dropped their arms, faced to the right, and started for the R.R. with hands up. Ah, that was a grand and glorious sight.*

*Just previous to this, and before the visibility was such that one couldn't tell much about what was going on, I received a message from Herlihy stating that W platoon had fallen back from the river, and that the B were coming then between the two companies. [The weak always yell for help before they are hurt], and, as luck would have it, just at this time, a platoon of I Company emerged from the ravine, east of M, where they were stationed, as company reserve, and wanted to know what was going on. Lieutenant Bush said he heard the racket, and if there was a fight, he wanted to get into it. He was ordered to [fall in] between G and I, reporting to Herlihy. I have often regretted that this coincidence occurred, for, fifteen minutes later, I would have known that this was a false alarm, and this platoon would have been invaluable to Reid. However, "Il n'y a pas de quoi."*

*What about Reid? That was what was worrying me now. Murray went on a search for him, and after killing a Boche in a shell hole in the rear of our line, he brought me the news that F Company had had a big fight just in front of their trenches, and had succeeded in driving the Boche back, but that they were suffering from M.G. fire from those of the Boche who had advanced over the French territory, and were now firmly settled in the woods to the east of their position. So, I sent Reid's other platoon to him, with a message of congratulation and encouragement, also informing him of the situation elsewhere.*

*It was now about 4:50 a.m., and I sent you the following message: "The Boche have penetrated Messy and the French are falling back on my right. Will you guard my flanks." —Rowe, Maj.*

*Now came the period of waiting and watching, during which we were the silent and helpless witnesses of losses from our own artillery; and during which came numerous pleas for help from Reid, and for mercy from Herlihy and Dineen, due to the artillery. We shot all of our rockets for the benefit of the artillery, with no result, and at last sent back word by the sole surviving member of the artillery liaison group, and he apparently got back safely, for in due time this particular situation improved. Along about 8:30 a.m., the situation on the right looked so serious and no word came from you, that I sent my carrier pigeon message which was practically a duplicate of the above message to you.*

*By the way, Colonel Adams told me that this message was the first information that the French Army HQ'rs had that the Germans had crossed the Marne.*

*At nine o'clock I sent this message to you by T.P.S.: "Can I have any assurance that my right will be protected?" —Rowe*

*Still no reply, but when things looked the blackest, along came Keeley. He wanted to know what was going on, and stated that he could not get in touch with you, and that he placed himself under my command. Just prior to his appearance, I had written the orders for a gradual withdrawal, but revoked them when I saw him coming. How about that for luck? Hastily, I told him the situation, and indicated Reid's position on the map, and ordered him to come up from the woods in rear of F Company, with his two companies, clearing them of Boche, and then take position on right of Reid. I also informed R of this much-desired succor.*

*In due time, R reported that the two companies were not to be found, and I sent back the following, at 10:00: "Maj. Keeley is on his way to organize the two companies on your right. You most close the gap between you and E—at least, keep it under close observation, for our line must not be pierced." —Rowe, Maj.*

*It is still my impression that if this move had been successful, and Keeley had persisted, there would not have been any reason for the later withdrawal, for, at that time, the Boche were not so numerous, and if others had been prevented from reaching them, those already there could have been cleaned up by Lough and Keeley. Imagine my shock, then, when I received a message from Keeley, stating that he was back on the Aqueduct line, and giving no reason, nor telling me the situation that he had left. The next hour or two are rather hazy as regards sequence, and as regards data. Very shortly, after the above, your first message arrived, which was full of praise and encouragement, warning me to be watchful of my flanks. A good comforting sort of message, that made us want to stick [it out] to the end.*

*Shortly after this, Reid paid me a call and told me all his troubles, and said that he couldn't hold on much longer, but when I got through with him, he left with the determination to hang on as long as he had any men left.*

*All this time, no message from Wooldridge; I could see that he was still on the job, but I couldn't see the trouble that he was having on his flank, although we saw some activity around the rock pile, but couldn't make out what it was all about. Then came his first message, written on a captured German postal card, and which was a wonder. I cannot find it, and only trust that it will turn up in the baggage, wherever that may be. It told me all about himself and how cleaned out he was, but asked for no help, and closed with an expression of determination to stick [it out] as long as he had anybody left, and added that at present rate of loss, this would not be long. He certainly deserves the M.H. if anyone does, "Go to hell Whittlesey" not excepted. I have a copy of my reply, but it is so blurred that I cannot connect it up to make sense.*

*Then I sent you another message, trying to describe our plight, but in which you must have seen no signs of weakening, for you came back with a stiffener, saying, amongst other things, that a definite hold to the end would be sure of its reward. Maybe this will help you to remember your exact words; it's all hazy to me except that one passage, and I have not expressed that very well.*

*Anyhow, at two-thirty, I sent this reply: "We have no intention of withdrawal until we are completely outflanked. At present a Boche M.G. is troublesome on right flank. If French counterattack in time, we are all O.K. We must thicken our line tonight, and have ammunition and food and carrying parties from the rear. There are many German rowboats on the river that should be destroyed before night. We are weary but proud." (I am rather ashamed of this message; too much demand and too little intention.)*

*Prior to this, I had received a message from Young that the French were to counterattack at four o'clock. He omitted what date, and thus saved himself later embarrassment. Keeley also warned me about my flanks, and at 2:35 I sent him the following: "We know that our flanks are in danger and look to you for protection. The Boche have advanced against the 30th without much opposition. Young has notified me that French are to counterattack, but they may not be in time. Protect that right and we can hold on forever. I have sent Frenchman to establish liaison."*

*Sometime later, the following to Keeley, without heading; I don't remember the reason, or motive: "The Boche are attacking my fight flank. Can I depend on you for immediate assistance?"*

*The next was from you, with orders to retire. No explanation, and here we were, expecting to hear the French at any minute. That was a sad moment, but we knew that you knew best, and so hastened to comply. When that was received, Herlihy was with me, telling me all about it. I ordered him to notify*

Wooldridge, and then to lead out in single file along the Surmelin, with Wooldridge to bring up the rear. These two companies were to take up the position along the river, as ordered by you. Then to Dineen to pull out, and follow the western slope of ridge east of Moulin, and warned him to get in touch with Reid, who would cover his rear and flank. Of course, he indicated his next position, and then issued the same orders to Reid.

Let me say right here that in spite of all the hell that all [of us] had been through, and in spite of fatigue and hunger, this movement was carried out with a minimum of loss, and with all taking up their new positions without confusion, or misunderstanding. I am very proud of that.

Herein, I have told the whole truth, as it appears after these months, and please use what you see fit. I am sorry that it is incomplete in some particulars, but that cannot be helped. How fate does work—the arrangement of companies so that the best two should be right where they were needed, and that the one which was without a leader should have had but little to do, was surely due to good fortune, as much as I would like to claim the genius. The German plan of attack fitted so thoroughly with our plans, and the good old-fashioned trenches were just the thing to resist that bombardment, and hold the defenders against such an onslaught.

All of which proves, though, the truth of that military truth, viz. "Great results can be gained by a few determined men," and I am proud to have commanded those determined men, who, although [they] could see certain death staring them in the face, still placed duty above all, and cheerfully gave all that they had in them to give, believing, I hope, that they were just where they belonged, and that they had not been forgotten. That battle was the best little bit of American propaganda of the war, and there was no other nationality represented on the Western Front at that time who were so willing to give their all, who made the other fellow pay so heavily. My only "brag" is of our Americanism, which was so wonderfully vindicated in the little valley of the Surmelin.

My dear general, that is all. This has been a real labor of love, for you and that gallant thousand, written during leisure hours, between nursing and other household duties. If this meets with your approval, I would much appreciate a copy of your story, at your convenience.

Yours very truly,

Guy I. Rowe

General Ludendorff said:

*All [German] divisions [along the Marne] achieved brilliant successes, with the exception of the one division on our right wing. This encountered American units! Here only did the Seventh Army, in the course of the first day of the offensive, confront serious difficulties. It met with the unexpectedly stubborn and active resistance of fresh American troops.*

*While the rest of the divisions of the Seventh Army succeeded in gaining ground and gaining tremendous booty, it proved impossible for us to move the right apex of our line, to the south of the Marne, into a position advantageous for the development of the ensuing fight. The check we thus received was one result of the stupendous fighting between our 10th Division of Infantry and American troops.[1]*

For his actions in World War I, Maj. Guy Ichabod Rowe, US Army, was awarded the Distinguished Service Cross.

### Citation

*The President of the United States of America, authorized by an Act of Congress, July 9, 1918, takes pleasure in presenting the Distinguished Service Cross to Major (Infantry) Guy I. Rowe, United States Army, for extraordinary heroism in action while serving with 38th Infantry Regiment, 3rd Division, AEF, east of Château-Thierry, France, 15 July 1918. For fourteen and a half hours on 15 July 1918, Major Rowe held his battalion in an advanced and exposed position on the Marne, although violently and persistently attacked on his front and on both flanks by greatly superior enemy forces.*

The German attack to the east failed to reach its objectives and was halted at 11:00 a.m. on the first day, with no prospect of being resumed. The offensive to the west of Reims proved to be more successful, breaking through the French 6th Army and crossing the Marne at Dormans. Ludendorff succeeded in driving a huge salient into the Western Front but failed to achieve substantial results. The successful German penetrations were largely due to their improved tactical doctrine and use of storm troopers, but this advantage was negated due to poor coordination. The Germans had, however, established a bridgehead nine miles in length and four in depth before the French 9th Army, supported by British, American, and Italian troops, managed to halt this advance on July 17. The poor German coordination presented Foch with the opportunity to sufficiently repair his defenses and prepare a consolidated Allied counterattack.

## CAPT. JESSE WOOLRIDGE, 38TH INFANTRY, 3RD DIVISION

*Newly captured prisoners began to give real information—a grand offensive was to be made [where] the Marne was only about fifty yards wide. . . . We had six hundred yards of [this] front all to ourselves . . . [When it began] it seemed [the Germans] expected their artillery to eliminate all resistance . . . French officers attached to our brigade stated positively [that] there was never a bombardment to equal it at Verdun.*

*At 3:30 a.m. the general fire ceased and their creeping barrage started, behind which—at forty yards only, mind you—they came, with more machine guns than I thought the German Army owned. . . .*

*The enemy had to battle their way through the first platoon on the riverbank; then they took on the second platoon on the forward edge of the railway, where we had a thousand times the best of it—but the [Germans] gradually wiped it out. My third platoon [took] their place in desperate hand-to-hand fighting, in which some got through only to be picked up by the fourth platoon, which was deployed simultaneously with the third. . . . By the time they struck the fourth platoon, they were all in and easy prey.*

*It's God's truth that one company of American soldiers beat and routed a full regiment of picked shock troops of the German Army. . . . At ten o'clock . . . the Germans were carrying back wounded and dead [from] the riverbank, and we in our exhaustion let them do it. They carried back all but 600, which we counted later, and 52 machine guns. . . . We had started with 251 men and 5 lieutenants . . . I had left 51 men and 2 second lieutenants.*

### Distinguished Service Cross

*The President of the United States of America, authorized by an Act of Congress, July 9, 1918, takes pleasure in presenting the Distinguished*

*Service Cross to Capt. (Infantry) Jesse Walton Wooldridge, United States Army, for extraordinary heroism in action while serving with 38th Infantry Regiment, 3rd Division, AEF, east of Château-Thierry, France, on 15 July 1918. With rare courage and conspicuous gallantry Captain Wooldridge led a counterattack against an enemy of five times his own numbers: 189 men entered this counterattack, and 51 emerged untouched. More than 1,000 of the enemy were killed, wounded, or taken prisoner.*

With the Germans having ultimately failed in their efforts to break through, Ferdinand Foch authorized a combined Allied counteroffensive commencing on July 18. Twenty-four French divisions supported by US, British, and Italian troops, and around 350 tanks, moved in for the kill. This was the one that was going to become the classic template for the modern pitched battle. The ultimate purpose of the attack was to eliminate the large German salient that jutted out among the French lines.

Foch's attack proved calamitous for the Germans. With General Mangin's French 10th Army and Degoutte's 6th Army leading the way, the assault advanced a full five miles on the first day alone. Berthelot's French 5th Army and Eben's 9th Army launched subsidiary attacks simultaneously in the west that also had desired effects. Reeling from the force of this Allied onslaught, during the night of July 19 the German High Command promptly ordered a withdrawal from this section of the Aisne-Marne salient. Forcibly ejected from their footholds south of the Marne, they began to retreat across previously German-held ground that was captured in the Aisne offensive. Ludendorff was now faced with the real possibility that his armies in the salient could become isolated and surrounded. He had scant options other than to order a retreat northeast out of the salient to a new line along the rivers Aisne and Vesle.

Although Ludendorff's five offensives had been a calculated gamble from the outset, they had come close to breaking the Allied line. He was now fully aware that literally millions of American soldiers were gathering in France. If Germany was to have any hope at all of bringing this war to a favorable conclusion, it would have to be before all of those fresh troops had a chance to enter the line. The Germans had suffered around

800,000 irreplaceable casualties during Ludendorff's offensives. While the Allied losses were equally high, their losses could be replaced—a luxury the Germans couldn't afford. By August 3 they were back where they had started at the launch of the great 1918 spring offensives.

Reoccupying the salient provided the Allies with improved lateral communications and greater flexibility in deploying troops. The attack launched on July 18 was the beginning of real Allied cooperation along the Western Front, which would ultimately transform the way the war was being fought, and the boundaries of this seemingly unbreakable trench line that stretched from Nieuwpoort (Nieuport) in Flanders all the way down to the French–Swiss border. Although trenches would still play a part on the battlefield, the Great War would never be the same again.[2]

## CHAPTER ELEVEN

# Doughboys Getting Around

## ITALY

MOST PEOPLE ASSUME THAT ALL AEF BATTLES OCCURRED IN FRANCE on the Western Front. While it's fair to state that most of them did, there were a few exceptions.

In response to urgent requests from the Italian government in July 1918, the 332nd Infantry Regiment, 83rd Division, with attached medical and supply units, was sent to the Italian front. The main purpose of this move was to give the impression that Americans were arriving in significant numbers, which would help build the Italian Army's damaged morale, and in the process provide them with a distinct psychological advantage over the Austrians. The 332nd Regiment was first stationed near Lake Garda, where it trained to use new methods that would correspond with the style of fighting in the problematic mountain terrain where the majority of the fighting occurred in the Italian theater of operations.

When the regiment moved to the Piave River front in early October, they actively participated in a ploy that was solely intended to deceive the Austrians into thinking there were more Americans in Italy than the actual number. It was an expertly conceived and executed deception that entailed battalions from the 332nd marching from Treviso in broad daylight. They followed a circular route, and each time they marched they would wear different articles of uniform and equipment, leaving the city each time via an alternative route. These little marches would continue throughout the day, and then under cover of darkness the battalions would surreptitiously return to their base in Treviso.

## LONGSHAW KRAUS PORRITT, AMERICAN AMBULANCE FIELD SERVICE

*To bolster Italian morale, and prevent her from making a separate peace with the Central Powers, American military authorities in Paris were anxious to get some Americans on the Italian front. But, because we had not at that time declared war against Austria, American soldiers could not be sent to this Italian front. To meet this emergency, the American Army authorities in Paris requested the American Red Cross to organize as quickly as possible, four or five ambulance units, to be equipped with Ford and Fiat ambulances, with American drivers; and get them down to the Italian front. At that time there were quite a number of American Ambulance Field Service drivers who had finished their term of service on the Western Front and were looking for openings in other branches of US military service.*

*I was in the hospital at Brest, waiting to be sent back to Moutchic. Learning that I had previous ambulance experience, I was told that if I cared to switch over from naval to army service I would be given an honorable discharge from the navy, provided that I would accept the army's offer of a second lieutenant's commission and pay. Those who would enlist in these emergency ambulance units were to be sent under the jurisdiction of the American Red Cross, to the Italian fronts. I accepted this offer, for one reason because it promised an immediate pay raise. I was sent down to Italy in January 1918, as a member of Section 4. I served more than a year, participating in the Battle of the Piave in June 1918, and the Battle of Vittorio-Veneto in October 1918. I was awarded the Italian Croce al Merito di Guerra for outstanding service in the first of these two major battles. In the concluding weeks of the war, I was promoted to First Lieutenant, US Army. I am fully aware that my months of service with the French Army do not count in qualifying for the Connecticut World War I bonus. Also that my service in the US Navy was for only 89 days, and 90 days are necessary to qualify. But I was commissioned as a second lieutenant in the US military service in December 1917 and served on the Italian front.*[1]

The 332nd regiment was held in reserve with the Italian 31st Division when the Italian Vittorio-Veneto offensive jumped off. They participated in the active pursuit of retreating Austrians on October 29. For this coordinated action they were designated to be part of the British XIV Corps of the Italian 10th Army, and allocated the task of forming the corps advance guard. They encountered further action on November 3, when they successfully overcame an Austrian rear-guard battalion that was defending the crossings of the Tagliamento River not far from the village of Ponte-della-Delizia. On the following day the regiment crossed the river along a narrow footbridge and subdued all Austrian resistance that was established on the riverbank. At 3:00 p.m. on November 4 the Austro-Hungarian Army signed an armistice with Italy, bringing all hostilities to an end. The total cost to the 332nd Regiment was one man killed and four wounded.

## SIBERIA

As far back as 1754 the Czar of Russia was dispatching undesirables, petty criminals, and political opponents to eastern Siberia. They were mostly sentenced to serve their time doing hard labor (*katorga*). The journey to this foreboding destination would have been mostly on foot and could take up to three years. About half died before they even caught sight of their destination. The name *Siberia* still evokes images of frozen arctic tundra in a barely habitable wasteland of vast proportions. The country is immense; it occupies about 5.2 million square miles and reaches from the borderline of Europe in the Ural Mountains to the very east of Russia at the Pacific Ocean and from the Arctic Ocean to the borders with China and Mongolia.

In 1918 President Woodrow Wilson had decided that the United States must send troops to Siberia to protect its investments. It had nearly a billion dollars' worth of American guns and equipment strewn along a segment of the Trans-Siberian Railway between Vladivostok and Nikolsk. At that time civil war and murderous gangs who could operate with virtual impunity roamed freely around the region. It had devolved into an anarchic, lawless society where literally no one was safe.

Giving his approval to send eight thousand American troops to that cold, forbidding part of Russia was a decision that Wilson didn't take lightly. The World War was still raging in Europe, and Russia was still beset by civil war. Even though the Bolsheviks had ousted Alexander Kerensky in November 1917, a few months after the Mensheviks had deposed the tsar that spring, there was still no legitimate government in power with whom the United States could do business. Meanwhile, the Allies clung vainly to the hope that the Czech Legion and even some White Russian and Cossack forces could still be instrumental in helping to defeat Germany and Austria by creating diversions in western Russia and in eastern Siberia. They hoped this activity would cause the Central Powers to divert forces from the Western Front back to Eastern Europe. Meanwhile, the Red Army in Russia continued fighting for its very survival on at least four fronts.

The overall campaign was referred to as the Polar Bear Expedition, but was also known as the Northern Russian Expedition, the American North Russia Expeditionary Force (ANREF), or the American Expeditionary Force North Russia (AEFNR).

Maj. Gen. William S. Graves, a Texan who had been decorated for bravery during the Philippine Insurrection in 1900, and had served with Pershing on the Mexican border, was selected to lead the American component of the Allied Expeditionary Force. After serving with distinction on the army staff, Graves had just assumed command of the 8th Division at Camp Fremont, California, when he was summoned by coded message to meet Secretary of War Newton D. Baker at the Baltimore Hotel in Kansas City. The message gave no reason for the meeting, and Graves did not know if he would be returning to California afterwards. He hastily departed Camp Fremont by train, meeting the secretary in Kansas City as ordered. Baker conveyed the president's orders: that Graves take two infantry regiments then stationed in the Philippines (the 27th and 31st) to Vladivostok. Most of his staff, and five thousand fillers, would be drawn from the 8th Division.

The American Expeditionary Forces in Siberia had a nickname—or, rather, nicknames. That far-off group of Americans, consisting of the

27th and 31st Infantry Regiments, Ambulance Company No. 4, Field Hospital Company No. 4, a telegraph company, and several supply units, became known as the "Wolfhounds," or the "Snowdogs"—although the former nickname was more commonly used. The 31st Infantry's first combat action occurred on August 29, 1918, at Ugolnaya, when a patrol came under fire from local partisans, inflicting the first American casualties on Siberian soil. Under orders from the Allied expedition's Japanese commander, Gen. Kikuru Otani, the 27th Infantry Regiment was dispatched to Khabarovsk and the 31st was ordered to follow. When General Graves reached Vladivostok on September 1, he rescinded Otani's order, making it clear that US forces were under Graves's command, not Otani's. General Graves soon issued instructions to relocate several strongpoints.

By the end of 1918, the Allied force in Siberia included roughly 72,000 Japanese, 70,000 Czechoslovaks, 12,000 Poles, 9,000 Americans, 4,200 Canadians, 4,000 Romanians, 4,000 Russian auxiliaries, 2,000 Italians, 1,600 British, and 760 French. Rather than going home to fight the Germans, the opportunistic Czechoslovaks had taken over a large segment of the Trans-Siberian Railway between Lake Baikal and Yakutsk and run it as their own. Because of their numbers and the arms they had looted from abandoned Russian stocks, no army was strong enough to force them out.

Drinking water for the Vladivostok garrison was drawn by cutting ice blocks from a quarry in the mountains, sliding the ice down the mountainside, and hauling it to the kitchens where it was melted and boiled. Barracks life left much to be desired. Before the buildings could be occupied, squatters had to be evicted and the incredible filth left by the previous inhabitants had to be cleaned out. Although barracks buildings were substantial brick structures, windows were ill-fitting, and potbellied stoves heated little more than their immediate surroundings. Mattresses were straw-filled, creating a home for bugs of every description, and a serious health hazard. They were also a fire hazard, causing the replacement battalion's barracks to burn down when sparks from a coal stove caught a mattress on fire and spread throughout the building before anyone could find water—that was not frozen—to extinguish the blaze. Latrines were outdoors, making every morning a new challenge. Depending on the time of year, ice, mud, or powdery dust covered the barracks' exterior grounds. Yet despite the irritants, soldiers in Vladivostok and other garrison towns lived as comfortably as their counterparts in barracks back home.

Soldiers and most leaders remained uncertain of the actual purpose of their mission. Some believed their primary responsibility was to help the Czechs fight their way back home. Others assumed they were to round up German and Austrian prisoners of war, running loose all over Siberia. Most believed they had been sent to fight the Bolsheviks, derisively nicknamed "Bolos" by American troops. The "brass" had other ideas. When General Graves learned that a soldier had arrested a Russian simply because he was a Bolshevik, he issued the following statement: "Whoever gave you those orders must have made them up himself. The United States is not at war with the Bolsheviki or any other faction of Russia. You have no orders to arrest Bolsheviks or anybody else unless they disturb the peace of the community, attack the people, or the Allied soldiers."

After World War I ended in November 1918, the rationale for keeping American troops in Siberia came into question. The mission no longer had anything to do with getting Czechs back into the war against Germany. While Allied governments openly favored Russia's Whites over the Reds, American troops trusted neither because Russian leaders on both sides were thoroughly corrupt and brutal. As one officer put it, "The peasantry lives in a constant state of mortal fear, never knowing when the blow will descend on them. No crops are raised—nothing. To do so would be merely to take one's life in hand in protecting them from bandits and guerrillas."

In April 1919, reacting to increasing Bolshevik assertiveness and general lawlessness along the Trans-Siberian Railway, the Allies agreed to assume responsibility for the rail line's security and operation. Bolsheviks interpreted the agreement as pro-Kolchak. Their view was reinforced on May 21, when troops of the 31st Infantry began rousting an ill-disciplined band of Bolshevik partisans out of the town of Maihe on the Suchan spur. The three-day action resulted in several exchanges of fire, but no American casualties. The AEF wasn't withdrawn from Siberia until January 8, 1920. On receipt of the withdrawal order, the 31st Infantry began its departure from the Shkotovo District. In bitter cold amid a blowing snowstorm, the evacuation was completed despite two partisan attacks.

As a result of the fighting against Soviet Bolshevik forces around Archangel in 1918–1919, there were many casualties, and eyewitness accounts of hundreds of US, British, and French personnel who disappeared.

### CORP. NOBLE RUST, 27TH INFANTRY INTELLIGENCE UNIT

*I had been transferred to intelligence headquarters from the 16th Company, Coast Artillery Corps, Regular Army, stationed at Fort Mills, Corregidor, Philippine Islands, because of my ability to speak and read German, which I had studied at Bethel College, Kentucky. Soon afterward, I was assigned to the intelligence unit under Col. D. P. Borrows, Captain Brazina, and Lieutenant Kosilski, which landed at Vladivostok with the 27th Infantry under general command of General Graves. There we were stationed at the palatial "German Club" building on Svetlonskaya Street. We served as guards, interpreters, orderlies, dispatch riders, and military police to the general staff, being formed into a headquarters company by Lieutenant Mills. The boys will remember me by my nickname of "Ding Hai." I led a patrol of ten men from headquarters and fifteen men from Company B, Replacement Battalion, during the Kolchak and General Gaida revolts at Stancion during the month November, 1919.*

Companies A, B, C, D, K, L, and M of the 339th Regiment were ordered to Russia. They were accompanied by the 338th Regiment's machine-gun company and eighteen twelve-pound guns from the artillery, which later proved almost worthless. The men sailed from Dundee, and after a stormy voyage of fourteen days arrived at Archangel, on the Marman coast.[2]

### PVT. 1ST CLASS CORIE VINAL, COMPANY K, 339TH INFANTRY, 85TH DIVISION

*The men were given Russian rifles and Russian ammunition, which jammed at nearly every shot. We fought in ice, water, and mud, with the temperature*

*25 below zero. Transportation facilities and support were such that we could not hold [our] own, even though five of our men were able to lick every fifty "Bushwicks" we went up against. At the start of the advance the temperature was 20 below zero, and while the Bushwicks had furs swathed about them, we did not; therefore, we suffered from the cold. Then advance against the Bolshevik started, in which we gained ground readily. We found that the heavy guns brought by the artillery to protect our advance would be no good, as we could find no way to drag them inland.*

*The Russians were apparently using German equipment, and they were reinforced by many sailors. For fourteen days we were in action against them back along the Dwina River. At times it would rain and snow, and we were without dry clothing for days at a time. It seemed every bullet would choke our rifles, and they were nearly useless.*

*After fourteen days, the Bolshevik made a stand at a bend in the Dwina River, and we dug in on the opposite bank as best we could. The ground was frozen hard. The enemy planted machine guns opposite and made it mighty uncomfortable for several days. They also used shrapnel and we lost many men. Finally, several companies managed to cross the river below us, and they executed a flank movement. Taken by surprise at the rear, the Bolshevik forces loosened their hold on the bridge at that point and the Allied soldiers swarmed across. We were then about 120 miles from Archangel.*

*The Bolshevik continued their retreat after that, and our forces followed them. We traveled in wagons, in sleighs, and on foot, over windswept hills and through snow and ice. Late in August we reached the town of Kadish, drove the Bolshevik out of that place, and ten miles beyond the town. We were outnumbered along the route from Archangel, but from what we saw of their fighting ability, one of our men was better than ten of theirs. However, after reaching a point ten miles beyond Kadish, the enemy received heavy reinforcements and they made a fresh stand. This was about 150 miles from Archangel. Notwithstanding our poor equipment, we held our lines for two weeks before our retreat was decided upon.*

*When the main force fell back, my company was placed on outpost duty; we were at the apex of the Allied line. All the American doughboys were disgusted at such a thing as having to retreat, but it was inevitable, since the Bolshevik had received such strong assistance and new supplies. We fell back to the river, where we entrenched again, and it was decided to go back no further. After having had many narrow escapes from death by exploding shells, I fell victim to the influenza after reaching the river. I was taken to Archangel and, believe me, I thought I would never see the good old USA again. It was a terrible trip. After being carried aboard the Red Cross hospital ship, my luck kept with me, for the boat was shelled by a land battery several miles away and part of the upper deck was carried away. Two days after I reached Archangel my company returned to that place, having been relieved by Company L and five hundred loyal Russians.*

## CHAPTER TWELVE

# Saint-Mihiel

THERE'S A WOODED PLATEAU IN NORTHEASTERN FRANCE KNOWN AS THE Argonne that has an elevation of around 320 yards. It descends into the Champagne region south of the Ardennes, near the border with Belgium between the Meuse and the Aisne rivers. At this location in 1918, the 5th German Army was on familiar territory, because it was one of the areas that they had traversed without significant opposition on September 4 and 5, 1914, shortly after hostilities commenced. The battles that occurred there were part of what is known as the Hundred Days Offensive that began on August 8, 1918.

September was a seminal month in the life of the AEF during the Great War. For General Pershing and the AEF this was going to be their greatest battle to date and the one in which they would incur the most casualties. The previous months had provided a painful learning curve for the Americans, on some occasions that curve had defiled geometry and many American soldiers had been inadvertently punished for their inexperience.

Relations between the Allied commanders were not particularly healthy in the late summer and fall of 1918. The ties that bound this alliance were on occasion gossamer-thin. Foch visited Pershing's headquarters on August 30 to explain his plan to reduce the Saint-Mihiel salient and then push the Germans back along the whole front. Relations between these two generals had never been amicable, and at this moment in history, they had reached their nadir. Pershing secretly despised the French commander's arrogance, and was fully aware that his tactics during the early years of the war had brought the Allies to the brink of disintegration.

There was no love lost between Pershing and British commander general Douglas Haig either. Haig wrote frequently of his contempt for Pershing in his personal diary, describing the AEF commander as "very obstinate and stupid." In his memoirs, Foch includes a scathing letter that was sent by French prime minister Clémenceau, wherein he bitterly castigated the American forces for what he called "marking time," and actually went so far as to suggest an appeal to President Wilson to remove General Pershing from his command. Foch responded sagaciously on that occasion, and actually paid due tribute to the immense effort made, and results achieved, by Pershing and the AEF. For all of his faults, Foch understood that he needed Pershing's AEF, and as the appointed Allied commander, he also needed to maintain cohesion and unity, even though diplomacy wasn't his finest trait.

The two commanders were destined to clash yet again. During another meeting Pershing became enraged at the mere suggestion of dividing American forces at that juncture. He vehemently tabled counterproposals, which Foch characteristically dismissed as impractical. Foch stared at the American general and asked straight out, "Do you want to go into battle?" to which Pershing abruptly replied, "Most assuredly, but as an American Army, and in no other way. If you assign me a sector I will take it at once." He went on to tell Foch in no uncertain terms that there was absolutely no way that he would yield command to either the French or the British. On this occasion they had reached a stalemate that prompted Foch to leave the meeting in a huge Gallic huff.

Later on Pershing turned to his friend Marshal Pétain for advice and support on what he considered a most pressing matter. Pétain, the man whose military career would eventually culminate in ignominy, was at that time regarded as a sound friend by Pershing. He encouraged Pershing to stick to his larger operation against the Saint-Mihiel salient on the grounds that Foch would have little or no say at all in the plan once it had been set in motion. Pétain also disapproved of the option of dividing American forces by placing them on both sides of the Aisne, because in his opinion the terrain was too inhospitable. On the other hand, Pétain pointed out several times that going against Metz was not possible as long as the area around the Meuse River was dominated by German guns. At this stage in the war, in that sector, the German trench boundaries started in the French fortified area southeast of Verdun, and protruded south toward Saint-Mihiel, and then east to Pont-à-Mousson.

After a lot of negotiation a compromise was reached. Foch suggested that Pershing should indeed take over the whole sector from the Moselle to the Argonne, but for obvious reasons, the defense of Verdun should remain entirely in French hands. The French Army would remove 100,000 men from the line, knowing that Pershing would be able to replace those men with 600,000 Americans. Now that sufficient American military manpower had arrived in France, the American 1st Army was activated as a field army. It was the fulfillment of Pershing's ultimate ambition: the formation of an independent American Army that combined American corps and American divisions. As an element of the AEF during the closing months of the Great War, it was in effect the first of three field armies established under the AEF.

Sometime later, Foch, in a considerably more affable mood, met British commander Field Marshal Haig and listened to his proposals and suggestions concerning the way forward. On the basis of this meeting Foch decided to reconsider his plan and set new objectives. He planned to launch a series of converging attacks against the Germans' lateral lines of communications. This plan envisaged British forces attacking in a southeasterly direction and the Franco-American forces attacking northward from the Meuse-Argonne region in a massive pincer movement that would finally seal the fate of the German forces on the Western Front—at least, that is what they hoped to achieve.

A further meeting was called for with Pershing and Pétain in Bombon, on September 2. On this occasion the atmosphere was less acrimonious, and Pershing finally got his way when he was given control of the sector that he wanted, from which he could organize the attacks and operate autonomously, beyond the constraints of British and French control. The generalissimo finally agreed that the Saint-Mihiel attack could go forward—its elimination was imperative before any great Allied offensive could commence against the Metz region or northward, between the Meuse River and Argonne Forest—but he added that its objectives would be strictly limited, allowing the AEF to undertake another major offensive set to go about ten days later, on the front between the Meuse River and the Argonne Forest.

Allies would employ a "limited objective" strategy that would ultimately be to their detriment. Pétain, among others, advocated limited-objective attacks, designed to reduce systematically an enemy's position in small portions rather than sending whole regiments over the top en masse.

German high command knew full well that another offensive was imminent, but there was disparity as to precisely where the Allies would strike next. Although the recent reduction of the salients had seriously affected German morale, they were now well dug in behind strong defensive lines. The presumed door to breaking these lines was firmly shut and bolted, but its hinges hung on the Meuse River, east of the Argonne Forest. The plan now was to push open this proverbial door by throwing forces against it all along the line that would simultaneously dislodge the hinges by battering through on the Meuse-Argonne front.

The AEF was prepared—in theory, at least. At their disposal they had 2,700 artillery pieces, mostly 75mm field guns and 155mm howitzers, both borrowed from the French. Maj. Gen. Charles P. Summerall, a specialist in artillery, had introduced some flexibility in the use of artillery as a weapon in support of the infantry. More often than not, the guns were stuck on rough and congested roads way behind the infantry. The AEF had the advantage regarding numbers of men and available equipment, but the Germans held the high ground. The terrain in front of them wasn't really conducive to the type of large-scale frontal attack that had been planned, and dense foliage, along with almost-impenetrable undergrowth, would make fighting there a daunting prospect indeed.

The AEF staff began the final planning for the operation that would commence with the Saint-Mihiel offensive. The Saint-Mihiel salient was a two-hundred-square-mile triangle that protruded between the Moselle and Meuse rivers, fourteen miles into the Allied lines. The reduction of this salient was the first task assigned by Marshal Foch to General Pershing, who gathered together fifteen American divisions for the attack. Of these, nine were earmarked for the assault and six were to be retained as tactical reserve. Marshal Foch added four French divisions to this force. The terrain was mostly rolling plain interspersed with small, densely forested areas. Eight German divisions defended the salient, with five more in reserve. They had occupied this area for more than three years, and in that time they had transformed it into a veritable fortress, complete with strong artillery, machine-gun emplacements, and fields of barbed wire fixed with screw pickets. Attacking this position was the first item on the agenda. The engagement was the first battle in which American-led forces employed an operations order that allowed independent initiative from their frontline commanders. To actively encourage frontline commanders to use their initiative and make command decisions based on the situation at hand was almost unprecedented in World War I.

One of the combat commanders participating in the operation was a young colonel by the name of George S. Patton Jr. He and his subordinate officers believed that by rapidly adapting to a situation as it evolved, they could influence events on the battlefield. During World War II, General Patton would draw on this experience again when he prepared for an attack on the German salient in the Ardennes Forest during what became known as the Battle of the Bulge. At the Battle of Saint-Mihiel, Patton's 174 tanks spearheaded the attack, but only 70 made it to the German positions. It was during that first day that Patton met the colonel of the 84th Brigade, Douglas MacArthur. According to Patton they didn't have a great deal to say to each other at the time.

Initially Pershing was against using the standard preparatory artillery bombardment because he wanted to maintain the element of surprise. Eventually he decided to use a four-hour bombardment along the southern flank and a seven-hour one along the western flank. It was the greatest artillery concentration ever assembled on the Western Front to date, and it erupted with a pugnacious, deafening roar that shook the earth to its very core. A few seconds later innumerable tons of explosives were being launched and lobbed into the German frontline positions. While the gas and smoke created an eerie mist, the whole sky appeared to ignite with the reflecting flashes of the thousands of guns that amalgamated into one another. At the suggestion of Pétain, an elaborate scheme had been devised to deceive the Germans into thinking that the American first blow would come to the south near Belfort. The deception worked, because the Germans deployed three divisions to that sector.

The weather section of I Corps operation order stated: "Visibility: Heavy driving wind and rain during parts of day and night. Roads: Very muddy." The terrain would prove to be the biggest obstacle to the attacking forces. After five days of rain the ground became almost impassable to both the tanks and infantry. Those French Renault tanks were designed to cross six-foot trenches in dry weather; now they would be required to navigate line after line of trenches that were eight feet deep and ten to fourteen feet wide, in debilitating deep mud.

The attack on Saint-Mihiel began at 1:00 a.m. on September 12, 1918, when two American corps, the I and the IV, respectively, launched the main assault against the south of the line. The second wave was provided by the French 26th Division, the French 15th Colonial Division, and the 8th Brigade. At Saint-Mihiel between September 12 and 16, the Western Front in France would experience one of the most significant battles of World War I.

Meanwhile, at 8:00 a.m., as timid crepuscular rays of light began to hail the dawn, the artillery barrage increased in intensity. The V Corps began its attack, and also made excellent progress. It should be noted that AEF tactical doctrine left much to be desired, mainly because despite all the training, strategy was still based on 1917 Field Service Regulations, which had hardly been revised from the prewar 1911 version. The manual specified that the attack should be conducted under the conditions of fire superiority, with advance achieved by infantry rushes. Fire superiority was to be gained by antiquated theories based on accurate rifle fire. The bane of all forces during the Great War was the machine gun, and little attention had been paid by the AEF to the devastating potential of this weapon.

The basic ambivalence in the AEF's tactical doctrine ensued from the fact that while Pershing—along with other Allied commanders, such as former cavalry officer, British commander Douglas Haig—advocated open warfare. This contrasted dramatically with the reality of the Western Front. Pershing and the War Department had prepared an army whose fundamental capability wasn't designed for a war of movement, but lay in inflicting casualties on the Germans in a static, grinding war of attrition.

It was just such ambivalence that confused Pershing's subordinate commanders as they sought to train their units for combat. The AEF's best corps commander, Maj. Gen. Hunter Liggett, was prompted by this ambivalence to prepare a memorandum outlining his ideas on a tactical doctrine of "open warfare" that would permit his units "to train upon some practical line." There was a definite contradiction between Pershing's stated preference for the tactics of open warfare and his design of an army more suitable for sustained attrition. The Germans had developed and successfully used infiltration assault tactics for their 1918 spring offensives, but Allied commanders hadn't responded by applying similar tactics to their armies. This glaring lack of inspirational military planning on behalf of the Allies frequently culminated in failed offensives based on unsound tactics.

The most prolific and most costly error of the war was the Allies' insistence on mostly futile "frontal assaults." The AEF continued this trend of sacrificing men, wave after wave, in bloody charges against entrenched German positions. A general lack of adequate training for the AEF was also largely detrimental to their tactical ambitions. Like the British "Pals" battalions decimated at the Somme—because according to some callous British commanders, they weren't capable of doing anything but walking toward the German positions, their Lee-Enfield rifles held at high port—American soldiers would also pay dearly for their inexperience. Haig wrote in May of 1918: "It is ridiculous to think such an army could function unaided in less than two years' time." After four years of war, tactics still relied heavily on the time-honored preparatory artillery barrage followed by men scrambling out of their trenches and going over the top.

The actual effectiveness of these artillery preparations remained dubious at best. The Battle of the Somme, for instance, was preceded by a weeklong artillery bombardment. Approximately 1,738,000 shells were fired along a frontage of 25,000 yards. Despite the length and intensity of this barrage, it failed in its objective to destroy the German positions. If one was on the receiving end of an artillery barrage, the first thing you would experience would be the concussive force of the explosion, caused by the rapid release of energy compressing the air particles. This is often referred to as "overpressure." Soldiers often said that it felt like the air had been sucked out of the area, causing a tightening of the skin and pulsating of the eyes.

Seconds after the overpressure struck and radiated outwards, it was followed by shock waves that created a vacuum in the immediate area of the explosion. Oxygen is pushed out, sucked back in, and then immediately pushed out again into a stomach-wrenching wave of energy. The blast wave followed by the shock wave had the possibility of wreaking havoc on internal organs, brain, lungs, and stomach, often pulverizing them if the victim was too close to the point of impact. Air sucked out of the lungs would often leave the soldier gasping for breath. Blood is forced out of organs and arteries upward, toward the brain. After successive blasts, eardrums could rupture, causing bleeding out of the ears. Those closest to the explosion would simply disintegrate into shards of bloody flesh. Heads, arms, and legs would be literally blown apart.

Attrition and trench warfare reemerged in 1918, but now it had been refined, and new tactics had been introduced that maximized the effect of the weapons. Artillery wasn't used simply to blast the enemy from its defenses, or even necessarily to kill his troops. Instead, short, but intense, barrages, mixing high explosives and gas, would neutralize the enemy's ability to resist, sever communications, suppress his artillery fire, and disorient the men. German colonel Georg Bruchmüller developed a form of a double creeping barrage, with the first line of the barrage consisting of gas shells. His ideas were applied on the Western Front in the Spring Offensive of 1918; using this method, combined with highly trained assault troops, the Germans achieved significant breakthroughs in the spring and early summer of 1918. Artillery remained a vital element of offensives and battles throughout World War I, and the Allies were able to combine its power with large quantities of tanks and superior numbers of aircraft.

The culmination of three years of innovation and tactical development finally led to the breaking of the deadlock on the Western Front. The tactical lessons of 1914–1917 had been learned only with great loss of life. When mobile warfare returned, it brought with it casualties that rivaled the slaughter of those first three years. This was the inescapable nature of a war fought with modern weapons. In the words of French general Charles Mangin, "Whatever you do, you lose a lot of men."

The Second Battle of the Marne demonstrated admirably how a strategy based on movement with artillery tank and air support could achieve astonishing results by Great War standards. AEF troops did a lot of learning on the job, and relied heavily on the experience of other Allied units for tactical training. One Allied commander wrote: "The AEF succeeded not because of imaginative operations and tactics, nor because of qualitative superiority, but by smothering German machine guns with American flesh." The effect of having tanks advancing with Allied infantry provided a distinct psychological advantage, but it should be noted that in the French Tenth Army, commanded by Mangin, 346 tanks were available, but only 225 actually made it across the line of departure, and 102 were knocked out. On the following day, 195 were operational, and 50 of those were knocked out that day. By the third day, the French had only 32 operational tanks.

Maj. Gen. Hunter Liggett complained in April 1918 that he could find no definitive US instructions on how to conduct open warfare. There was little doubt that all the US officers talked about it, but when one attempted to find precise doctrine for its execution, the existing literature was mostly absent. Liggett voiced his concern to Pershing's headquarters, and action was eventually taken to amend this deficiency. Liggett prepared a comprehensive memorandum outlining his ideas on a tactical doctrine of open warfare that would permit his units to train along practical lines. Throughout the subsequent six months, Liggett held administrative control over four American divisions, supervising their training and intervening on their behalf with the French commanders. With the assistance of his effective chief of staff, Col. Malin Craig, he also ensured that his corps and headquarters staff were suitably trained in accordance with his requirements.

## NORVEL PRESTON CLOTFELTER, COMPANY A, 344TH MACHINE-GUN BATTALION, 90TH DIVISION

*September 10, 1918: Rained all a.m. and part of p.m. Were told that Co. had moved, so we went up, two at a time, and got our stuff. Wet. Road is full of trucks and wagons, bringing up ammunition. Big drive will soon be on. More troops coming in too.*

*September 11, 1918: Rainy day. Trucks came this morning, and we loaded up reserve rations. We left with the trucks at 8. We got stuck in the mud but finally pulled out. Lost truck [that] was leading and rode back and forth between Manonville and Dumevre. Finally went back to Saint-Jean at 1:30 p.m. and got new directions. Back same way, only kept on from Dumevre to Gezencourt. Unloaded there. Hiked out to find [battalion] P.C. Rainy and black as pitch. Sgt. Maj. got lost from us. Two cooks and myself pitched our tents and tried to sleep. I had one shoulder in water and could not sleep.*

*September 12, 1918: Hell broke loose at 1:00 a.m. Big barrage started. One continuous roar of guns of nearly all calibers. Must be fierce on Heinle. Aroused at 7. Several of our party lost in brush last night. Could see them all around this morning. Made up our rolls and found kitchens. Learned that 3rd [Battalion] had gone on the big drive. Walked around [in] a.m. and part [of] p.m. with Lieutenant Nicholson, trying to locate 3rd [Battalion]. No success. Helped move kitchen and rations. Prisoners coming in all day, sometimes as many as a [battalion]. Sammies are moving right along. French have some big guns here, kilo from Mamey. Lay on wagon endgate tonight but could not sleep. Everything wet. All roads near here so congested that a wagon can hardly pass.*

*September 13, 1918: Rainy. Not much done but keep out of rain [in] a.m. Kitchen moved up to front[in] p.m. Started at 1:00 p.m.; arrived at 9:00 p.m. Delay on congested roads. Kitchens fired up and from 12 [midnight] on, I, with about twelve others from I, K, L, and M companies, carried hot rations to men out in lines. Dark as pitch and woods thick and dangerous. Found many hungry men who had not eaten for two days.*

*September 14, 1918: Did not go to bed last night. Carried rations until nine this morning. Could never get as far as Co. L. [They have pushed too far ahead]. Americans on this front have advanced about five miles, and taken eight thousand prisoners. More trouble with M.G. [machine-gun] nests and snipers than any other thing. Dead Germans lying all through the wood. Some Americans too. Was preparing to rejoin Co. this evening but Mess Sergeant Canning thought that he had a spy located, and we went to warn companies. While there German snipers got busy with [machine guns] in trees.*[1]

During the attack at Saint-Mihiel the Germans defended stoically, long enough to make an orderly retreat. By the end of the day the 1st Division, advancing from the south, was within striking distance of Vigneulles, and ten miles from the advancing columns of the V Corps' 26th Division. With the capture of Vigneulles and the linkup of the two converging American columns, the most critical part of the operation was over. The AEF was in a celebratory mood because by the close of the following day, the 1st Army had succeeded in taking practically all of its objectives. In two days the American soldiers had reduced and cleared a salient that had remained virtually undisturbed for three years. What the Allies didn't know was that the German forces there had been ordered to pull back from this position on September 8, and had been slow in actually complying with the order from High Command.

African-American troops under French command fought valiantly at Château-Thierry, Saint-Mihiel, and Soissons. They proved proficient in the use of bayonets, knives, and even fists. The 370th Infantry—formerly the 8th Illinois National Guard—were all African Americans. After remaining at a camp near Grand Villa, they were sent to Saint-Mihiel, where they remained under almost constant fire. In that time these excellent troops won the admiration of the Allied officers, and several times the division was cited for gallantry. Throughout the Saint-Mihiel offensive the 370th never failed to take any of the several objectives allocated to them. During the summer the 370th Infantry served with French units in both the Saint-Mihiel and Argonne regions. They lost many men during that time, but fought the Germans hand to hand on numerous occasions.

After the Saint-Mihiel campaign, the division was sent to rest billets behind the lines, where it remained a few days before being sent to Château-Thierry, where once again these indomitable soldiers lived up to their reputation as fighters. They were brigaded with the French, and for several weeks participated in the drive that preceded the smashing of the famous Hindenburg Line. After leaving Château-Thierry they were transferred to Bar-le-Duc, behind the lines, where they rested for two weeks before going into action at Soissons. They went "over the top" in that sector on September 1. They advanced a full five miles through shells and machine-gun fire to reach their objective, earning even more gratitude from the French Army.

Over 550,000 American and roughly 110,000 French soldiers participated in this offensive. Allied air support was comprised of 1,481 airplanes, the greatest concentration of airplanes ever assembled during the Great War. The army had about 400 French tanks available, and Americans manned 144 of them. Although the Western armies had numerical superiority over the Germans, by the late summer and early autumn of 1918, the strategic situation was in danger of becoming less fluid, descending once again into a murderous war of attrition.

The 95th Aero Squadron was one group of the 1,481 airplanes over the skies during this period, and for pilot Waldo Heinrichs, this fight would prove to be almost his last.

## WALDO H. HEINRICHS, 95TH AERO SQUADRON

*On September 17, the second flight of the 95th Squadron, then stationed at Rembercourt in the Verdun sector, was scheduled for a 2:30 p.m. patrol over the German lines on the Saint-Mihiel side. The object of the flight was to down enemy balloons. The airmen left the field in two echelons—three in the lower echelon, and four in the upper. I was flying in the lower echelon with Captain Mitchell, who led the formation, and Lieutenant Holden, who carried the balloon gun. We were at an altitude of 3,000 meters when we sighted seven German Fokkers, of the type D.VII.*

*Captain Mitchell gave the signal for attack, and he and I alone went down on the rear man. I never saw any of the other members of our patrol after the signal was given. Captain Mitchell fired a few rounds with his guns, the new American Marlin, with which our squadron was equipped, when they jammed. I followed the attack. By this time the seven German machines had me surrounded, and two of them attacked. It was while dodging one that I ran through the burst of fire of the man in the rear.*

*I have an official document from the German doctors showing that I had wounds in the following places:*

| | |
|---|---|
| *Explosive bullet* | *Right heel* |
| *Ordinary bullet* | *Left ankle* |

| | |
|---|---|
| *Explosive bullet* | *Left thigh* |
| *Explosive bullet* | *Left elbow; fracture above and below joint* |
| *Explosive bullet* | *Left cheek; fracture upper and lower jaw, loss of fifteen teeth* |
| *Explosive bullet* | *Right hand* |
| *Ordinary bullet* | *Finger of right hand* |

*I landed fifteen kilometers behind the German lines near the town of Gorze. My motor was hit and useless, and therefore I had no possibility of returning to [my] own lines. I landed in an open field in the midst of some woods by diving under telegraph wires and tried to set the plane on fire, according to War Department orders. We carried safety matches, but I was unable to strike them because of the loss of the use of one arm, and was covered by German rifles before I was able to accomplish my purpose.*

*I surrendered to a German first lieutenant and a detachment of about forty men. They treated my wounds immediately, and were very kindly in their treatment. They disposed of the plane and I never saw it again. I was left lying on the ground within sight of our own balloons for fully an hour before the stretcher bearers came and carried me to a German field-dressing station. From the dressing station, where they applied a splint, I was taken to a field hospital and given an anesthetic. The German orderly at this place stole all my clothes, personal belongings, and personal photographs, contrary to the treatment which we offered their prisoners.*

*I was laid in a bed next to an American private who was severely wounded in the stomach. We were both parched [with] thirst and called for water the whole night long, but the German orderly refused to give it to us. The doctors whom I met were uniformly courteous, never kind, but were limited by lack of equipment and overwork.*

*The next morning, September 18, I was taken to the Intern Hospital for Allied Wounded in the city of Metz, named St. Clemens. At that time there were fourteen officers in the hospital and some six hundred soldiers more or less wounded. To minister [to] this [population were] a few nurses, two doctors, and one attending physician.*

*It was on the third day, after a diet of bread and water, that we were taken to the information officer and questioned for half an hour to receive information regarding our unit. The only two questions that I answered were my name and squadron, according to War Department instructions. To all the other questions which he put to me, I made the uniform answer, "I do not know," or "I refuse to answer." The German information officer, however, seemed to have more information regarding our air service than I had myself, and told me the location of my squadron, number of hangars, the officers, and other minor details.*

*The food at the Metz hospital was plenteous for the officers. We received the usual menu of sausage, 250 grams of bread, wine, burnt barley coffee, horse-meat, potatoes, and carrots. The men, however, received two soup rations per day, and time and again they were compelled, through scanty rations, to eat [what] we were forced to leave.*

*The medical attention was necessarily limited by their lack of equipment and personnel. They had no oils, all the bandages were of paper, and they seldom used disinfectants or sterile bandages. All of the work in the hospital was done by convalescent wounded, and the treatment of British and American prisoners was not only unkindly but often brutal. There were many Russian prisoners who came in in frightful condition and died in great numbers. The French were uniformly well treated, while the British and Americans seemed to inherit all the hatred which they could shower upon us, although they didn't express it in brutal acts to the officers.*

*The doctors and nurses were, in general, courteous and helpful, but we only saw them once a day, and whatever medical attention we got during the day was extremely hard to secure. There were no means of communicating our wishes to them, nor theirs to us, with the exception of the little German which I was able to speak. There were many instances among our enlisted men, of whom there were about forty in the hospital, of gross neglect and serious mal-treatment. There were three cases resulting in death which I personally know of, where the soldiers died of blood poisoning due to the fact that the German doctors had not operated in time. They passed this off with the excuse that the soldiers had worried themselves to death.*[2]

# WILLIAM B. VAUGHN, COMPANY F, 313TH INFANTRY, 79TH DIVISION

*Our artillery threw out an all-night barrage and we went over the top at five o'clock on the morning of the 26th. No one will ever describe the scene in a way to be appreciated. It seemed that all hell broke loose. There were the whistle of shells, the drumbeat of the machine guns which sounded like a huge wireless outfit as the Germans swept up, and the "punk" of the snipers' bullets. That continued for six days.*

*One sniper whom I saw ducking behind a bush took a shot at me. The bullet struck my helmet and glanced off, or I would not be here to tell of it. Another bullet gouged the leather from my scabbard. Four of our tanks were destroyed by direct hits, blowing them up. We kept plugging away, going two days without food. On one of the six days I came across a destroyed tank and found a can of tomatoes and a can of beef. The tomatoes had spoiled, but the beef made a banquet.*

*During the time we were in this battle we lost nearly all our officers and a large number of men. We had two platoons left out of four when we emerged from the woods on the sixth day and hiked back to a supply station. Then we marched for a French rest camp eight miles from Verdun, but left the same day for a town on the Meuse River, where we met the 26th Division. We remained three days and went to Saint-Mihiel, where we were billeted in an old mine. That sector was then quiet and we marched to Verdun.*

*We had only one lieutenant left. Our next hike took us to a woods north of Verdun, where November 1 found us in the midst of battle again. We lost heavily again, but reached our objective. It was on top of a hill, and the following morning a German airplane spotted our location, and for an hour we were in the center of a barrage fire. I saw men killed and maimed in the most horrible manner in that barrage. That sector was a series of hills, several of which we captured.*

*On the morning of November 7 our barrage opened and we advanced with it. We reached what we supposed was our objective and dug in. Three hours later we were told our objective was in a woods on the next hill, and we started again. Just then a sniper's bullet hit my left leg, breaking it. I crawled to the nearest shell hole and dropped in. I left my rifle, but kept my .45 caliber pistol. That night was the longest in my life. I could hear men moving past the hole, but was unable to tell whether they were Germans or Americans. I kept my gun pointed toward the sky, and if any Huns had dropped over into that hole that night, they would have been dead birds. Shells and flares passed over the shell hole all night. When morning came I peeked over the ground and saw our men lying along a ditch. I called and two of them came. They carried me nearly two miles to a dressing station. From that place I was driven over shell-wrecked roads to a hospital near Verdun. Just as the surgeons were preparing to take an X-ray picture, there was a cry of fire. In a few minutes the place was ablaze. There were many patients in the building, but they were all rescued.*

*On November 11 I was taken to a railroad station where I lay in a shed all day. It was there I heard of the armistice being signed. We went through horrible hardships, but it was well worth the price. I wish that every American boy could have been out there in No Man's Land. War has its horrors, but there was an amusing incident here and there.*[3]

## John R. Breckinridge, First Aid Man, 109th Field Artillery, 28th Division

*After a brief rest we reached the Argonne on September 22 and we swung into position there unobserved by the Germans. On the night of the 26th, 1,500 guns opened a stupendous barrage, which lasted several hours. Our infantry advanced to Rennes, but the fighting was so hot the Germans retreated as far as Apremont before they made a stand and drove us back. We brought up our artillery and they retreated again. However, it was nerve-racking to bring up and place guns in that shelling.*

*It was there that I attended to fifteen casualties in two hours, each man from different companies. I was standing above a trench that night when a shell exploded inside. I found that eight men had been wounded. Col. Asher Miner was supervising Battery F, when a shell carried away one of his legs. Lieutenant Colonel Harvey was hit by a piece of shell which struck his pistol and was deflected into his side. Battery F was advancing when a shell killed the horses, drawing one of the guns, but did not damage the gun. That night we held our position and the next day advanced into the woods. We arrived at three o'clock, had emplacements ready by six, and prepared for another long duel, but received orders to move at eight. We advanced to the top of the hill, pulling up the guns by ropes. That, however, was the last of the Argonne for us, as we were relieved and sent to Flanders. There, under the command of King Albert of Belgium, we fought on the pockmarked fields near Ypres. That was a horrible sight.*

*The stately trees along the roads had become charred dwarfs; shell holes lay so close that sometimes walking was impossible. It rained constantly and the trenches were filled with mud. The bleaching bones of horses and men, and the broken rifle butts, the soldiers' tombstones, showed where death had won. A Belgian soldier with his wife and child lived with us in a dugout. I asked him where his home was, and he answered that not a brick of it was left. That was our foreground.*

*One night as I lay dozing in my trench I had a premonition of something happening to my brother George. I learned later that a shell had exploded in his trench, killing three soldiers who had been talking to him, but miraculously, he was not wounded. On November 11 we were informed that the armistice had been signed. Instead of cheering and rejoicing we lay down and slept, we were so tired.*[4]

Saint-Mihiel was the last great salient on the Western Front. Due to the incessant shelling, the terrain in No Man's Land resembled a moonscape, with craters in such close proximity to each other that in most places they overlapped. The roads had almost completely disappeared, and surrounding hills had been plundered of every blade of grass. Former woodlands had been transformed into skeletal wastelands, with the odd protruding bullet and shrapnel-raked tree stump standing forlorn and abandoned among the regurgitated white-chalk subsoil.

As critical as some Allied commanders were about the methods employed by AEF units, there were some solid facts that they couldn't dispute. Pershing wrote: "It was my opinion that the victory could not be won by the costly process of attrition, but it must be won by driving the enemy out into the open and engaging him in a war of movement. Instruction in this kind of warfare was based upon individual and group initiative, resourcefulness, and tactical judgment, which were also of great advantage in trench warfare. Therefore, we took decided issue with the Allies and, without neglecting thorough preparation for trench fighting, undertook to train mainly for open combat, with the object from the start of vigorously forcing the offensive."[5]

These young American soldiers may have been lacking in some areas of training, but they brought a vigor and zeal to the Allies that had long since dissipated in the ranks of their war-weary armies. They brought enthusiasm, courage, and spontaneity to a conflict that had sapped the will from almost every combatant. In the summer and fall of 1918, the AEF encouraged independent thinking and actively expanded on certain tactics, such as advances by rushes or by infiltration of small units, which previously only officers had directed. Skirmish lines, for example, were to "cross open, fire-swept areas by advance of individuals or squads," with platoon leaders resuming command only after some predetermined terrain feature had been reached. All of these measures reflected a tactical decentralization and encouragement for initiative undreamed of in other Allied armies.

The Battle of Saint-Mihiel proved innovative in many ways: It was to be the world's first major air offensive. The skillful and daring leadership, combined with imaginative operational planning, still resonates with modern military commanders. Another major factor in the victory was the continuation of detailed preparation that allowed officers to interpret their commander's intent to their own designs. If Pershing had been allowed to conduct his offensive as planned, the First American Army probably would have penetrated German lines even further, altering the strategic situation along the entire Western Front.

# CHAPTER THIRTEEN

# The Meuse-Argonne

## SECRET ORDER OF GENERAL VON DER MARWITZ, COMMANDING, GERMAN FIFTH ARMY

*September 15, 1918: According to information in our hands, the enemy intends to attack the Fifth Army east of the Meuse in order to reach Longuyon. The objective of this attack is the cutting of the railroad line Longuyon–Sedan, which is the main line of communication of the Western Army. Furthermore, the enemy hopes to compel us to discontinue the exploitation of the iron mines of Briey, the possession of which is a great factor in our steel production. The Fifth Army once again may have to bear the brunt of the fighting of the coming weeks, on which the security of the Fatherland may depend.*

*The fate of a large portion of the Western Front, perhaps of our nation, depends on the firm holding of the Verdun front. The Fatherland believes that every commander and every soldier realizes the greatness of his task, and that everyone will fulfill his duty to the utmost. If this is done, the enemy's attack will be shattered.*

The battle in the region of the Meuse-Argonne would come to represent the zenith of the AEF's contribution to the Great War. It would be the place where legends were cemented and heroes were made. It was a remarkably intricate operation that entailed involving AEF ground forces fighting through rough, hilly terrain, which the German Army had spent four years fortifying. The purpose and objective of the offensive was the capture of the railroad hub at Sedan. Seizure of this location had the potential to completely dislocate the rail network supporting the German Army in France and Flanders, and to force their withdrawal from the occupied territories. One of the great logistical accomplishments of the Great War was the transference of American troops from the Saint-Mihiel salient to the new section of the Front that extended thirty miles east to west, and was situated to the north and northwest of Verdun.

The AEF was required to relocate forty miles to a location along the west bank of the Meuse River. Throughout the next two weeks, a massive movement of troops, artillery, and supplies took place, syphoned along three roads into the area that would become the new battleground. This movement was completed over only three roads. To avoid unwelcome enemy attention most of the transportation occurred during the hours of darkness. These logistics were expertly organized and coordinated by Col. George C. Marshall, who would eventually become secretary of state and orchestrate the famous Marshall Plan after World War II. In September 1918 Marshall was on the staff of the AEF and had been a significant planner of American operations on the Western Front. The operations at the attacks would constitute part of Marshal Foch's larger offensive against the Germans. The AEF would be launched simultaneously along with concentric attacks of the British toward Mons, while the French would attack in the center and provide support for the Allies in their operations.

By September 1918, after sustaining heavy losses, the Germans had committed all of their available reserves. Meanwhile, the Allies were still receiving a steady stream of reinforcements. If a breakthrough on both flanks of the enormous salient held by the German armies in the north of France could be achieved, this offensive would be decisive in ending "the war to end all wars."

According to the plan, during the first phase, US forces would penetrate the third German line, advancing about ten miles and clearing the Argonne Forest, to link up with the French 4th Army. The second phase would consist of a further advance of ten miles to outflank the enemy positions along the Aisne, and prepare for further attacks toward Sedan and Mézières, on the Meuse River. Additional operations were planned to clear the heights along the east bank of the Meuse. It looked good on paper.

By the end of the Saint-Mihiel offensive, many Allied commanders somewhat erroneously agreed that American units had evolved sufficiently to be regarded as trained combat units. The AEF had successfully eliminated the Saint-Mihiel salient, and with a comparatively small loss by Great War standards. Now they were confronted with the much more serious task of attacking the enemy's line from the Argonne to the Meuse River. Holding this line was of vital importance to the German forces. At that moment in time, the German Army had five divisions holding the line from the Argonne to the Meuse River. One of the German divisions was commanded by Prince Eitel Friedrich, the Kaiser's second son, who had the rank of major general. His division came from the Russian front in the latter part of 1917 and early 1918.

Between September 14 and 26, the bulk of the American Army was transferred to the new staging area in preparation for this momentous attack. The plan as envisaged by Foch was for the British to attack north and storm the Hindenburg Line, then capture the important railway hub at Aulnoye. The French would simultaneously conduct an assault in the south with the purpose of breaking the Kriemhilde Stellung (a fortification that constituted part of the Hindenburg Line), after which they would retake Mézières and Sedan, cutting the railway network that supplied the German armies from Metz. The offensive would bring many troops into the proximity of the Ardennes Forest; although regarded at the time as being virtually impenetrable, it was in fact intersected by numerous roads and railways.

Pershing and the AEF staff were in a buoyant, almost triumphalist mood, greatly anticipating this latest offensive. It didn't appear to be a major concern that some of the American divisions were not "battle-ready." The 91st Division, for instance, had only experienced one month's training when it was generally assumed that each division coming into the line needed at least three months to prepare. The 91st was part of the US Army's V Corps, and one of nine AEF divisions earmarked to participate in the initial Meuse-Argonne attack. The 37th Division, also under V Corps, was to its right, and I Corps' 35th Division was on its left. The sector allocated to the 91st was on a seam between the German Crown Prince's 1st Guards Division and the 117th East Reserve Division, under the overall command of General von Gallwitz. Shortly after the offensive began, the German Army added the 5th Guard Division in between the 1st and the 117th.

On September 25, at 11:30 p.m., the American divisions comprising roughly 26,000 men each were waiting anxiously to go over the top as 2,700 guns thunderously opened the initial barrage. One of the officers responsible for some of the shells being lobbed at the Germans was future US president, Harry S. Truman. Truman had been promoted to captain in France and assigned to Battery D, 129th Field Artillery—the outfit with the dubious distinction of being the worst-disciplined in the whole AEF.

The artillery preparation gave the sky above the German positions an eerie red glare as the shells impacted their targets. The AEF troops were organized in three corps, facing north from the edge of the Champagne in the west to the Meuse River in the east, primed and ready to attack at dawn the next day. The German Army had spent four years fortifying this region, and they weren't going to relinquish it without a fight. Previous notions of the German Army's impregnability had been seriously devalued during the recent AEF victory at Saint-Mihiel, but they were still more than capable of defending their positions.

Pershing somewhat ambitiously envisioned this latest offensive occurring in three distinct phases rather than the two phases initially planned. The intended American Army's area of operations was between fifteen to twenty miles wide, bounded by the unfordable Meuse River on the east and the dense, rugged Argonne Forest and the Aire River on the west. The first attack would involve a drive up the Aire River valley on the left, compelling the Germans to evacuate the Argonne Forest, while in the center, Montfaucon was to be seized before the advance proceeded to the heights of Cunel and Romagne. The ultimate objective for the first phase was to achieve a line stretching from Dunsur–Meuse in the east and Grandpré, along the banks of the Aire, in the west, within thirty-six hours. Speed would be of the essence.

The second phase would entail the 1st Army making a somewhat optimistic ten-mile advance to a line stretching from Stenay, along the banks of the Meuse River, to Le Chesne. If this could be achieved it had the potential to flank and compromise German defenses on the Aire, allowing the French 4th Army to capture Mézières and Sedan.

The third and final phase entailed the 1st Army navigating the Meuse River, and once the crossing had been achieved, clearing German artillery from the heights. Finally, they would cut the Carignan Sedan railway line. By doing so, the Americans, along with the French and British, would oblige the Germans to withdraw all the way back to Berlin.

News arrived in late September that German ally Bulgaria had sought and been granted an armistice. At a crown council convened by Kaiser Wilhelm II in the Belgian Ardennes town of Spa on September 29, General Ludendorff appeared to lose his composure, demanding that the German government seek an immediate armistice based on the "Fourteen Points" outlined by US president Woodrow Wilson the previous January. Up until that point Ludendorff had vehemently claimed that his forces were far from defeat, but with this direct appeal to the Kaiser, he had incurred the displeasure of Reichstag politicians and given them grave cause for concern.

## PHASE ONE

The morning of September 26 was especially foggy in the low ground just west of the commanding terrain of Montfaucon (Mount Falcon) and east of the Argonne Forest. The smoke from the massive artillery barrage contributed to the poor visibility; it was reported that troops could see no more than fifty feet ahead throughout the morning. The atmosphere would have been incredibly tense that late September morning as thousands of young American soldiers fixed their bayonets and wished each other good luck. Some shook hands, while others closed their eyes and muttered prayers. Officers would survey No Man's Land furtively with their periscopes or field glasses while intermittently looking at their watches to ensure that the whole thing went off on time. Those few minutes before leaving their positions would have been the ultimate test of a man's endurance.

Then the whistles would blow and the order was given to go "over the top," to clamber out of their trenches, or move out from their positions carrying loaded weapons and heavy equipment, and head toward the enemy's murderous "field of fire" over shell holes and complex networks of barbed wire, keeping low to the ground for safety. Many soldiers described walking out into No Man's Land as the most petrifying, mind-numbing experience of their young lives. Those first few moments divested of shelter, away from their cover, they would feel bereft of humanity, completely vulnerable and exposed. Suddenly, with the prospect of instant death or a slow agonizing wound, senses would sharpen and ultimately dispel the effects of sleep deprivation from the previous night. The initial surge of apprehension would be replaced by sheer terror as they stumbled into the dawn mist and a very uncertain future.

## GEORGE N. WISE JR., 310TH MACHINE-GUN COMPANY, 79TH DIVISION

*We got near the top of the hill to where a road crossed. There the bullets began to plow up the ground about us. Snipers were busy picking off our boys and shells were dropping every minute. We carried our machine guns to the roadside and let loose to Jerry, clearing a path for the infantry. This was on November 6, and we were to be relieved, but the shelling was so heavy that our relief could not reach us. It was so heavy that the woods [were] laid bare, and four of our heavy army trucks were demolished. That night we were told we must carry on the advance in the morning, and we lay along the road until daylight.*

*At ten o'clock the guns began to run out of ammunition, and Private Decker of Baltimore and myself went back to our ammunition stores. We got back to the guns when the Germans put over a heavy barrage. We dropped into the ditch and lay flat. After lying there about ten minutes a shell struck near us. One of the fragments tore through my right thigh, struck the left knee, and, bouncing off, hit Decker in the leg. There were no first-aid men in sight, so I tied a towel about my leg and lay in the ditch. The shellfire was so heavy that the ambulances could not get near the Front, and I was carried back several miles. Since that time I have been in several hospitals in France.*[1]

Dislodging the Germans from these expertly organized positions was going to be no mean feat. Looking down from the high ground on either flank of this uneven, rugged terrain provided the Germans with excellent observation points to enable showering the attacking infantry with accurate artillery barrages. During the years that they had occupied this area, they had developed a highly elaborate defensive system comprised of four fortified lines featuring a dense network of machine-gun positions with interlocking fires, and reinforced concrete pillboxes all fronted by reams of hideous barbed wire. Interspersed between the trenches they had installed a series of intermediate strongpoints in the numerous wooded areas. The whole defensive position was approximately fifteen miles deep, manned by five divisions in the line and a further seven in reserve. The four lines were named after the witches in Richard Wagner's operas: the Giselher Stellungen, three miles north of the front lines and incorporating Montfaucon; the Kriemhilde Stellung, a part of the larger Siegfried Stellung, also known as the Hindenburg Line to the Allies, which was, in effect, the strongest of the Stellungen (fortifications), encompassing the village of Grandpré and the Heights of Cunel and Romagne; then, five miles further north in the less-defensible plateau, the somewhat less fortified Freya Stellung.

The American 1st Army commenced the attack with nine divisions and held a further five in reserve. On the first day the attack went in at 5:30 a.m., with the 91st Division moving out with three regiments abreast—from left to right, the 363rd, 361st, and 362nd. The 364th Regiment followed in support of the 363rd, on the far left of the division sector. The Germans were surprised on the first day of the Meuse-Argonne Offensive, and consequently, resistance was relatively light—but there were some worrisome signs that this was not going to be the modus operandi for the coming days.

## Morris Albert Martin, Company D, 361st Infantry Regiment, 91st Division

*This area of France had seen heavy fighting since the beginning of the war. After the last major battles in this sector in 1916, it became the scene of routine trench warfare, including minimal local attacks and counterattacks, raids, mining, shelling, and gassing.*

*The 91st Division, together with the other divisions, came into the sector on September 19–20 and was placed in bivouac in the Hesse Forest, an*

*extension of the Argonne Forest. On September 21, the division received orders
to attack almost due north on "V" day, through the Cheppy and Very woods
(other extensions of the Argonne), and into the broken country beyond. These
woods and forests were thick, heavy underbrush and cut by numerous ravines.
The final orders came on September 24, and on the evening of September 25,
the American troops moved forward into the very front line, relieved the screen
of French soldiers by midnight, and lookup positions for the jump-off. "D"-day
was set for September 26, and "H" hour was 5:30 a.m.*

*Late in the evening of September 25, Lieutenant Proctor had received
word of some extra bread and jam to be had down at the ration dump, about
a mile to the rear. He detailed me, together with three others, to go back and
get our share for the First Battalion liaison group, of which we were members
Although we [went] as fast as we could, when we reached the dump, it was
a scene of wild confusion. It seemed that detachments from every unit in the
regiment, and perhaps the division, were there, scrambling for bread and jam.
After perhaps an hour of pushing, shoving, and milling about, we got our
allotment and started back toward the outfit.*

*Upon arriving in our sector we were dismayed to find that all the compa-
nies of our battalion, including our liaison group, had moved up into position
for the jump-off next morning. Only the machine-gun company in command
of Captain Doherty was in sight. To make the situation more embarrassing,
and serious, the other members had taken our equipment with them, including
our rifles. We had been ordered to leave them when we went after the extra
rations, so we wouldn't be burdened too much in our scramble for eats. Fortunately we still had our gas masks, which of course we carried at all times.*

*It was dark by now, and we knew it would be virtually impossible to
find the group in that wilderness, so I, being in charge, reported to Captain
Doherty, and explained the situation to him. He said that the company would
remain in the present position until the zero hour, 5:30 in the morning, and
we could go into action with him, and that he would try and at least find us
some guns. If not, we could carry ammunition for the machine guns. So we
prepared to make the best of it and wait for the jump-off, hoping to find our
group with our equipment.*

*We tried lying on the ground while waiting, in order to get what rest we
could, but it was quite damp, and the night had turned cold, so that we could*

not keep warm. In order to keep as comfortable as possible and help quiet our jumpy nerves—a few big shells were coming over—we alternately tramped back and forth and lay on the ground, relaxing as much as possible, waiting for the zero hour.

At 11:30 p.m., the long-range guns of the army artillery opened fire on selected targets in the rear of the enemy lines. At 2:30 a.m., guns of corps and divisional artillery opened up together. We were near one of the large naval guns and when it would fire, the entire area would be lighted up as though by immense floodlights. The bombardment was so stunning and the noise so overwhelming, that only those who have experienced it can appreciate our reactions. The concussion of the air was terrific, and the ground trembled so violently that we could not lie down, and it was only with difficulty that we could breathe, and keep our feet.

The bombardment grew in intensity throughout the night. Presently the sky began to grow lighter, and we knew that zero hour was approaching. Captain Doherty was walking around among us, explaining our objective and encouraging us to do our best. By now it was early daylight. Suddenly, the captain looked at his watch, signaled to his sergeants and guides, who ordered us to fall into a single file, we stragglers taking our position in the rear of the columns. At 5:30 a.m. the whistle blew, the guides picked their respective paths in the woods; Captain Doherty yelled, "Let's go," and we plunged into the thundering, crashing inferno ahead of us.

The file in which we four had taken our places had barely started down its path when there was a terrific explosion and flash of fire. It seemed to be in our very faces, and we instinctively fell away from it to the right. We thought a shell had landed in our midst, but it proved to be a six-inch gun hidden in the woods, and we happened to be passing under its muzzle when it fired. We were all stunned and unnerved by this first introduction, but we quickly recovered and resumed our way into No Man's Land.

By the time we passed through the first patch of woods and emerged into more-open country, the sun had risen, although quite heavy fog hung overhead, making visibility rather poor. We now began to see evidence of four years of fighting, which had taken place intermittently in this sector. The ground was torn and upheaved into mounds; trees were shattered, and only stumps remained; great shell holes yawned here and there, and occasionally a long concrete pillbox would be seen still standing. And entwined through all this debris were great quantities of tangled barbed wire, which had been battered down by artillery fire. Our putties were soon torn to rags.

Being in the last wave of the advance, we presently began to see results of our barrage. Fresh shell holes, still smoking; newly splintered trees; and occasionally, a dead German. To add to the confusion, the shells of our artillery were screeching and whining overhead on their way into enemy territory. A little farther along I saw a pack and rifle lying beside the path, and when I picked them up I was astonished and pleased to find that they were my own. The fellow who had been carrying them despaired of me ever finding him, and had thrown them down. In a short time, two of the other fellows likewise found their equipment, leaving only Riddell still without any. A little farther on he found a dead American, and he took the pack and rifle from the body, although he was not a member of our division. As I recall, he belonged to the 37th Division, but had wandered into our sector. We stragglers were equipped now, and we began to watch for our own outfit. In the meantime we had crossed the large open space and entered another patch of woods. As we started down a road we came upon our regimental group, including our colonel, operations officer, and several staff officers.

We then decided to part company with the machine-gun outfit and attach ourselves to this group, knowing that eventually we would find our own section. Evidence of some real fighting began to appear now. Bodies of both German and American soldiers were seen frequently. In spite of all that I had been trained to expect, I experienced a decided shock when I saw these first Americans, lying there cold in death. They who had come to this frightful and violent end in a strange land, fighting for a cause they thought was just. We were beginning to be impressed by the grimness of our task, although we could not as yet appreciate what lay in store for us in the days to come.

The first two waves had passed hurriedly over this ground toward the first objective, leaving the mopping up to the following wave. Snipers hidden in the trees, which had been overlooked by the first waves, were a constant threat, and each one had to be dealt with separately. Occasionally one would be armed with a machine gun hidden in a tree. After our third wave had gone by he would start shooting from the rear. Then there would be an exciting time, with a squad or so of soldiers circling that particular tree. Like a pack of hounds with *a treed coon. Presently the sniper would be spotted, and after a few shots he would come tumbling out of the tree, either dead or wounded. They never gave up without a struggle, as they were picked men from selected veterans, and had orders to sacrifice themselves if necessary in order to hold up our advance as much as possible.*

*At one point in our advance through this piece of woods we came upon a cleverly constructed trap the Germans had built to capture a tank. They had dug a pit about twenty feet square and eight feet deep. It had then been covered with a piece of wire netting and gray-colored canvas. A tank lumbering down this road in the dense woods would ordinarily have plunged into this pit and been helplessly caught. Fortunately one of the very few tanks in our sector had spotted this trap in time and had driven around it, making a new road for others to follow. The cover had been stripped off the pit and a log tossed across the road to warn other tanks or trucks.*

*It was shortly after this that we met our first group of German prisoners. Four proud doughboys, with bayonets fixed, were escorting about forty pris-oners back to the prison cages in the rear. The Germans were a hard-bitten-looking bunch, although they did not appear to be downcast; rather, they seemed to be happy that it was all over for them. Striding arrogantly along at the rear was a giant, handsome-looking German officer smoking a cigar. However, the doughboy urging him along with his bayonet didn't seem to be very highly impressed by this officer's attitude, but was telling him to "Shake it up."*

*As we came out of the woods into a large, cleared space we found evidence of a long residence here. There were well-equipped dugouts, a light plant water system, narrow-gauge railroad, and other indications [that] the Germans had settled down here for a long and comfortable sojourn. Our shells had found some of these dugout entrances, some of the tracks were torn up, and gaping shell holes were here and there. Up to this point our barrage had been so terrific that the enemy had offered very little resistance. The infantry had followed so closely behind the exploding shells that when the Germans recovered from the first shock and came up out of their dugouts, they found the hard-boiled doughboys waiting for them. If they were a little too slow in coming out, an occasional hand grenade was a good persuader.*

*It was now about noon and a warm, bright sun was shining overhead. After leaving the group of dugouts, we came to broad road leading directly to the north. At this point we found our battalion liaison group with Lieutenant Proctor in command, and we were certainly glad to be with our outfit again. The lieutenant explained that shortly after we left for the ration dump, he had received orders to move up into position at once, and could not wait for our return. Lying along the road sleeping or otherwise resting were hundreds of exhausted soldiers. They had had very little if any sleep or rest the previous night, and had been in the first waves to go over the top. They had struggled forward for several miles at a fast clip, and under terrific strain. Small wonder they were exhausted. We also noticed from the regimental numbers on packs that a great many of these men were not members of our division. Owing to the dense woods and rough terrain over which we had been passing, many men from divisions on our right and left had lost their bearings and were now in our sector. They later were returned to their own outfits, or were organized into our units so that they would not lose their effectiveness or become stragglers.*

*After following this road for about a mile, we left the woods and came out into open country once more. Glancing to our right and left as far as we could see were long lines of American soldiers pressing eagerly toward their objectives. In this bright sunshine, with green woods as a background, these long lines of khaki-clad figures advancing brilliantly across the grassy plain gave me a thrill, which I shall never forget. Had it not been for the crash of exploding shells, the rat-tat-tat of machine guns, and the musical chirp of machine-gun bullets, I could well imagine myself back at Camp Lewis, watching a well-executed maneuver.*

*It was here that we suffered our first casualty in our detachment. We were advancing across the open country in the face of a terrific machine-gun barrage, going forward by rushes, dropping into the slight depressions caused by ages of plowing fields in the same direction. As we rose after a slight breathing spell preparatory to making another rush, Cloward, detached from C Company, gave sort of a groan and settled down in the grass. He had been behind me and slightly to my left. As he fell his bayonet barely missed my leg. I knelt down beside him and asked where he was hit. He motioned to his stomach, and asked for a drink. I took out his canteen and gave him one. We were on a slight ridge exposed to the full sweep of the withering hail of machine-gun bullets, so I pulled him back into a lower spot and removed his pack. He said his back was hurting, so I pulled up his shirt and there was a small bluish hole about an inch from his spine, with a slight trickle of blood from it. The bullet had passed through his gas mask and completely through his body. I gave him another drink and made him as comfortable as possible under the circumstances, and went on, after directing a medical corpsman to his position.*

*We advanced steadily northward as the afternoon wore on. The Germans had recovered somewhat from the first shock of our devastating barrage, and were now offering stiffer resistance, particularly with machine guns and bench mortars. We had also passed the extreme range of all but our heaviest guns, so we had no artillery support, but were entirely on our own: no tanks; no airplanes; nothing but our own machine guns, and a few one-pounders. Fortunately we did not realize how precarious our position might have been had the Germans had the necessary reserves to have made a strong counterattack. The boys were still flushing out an occasional sniper in a tree, or machine-gun nest spotted in a shell hole, while the leading waves were perhaps a quarter of a mile in the lead.*

*About one mile north was a ridge running east and west, parallel to the one we were crossing. A series of trenches ran along this ridge, with a belt of wire out in front. Between the two ridges was a narrow, shallow valley with a small creek running through it. Our advance elements had reached this trench system at the left end. Apparently the Germans in the trenches were not offering any real resistance, but were coming out in bunches to surrender.*

*An incident occurred here that would have been amusing had it not been so tragic for the one involved. At the opposite end of the trench from where our soldiers were, a lone German suddenly appeared and started trotting toward our men with the evident purpose of surrendering, along with the rest of his comrades. A one-pounder on our ridge started firing point-blank at him. A one-pounder shell explodes upon contact, and as each shell would strike near this fellow it would explode, enveloping him in a cloud of dust and smoke. He never was hit, and as each shell exploded in his very face, he ran faster until the men firing the one-pounder got to laughing so hard that they had to stop shooting and the runner escaped. I was glad, for he deserved a break after that heroic race with death.*

*The resistance of the Germans became stronger as the afternoon waned, and many trench mortar shells fell in our midst. As our liaison detachment was crossing the little valley, we heard the peculiar whistle of one of these shells, and glancing up saw it descending in a short arc with its end-over-end motion. It appeared that it was going to strike squarely in the middle of our group. The lieutenant yelled for us to run. We needed no further urging, and after running as far as we could before it should explode, we flopped down on the ground with our faces buried, expecting the worst. Fortunately it was a dud and did not explode. We took a look at it, half-buried in the ground, feeling that we were exceedingly lucky in this instance, but wondering what the future had in store for us. We were thinking of the lifeless mangled bodies of our comrades we had seen scattered across No Man's Land.*

*It was now sundown and orders were issued to dig in and strengthen our position, anticipating that the Germans would get organized and attempt a counterattack either during the night or early in the morning. Outposts were taken out and placed and we runners were instructed to locate the various units so that we could carry messages back and forth. Early in the night orders came to retire back across the valley and up the hill, to the top of the first ridge to the south. There were a series of old trenches still in fair condition, protected by a good belt of barbed wire. This location would give us a more-strategic position from which to repulse a counterattack if it came, as we expected it would.*

*There was no overhead shelter available, of course, and we had no over-coats in our packs. We had gone over the top with tight packs, with the theory, I presume, that it was to be a forced drive, and we shouldn't be encumbered with any extra weight. Curry the bugler and I picked out a shell hole about three feet deep and four feet across and tried to make the best of it. A cold wind sprang up and we twisted and squirmed, trying to keep warm. Finally we took out our bayonets and dug out dirt and piled it in ridges in the direction from which the wind was coming, to act as our windbreak. We curled up together like a couple of pups, after taking our blouses off and using them as blankets. However, it was no use, and we continued to shiver until morning.*

*About daylight a cold rain commenced falling, and the Germans started to shell us viciously. This was rather disquieting, for we realized that they had been able to bring up some big artillery, which they did not have before. This wasn't going to make our job any easier, especially in view of the fact that our own artillery had not been able to come up to a point where it could give us any support. After the opening barrage had been completed and the infantry had passed beyond the range, the artillery would have to take to the Avocourt-Very* road and fight its way forward in competition with the ammunition trucks, horse-drawn vehicles, motorized machine-gun outfits, rolling kitchens, and marching reserves. It would be several hours before we could expect any artillery assistance, and plenty could happen in that length of time.

Well, we had been led to believe that this was no Sunday School picnic we were on, so we tightened up our belts and started down the hill and across the valley once more. As we crossed the little creek, I dodged into the willows and filled my canteen with water. Although we had been cautioned not to do so, fearing that the water might have been poisoned, I decided that I would just as soon die from drinking poisoned water as to suffer from the lack of water. Later in the day I had reason to feel thankful that I had violated orders.

As we left the creek and approached the hill we were met by a terrific barrage of trench mortar shells and machine-gun fire. There was no cover to be had, so we had to press forward until we reached the foot of the hill where we would be comparatively safe from all fire except trench mortars. The range was so short that the trajectory of other shells would carry them farther to the rear and mess up the reserves. We could see the rest of the division strung along the foot of the hill, far to the left. Some had climbed part of the way up the hill. We were on the extreme right of the division sector, and the hill in front of us was rather low, with an easy slope. However, to the left, the other brigade had a steep hill to climb before emerging into the flat plain before Eclisfontaine. Epinonville lay in front of us about a quarter-mile from the top of the hill. I saw one of our men who had been severely wounded and was lying with his head downhill. He was near Curry, and I called to him to turn the poor fellow around with his head uphill, so he would be more comfortable.

A well-kept military road ran along the foot of the hill before us, and as it reached our sector it swung up the hill into Epinonville. It was floored with heavy planks in order to make it passable in wet weather, and where it passed in front of us it went through a cut about four or five feet deep. This cut came in rather handy for us for a time, although later it almost became a fatal trap. The advance units were in this sunken road, but were unable to make much headway. Every time an attempt was made to leave this shelter and enter Epinonville, the men would be met by a blistering fire from machine guns, and snipers hidden in nearby trees. Without some artillery fire to prepare the way, it looked like a hopeless task. A one-pounder section was brought up and fired on some of the buildings suspected of sheltering machine-gun nests, but without any effective results. In the meantime, the German shelling was growing in intensity, and several times groups of Germans were seen concentrating preparatory to launching a counterattack. Fortunately, each time our alert machine-gun units broke up these attempts.

Our group had become split. Part of it was with the battalion adjutant in the sunken road. The part I was with was at that moment in a shallow shell hole about one hundred yards south of the sunken road. It was raining steadily, and a sniper in a nearby tree had us spotted. Every effort to leave this uncomfortable hole and get into the road was met with deadly fire from this fellow. I distinctly remember peeking up once to size up the situation when a shell from this sniper plunked into the bank right in front of my face and filled my eyes with dirt. Needless to say, I hugged good old earth for some time after that. Something must have happened to the sniper, for presently he no longer gave us his attention, and one by one we were able to get to our feet and dash madly for the sunken road and fling ourselves into it like a diver plunging into a pool of water.

We made our way down the road to the battalion command post where lieutenants Able and Bates were in a huddle, trying to decide the next move. Some men were crawling forward in the grass and weeds to reconnoiter our position. Those who weren't shot came back to report that some artillery preparation was absolutely necessary before any impression could be made on Epinonville. Corporal Sylvester raised up to peek out of the road and a bullet struck him squarely between the eyes. In the meantime, scouts reported that there appeared to be a heavy concentration of Germans in the rear, and the artillery fire was demoralizing. Our protection in this road was fast becoming untenable. If the enemy should be able to get into one end with machine guns, they could mow us down like grass before we could retire.

Accordingly Lieutenant Able decided to send a message back to Captain Doherty, asking him to bring his machine-gun company to a point where it could protect the exposed end of the road. He wrote the message and asked who was going to carry it. No one replied, and after an interval of waiting, I said I would take it and attempt to deliver it. As I climbed out of the road and started back to where I might expect to find the machine-gun company, the air seemed to be full of angry hornets. Leaves were being clipped off the apple trees in the old orchard, blades of grass were suddenly falling over, and as I stepped up on a section of the plank road, a bullet tore out a splinter a foot long near where I was standing. I needed no further command to move out of there.

Noticing a bomb of mounted machine guns off to my left, I hurried over, but found that they were members of the machine-gun battalion supporting our brigade. They looked very businesslike and gave me more of a feeling of safety than I had had for the past several hours. I had just asked an officer if he knew the whereabouts of the machine-gun company when the cry went up that the Germans were coming in behind us. I looked back to the south and there was a body of about two hundred men coming over the ridge. Some of the machine gunners immediately reversed their guns, but before they could commence firing, an officer, looking through his field glasses, said they were Americans. What a relief. When they came up we found they belonged to the 35th Division, but had lost their way, and could not make contact with their outfit. One of our officers told them to fall in with us and be prepared to do some fighting.

Swinging down the hill and slightly to the west, I soon found the machine-gun company and delivered my message to Captain Doherty. He immediately began assembling his men to advance to the support of the men in the sunken road. A large number of men from the different units were assembled at the foot of the hill, and there was a particularly large group bunched in a small draw running south. Large numbers of shells were coming over, and one exploded at the head of this draw. Someone yelled to these men to scatter out, as German aviators flying overhead had been directing the artillery to this position, and the shells were getting too close to be comfortable. It seemed that the German airmen had complete control of this section, and in addition to directing the artillery to these concentrations of men, were also harassing us with their machine guns.

An emergency dressing station had been established nearby, partially protected by the hill. Large numbers of wounded men were being brought in, attesting to the viciousness of the German resistance. After delivering my message I started back up the hill to find battalion P.C. I had seen our colonel striding back and forth at the top of the hill, apparently oblivious to all the screaming and exploding shells, and the hail of machine-gun bullets. I stopped to speak to Turner of the gas detail a moment. As I started to leave him there was a blinding flash and a terrific explosion as a shell exploded in the draw, in the middle of a large group of men. I saw arms and legs and mangled bodies flying in every direction. It was the most horrible sight I had seen yet.

I started off in a diagonal direction, heading for the top of the hill, where I had seen the colonel a short time before. Hearing a shout I looked up, and at that moment a shell coming from the rear passed just over my head and crashed into the side of the hill just in front of me. I noticed then that I was among D Company men. This was my own company, and Captain Dickson was yelling to the men to get down and dig in, realizing that our own artillery, which had just gotten into position again and opened fire, had a short range and was firing into us. The range changed soon to our relief, and our shells began to sail over, dropping into the German lines around Epinonville. That was a tough situation for a while—terrific fire from the Germans in front, and our own shells crashing into us from the rear.

I had dropped down momentarily while our shells were coming overhead, but being anxious to find the liaison section, I again started toward the top of the hill. I had taken but a few steps when, hearing a crash and a whining noise slightly to my left, I turned partly around. Something struck me a crushing blow on my left arm, whirled me halfway around, and knocked me to my knees. My arm felt dead and I could not lift it, although I felt no particular pain. I grabbed my left wrist with my right hand and pulled my arm up in front of me. It was then that I noticed the blood gushing out and running down the front of my blouse. I realized that I had been hit by a piece of high-explosive shell.

Turner, whom I had just spoken to, was about a hundred yards away and saw me go down. He came running over to assist me. He and another fellow proceeded to cut the sleeve out of my blouse and the two shirts I was wearing in order to bandage the arm. I took my handkerchief out and had them tie it around my arm, just at the elbow, running my bayonet through the loop and twisting it in order to stop the flow of blood. I noticed that the wound was about midway between the wrist and elbow, and it was bleeding badly. I was on the verge of passing out when Turner pulled out my canteen and gave me a drink of that cold water that I had taken from the creek earlier in the morning, in violation of orders. It was the best-tasting water I had ever drunk.

After bandaging my arm and placing a temporary splint on it, the men helped me down to the dressing station nearby. They had just brought John

White in, with both feet almost completely shot away. I had talked with him not more than fifteen minutes earlier, and we had both laughed about how rough the Germans were playing. Now he was seriously wounded, and I had just gotten mine too. I picked out a spot and lay down until I could get over the shock, as I had lost considerable blood, and the arm was beginning to throb.

The battle was raging fiercely. Our men had succeeded in taking Epinonville but could not hold it, and were forced to retire temporarily. I think they took the town three times that day before they were able to withstand the vicious counterattacks the Germans launched. General McDonald, our gray-haired brigade commander, had his command under a tree a short distance from the dressing station. We could hear him and Colonel Parker discussing the situation. They were debating the possibility of sending men around to the right of our position [to] try to outflank the Germans defending Epinonville. However, the 37th Division had not been able to come abreast of us on our right, thereby leaving this flank exposed to attack. Our position in this respect became more serious as the attack advanced. About the fifth day our division had advanced while the divisions on our right and left had fallen back. In order to protect our flanks, we had stretched our line in the shape of a horseshoe, until instead of a two-kilometer sector, our line was about ten kilometers long. We actually had to give up some dearly captured ground and retire in order to shorten our line.

Wounded men were coming in, or were being carried in, in increasing numbers as the day wore on. About two o'clock in the afternoon we began to wonder about something to eat. I told one of the fellows that was able to walk where I had left my pack. He went out and found it and brought two cans of corned beef, which we divided up and ate with relish. German planes were flying over our position at short intervals, and invariably when they returned to the German lines, a furious bombardment of our dressing station would begin. We realized that the fliers were giving our position to the German artillery.

However, we were down at the bottom of the hills, and trench mortar shells were the only ones that would drop near us on such short range. During the rest of the afternoon shells dropped all around us, and we expected any moment to have one drop squarely in our midst. As we would hear one of them with its peculiar whistle coming, we would tense ourselves for the shock, heaving a tremendous sigh when it missed again. One German aviator flew over several times, so low that we thought surely he would crash into the trees or into the side of the hill. He would lean out of the cockpit of his plane and fire point-blank into our faces with a revolver as we lay helpless on our backs. However, we were more or less resigned to the inevitable, feeling that if he didn't get us, one of those shells would eventually, and it would probably be much more messy anyway. I saw two men coming across the valley when suddenly a shell exploded right between them.

As I lay on the ground I could see Montfaucon to my left in the distance, not knowing at that time what a bitter fight the boys of the 79th Division were having. We were later to learn of this great drive and of the heroic conduct of all the splendid divisions involved in that titanic struggle. American history was being made here on this day, and other days to come. But I was through, and destined not to take a very large part in the victorious drive that eventually brought Germany to a surrender.

About three o'clock I saw the flash of a gun to the south and presently heard a shell whistling overhead. We knew at last that some of our guns were getting into position after their struggle along the Avocourt-Very road. It gave us a great deal of assurance to know that some of our shells were again dropping into German territory. We who were there wanted to see the enemy driven back past Epinonville at least. That front line was altogether too close for comfort. We had been cheerily informed that it might be several days before any ambulance could reach us. Toward evening the firing diminished somewhat, or rather became fainter, and we learned that our men were pushing the Germans farther back, which was good news to us.

Presently one of the doctors came along and inquired if any of us could walk. He said if we could, we had better start walking back to the rear. We would be able to find some warm food somewhere, and probably be evacuated sooner. The first ambulances to arrive would naturally take the most seriously wounded. I had a doctor adjust my bandage and splint, and I got onto my feet to test out my legs. Finding that I felt fairly strong, I started walking down the road toward Very. Presently the men began shouting to pass the word back to our artillery to raise the range—that they were again shooting into their own men.

The fighting had been severe in the sector of the other brigade through which I had to pass. Lots of men were wounded and dead. The canyon was quite narrow here, preventing the men from spreading out, and the German shells had done plenty of damage. I passed a supply wagon with four mules and two drivers—or rather, what had been a supply outfit. A shell had just recently struck both men and the mules, blowing most of the wagon away. The bodies of the mules were still steaming, and the whole thing was a ghastly mess. I sat down beside the road at the edge of Very to rest. A military policeman came along and said, "Buddy, you better move out of here—the Jerries are shelling this place regularly every ten minutes." That's all I needed to hear, and I was on my way again.

I hiked on back toward the rear. Other walking cases were strung out as far as I could see, some barely able to walk, but anxious to reach a place where they could get attention for their wounds, and something to eat. As I came up the slight hill from the valley, I was close to the battery of artillery which I had seen commence firing earlier in the afternoon. It was a short distance off the road, and as I stopped to watch it fire, a German plane suddenly swooped down over it, firing at the gunners. A doughboy who had been sitting beside the road jumped up and started shooting at the plane with his rifle. The barrel of the gun must have been wet, for suddenly it exploded and blew most of the fingers off his left hand. He threw the gun down and started back toward a first-aid station on the run.

An ammunition wagon came along and the driver asked me if I wanted a lift. I climbed on and rode a mile or so to where he stopped. Some company had just eaten, and I walked over and asked the mess sergeant about getting something to eat. He said they had cleaned up everything except some bread and jam, but that sounded good to me. He fixed me up a sandwich and I had taken about two bites when a shell landed right near us. Someone yelled "Gas!," and I had to drop my sandwich and start pawing for my gas mask. I managed to get the mouthpiece in my mouth with one hand, and then some fellows who had theirs on helped me get mine the rest of the way on. After a little while someone said "No gas," and we took the masks off. I was afraid my sandwich might have gas on it, so I was afraid to eat it. Still hungry, I started back along the Avocourt-Very road.

Just at dark I came to a company of the 316th Engineers lined up in the woods ready to eat. I went over and asked the mess sergeant what the chances were for a handout. He said, "Sure, get right there in the head of the line and

*I'll fix you up." First time I ever crashed a chow line. He had no extra mess kit, but he found a big lid off of some dish, and proceeded to fill it with a generous helping of hot hash of some sort. He also gave me a big dipper full of scalding hot coffee. Seeing that I was handicapped by having the use of only one arm, he helped me to a position nearby with my back to a tree. I proceeded to stow that food away in a hurry. I would like to see that buddy someday to thank him, and tell him that nothing I have eaten since tasted as good as that chow and coffee of his. It was the first food I had had for three days, except some hardtack and cold corned beef.*

*A few large shells were exploding occasionally along the road. The Germans had this country thoroughly mapped, and knew very bridge, crossroad, and clump of woods. A six-inch gun in a batten just off the road had suffered a direct hit, and was turned upside down in a shell hole. Dead horses and mules were lying about. Tragic victims of this war. A full ammunition cart had been hit and exploded. All that remained was the metal tires and some bolts. Parts of the mule were strewn about and the unfortunate driver was lying nearby, thoughtfully covered with a piece of canvas, by someone.*

*Having appeased my hunger and rested, I started once more to make my way along the road toward the rear. By this time the road was literally choked with all kinds of traffic, moving at a snail's pace. Everything would move forward a few paces, then stop. Perhaps a culvert had been blown up or a truck wrecked by a German shell. Immediately the engineers would plunge in to repair the culvert, or the truck would be dragged off to the side of the road. Then the traffic would slide forward a few more feet. Mule skinners lounged beside their animals, while truck drivers dozed in their seals.*

*We walkers naturally had to struggle along at the side of road the best we could. I was continually stumbling into holes, which were now filled with watery mud. My canteen was long since emptied. Since I was now running some temperature caused by lack of attention to my wound, I required a great deal of water. I was forced to ask the fellows along the road for a drink quite often. And may it be said to their credit that none of them along that long, weary road to Avocourt refused me that night. Of course, they were all interested to know what was going on up front.*

*We had the only firsthand news available, and so we spread what little news we had along the road that night. A soldier in the thick of a battle never knows what is going on beyond the range of his immediate sector. He is busy doing his allotted task to the best of his ability. However, the fact that we were wounded convinced the men along the road that there was something going on up front.*

*About nine o'clock that night I arrived at Avocourt. I had been on the road [for] four hours, and walked several kilometers. It had been twelve hours since I had been hit. My arm was badly swollen and the broken bone was causing me a great deal of pain. I was also running a considerable temperature. The ambulance station in Avocourt was in a dugout, which was about all there was left of this town. The attendants gave us a drink of hot chocolate and a blanket and told us to make ourselves as comfortable as we could until our turn came to get into an ambulance. There were quite a number of wounded lying around, and more straggling in. Some of the more severely wounded were moaning, while others were grimly bearing their suffering. I don't recall if one of the medical corpsmen gave me a shot to ease my pain. The next thing I remember was being wakened by someone shaking me and asking if I was a 91st Division casualty. I told him I was, and he asked to see my identification card, which had been fastened to me on the battlefield. When he had satisfied himself that I was a member of that division, he said, "Come on, we have two small ambulances here and room for eight men."*

*We eight were led out and helped into the two Ford ambulances. It was about midnight, and the blackest night I ever saw. Of course, there were no lights. They weren't taking any chances on an air raid or even a long-range shell dropping in to see us. Each car had a small blue light real low down in front, shielded so that it threw no light up at all. There were two drivers with the car. And so we started out for as wild a night ride as I've ever taken. Of course, the road was churned to pieces by shells, and roughly repaired just so traffic could get over it. When we would come to a particularly rough spot one of the men would get out and walk along in front as a pilot until we came to a better stretch. And if we heard a shell coming, the driver would stop and wait to see where it was going to land. We sat on a lengthwise seat, two on a side facing the other two, with our feet braced, and our teeth clenched, hanging on with grim determination.*

*Presently we emerged from the woods onto a stretch of smoother road and stopped in front of a tent set up in the remains of an old stone building. We were helped out and into this tent, which proved to be a field hospital. We were each given a drink of hot soup or broth. Then one of the doctors motioned me to get up on one of the tables and lie down. He brought up a hypodermic needle that looked like an ice pick to me, and said, "Grit your teeth and hang on, because this may hurt some." He opened my shirt and eased this needle into my chest, and then made a cross with an indelible pencil on my forehead. He said this was done so the next station down the line wouldn't give me another shot. We were told that this shot was a serum to prevent lockjaw.*

*When we went out to resume our journey, we found several large GMC [General Motors Company] ambulances waiting. So we were doubled up and eight of us placed in each car. We hit some good smooth road then, and that driver certainly opened her up. But that wasn't any too fast to suit me, for I was getting pretty groggy by this time, and the old arm was hurting something fierce. We met several columns of marching troops, and when we slowed up once and asked them, "What outfit, buddy?" someone replied that it was the First Division. This was nothing new for this outfit, for those boys had seen plenty of action.*

*We arrived at the first evacuation hospital about 3:00 a.m., and were unloaded and ushered into the waiting room. It didn't take long to get our history, and we were shortly prepared for the operating room, the most seriously wounded ones to go first. I was placed on a stretcher and carried across the street to a small waiting room and set down on the floor. Presently two orderlies came from the operating room and asked who was next. I gave them a high sign, and they picked me up and in I went.*

*My first impression was that I had been carried into a slaughterhouse by mistake. There must have been fifteen or twenty operating tables, and they were all occupied. They slapped me onto a table and I had a few moments to glance around before they started to pouring the ether into me. It was a horrible sight. Blood, mangled arms, legs, heads, and bodies. Some limbs had been shot off; some were being taken off, and the nauseating smell of blood, mixed with ether, was all over the place. I was thankful when I lost consciousness, and drifted off to blissful forgetfulness.*

*When I came out from under the influence of the anesthetic I was in a large ward and the sun as shining. It was a bedlam, though. Different people act differently. Some were laughing; some were crying, while some were swearing like the proverbial sailor. Everything was nice and clean, and pretty soon they brought me a nice hot stew and coffee. I found my personal belongings, such as my razor, watch, fountain pen, and billfold, tied up in a napkin at the head of my bed. When I had been going under the ether in the operating room, I had requested the doctor to save the shrapnel for a souvenir if he found any in my arm. However, there was no sign of any among my other things, so I concluded that it had gone through my blouse, shirts, and arm, and merrily on its way elsewhere.*

*I could occasionally hear the roar of the big guns, and I knew that the rest of the boys were still pushing on. Lying there in the nice clean bed, I gave myself over to some reflections. I recalled what Turner had said the day before when he was helping to dress my arm. Something about getting out of this hell and having a chance to rest and get enough to eat anyway. Those boys up there were still in that hell, and the end wasn't in sight yet. Closing my eyes, I could still see those mangled and bloody bodies of my buddies, and I began to wonder what it was all about.*

*A nurse came along shortly and said that those who were able to be moved would be sent farther back to the war, to some base hospital. She asked if I felt like being moved, and I told her I felt like running if necessary. I was carried out and placed aboard an American Red Cross train headed for somewhere at least a little nearer home. My trip to the rear was considerably different from the one toward the front. Then we rode in French boxcars, trucks with coolie drivers, or usually, walked. Marching all night until we were completely exhausted, and then hiding in the woods during the day to escape German bombers. How I was shifted from hospital to hospital during the next three months, gradually getting closer to the coast, and finally sailing for the good old USA in January is another story. I cherish the hope that some of the buddies who were with me on this trip will recognize the situations I have described, and perhaps I may hear from some of them. Suffice it to say that I was one of those who made the trip to Epinonville and back. Many did not come back.*[2]

The primary objective on Day One was Montfaucon. At an elevation of 1,122 feet (342 meters), taking this position that dominated the surrounding countryside was an irrevocable imperative according to Pershing. To achieve his aim he sent in the untested 79th Division who assaulted it from the front, the intention being to keep the Germans distracted while the "Ivy Men" of the veteran 4th Division advanced past Montfaucon to conduct a turning movement from the east, taking it from behind. These two divisions were from different corps. The 4th was attached to III Corps, while the 79th was part of V Corps. Two very different commanders who didn't particularly see eye to eye ran these two corps. Contemporaries regarded V Corps commander Maj. Gen. George H. Cameron as a soft-spoken, unimposing character who fervently disliked bombastic "ring-thumpers" like Bullard, who pounded their West Point class rings on map tables to draw attention to their lineage and military sagacity. Maj. Gen. Robert Lee Bullard, III Corps commander, was his antithesis. There's no doubt that Bullard was hungry for glory, and on occasion even capable of bending the rules to get his own way. He displayed this capacity during the attack on Montfaucon, whereupon he simply decided to ignore military protocol and repeal the order.

The confusion that arose from this situation caused chaos among the regiments. Maj. Gen. Robert Alexander, commander of the 77th Division, insisted on the application of open warfare and ordered a straight push forward of the whole line across terrain that was far from conducive to this purpose. Although progress was made on that first day, it was more due to German concessions than military aptitude from the AEF division commanders.

The 1st Army's situation also gave rise to ominous foreboding, but this was mainly due to some serious logistical problems they encountered while attempting to get to the Front. What few roads were available for these purposes were not in good condition, and throughout the whole of that first day they were completely congested with incoming traffic heading to the Front—bearing in mind that a significant percentage of this traffic was due to horses that were used extensively for military trains. They were used to pull ambulances and carry supplies and ordnance, among other things. Despite the initial AEF successes against these somewhat demoralized adversaries, different tactics would now be required; but even then, the results would be less than satisfactory.

Montfaucon was taken around noon on September 27, but it was a shallow victory, because the Germans had chosen to retire from this position and reinforce other tactically advantageous positions to the north of that hill. By the third day many AEF troops began to complain about lack of food and water due to supplies not reaching the Front, but despite this, Pershing urged them to push on. Bolstered by good artillery and tank support, the Americans advanced roughly one and a half miles. Relatively good progress was made everywhere except in the Argonne Forest. The position achieved by the evening of September 28 by III and V Corps extended beyond the German second line of defense, but brought the AEF into dangerous proximity of the infamous Hindenburg Line.

Incessant heavy rain on September 27 and 28 impeded the progress of the tanks; in some cases, they became irretrievably bogged down in the mud, like the British tanks at Passchendaele a year earlier. The AEF's 1st Army had managed to advance eight miles into the German lines by the end of September, and had gone up against some of the most heavily fortified German positions on the Western Front. In the process they had captured nine thousand prisoners, vast amounts of war supplies, and around one hundred guns, but at a cost. Lack of coordination between corps and regimental commanders combined with poor intelligence regarding the terrain left Pershing with few options.

Foch's general offensive had ground to a shuddering halt. Up north in Flanders Fields, history was repeating itself, as British attempts to advance became mired in thigh-deep, light brown mud. The French Army holding the center hadn't even left their positions. There had been some progress made in proximity to the Somme against the Hindenburg Line, where the British—supported by the 27th and 30th Divisions of AEF's II Corps—had managed to breach these tough German defenses. As September expired and October began, the British had halted their drive to improve their lines of communications. Using this all-too-brief hiatus, Pershing decided to rotate his less-experienced divisions with three battle-hardened ones. This decision would entail replacing the 37th, 79th, and 35th with the 3rd, 32nd, and 1st, in preparation for the second phase of the offensive. The 91st Division was retained in the line despite protests that many of the men were suffering from exposure and rampant diarrhea. The numerical odds that had up until that juncture distinctly favored the Allies began to level out as the Germans also used this time to strengthen their position by introducing six new divisions into the area, bringing their total to eleven.

## October 4, 1918

Although the 1st Division progressed three miles in the west on that first day, they quickly descended into a brutal slogging match that tested the resilience of the hardiest veterans. The AEF continued to launch punitive frontal attacks against well-protected German defenses that inevitably culminated in massive casualties for the Americans. I Corps captured a strategically important ridge on the east edge of the Argonne, but progress became painfully slow. Maj. Gen. Robert Lee Bullard's III Corps—comprising the 80th Division on the left, the 4th in the center, and the 33rd on the right—were presented with some particularly tough objectives.

Some of the stiffest resistance was meted out to the 80th Division as they attacked the Bois des Ogons, an outpost of the Kriemhilde Stellung, which was in the center of the Meuse-Argonne sector. Bullard displayed incredible insensitivity when he insisted that despite sustaining heavy losses, the 80th Division keep pushing forward after being repeatedly repelled. The division was close to breaking point when division commander, Maj. Gen. Adelbert Cronkhite, pleaded with Bullard to repeal his order to orchestrate a third attack. Bullard even went so far as threatening Cronkhite with dismissal if he refused to execute the order, insisting that one more attack would clear the Germans out of the woods. It actually took more than one attack, but by the evening of October 5, the Germans had simply decided to abandon the position. It has been well documented that Bullard hated complex orders requiring close coordination, and firmly believed that one could win battles just by charging straight ahead. For many, Bullard provided the style of leadership necessary during the Great War. This West Point graduate spoke fluent French, and his contemporaries frequently praised his diplomatic skills in his dealings with his French counterparts during joint US–French operations.

Military historian Alan Clark said of British general Douglas Haig: "If the dead could march, side by side in continuous procession down

Whitehall, it would take them four days and nights to get past the saluting base." World War I generals were not known for their compassion, nor, in many cases, for their strategic acumen.

## THE LOST BATTALION

The story of the Lost Battalion was one of courage, tenacity, and survival. The Allies' push forward during the Meuse-Argonne Offensive into the Argonne Forest started to break German positions, but several companies of the 77th Division were caught up in an epic battle which proved the fighting spirit of the American Expeditionary Force.

The word *lost* is not the correct word here; the words *surrounded* or *cut-off* are actually better suited for the battalion's situation. Maj. Charles Whittlesey, a Wisconsin native and New York lawyer, was central to the Lost Battalion's story. He was an American hero, awarded the Medal of Honor for his role in the Argonne Forest, which would sadly lead to his untimely death.

The *New York World* newspaper provided a brief biography of Whittlesey shortly after the battle in the Argonne Forest:

> *Major Charles W. Whittlesey, leader of the battalion of several hundred men, who for five days floundered through the Argonne Forest after they had been encircled by the Germans, and were finally found by a searching party, lived in this city at No. 136 East 44th Street. Major Whittlesey was a lawyer before he enlisted, and was but recently graduated from Williams College. He enlisted in the first Plattsburg officers' training camp. After receiving his commission, he was sent to Camp Upton. He sailed for France in September.*
>
> *It was because of the major's leadership that the battalion finally slipped through the circle the German army had drawn about it and met the searching body sent to their aid. Army authorities have permitted it to be known that the 77th New York has been in the Argonne fighting, and the naming of Major Whittlesey has had many in New York believ[ing] that it was a battalion of the 77th which was surrounded in the Argonne.*

*Major Whittlesey is a nephew of Charles W. Whittlesey, a lawyer of No. 51 East 58th Street. "He is the last man in the world we expected to do something heroic in this war," said Mr. Whittlesey to a World reporter yesterday. "He was a very quiet fellow—shy, you would call him—and he detested any form of publicity. He was the most peaceful fellow in the world, too, and before the United States entered the war, he often said he did not believe in war. But when he did get in, he was among the first to volunteer at Plattsburg." Major Whittlesey is a member of the Harvard and Williams clubs. He is a native of Pittsfield, MA.*

## AFTER ACTION REPORT, 77TH INFANTRY, NATIONAL ARCHIVES

An excerpt from the 77th Infantry "After Action Report" reveals further details about what transpired during this fateful battle:

*During the first phase of the World War the French made an attempt to clear the "Forest of Argonne" of the enemy, and had lost many men in the endeavor. Thereafter further attempt was made, until the Allied Offensive, which was launched September 26, 1918. It had remained unmolested for nearly four years in the hands of the enemy, who had early in the war occupied it, and had skillfully developed its natural features into one vast impregnable fortress.*

*The "Forest of Argonne" was an area of densely wooded hills and slopes with many ravines, gullies, and swamps, all of which were covered with tangled underbrush; consequently the Germans were able to place their machine guns to command all roads and paths traversing it, and had located them in positions which enabled the gunners to place a series of interlocking bands of fire between trees and along systems of barbed wire, which they had cleverly constructed and concealed, during their unmolested occupation. All of this, combined with his cleverly concealed artillery positions, his hidden observation posts, and infantry with supporting weapons, rendered the "Forest of Argonne" most inaccessible to direct attack and hostile penetration.*

*The most impossible task of clearing the "Forest of Argonne" by direct attack was recognized by the Allied Command, and during the discussion of the Meuse-Argonne Offensive, plans were discussed as to how it could be taken without a heavy attack in that difficult region. It was decided that the right of the Fourth French Army, which was the 39th French Corps, operating on the west of the Forest, and the American divisions, operating on the east of the Forest, would advance, simultaneously, launching a scalloping movement on the east and west outskirts of the Forest, thus creating and developing a pocket from which the enemy would be obliged to withdraw in order to avoid capture.*

*As a result of this plan, a speedy withdrawal of the enemy from their Forest stronghold was anticipated, and very little resistance was expected. For the above reasons was the 77th Division assigned such a wide zone of action, with the mission of mopping up the forest as the enemy withdrew. Information has also been obtained that the enemy troops occupying the "Forest of the Argonne" were organizations of the "Landwehr Reservers"—"old fellows," they called them—and it was thought that they had lived lives of ease and comfort for nearly four years, while unmolested and secure in their forest fastness, consequently would not offer a great deal of resistance. Contrary of supposition, these troops were determined and stubborn in the conduct of their defense and resistance, and proved to be among Germany's best troops.*

*It is very true that they had remained in the Forest for a long period, but they had not remained idle, nor were they so elderly, for they had perfected and developed a system of defense which was most difficult to overcome. The "Landwehr" divisions were reinforced by the 76th German Reserve Division, which greatly strengthened the enemy resistance. Both the "Landwehr" and the 76th Reserves were fresh troops, unworn by long service at the Front, and they fought courageously, contesting every foot of ground after falling back upon their main line of resistance. From the morning of September 27th, their resistance commenced in earnest, and from then on new enemy divisions appeared on the Front.*

*Returning to the plan of attack, the American divisions operating on the east of the "Forest" advanced rapidly, as planned, but the right of the Fourth French Army, operating on the west of the "Forest," was unable to advance, owing to the organization and defense of the enemy territory to its front, which consisted of well-constructed trench systems organized in depth, surrounded by solid masses of barbed wire, and covered with second-growth brush. Also, the strong enemy defensive positions at La Palette Pavilion, and those extending west, dominated all of the ground in front of the right of the Fourth French Army.*

*The liaison mission between the right of the Fourth French Army and the left of the 77th Division, charged to a Franco-American liaison group, composed of American colored troops and a like number of French troops, and operating under the 38th French Corps, was not accomplished, owing to the unforeseen and determined opposition by the enemy on the left of the Forest, and at all times during the operation the right of the Fourth French Army remained to the left rear of the left of the American line.*

*Consequently, the contemplated pocket was not formed, and the enemy did not withdraw. Thus we find that the 77th Division faced the "Forest of Argonne" and its occupied defenses with the left flank exposed to the enemy territory to the left and left front, and holding a seven-kilometer zone of action. Due to the combination of circumstances, as stated above, the 77th Division became much involved in the Forest, and many times during those memorable days, regiments, battalions, and even companies were obliged to settle their own disputes with the enemy. Is it so astonishing, then, that the organizations of the 77th Division should have found themselves engaged on various occasions with both flanks open? It was the indomitable courage, optimism, and determination of the personnel of the division, from its commander, whose efficient leadership and will carried the division forward, to its last private soldier, which enabled it to realize upon emerging from the Forest before Grandpré, eighteen days after it entered, that success had crowned its efforts.*[3]

Major Whittlesey could not have gotten his command lost, as its name would imply, for his designated line of advance led one flank of his force along a well-defined ravine. This ravine runs north and south, perpendicular to and into the head of the Charlevaux ravine, near the Charlevaux Mill. It runs south, past the Moulin de l'Homme Mort, and on past the Dépôt de Machines. This ravine also divided the regimental subsector of the 308th Infantry, and it was only necessary for Major Whittlesey to conduct his command north along its slopes in order to reach his position. He could read a map like a book, was intelligent, and exceptionally cool under fire. He bore the same hardships as did his officers and men, and they stood with him to the last. He conducted his command to the objective designated for him by the division commander, occupied the position assigned him, and organized and held that position until the remainder of the division, on the right, and the French, on the left, were able to move up on his flanks five days later.

## MAJ. CHARLES WHITTLESEY, 308TH INFANTRY REGIMENT, 77TH DIVISION

*We were twice cut off in the Argonne Forest. The first time was September 26. The second time we were penned in from October 3 till the night of October 7. We advanced into the heart of the forest, an almost impenetrable jungle of undergrowth with about six hundred or seven hundred men of the First and Second Battalions, 308th Infantry, an outfit of New Yorkers and Westerners. We had exhausted our rations, and before the fresh supply had been served to more than half of our men, we got the order to advance. Each man carried 220 rounds of rifle ammunition.*

*The following day we ran into stiff resistance at a hill where the Germans were entrenched and had mounted many machine guns. Our course lay through the deep ravine with hills two hundred feet high rising from its bottom. A Company attacked the hill and lost all its officers and more of its men. The next morning, we went forward, reaching our objective—a road running along the hillside—at 6:00 p.m. There we bivouacked, throwing out outposts.*

*The spot we occupied was perhaps three hundred yards long and was thickly wooded. You could see no one ten yards away. To the north the hill rose sharply above us. The Germans were hidden there. Below us was a swamp and marsh to which, fortunately, we could make our way at night for drinking water, crawling through the machine-gun fire, which the Boche sprayed about the pool.*

*Lieutenant Leak came back from an attack on the hill led by Lieutenant Wilhelm, with ninety men. Lieutenant Leak had with him eighteen men. He reported that Lieutenant Wilhelm had been surrounded with the rest, while crossing the ravine, but that they had cut their way to regimental headquarters. Many of his command were lost, however.*

*That morning, October 3, runners whom I had sent to our outposts returned to tell me the outposts had been cut off or captured. We knew then that we were surrounded, and it was then simply a matter of sticking there until reinforcements came up. "Simply a matter of sticking there" was the modest phrase employed by Major Whittlesey to describe one of the most heroic decisions of the war.*

*"The Germans attacked every afternoon," Whittlesey continued. "They would come down the hillside through the brush, yelling like ten thousand devils. It was useless to look for a target through that brush. They heaved down hand grenades, called potato mashers because of their shape, and swept us with machine guns. It was impossible to say how many of them we accounted for with our return fire. They dragged their dead and wounded away each night, but we found bodies in the brush afterward. Of our own number, 107 were killed. It was impossible to bury them properly in the rocky hill and their bodies were later taken back for burial. The afternoon of October 7 they sent a messenger to us. He was blindfolded and carried a white flag. He brought a typewritten message, reading, as nearly as I can remember: 'We have heard the cries of your wounded. It is impossible for you to escape. Why do you not surrender, in the name of humanity? Send back your reply by messenger carrying a white flag.'*

*"Well, we didn't send back any message at all. We simply told that messenger to 'Go to hell.' Perhaps he went. I don't know. The Germans must have been informed by their scouts [that] the relief was advancing toward us, and hoped to get us to surrender before our regiment came up. We ourselves did not know that help was so close at hand. But we stuck on, and that evening a battalion of the 807th made its way to us. Then the Germans retired. Back of us came the 77th Division advancing along the entire line.*

*"We marched out with 87 of my battalion, the First, and 107 men of the Second under George McMurtrie, who were unwounded. All of the rest of our*

*men were killed or wounded. Captain McMurtrie was a wonder. I don't know what I should have done without him. He used to be a New York broker. He was wounded in the knee the second day of our advance but kept right on, and later he was wounded by the handle of a potato masher, which was driven into his back. But he still kept the men going in glorious fashion.*

*"And those runners! After several had been killed trying to get word to headquarters, I asked others if they cared to take the risk. 'Why sure,' they always said. That's the way they all were. When we were relieved we had not had a bite to eat for four days."*[4]

In newspapers—both locally, such as in Pittsfield, Massachusetts, where Whittlesey and his family were residing, and internationally—Whittlesey's story of leadership and courage became the story of legends. Here is just a small sampling of the stories released at the time.

### Berkshire Evening Eagle, *October 11, 1918*

*"Whittlesey Not Kind of Boy Who Surrenders to Germans"*

*"Go to hell" was the reply of Maj. Charles Whittlesey, the Pittsfield boy in command of a battalion of the 77th Division fighting northwest of Verdun, when called upon by German headquarters to surrender with his band of men who became lost in a thicket during the fighting early this week. This reply may sound a little strong to some friends of "Charley" Whittlesey, but not to the people who know him the best. These people know that it was the reply that best fitted the occasion.*

*"Charley" Whittlesey, as he is best known to Pittsfield people, or Major Whittlesey, as he is known to the world at large today, was the man for the place. He is entitled to all the pleasant words that are being showered upon him, but a man who probably knows him better than say, any other man today, said if Major Whittlesey was in a position to answer all of these congratulations, he would say, "The men and their officers did simply what their country expects. It was their good fortune to exemplify the spirit of America: to show what thousands of other Americans would do under life circumstances."*

### Reported Promoted

*It was reported today that Major Whittlesey had been promoted to lieutenant colonel, but this report has not been confirmed. Friends are confident that if a promotion has not been made, it will come in due time.*

### The "Lost Battalion"

*The battalion of American soldiers "lost" in the Argonne Forest knew where they were; only, being surrounded by foes, they could not get supplies or ammunition or link their lines with their comrades. The proper thing for them to do in that case, as any tactician might have explained, was to surrender and wish for better luck in the next war.*

*But this battalion, being ignorant farm boys, dry-goods clerks, and so on, without the advantages of long military training, and strong in the purpose that there shall not be any next war, made other arrangements. They felt at home in those woods, so they stayed. Having healthy young appetites and nothing much to eat, after the "iron rations" disappeared, they experimented with the leaves of fallen trees. Presently other "Yankees" just like them began swooping above them in airplanes, dropping encouraging messages and even things to eat, and munitions gentled down on little parachutes.*

*In the end it turned out that the men of this battalion were not lost at all, but merely out of line. It took their friends five days to struggle up to them; the Germans fought for every inch. By that time the boys were something more than merely hungry, but after about two square meals they were ready to fight again. And they did. What is the German High Command, which has studied the art of war for years, going to do with a lot of crazy youngsters like that, who simply will not fight according to the rules?*

The *Canadian Press* carried the following story under the dateline "With the Canadian Forces Northwest of Verdun":

## Canadian Press, *October 11, 1918*

### *"Maj. Whittlesey's Stand"*

*The brightest spot in the heroic and amazing story of the now-famous "Lost Battalion," which belonged to the 77th Division, as yet untold, was the climax to the fourth day of the troops' siege in the Argonne Forest.*

*None of the battalions could know that relief would come within twenty-four hours: none felt very sure that it could come at all before it was too late; but the same spirit animating them to plunge ahead in the forest to their perilous position maintained them at that moment, and every living man, wounded or well, in the battalion enthusiastically approved Major Whittlesey's abrupt answer when the news of it was circulated through the position.*

### Fell into Enemy Trap

*A composite story gleaned from a dozen recitals reveals that the battalion when ordered to advance last Friday pushed its way rapidly ahead through the forest, and in its eagerness to catch up with the retreating Germans, gradually spread out and widened its ranks. This allowed the Germans to infiltrate unseen behind the Americans and they fell directly into a cunning trap, which the Germans had set for them. The enemy had planned to catch the Americans in a hollow surrounded all four sides by heights, the greatest of which was a steep hill directly ahead. The Americans, who were not accustomed to forest fighting and were filled with eagerness, dashed into this hollow without stopping to think that the enemy might be awaiting them. The members of the battalion were at first checked by their own artillery barrage, which had worked steadily forward.*

*Nevertheless, it had not worked as fast as the troops themselves, and the battalion proceeded halfway up the hill, and there they waited for the barrage to pass in front of them. Then they discovered that the Germans on both sides had jointly flanked them and had closed in upon their rear. Sheltered only by shallow and hastily constructed trenches, the men were subject to a grilling, sniping machine-gun fire, as well as a trench mortar bombardment, every time they showed themselves. Only with the greatest difficulty and with extreme caution could they move from place to place and keep guard against surprise attacks. The battalion had started with meager rations, expecting more to reach them later. These of course could no longer be transported. They sent back volunteer scouting parties, but if these reached the positions in the rear without being captured or killed, they could not tell, for none ever returned.*

## Dared Not Show Themselves

*Daily American aviators, searching vainly for them, flew overhead, but no outcry the men could make brought anything but a volley of shouts and laughter from the Germans in front and behind and to the right and left of them.*

*The beleaguered men discovered there were German machine-gun nests all around them, every 175 feet or so, and a man to show himself ever so briefly was the signal for a sweeping rash of bullets. If a man made an unusual noise, trench mortars pounded the vicinity viciously. Just for diversion the enemy made a practice of sweeping the whole terrain—the hillside where the improvised trenches were located, and the valley in which the men crawled to get leaves and water—regularly, and then irregularly, with machine guns.*

*There was not a man in the battalion, wounded or otherwise, hungry or starved, but scouted the idea of surrender. Their ammunition was depleted to a point where the few machine guns in the outfit had but one belt of cartridges apiece, and the rifle ammunition was running so short that they had received orders not to fire at any one attacking until within such short range that his death or serious injury was almost inevitable.*

*Major Whittlesey had his entire battalion behind him to a man. Capt. Leo Stromee of San Bernardino, California, told the Associated Press [that] his men jeered at the idea of surrender, and the men who came out of the four days' siege are united in declaring that they never would have given up.*

## "LEADERSHIP DID IT!": JAMES V. LEAK, COMPANY E, 308TH INFANTRY

*In the outset may you understand that the "Lost Battalion" is entirely a misnomer. First, it was not a battalion, but was composed of seven companies of infantry and one machine-gun company. A battalion is composed of only four companies. Second, it was not "lost." We knew exactly where we were, and went to the exact position to which we had been ordered. This organization was under the command of Maj. Charles W. Whittlesey. It consisted of companies A, B, C, E, G, and H, 308th Infantry, Co. K, 307th Infantry, and Co. C, 306th Machine Gun Battalion. All told there were slightly less than 700 men in it. A war-strength company was 250 men.*

*The 77th Division, of which we were a part, had been ordered by the commanding general to advance to the Binarville-Charlevaux Mill road and to take that road. The 308th Infantry position was on the left flank of the Argonne Forest. This forest had been established as a game preserve during the reign of one of the French kings, and had been so maintained to the World War. It was approximately five to nine miles wide and twenty-five miles long, covered by forest as dense as the Big Thicket, and in terrain quite similar to the Hill Country of Texas. At the intersection of the sector assigned to the 308th Infantry, the Binarville-Charlevaux Mill road was about two-thirds of the way up a hill.*

*Late on the afternoon of October 2, 1918, the 308th Infantry stormed and captured the German trenches about one mile south of this road and pushed its way to Hill 198, just south of the "Pocket." Under cross machine-gun fire we crossed Charlevaux Creek on a narrow bridge. We dug "foxholes" in the hillside immediately under the road. The Germans were on top of the hill above us. Neither the French troops on our left nor the 307th Infantry on our right were successful in their attacks on the German trench a mile to the south of us. During the night German troops again occupied that part of the trenches over which we had come that afternoon. Thus we were a mile behind the German line, cut off and surrounded, but not lost.*[5]

Throughout the rain-drenched month of October, AEF divisions slogged away, incurring unprecedented casualties. October 8, the day that the Meuse-Argonne Offensive was expanded to the east of the Meuse River, saw some of the 82nd Infantry Division pressing home an attack that brought them into the Argonne Forest, where they intended to out-flank German positions. Among the ranks of the "All-Americans" was a then-unknown acting sergeant from Tennessee by the name of Alvin York (profiled further in chapter 18).

Bullard kept impetuously demanding attacks from his III Corps, often with little or no preparation. When the 4th Division gained ground, he neglected to order counterbattery fire, let alone trying to deal with the German control of the air over the Front. As new American divisions were rotated into line, the Germans continued to reinforce their positions, and by October 6 they had no less than twenty-seven divisions in the area. On October 14, while the 1st Army prepared to launch a general assault along the German lines, III and V Corps made a further attempt to capture the fortified hills and forests of the Cunel-Romagne front. At that time the 1st Army had become almost unmanageable, fielding over a million men strung out along an eighty-three-mile front. Pershing personally organized the 2nd Army and appointed Bullard as its commander. Bullard and his army assumed control over a thirty-four-mile stretch of the Front, regarded as a relatively quiet sector south of Verdun, between the Meuse and the Moselle rivers. Meanwhile, the increasingly active Meuse-Argonne sector remained the 1st Army's responsibility, and there was still work to do if this war was going to be won.

## PHASE TWO

The second phase of the Meuse-Argonne Offensive commenced October 16 with the attack on Grandpré on the River Aire, and culminated with AEF troops reaching the northwestern corner of the Argonne. Pershing directed General Liggett to take immediate command of the 1st Army. Liggett reequipped and remodeled the 1st Army to his own design. He took particular care in retraining his infantry and artillery, along with providing adequate supplies for their daily sustenance. His incessant emphasis on preparation allowed him to redefine the stereotypical, unimaginative generalship that too often characterized World War I commanders.

Under his leadership the 1st Army was earmarked for a major assault, along with a series of coordinated local attacks, with the purpose of straightening the American front from Grandpré in the west to the east bank of the Meuse River. Now that the third German defensive position, the Kriemhilde Stellung, had been breached, Pershing instructed the 1st Army to make preparations for a general offensive scheduled to commence October 28. Prior to the day of the attack, local assaults were organized to secure advantageous lines of departure. The deadliest of these local operations was the ten-day slogging endured by I Corps in their efforts to capture Grandpré. General Liggett had remarked before the attack went in that capturing this objective would incur frightful losses. That didn't stop him from pressing ahead as planned.

So by the third week of October, the 1st Army had breached the German third line of defense and cleared most of the Argonne, in the process achieving the majority of predetermined objectives outlined for the first phase of the campaign. The reorganized 1st Army, now under the command of General Liggett, began the final pursuit to Sedan. AEF divisions were reorganized once again, as a necessary major road construction program was undertaken during October to improve the logistical situation of frontline troops.

By October, while German troops were fighting and dying at the Front, their country was on the verge of total collapse. Mass desertions were occurring, and the morale of the German Army was at an all-time low. Due to the fact that the Allied forces refused to negotiate with the Kaiser and insisted upon dealing with parliamentary representatives of the German people, Paul von Hindenburg and Erich Ludendorff actively coerced Kaiser Wilhelm II into establishing a constitutional monarchy, which for all intents and purposes would reduce the Kaiser to a mere figurehead. As early as October 12 the German government announced that it had accepted President Wilson's requirement, and that it would withdraw its forces from France and Belgium. Despite the announcement, fighting on the Western Front continued unabated, although the end was definitely in sight.

However, Pershing found the prospect of an armistice with Germany abhorrent, and insisted to the other Allied commanders that the war should continue until Germany was decisively and unreservedly defeated.

## Pvt. James V. Schairer, 147th Infantry Regiment, 37th Division

### *Distinguished Service Cross Recipient*

*On July 24, 1917, the nearly twenty-three-year-old James, called "Jimmy" by his friends and family, enlisted in the Ohio National Guard. He was attached to the Medical Detachment of the 147th Infantry Regiment, 37th Division. His detachment was deployed at the Meuse-Argonne defensive sector of the American Expeditionary Force in France. In 1919, the Distinguished Service Cross was conferred posthumously upon Private Schairer for extraordinary heroism in action near Montfaucon, France, on September 26, 1918.*

*Seeing two men fall wounded, Private Schairer immediately went to their assistance, unmindful of the extreme danger to which he was exposed; and, after dragging the men to a shell hole, administered effective first aid. For his valor, he also received the French Croix de Guerre. In precedence for valor, the Distinguished Service Cross ranks immediately behind the Medal of Honor. Unfortunately, he never got a chance to wear the cross. He was killed a month later in the performance of his duties, at the age of twenty-four.*

*It was on October 30 that Jimmy was killed by a piece of German shrapnel. His regiment joined the 37th Division for the first offensive in Belgium, and while he was in his dugout, a German shell made a direct hit. He received a concussion to the skull and died that night as he was being rushed to the field hospital. He was buried with military honors at Dentergem, West Flanders. After the war, Private Schairer was reburied at the Flanders Field American Cemetery at Waregem. This is the only American World War I cemetery in Belgium, and 411 American servicemen are buried or commemorated there. As with all Allied war cemeteries, the land was provided in perpetuity by the Belgian government.*[6]

## Phase Three

V Corps in the center advanced six miles during those first days. The Germans were shocked, and ordered a withdrawal. On November

2–3, the 2nd Division marched right through the enemy positions and advanced another five miles. On November 3, 1918, III Corps on the right forced a crossing of the Meuse, south of Dun-sur-Meuse, with the 5th Division forcing the bridgehead. On November 5, 1918, leading US units reached the hills overlooking Sedan. The 1st Army boundary was ordered to be shifted to the east to allow the French 4th Army the honor of capturing Sedan, the site of a defeat in 1870, and the 1st Army's route of advance was redirected.

From November 7 through 11, 1918, the units already east of the Meuse continued advancing northward, and the 1st Army Headquarters laid plans for taking the old fortress of Montmédy, the next logical objective. As part of the 1st Army's shift eastward, units of the 2nd and 89th Divisions began a west-to-east crossing of the Meuse. The final Allied push toward the German border had started on October 16–17, 1918. As the British, French, and American armies advanced, the alliance between the Central Powers began to disintegrate. Turkey signed an armistice at the end of October, followed by Austria-Hungary on November 3. Germany began to implode and dissolve from within. Faced with the prospect of returning to sea, the sailors of the High Seas Fleet stationed at Kiel mutinied on October 29. Within a few days, the entire city was in their control and revolution began, soon spreading throughout the country.

By November 4, the 1st Army had secured positions along the heights overlooking the Meuse and brought the railroad from Sedan to Mézières under artillery fire. With this action it is fair to say that the Americans had achieved their objectives, but at a heavy price. In six weeks the AEF had lost 26,277 killed and 95,786 wounded, making this in effect the biggest American land battle to date.

Continued Allied attacks, spanning almost the entire front from the Meuse River to the North Sea, triggered massive disorganization among the German forces. Bullard, who had been appointed commander of the 2nd Army on October 12, was ordered to keep close watch of the enemy for any indications of a withdrawal. Two days before the armistice was signed, Marshal Foch issued urgent orders, instructing all units on the Western Front to maintain the pressure on the Germans so that they wouldn't be allowed time to rest or reorganize.

On November 7, the new German Republic formally asked Entente allies for a ceasefire to discuss a possible surrender. They didn't get a reply. On November 9, the Kaiser abdicated and surreptitiously made his way across the border into the Netherlands, and exile. Foch despised the Germans, blamed them for the war and the devastation in France, and had every intention of making them pay dearly. There would be no ceasefire, Foch informed the German delegates. Furthermore, the German government had to unconditionally accept a list that contained thirty-two demands, including withdrawal from all occupied territories, the destruction or surrender to the Allies of the entire German Navy and Army and all its equipment, and a formal acknowledgment that Germany was responsible for the war and would pay full reparations for all war damages incurred. If Germany did not agree to these terms within seventy-two hours, Foch announced, the fighting would go on until Germany had been invaded and occupied.

On November 10, the German delegates were back. Despite the humiliating conditions imposed by the Allies, the Germans were left with no other option than to accept all demands and give in. The terms and conditions would resonate with the Germans for many years to come. A young German corporal by the name of Adolf Hitler was convalescing in a Berlin hospital after being gassed near Ypres. The news of Germany's capitulation brought him to tears. He became obsessed with attributing blame for this humiliating defeat to the Jews and Marxists in Germany whom he claimed had undermined the war effort. To Hitler, and so many others, the German politicians who signed the Armistice on November 11, 1918, would become known as the "November Criminals." Someday Hitler would exact his terrible revenge.

At 5:10 a.m. on November 11 the Armistice was signed between the warring parties, in a railroad carriage that was parked in Compiègne, within earshot of the front lines. To give everyone enough time to contact all of their forces in the field, the terms of the agreement called for the cessation of all hostilities along the entire Western Front to take effect at precisely 11:00 a.m. that morning. Foch had picked that time because it was poetically the eleventh hour of the eleventh day of the eleventh month. After more than four years of bloody conflict, the Great War was finally over.

On November 11, 1918, Marshall Foch's armistice instructions arrived at 6:00 a.m. Neither the French nor British nor American commanding generals had issued any orders as to what was to be done in the meantime. Foch wanted to exact his revenge on the hated enemy right up to the last minute, while Pershing vociferously opposed any peace treaty at all; he wanted the war to continue until Germany was conquered and destroyed. British commander Sir Douglas Haig shared Foch's attitude that Germany should be punished for as long as it took. In the absence of any specific orders from the commander in chief as to what was to be done, decisions were left to the subordinate officers. Most of them, sensibly, ordered their troops to stand down. News of the ceasefire didn't reach some US units until about noon. Consequently, on that very day, AEF troops on the Western Front in France suffered more than 3,500 casualties, although it had been unofficially known at Allied command for two days that the fighting would end at 11:00 a.m. on November 11.

Almost a year later, on November 5, 1919, Gen. John J. Pershing, commander of the AEF, found himself testifying on the efficiency of the war's prosecution before the House of Representatives Committee on Military Affairs.

It was the AEF doughboys that had carried on the war with the most enthusiasm. American officers launched several different attacks that morning. At 4:00 a.m., the 5th Marine Division was ordered to cross the Meuse River on pontoon bridges, and they came under artillery and machine-gun fire. The marines suffered more than 1,100 casualties. The US Army's 89th Division was ordered to storm the town of Stenay because, the commander later explained, it had a number of bathhouses, and he didn't want the Germans to have them after the war was over. It cost the Americans 61 dead and 304 wounded to take Stenay. The African-American 92nd Division, a unit with white officers, had been scheduled to make an attack on the morning of November 11. When Gen. John Sherburne heard that the Armistice had been signed, he contacted his superiors to ask if the planned attack should be canceled.

He was told in no uncertain terms that the advance should proceed. The result, he bitterly declared, was "an absolutely needless waste of life."

In the 81st Division, the commanding officer ordered his men to stand down; at 10:40 a.m., less than half an hour before the war was to end, his superior countermanded that order and told the men to advance. The division lost 66 killed and 395 wounded. At 10:44 a.m., sixteen minutes before the end of the war, the 313th Regiment was ordered to clear out a German machine-gun post at the village of Ville-devant-Chaumont. As the American troops advanced, the Germans, in utter disbelief, first waved at them frantically, then fired over their heads to try to get them to stop, and finally in desperation fired a short burst directly at them. Pvt. Henry Gunter, who had arrived in the trenches four months ago, was struck in the head and died instantly. He was the last American killed in the war, at 10:59 a.m. But he was not the last soldier to die.

At 11:00 a.m., as the guns fell silent, a German junior officer named Tomas left his trench and approached a group of American troopers in No Man's Land to tell them that they could find shelter in the remains of the bombed-out house that he had been staying in. The Americans, however, had lost their field telephone and were not aware that the war was over. As Tomas approached, they shot him. It was 11:02 a.m.

In all, the six hours between the time the armistice was signed and the time it went into effect cost over 10,000 casualties on all sides, the French losing about 1,200 killed and wounded, the British, 2,400, the Americans, around 3,000, and the Germans, 4,100.

Col. Thomas Gowenlock served as an intelligence officer in the American 1st Division. He was on the front line that November morning, and wrote of his experience a few years later:

*On the morning of November 11, I sat in my dugout in Le Gros Faux, which was again our division headquarters, talking to our chief of staff, Col. John Greely, and Lt. Col. Paul Peabody, our G-1. A signal corps officer entered and handed us the following message: Official Radio from Paris, 6:01 a.m., Nov. 11, 1918. Marshal Foch to the Commander in Chief. 1) Hostilities will be stopped on the entire Front, beginning at eleven o'clock, November 11 (French hour); 2) The Allied troops will not go beyond the line reached at that hour on that date until further orders. [Signed], Marshal Foch, 5:45 a.m.*

*"Well, fini la guerre!" said Colonel Greely. "It sure looks like it," I agreed. "Do you know what I want to do now?" he said. "I'd like to get on one of those little horse-drawn canal boats in southern France and lie in the sun the rest of my life."*

*My watch said nine o'clock. With only two hours to go, I drove over to the bank of the Meuse River to see the finish. The shelling was heavy and, as I walked down the road, it grew steadily worse. It seemed to me that every battery in the world was trying to burn up its guns. At last eleven o'clock came, but the firing continued. The men on both sides had decided to give each other all they had—their farewell to arms. It was a very natural impulse after their years of war, but unfortunately, many fell after eleven o'clock that day.*

On November 11, 1918, in cities, towns, and villages throughout the world, jubilation and celebrations erupted as people began cheering, dancing in the streets, drinking copious amounts of alcohol, and welcoming the end of that terrible war. Meanwhile, the men who had endured the brutal fighting sat in their trenches and dugouts and spoke in hushed tones. Was it really all over? Many believed the Armistice was only a temporary measure and that the war would start up again sooner or later.

Not everyone celebrated. In millions of homes, hearts had been irreparably broken at the news that a loved one wouldn't be coming back. The empty place at the dinner table or the empty chair beside the hearth, children bereft of their fathers, wives bereft of their husbands, while mothers and fathers silently wept for the son that would never return. The boy that joined the army in a burst of patriotic fervor only to be blown to pieces, drowned in the mud, or have his bullet-riddled young body splayed on the barbed wire in No Man's Land. Then the endless parade of men missing limbs or hiding grotesquely disfigured faces behind porcelain masks. Did they feel like heroes? For some, the "war to end all wars" would never end.

# PART IV
# FRAGILE PEACE

# Chapter Fourteen

# A Monstrous Lie

AMERICA WOULD EMERGE FROM THE GREAT WAR AS A GLOBAL SUPER-power, assured of its place in the world. President Wilson would stand by his "Fourteen Points" plan announced on January 19, 1918, secure in the knowledge that it would provide a framework for what everyone hoped would be an equitable and enduring peace in Europe. The nations of the world would disarm, many would renounce their colonial claims, and the map of Europe would be revised so that all major ethnic groups, such as the Poles, Czechs, and Serbs, would each have their own self-governing nations. The war was over; empires had collapsed, and monarchies had been deposed. Wilson's visionary ambition now was to establish a League of Nations that would guarantee that the just provisions of this treaty would be enforced, by pledging themselves to protect one another from external attack by any aggressive country. It all sounded good on paper.

Negotiations between the Allied powers that would cement the peace began on January 18, 1919, in the Salle de l'Horloge at the French Foreign Ministry in Paris. In attendance were seventy delegates representing twenty-seven nations. Germany, Austria, and Hungary were excluded from the negotiations. Russia was also excluded because it had negotiated a separate peace with Germany in 1918. The terms of the treaty were punitive for the former Central Powers, and provided that the Rhineland would be occupied by Allied troops for a period of not less than fifteen years. Furthermore, it stipulated that former German emperor, Wilhelm II, would be tried as a war criminal with supreme offense against international morality. Article 231 (the "War Guilt Clause") laid sole responsibility for the war on Germany and her allies, making them accountable for all damage to civilian populations of the Allies. There was absolutely no ambiguity regarding article 227, which stipulated:

*The Allied and Associated Powers publicly arraign William II of Hohenzollern, formerly German Emperor, for a supreme offense against international morality and the sanctity of treaties.*

*A special tribunal will be constituted to try the accused, thereby assuring him the guarantees essential to the right of defense. It will be composed of five judges, one appointed by each of the following Powers: namely, the United States of America, Great Britain, France, Italy and Japan.*

*In its decision the tribunal will be guided by the highest motives of international policy, with a view to vindicating the solemn obligations of international undertakings and the validity of international morality. It will be its duty to fix the punishment, which it considers should be imposed.*

*The Allied and Associated Powers will address a request to the Government of the Netherlands for the surrender to them of the ex-Emperor in order that he may be put on trial.*

Germany would be compelled to yield control of its colonies, and lose numerous European territories. Most of the province of West Prussia would be ceded to the restored Poland, thereby granting it access to the Baltic Sea via the "Polish Corridor," which Prussia had annexed in the Partitions of Poland. This effectively transformed East Prussia into an exclave, separated from mainland Germany. The fertile agricultural pastures in the area of Eupen-Malmedy were given to Belgium as part of the war reparations, along with Alsace and much of Lorraine, which were both originally German-speaking territories.

Herein lay the tentative seeds of World War II. On August 1, 1923, a young, disillusioned World War I veteran named Adolf Hitler declared: "The day must come when a German government shall summon up the courage to declare to the foreign powers: 'The Treaty of Versailles is founded on a monstrous lie.' We fulfill nothing more. Do what you will!

If you want battle, look for it! Then we shall see whether you can turn seventy million Germans into serfs and slaves!"[1]

At the conclusion of the treaty signing, Clémenceau, acting on behalf of the Allied and Associated Powers, requested the extradition of the Kaiser from the Netherlands so that he could stand trial, but the Dutch government refused to cooperate, and consequently this request was politely refused. The Kaiser would die in exile in the Netherlands on June 4, 1941, at the age of eighty-two.

John Maynard Keynes, a respected British economist, resigned his position at the British Treasury in protest at the terms dictated in the treaty. He said, "I cannot leave this subject as though its just treatment wholly depended either on our own pledges or on economic facts. The policy of reducing Germany to servitude for a generation, of degrading the lives of millions of human beings, and of depriving a whole nation of happiness should be abhorrent and detestable, abhorrent and detestable, even if it were possible, even if it enriched ourselves, even if it did not sow the decay of the whole civilized life of Europe."[2]

This was, however, the potential beginning of a new Europe. Economic, monarchic, and social ties that once held European infrastructure together were now shattered and no longer legal tender. This fabric, woven over centuries, that once bound these nations had been ripped at the seams. Along the Western Front cities and villages had been reduced to unrecognizable smoldering ruins. It would take more than seventy years to repair the visible scars inflicted on some towns, such as Ypres. Recovering from the Great War would take time, but in late 1918, people were starving, and many were homeless. The overwhelming human capacity for mass slaughter, carnage, and destruction caused by this war had shocked the world to its core. Now, publicity-hungry politicians jostled for position to express their sincere desire for a lasting peace. Precisely how to organize and guarantee that fragile peace was another matter entirely.

George Frost Kennan, an American diplomat and historian, correctly asserted that "The vindictiveness of the British and French peace terms; the exclusion of Germany and Russia from the peace conferences; the economic miseries of the postwar years; the foolish attempts to draw the blood of reparations and war debts from the veins of the exhausted peoples of the continent—these phenomena all assured that only twenty years after its ending, Europe would stand confronted with the nightmare of Adolf Hitler at the peak of his power, and . . . usher in a second vast military conflagration."[3]

When the "Big Four" met at the Paris Peace Conference—namely, US president Woodrow Wilson; British prime minister David Lloyd George; French prime minister Georges Clémenceau; and Italian prime minister Vittorio Orlando—they had no interest in an unbiased peace. They demanded and expected that punitive retribution would be imposed on the Central Powers, in the process completely ignoring Woodrow Wilson's "Fourteen Points" plan. They did, however, approve of his plan for a League of Nations. When Wilson eventually presented the details of the Treaty of Versailles to Congress, it was vehemently rejected.

Senate majority leader and chairman of the Senate Foreign Relations Committee, Henry Cabot Lodge, voiced serious reservations about the treaty, and eventually sabotaged the notion of the League of Nations covenant by declaring the United States exempt from Article X, which, among other things, required the United States to respect the territorial integrity of member states. Cabot had an agenda when he attached amendments and conditions to the treaty that rendered the document null and void. Congress became beset with intransigence, and consequently, the United States failed to ratify the treaty, or join the League of Nations.

In 1919 Wilson suffered a debilitating stroke that incapacitated him for the remainder of his term. Republican Warren Harding replaced Wilson, and pledged to continue opposition to the League of Nations; moreover, he forecast its failure in the United States. After rejecting the Treaty of Versailles that resulted from the peace conference, the United States remained technically at war with Germany until a separate peace was signed in the summer of 1921.

Nguyen Tat Thanh, a devoted Nationalist, settled in Paris after the Great War. He gained renown as the author of a petition addressed to the Allies gathered at Versailles that demanded independence for all countries under colonial rule. This man would eventually adopt the pseudonym Ho Chi Minh.

In the course of history, the Treaty of Versailles would be blamed for hyperinflation, political assassinations, the Depression, failure to obtain reparation payments, the fall of the Weimar Republic, and the rise of fascism in Italy, Germany, and Japan. Germany finally finished paying its Great War reparations in 2010.

## LETTERS FROM DWIGHT HARRIS DE GROFF, QUARTERMASTER 3RD CLASS, USS *NEW YORK*

*Dear Mother,*
*Just a few lines to let you know I am well and thinking of you all, and hope you are all well. I will break the news, as you have already seen. I have the name of the place on this sheet where we have spent most of our time in foreign service. Today was a historical day for us, and no doubt will be put down in the history of the war. It all began last night at twelve o'clock. Up all hammocks and secure ship for sea. Now the division I am in has the bow or front of the ship, so our division, the 2nd and the 1st, which has the other half of the forecastle, are the only ones who had to get up. We had a sandwich and some "java," which was good—in other words, "a wee hour lunch." We got under way at 3:30 a.m. for mid-ocean, where we were to meet the German fleet. We had a very good day, as the fog, which had been too heavy for a week, cleared away. We met the German high seas fleet at 9:30 a.m. and convoyed them back to Rosyth, but we had fourteen-inch shells and powder in our guns, ready for them if they should "play us dirty." Please excuse language and writing, but I have so much to write that I must hurry it up to finish it before hammocks—7:30 p.m.*

### Germans Simply Surrendered
*Well, they didn't do a thing, just simply surrendered; in other words, "Kamerad," as they did on land. We anchored this afternoon at four o'clock in there, and the Germans stayed outside the nets, I don't know why. Believe me, they have some fleet, but they can't compare with*

*ours and the other four American dreadnoughts, as our ships, the Texas and New York, are the best-equipped battleships Uncle Sam has. The German ships are to be manned by British sailors and distributed later to different countries. There were 17 battleships, 150 submarines, and a bunch of destroyers and other "jiggers."*

*The King and Prince of Wales were aboard yesterday. The boys are getting ten-day leaves right along. I think we shall parade in London [on] Christmas, if not before; also in Paris. The USS Florida in our squadron leaves us Sunday for "sunny" USA. We never see a "sunny" day over here. Am enclosing a few pictures of German ships we brought in.*

## Lost in Fog, November 23, 1918

*We had liberty yesterday afternoon. So foggy that our boat got lost, and we just got back this morning at 9:30 with the grand fleet.*

## Expects President Wilson, November 24, 1918

*Well, here it is Sunday morning. Am going to finish your letter now or at least will try to. Last night I had started it, and twenty of us had to go on the beach to dig around a boat so we could get her off the ground when the tide came in. It went aground on account of the heavy fog, which has lasted for two weeks.*

*We had a hard winter over here last winter, as it was so cold, and every two weeks we had to convoy supply ships to Norway—"the land of the midnight sun"—and believe me, it is cold up there. Besides making these trips in sleet and rain and cold, we went out every so often, as they would receive a message that the German fleet was out. The convoy trips lasted five days without stopping the engines, and on these other trips we would maneuver for three or four days in the North Sea and come back here to Rosyth and coal ship. When the fellow coals ship all day and all night, he is pretty tired, but I got so I didn't mind.*

*We have two gold chevrons now, which we wear on our left sleeve, for foreign service, and I think the King of England will give us some kind of medal for our services with the grand fleet. The king sent his regards to the admiral today, thanking us for our services.*

*He is satisfied with the way the crew keeps the ship cleaned up and always ready to meet the Germany fleet with our fleet. I am going to enclose a souvenir from "Bonnie Scotland," as we can send them now. We must paint ship and clean her all up, as President Wilson will come aboard soon.*

## Chapter Fifteen

# Thanks to the Great War

The Great War saw the introduction of many firsts in technological, scientific, and societal innovations. Tanks, for instance, were invented as a means of breaking the trench-warfare stalemate. Chemical weapons in the form of deadly poison gases were used for the first time, leading quickly to the development of the first gas masks. It also witnessed the first genocide. On a positive note, the war also saw the introduction of blood banks, mobile X-rays, aerial photography, and the inclusion of women in the military.

It was during the war that sanitary napkins for women were first invented. When America officially entered the Great War, Kimberly-Clark started to mass-produce the padding for the purpose of using it for surgical dressing. Red Cross nurses assigned in the battlefields discovered that this product was remarkably absorbent, so they decided to use it for their own personal hygiene; hence, this seemingly innocent item brought great fortune to the once-small firm. Kimberly-Clark's new invention of sanitary napkins were branded "Kotex," which stood for "cotton texture." They became available to the public in October of 1920, only two short years after the Armistice.

World War I saw the introduction of air traffic control when the US Army installed the first operational two-way radios in planes. In 1917, a human voice was first transmitted by radio from a plane in flight to an operator on the ground. It also gave birth to the fighter pilot. Airplanes were deployed en masse for the first time in both air-to-air combat and reconnaissance missions, and 1st Lt. Eddie Rickenbacker would become recognized as America's most successful fighter ace. Charles Kettering designed the world's first drone, an unmanned "flying bomb," known as the Kettering Aerial Torpedo, or the "Kettering Bug." It included an onboard gyroscope, and could hit a target at a range of forty miles.

In the winter of 1918, almost half of all children living in Berlin were suffering from rickets, a condition usually caused by extreme and prolonged vitamin D deficiency whereby bones become soft and deformed. At the time, the exact cause was not known, although it was associated with poverty. Dr. Kurt Huldschinsky decided to conduct an experiment on four of the afflicted children, placing them under mercury-quartz lamps that emitted ultraviolet light. As the treatment continued, Huldschinsky noticed that the bones of his young patients were getting stronger. In May 1919, when the sun of summer arrived, he had them sit on the terrace in the sun. The results of his experiment, when published, were greeted with great enthusiasm. Children around Germany were brought before the lights. In Dresden, child welfare services had the city's streetlights dismantled so that the bulbs could be used for treating children. Researchers later discovered that vitamin D is necessary to build up bones with calcium, and that this process is triggered by ultraviolet light. The undernourishment brought on by war produced the knowledge to cure the ailment.

The idea of putting the clocks back, or daylight saving time, began in World War I. On April 30, 1916, Germany was experiencing a coal shortage, so the Reichstag decreed that clocks should be moved forward an hour to give an extra hour of daylight in the evening. It was the country's way of saving coal and light. However, other countries immediately adopted this practice. Within three weeks Britain had followed Germany's example, and other European countries followed suit. On March 19, 1918, American Congress went on to form several time zones, officially declaring daylight saving time two days later, until after World War I ended. Although the practice of daylight saving time was discarded at the end of the Great War, the idea had been favorably accepted, and was eventually revived.

Gideon Sundback, who worked at the Universal Fastener Company in Hoboken, New Jersey, designed the modern zipper in 1913. He received the official patent for his "separable fastener" in 1917. When World War I broke out, US forces, particularly in the navy, used them for the soldiers' uniforms and boots. Sundback's design increased the number of fastening elements to ten per inch, and included two rows of interlocking teeth that would latch together with the help of a slider. His design was the first fastener to resemble what we now know as a zipper.

The flamethrower (*Flammenwerfer*) was first used in an attack during the Great War on July 30, 1915, near the shattered village of Hooge on the Ypres salient. A backpack version of the same fearsome weapon carried by single soldiers was jointly developed by reserve army captain Bernhard Reddemann and engineer Richard Fiedler. Its true potential was only realized during trench warfare. After a massed assault on enemy lines, it wasn't uncommon for enemy soldiers to hole up in bunkers and dugouts hollowed into the side of the trenches. Unlike grenades, flamethrowers could neutralize (or rather, incinerate) enemy soldiers in these confined spaces without inflicting structural damage. Bunkers and trenches used to change hands quite frequently.

Professor Jean Perrin of the Sorbonne invented the geophone in 1915, for the purpose of detecting enemy tunneling. The apparatus consisted of two discs with mica membranes holding mercury and attached to a stethoscope. By placing the discs on the floor or walls of a tunnel, sounds were magnified two and a half times. A skilled listener could estimate how far away and how deep the German tunnels were, giving warning of the enemy's activity or enabling counter-mines to be dug. Soldiers in tunneling companies earned four times more than their surface comrades due to the obviously precarious nature of their dangerous work. British mining culminated in the simultaneous detonation of nineteen giant mines at Messines in June 1917, which entombed ten thousand Germans in the biggest explosion in human history, before Hiroshima, which was bombed on the orders of American Great War veteran Harry S. Truman.

As the Great War carried on, the British military attempted to find a better metal for their guns. The problem was that after repeated firing, the barrels of the guns became distorted from the friction and heat of bullets. Harry Brearley, a metallurgist at a Sheffield firm, was asked to produce more-resilient alloys. He examined the addition of chromium to steel, and, according to legend, threw away some of the results of his experiments as failures—literally, on the scrap heap. But Brearley noticed later that these discarded samples in the yard had not rusted. He had inadvertently discovered stainless steel.

## Chapter Sixteen

# Animal Heroes

ONE PARTICULAR UNSUNG HERO OF THE MEUSE-ARGONNE OFFENSIVE was "Mutt," a courageous French bulldog that during some of the heaviest fighting carried boxes of cigarettes to frontline troops. YMCA workers would tie cartons around Mutt, and he would accompany runners to the front lines, where his visits delighted soldiers. Mutt was wounded twice, and spent most of the Great War boosting the morale of the US 11th Engineers. When the war ended most animal mascots were left behind, but the indomitable Mutt was informally adopted by one of the soldiers and smuggled on board a US troopship. Halfway across the Atlantic he was discovered by a sergeant, who threatened to throw him overboard. When he heard the story of what Mutt had done for the troops, he relented, and the dog was allowed to finish the rest of his journey in peace. He arrived in New York harbor with the 11th Engineers and spent the rest of his days as an honored guest of the United States.

Another canine hero of the AEF was "Rags." Sgt. Jimmy Donovan befriended this stray dog that he found on the streets of Paris. Rags became the mascot of the 1st Division. Much more than a scruffy face and a wagging tail, he learned to carry messages through gunfire, locate broken communications wire for the Signal Corps to repair, and alert soldiers to incoming shells, saving the lives of hundreds of American soldiers. He was wounded along with his guardian at the Meuse-Argonne. Despite being in almost constant danger, Rags brought inspiration to men with little hope, especially in the bitter last days of the war.

The most decorated dog in the Great War was undoubtedly the one found by Pvt. J. Robert Conroy while training for combat on the fields of Yale University in 1917. He named the pup "Stubby" because of his short tail, and soon the dog became the mascot of the 102nd Infantry, 26th Yankee Division. Stubby learned to recognize bugle calls, and could even perform a modified dog salute. Such was the positive effect on the morale of the Yankee Division soldiers that the dog was allowed to remain in the camp, even though as a rule animals were forbidden. When the division shipped out for France aboard the SS *Minnesota*, Private Conroy smuggled Stubby aboard. Hidden in the coal bin until the ship was far at sea, Stubby was brought out on deck where the sailors were soon won over by the canine soldier.

When the Yankee Division headed for the front lines in France, Stubby was given special orders, allowing him to accompany the division as their official mascot. The 102nd Infantry reached the front lines on February 5, 1918. Stubby soon became accustomed to the sounds of war. When he was injured due to gas exposure, he was taken to a nearby field hospital where he was nursed back to health. The injury gave him a particular sensitivity to any trace of gas that would inevitably come in handy. One fateful morning while most of the troops were asleep, the Germans lobbed over some gas shells. Stubby immediately sprang into action and ran through the trench, barking and biting at the soldiers, rousing them to sound the gas alarm, saving many from injury. During the course of his service Stubby developed a unique talent for locating wounded men in No Man's Land. He would listen attentively for the sound of anyone speaking English and then go to their location, barking until medics arrived, or he would lead the lost soldiers back to the safety of the trenches.

Stubby even managed to catch a German soldier in the act of mapping the layout of the Allied trenches. The soldier called to Stubby, but he put his ears back and began to bark. As the German ran, Stubby bit him on the legs, causing the soldier to trip and fall. He continued to attack the man until some doughboys arrived. For this remarkable feat Stubby was put in for a promotion to the rank of sergeant by the commander of the 102nd Infantry, becoming the first dog to actually be given rank in the

AEF. Sometime later, Stubby was injured during a grenade attack, receiving a large amount of shrapnel in his chest and leg. He was rushed to a field hospital and later transferred to a Red Cross Recovery Hospital for additional surgery. When Stubby became well enough to move around at the hospital, he visited wounded soldiers, boosting their morale. By the end of the war, Stubby had served in seventeen battles.

When he returned to the United States he led the American troops in a pass in review parade, and later visited with President Woodrow Wilson. This incredible canine was awarded many medals for his heroism, including a medal from the Humane Society that was presented by Gen. John Pershing. He was awarded a membership in the American Legion and the YMCA. When his master, J. Robert Conroy, began studying law at Georgetown University, Stubby became the mascot of the Georgetown Hoyas. He died in 1926.

Probably the most famous canine to emerge from the Great War was Hollywood legend Rin Tin Tin, who was born on a battlefield in the Meuse Valley, in eastern France, in September 1918. The precise date of his birth has never been ascertained, but when Corp. Leland Leroy Duncan found the puppy on September 15, it can't have been more than couple of weeks old.

Corp. Leland Duncan was among the first three hundred Americans sent to France as a member of the 135th Air Squadron, a corps observation (reconnaissance) squadron that took part in the battles at Saint-Mihiel and the Meuse-Argonne. According to his obituary, "[Duncan] had charge of the squadron's ordnance, and was the first American to synchronize machine-gun fire through aircraft propellers." Wounded in action and awarded the Purple Heart, Corporal Duncan was honorably discharged from the US Army on May 26, 1919. In World War II he personally trained more than five thousand war dogs for the army.

Director Steven Spielberg recognized the potential of one particular animal legend when he directed *War Horse*. Although fictional, the story is based on fact, and serves as a kind of metaphor for all the horses that participated in the Great War. It is estimated that between 1914 and 1917, one thousand horses per day were transported from the United States to England for the war effort. Many of these horses were half-wild, tousle-maned, and shoeless. Despite their flaws, however, they were resilient animals, and particularly suited to the variety of weather conditions they would experience during the war that cost the lives of roughly eight million horses and countless mules and donkeys. After the war, most of the horses were sold to butchers on the mainland, considered unusable for any other practical purpose.

One of the stories that may have inspired author Michael Morpurgo to write *War Horse* was that of a foal born on the Isle of Wight in 1908, called Warrior. This horse went to war on the Western Front with Winston Churchill's great friend, Gen. Jack Seely, in 1914. He survived every imaginable disaster, and was active in many famous battles, including those at the Somme and Ypres. Warrior returned to England four years later, in 1918, where he lived with his owner, Jack Seely, on his native Isle of Wight, reaching the grand old age of thirty-three. Warrior even won a point-to-point one year almost to the day after he had led one of the last great cavalry charges of the Great War, at Moreuil Wood. His obituary in the *Evening Standard* in 1941 was titled "The Horse the Germans Could Not Kill."

During the Meuse-Argonne Offensive, 442 pigeons were used to carry hundreds of messages. Probably the most famous of all the carrier pigeons was one named Cher Ami, which means "dear friend" in French. Cher Ami spent several months on the front lines during the fall of 1918. He flew twelve important missions to deliver messages, but perhaps the most important was the one he delivered on October 4, 1918, for the famous "Lost Battalion," dispatched by its commander, Charles Whittlesey.

As Cher Ami tried to fly back home, the Germans saw him rising out of the brush and opened fire. For several minutes, bullets zipped through the air all around him. For a moment it looked like the little pigeon was going to fall—that he wasn't going to make it. The ill-fated battalion saw their hopes spiraling to the ground, but Cher Ami managed to recover and fly beyond the range of the enemy guns to deliver his vital message.

On his last mission, Cher Ami was badly wounded. When he finally reached his coop, a soldier discovered the pigeon lying on his back, covered in blood. He had been blinded in one eye, his leg was hanging off, and a bullet had hit his breastbone. This little hero of the 77th Infantry Division gradually recovered, and when French Army commanders heard about his exploits, they awarded him the French Croix de Guerre with Gold Palm. The men of the division carved a small wooden leg for him. When Cher Ami was well enough to travel, the little one-legged hero was put on a boat to the United States, where the story of Cher Ami became a media sensation, and he became one of the most famous animal heroes of the Great War.

## Chapter Seventeen

# Survivors

As soon as the Armistice had been signed, Pershing initiated preparations to bring the doughboys home. Transporting all of these men and women back to the United States with the least possible delay was going to be no easy task. The Services of Supply was promptly reorganized to execute the intricate details that this operation would eventually demand. At the end of November, approximately 25,500 had sailed home, and by the end of the year, the number had grown to roughly 124,000—a mere fraction of the two million that had made their way to France. Some would be obliged to stay a bit longer. The 3rd Army assumed occupation duties commencing on December 1, 1918, in the region around Koblenz, between Luxembourg and the Rhine River. Eight US divisions organized into three corps participated in the occupation of Germany. The last 1,000 AEF troops from these occupation forces didn't depart until January 24, 1923.

Scores of the wounded were among those initially repatriated, and tragically, further deaths ensued when many of those who had been gassed succumbed to the devastating Spanish influenza pandemic that occurred in 1918. Having been gassed made their lungs more susceptible to this strain of flu, which severely afflicted the body's respiratory function. The AEF and the influenza pandemic were inextricably linked. The virulent virus traveled with military personnel from camp to camp, eventually making its way across the Atlantic. Between September and November of 1918, it is estimated that around 40 percent of US Army and Navy personnel succumbed to this virus. During the AEF campaign at the Meuse-Argonne, the pandemic was responsible for diverting urgently needed resources from the front lines. Influenza and pneumonia killed more American soldiers and sailors during the war than enemy weapons.

Then there was another debilitating condition to consider. The term *shell shock* first appeared in the British medical journal *The Lancet* in February 1915, and it would come to define the phenomenon we now recognize as post-traumatic stress disorder, more commonly known by its acronym, PTSD.

About 50 to 60 percent of AEF soldiers were returned to frontline duty within a week. This was common among all combatants during the Great War. These were times when society's zeitgeist proliferated masculine norms that preferred the "suffering in silence" ethic in men rather than the reporting of mental health problems. Some commanders, medical personnel, and soldiers sincerely believed that the outward expression of mental health symptoms was a sign of weakness, and even cowardice.

Numerous battle reports made reference to soldiers collapsing or becoming hysterical from the strain of continuous artillery bombardments. What compounded the condition was the horrific sight of bodies blown to bits, having to wear uncomfortable gas masks for hours, and, in many cases, sheer exhaustion. The 78th Division reported that after enduring twenty-four-hour-long bombardments during the three straight weeks they spent along the front lines in the Meuse-Argonne campaign, some soldiers "went into shock," or lapsed into comas from which they could not be roused. Corp. Paul Murphy later recalled: "These shell-shock victims fell down as if they had been hit, but actually they hadn't been touched; they were completely helpless, mumbling and trembling at each new explosion." Mutism and speech disorders were the most common form of war neurosis. At the time these afflictions were thought to be symptoms of a soldier's repressed aggression toward his superior officers.

Despite overwhelming obvious evidence to the contrary, the army refused to consider shell shock a legitimate war injury. According to the chief surgeon of the Medical Department, "the so-called 'shell-shock' patients are no more entitled to a 'wound' chevron than are soldiers who are seized with an acute medical complaint due to exposure in battle, to the elements, or to bad water or indigestible food." Men diagnosed with shell shock suffered from nightmares and panic attacks. Some could not sleep or speak. One doughboy arrived at the base hospital in such poor condition that the sound of a spoon dropping sent him frantically searching for cover under his bed. After resting and eating well for a few days, however, he returned to his unit.

Most soldiers who suffered from shell shock or battle exhaustion voluntarily returned to the Front after a few days' rest in a field hospital. If rest and food were not enough to convince men to take this step once the tremors had stopped and speech and memory returned, field psychiatrists played a coercive role in inducing these victims to return on the premise that they were "letting down their country" if they refused, or because "their comrades needed them." They usually added that the glory of victory would be lost to them forever if they failed to return to the Front.

In many cases the soldiers responded favorably to these appeals to their honor, masculinity, duty, and ambition, but whether they had recovered or been cured of their condition was another question entirely. Three out of every five beds in government hospitals were filled in the interwar period with veterans suffering from shell shock. Anecdotal evidence also underscores that many veterans experienced great difficulty forgetting the wartime horrors they had witnessed. Three years after returning home, for instance, many soldiers noted that they were still fighting the war in their dreams. Many other veterans described themselves as nervous, jumpy, and unstable for years afterward. When one particular soldier returned from the hell of the Western Front, he didn't sleep in a bed for almost twenty years, preferring the carpet in front of the hearth. That man was author Martin King's grandfather.

## O'NEIL BILODEAU, COMPANY C, 311TH INFANTRY 78TH DIVISION

O'Neil Bilodeau initially joined the French Army in the 26th Dragoons Regiment where he fought for a year. He later joined the US Army and fought in the Saint-Mihiel Offensive and the Meuse-Argonne campaign.

**Berkshire Evening Eagle**, *July 14, 1936: "O'Neil Bilodeau, Son of Mr. and Mrs. Peter Bilodeau, Was in Government Hospital for Years. Leaves Home While Mother Visits Husband at Hospital"*

*O'Neil Bilodeau, veteran of World War fighting, has disappeared from his home. Police of two states have been notified, and Saturday night WGY sent out a broadcast for his return or information leading to his whereabouts. He is described by his mother as being fairly tall, thirty-nine years old, weighing about two hundred pounds, with broad shoulders. When last seen Saturday afternoon he wore brown trousers and had a white shirt with a light brown stripe. He wore no hat or coat, as far as is known. He never swings his arms when walking and his legs are not strong. Peter Bilodeau, his father, is seventy years of age. For twenty-two years he has been an employee of the city, but is now seriously ill at Hillcrest Hospital. It was while Mrs. Bilodeau was visiting her husband that O'Neil disappeared. When she left home he was sitting on the back steps. A friend at the house said that he remained there for some time after her departure and presently was gone.*

*O'Neil Bilodeau has not been well since returning from the war. When Germany and France locked horns in 1914, he joined the French Army and fought through the early part of the conflict. Sick, he was returned to his home, but having recovered, he enlisted and served in France with the 76th Division. It was during the last days of fighting that he was shell-shocked and gassed. Since that time he has been under the care of the government practically all the time. For nearly four years he was at the Northampton Veterans Hospital, but a year and a half ago he came to his home here, where his mother had been caring for him. He has suffered from depression, his mother says, and continually broods on the fact that he is unable to work. Three months ago he left home but returned within twenty-four hours. It is thought that if he wandered far, he headed toward New York State, where his thoughts seemed to lie most of the time.*

**Berkshire Evening Eagle,** *July 31, 1936: "Missing Shell-Shocked War Veteran Found in Hospital in Middle West"*

*O'Neil Bilodeau, who disappeared from his home here three weeks ago, wanders to Detroit. Refuses to talk to hospital authorities, mother here learns—wide search found her son.*

*O'Neil Bilodeau, shell-shocked World War veteran, who has been missing for nearly three weeks from the home of his parents, has been found. A telegram was received early this afternoon by Mrs. Bilodeau, stating that her son was in Eloise Hospital, Detroit, Michigan. The telegram was signed by Dr. P. K. Kruber. Immediately upon receiving the telegram, Mrs. Bilodeau communicated by long-distance telephone with hospital officials at Detroit. She learned from them that her son had been found wandering on the streets. He would not talk much, but gave his name and address. The hospital authorities said that he appeared to be in good condition physically, and was not suffering from exposure or lack of food. Mrs. Bilodeau or some member of the family will go to Detroit later in the week and bring the young man back to this city.*

*O'Neil Bilodeau disappeared from his Bradford Street home Saturday, noon, July 12, and has not been seen by his parents since. Local and state police were notified, as well as police in New York State. Notice of his disappearance was broadcast over the radio on successive nights from radio station WGY at Schenectady, New York. Bilodeau was last seen by local people near the Runnals garage in West Pittsfield. He was walking on the main highway to Albany, New York. His parents thought he might be found in berry fields or woods near Richmond, and a search was carried on there by friends of the family, without results.*

British lieutenant general Sir Aylmer Hunter-Weston coldly stated that "Cowards constituted a danger to the war effort, and the sanction of the death penalty was designed to frighten men more than the prospects of facing the enemy." Men who presented symptoms of war neurosis were often disciplined through military justice, and in some cases in the

British Army, they were sentenced to death. As the war continued and the number of cases of war neurosis increased, treatment plans began to evolve. In 2006, the British minister of defense posthumously pardoned all 306 British World War I soldiers who were executed for desertion or cowardice.

In 1917, when the United States prepared for war, they made use of British experience in determining treatment methods for shell shock, also known as war neurosis. In an attempt to gain a better understanding of this condition, the AEF asked Dr. Thomas Salmon and other leading psychiatrists to develop a neuropsychiatric service plan for the army. After observing French and British centers, Dr. Salmon returned home and suggested that war neurosis be treated as close to the battle lines as possible. Almost 70,000 US men were permanently evacuated from the line, while more than 36,000 were hospitalized for long periods from its effects. All told, 158,994 doughboys were psychiatrically inactivated for some time, and 1,000 of them were recorded as having committed suicide. Military and societal ignorance of the effects of this condition often culminated in tragic events.

### Berkshire County Eagle, *September 30, 1931: "Youth Takes Own Life with Gun"*

*Arthur J. Burns, 29, had been melancholy for some weeks, ill for the past month, and despondent because of an infection in the index finger of his right hand which ultimately brought about the amputation of that member. Burns committed suicide by shooting himself in the yard of his home, 33 Monroe Street, last evening. Burns used a revolver, firing the bullet through his head. His body was discovered shortly after eight o'clock. The young man, who was employed by Goodbody & Company, brokers, had been attended at Hillcrest Hospital for the past month for the infected finger, which was amputated several days ago.*

*He had been working up to the time of his death, but had been melancholy for some weeks. Burns was born in this city and had always lived here. He was well known, and his many friends were shocked at the tragic occurrence of last night. He had planned to attend a church service with a group of friends during the early evening but failed to put in an appearance. The members of the group, Miss Eleanor M. Hynes, Miss Marion Coughter, Miss Julia McMahon of this city, and James F. Flynn of Lenox, went to the Burns home shortly after eight o'clock and discovered his body. Police captain John H. Hines responded to the emergency call with officers Camille Marcel and Michael Callahan.*

*The captain notified Dr. Henry Colt, medical examiner, who viewed the body and gave permission for its removal to the Meehan Funeral Home. Burns is survived only by his mother, Mrs. Anna Burns, widow of Thomas J. Burns, who was killed in a railroad accident at Richmond two years ago.*

**Funeral Notice**

*October 1, 1931. Veteran of World War Arthur J. Burns of 33 Monroe Street, whose funeral will be held at 8:30 tomorrow morning at the St. Mark's church, was a World War veteran. Despite his youth, Burns enlisted in the United States Navy during the war. Burial will take place in St. Joseph's Cemetery.*

British poet Wilfred Owen was treated for shell shock at Craig Lockhart War Hospital near Edinburgh, before being returned to the Front. He summed up the condition with this excellent poem:

### Mental Cases

*Who are these? Why sit they here in twilight?*
*Wherefore rock they, purgatorial shadows,*
*Drooping tongues from jaws that slob their relish,*
*Baring teeth that leer like skulls' teeth wicked?*
*Stroke on stroke of pain—but what slow panic,*
*Gouged these chasms round their fretted sockets?*
*Ever from their hair and through their hands' palms*
*Misery swelters. Surely we have perished*
*Sleeping, and walk hell; but who these hellish?*
*These are men whose minds the Dead have ravished.*

*Memory fingers in their hair of murders,*
*Multitudinous murders they once witnessed.*
*Wading sloughs of flesh these helpless wander,*
*Treading blood from lungs that had loved laughter.*
*Always they must see these things and hear them,*
*Batter of guns and shatter of flying muscles,*
*Carnage incomparable, and human squander*
*Rucked too thick for these men's extrication.*
*Therefore still their eyeballs shrink tormented*
*Back into their brains, because on their sense*
*Sunlight seems a blood-smear; night comes blood-black;*
*Dawn breaks open like a wound that bleeds afresh.*
*—Thus their heads wear this hilarious, hideous,*
*Awful falseness of set-smiling corpses.*
*—Thus their hands are plucking at each other;*
*Picking at the rope-knots of their scourging;*
*Snatching after us who smote them, brother,*
*Pawing us who dealt them war and madness.*

Wilfred Owen was killed on November 4, 1918, while attempting to lead his men across the Sambre-Oise canal at Ors. He was twenty-five years old. The sad news reached his parents on November 11, Armistice Day. There were those young Americans who returned, staring with hollow eyes, whose nights were plagued with abominable nightmares, and those who flinched when a car backfired or a firecracker popped. These were the mortally afflicted whose wounds were not always apparent. They tried to pick up the threads of their former lives, and although many succeeded, many succumbed. Their lives would be blighted by what they'd seen and done. The gentler souls who had no resources to fight and kill, but were compelled to—they were never cowards. The men who internalized the experiences were the ones who survived, but there were those who couldn't, who refused to digest the horrific reality of the Great War. They were referred to as shell-shocked, bomb-happy, or just plain crazy, depending on their rank. For many of them, the agony and tragedy of war would endure until they died.

# FOREST E. DAMON, COMPANY L, 104TH INFANTRY BATTALION, 26TH INFANTRY DIVISION

## Berkshire Eagle, *May 22, 1946*

*The body of Forest E. Damon, 60, of 1 Naples Street, a mechanic employed by the Boston & Albany Railroad, and veteran of World War I, was recovered in the east branch of the Housatonic River, near the GE dump this morning. Dr. Albert C. England, medical examiner, said death was caused by drowning. Damon had been missing from his home since Saturday, when he told his wife to inform his foreman at the railroad junction that he would not be at work that night. A General Electric Company employee saw the body on the north side of the river, south of Newell Street, this morning shortly after 8:00 a.m., and notified police. A detail of officers under the direction of Capt. Camille L. Marcel recovered the body, which was later removed to Newton and Barnfather's Funeral Home. Mr. Damon, who had been employed by the Boston & Albany Railroad for twenty-three years, was born in Northampton, Massachusetts, February 27, 1886, but lived in Pittsfield many years. Prior to going with the B & A, he was employed as a car inspector by the Boston & Maine for six years. He was a member of the Pittsfield Post, American Legion.*

## Chapter Eighteen

# World War I Films and Video Games

### Films
### *The Lost Battalion* (2001)

THE STORY OF THE CARRIER PIGEON CHER AMI WAS MENTIONED IN chapter 16, and the men that he saved by delivering that vitally important message have since appeared in a feature movie titled *The Lost Battalion*. The A&E Original movie recounts the heroic story of how Major Whittlesey and around five hundred men were trapped on the side of the hill in the Argonne Forest. They were completely surrounded by German soldiers and cut off from their regiment. By the second day only a little more than two hundred men were still alive or unwounded. Whittlesey dispatched several pigeons to inform his commanders of the gravity of the situation, but didn't get a response. All hopes rested on one last pigeon, Cher Ami, who succeeded in delivering information to HQ.

In the course of the afternoon American artillery had attempted to provide support for the isolated battalion by lobbing hundreds of big artillery rounds into the ravine. Unfortunately, they didn't have the correct coordinates, and many of the shells landed right on top of Whittlesey and his men, making a bad situation even worse. Major Whittlesey summoned a doughboy to bring him his last pigeon, Cher Ami. He wrote a quick and simple note, telling the men who directed the artillery guns where the Americans were located, and asking them to stop. The note that was put in the canister on Cher Ami's left leg simply read:

We are along the road parallel to 276.4.

Our own artillery is dropping a barrage directly on us.

For heaven's sake, stop it.

Although the movie script is relatively faithful to the actual story, obviously there is some poetic license involved. While a few scenes are entirely contrived for dramatic purposes, they don't detract from the actual story too much.

Whittlesey never asserted that his objective was suicide, but he did protest that his men were worn-out and needed rest. During the first day of the offensive, Whittlesey reached his objective, but discovered the next morning that his battalion was surrounded. Some carrier pigeon messages would have reached HQ, but they were unable to break through the German cordon and get reinforcements to Whittlesey and his men. When American artillery began bombing his location, he did indeed use Cher Ami, his last carrier pigeon, to tell HQ to stop the shelling.

The movie's depiction of General Alexander as a manipulative, heartless man who deliberately lied to Whittlesey simply to ensure that he could tell his superiors that one of his battalions had reached its objectives, is very misleading indeed. Also, the assertion that the action of this battalion helped to end the war is frankly rather silly. The scriptwriters also need a tap on the fingers for giving Whittlesey the abominable line, "Hold on, because this might end the war."

The character of Maj. Heinrich Prinz is very loosely based on Lt. Heinrich Prinz, a German officer who had been assigned to interrogate captured soldiers because he had lived in the United States for several years. This is entirely possible, but Prinz had no authority during the actual battle. All in all, it is a good, entertaining movie that misses some serious location details but conveys the story adequately. While commendably accurate, it does fall prey to typical cinematic hyperbole. It conveys the story well, but has a tendency to overstate the significance of the battalion's achievement; overall, well worth watching.

Charles Whittlesey was a deeply troubled man. Like the PTSD victims of the last chapter, he struggled to make sense of his experiences. Outwardly he maintained the stance of a stoic war hero, but inwardly he was battling some serious demons. On November 24, 1921, just three short years after the end of the Great War, Whittlesey booked passage from New York to Havana aboard the USS *Toloa*, a steamship. On

November 26, the first night out from New York, Whittlesey dined with the captain and then retired for the evening, around 11:15 p.m. It was noted that he was in high spirits. Whittlesey was never seen again.

He was reported missing the next morning. It is presumed that he committed suicide by jumping overboard, although no one had seen him jump, and his body was never recovered.

Several theories existed at the time as to what had pushed Whittlesey to such depths of depression. Those close to him believed that his death could be counted among war casualties inasmuch as it was his sensitivity to the constant reminders of the destruction of the war that drove him to eventual suicide. Some believed that his suicide was caused by feelings of guilt: the possibility that he had given incorrect coordinates to the "Pocket," thereby causing friendly fire, or having refused to surrender to the Germans, leading to increased loss among his men. Others believed that it was his modesty and inability to adjust to the life of a hero that caused the depression that eventually ended his life. Whatever the exact reason may have been, it is clear that Whittlesey's death was indirectly related to the unhappiness which befell him after his experiences in the war. His friends and comrades never forgot him.

### *Sergeant York* (1941)

This man of humble beginnings was eventually hailed as America's greatest hero. Pershing referred to him as "the greatest civilian soldier of World War I." When he died in 1964, President Lyndon Johnson issued a statement calling York "a symbol of American courage and sacrifice, who epitomized the gallantry of American fighting men and their sacrifices in behalf of freedom."

Alvin York arrived in France on May 21, 1918. His unit first saw major action during the Saint-Mihiel drive in September 1918. By this time York had been promoted to the rank of corporal and given command of a squad. Then, his division—the "All American" 82nd—moved on to the Argonne Forest. He earned his reputation on October 8, 1918, when the division went into action, reaching, and holding, positions against repeated German counterattacks. Situated astride a major road and light railway on the crest of a ridge, they held this position and denied the German Army in the Argonne Forest access to two hugely important lines of supply and communication.

During the night of October 8, the 82nd Division replaced the 28th Division at the Front, and in the course of the following two days, they dislodged the retreating Germans from the wooded heights. It was during the intense fighting at this location that Pvt. 1st Class Alvin Cullum York earned his reputation. As his regiment advanced across the valley beyond Hill 223, it was subjected to withering fire from machine guns placed on the wooded slope at the left end of the valley. York was one of a seventeen-man patrol instructed to get up the hill, circumnavigate the machine guns, and hopefully silence them.

Surreptitiously edging their way through the woods behind the enemy line, the patrol surprised a German battalion commander and a large group of men in a clearing. The American patrol opened fire, and within moments, most of the Germans had thrown up their hands to surrender. No sooner had this occurred that a number of German rifles and machine guns, on a hillside just a short distance away, opened fire, killing and wounding nine of the patrol. While the other members of the patrol took cover and then occupied themselves guarding the captured German soldiers, York, who was at that time in closest proximity to the firing, assumed command. Later Sergeant York wrote in his diary:

*There were about thirty of them. They were commanding us from a hillside less than thirty yards away. They couldn't miss. And they didn't! Those machine guns were spitting fire and cutting down the undergrowth all around me something awful. I didn't have time to dodge behind a tree or dive into the brush; I didn't even have time to kneel or lie down. As soon as the machine guns opened fire on me, I began to exchange shots with them. In order to sight me or to swing their machine guns on me, the Germans had to show their heads above the trench, and every time I saw a head I just touched it off. All the time I kept yelling at them to come down. I didn't want to kill any more than I had to. But it was they or I. And I was giving them the best I had.*

*Suddenly a German officer and five men jumped out of the trench
and charged me with fixed bayonets. I changed to the old automatic
and just touched them off, too. I touched off the sixth man first, then the
fifth, then the fourth, then the third, and so on. I wanted them to keep
coming. I didn't want the rear ones to see me touching off the front
ones. I was afraid they would drop down and pump a volley into me.*

York kept firing at the Germans single-handedly, maintaining this
fire until he had killed more than fifteen of them, forcing the remainder
to surrender. Forming the prisoners in a column, York distributed the
seven remaining men of his patrol along it and started back to the American lines with the German battalion commander in front of him. More
Germans were encountered along the way and were forced to surrender.
York returned to his regiment with 3 wounded Americans and 132 prisoners, among whom were 5 German officers. Thanks to York's exceptional
courage and clear thinking, his regiment was able to continue its advance.
The account of what happened that day was meticulously documented.
For his exceptional exploits Alvin York was awarded the Medal of Honor.

In 1941, the story of Alvin York was made into a movie starring
Hollywood icon Gary Cooper, who won an Academy Award for his
portrayal. The movie itself was nominated for eleven Academy Awards.
Alvin York worked on this movie as a historical consultant and adviser,
and ensured that the locations chosen were as accurate as possible to the
real places. The fictional York family is comprised of the doting Mother
York, Alvin, and a younger brother and sister, residing in a relatively
spacious single-room house. The real York family had eleven children,
although the two eldest sons had already left home when Alvin joined up.

There are a couple of scenes in the film where York drinks at a saloon
that had the Tennessee–Kentucky state line running right through the
middle. Apparently the Tennessee men would drink on the Kentucky
side of the saloon, and the Kentucky men on the Tennessee side, so that
the owner would not have to pay taxes. The movie suggests that the reason behind York's decision to stop drinking was to earn enough money to
buy a farm and marry his sweetheart, Gracie, whom he used to meet in
secret because of her parents' disapproval of York. In truth, the actual cou-

ple's courtship only began after York had relinquished alcohol. Although it isn't really shown in the movie, York was a wild borderline alcoholic in his early life. He frequently got into bar fights, and was actually arrested on several occasions.

York's family was devoutly religious, and although the movie reflects this to some extent, it also opts to focus on the romantic element, which was intended to give it a wider appeal. Or was it? The Warner brothers who produced this movie were Jewish. They preferred to play down the overtly religious elements of York's personal story. The "turkey shoot" is accurately depicted in the film. There are rumors that York was shocked into sobriety by the death of a friend in a bar fight, although these have never been substantiated. One particular scene where his captain and company commander try to convince York to accept a promotion to corporal is extremely faithful to the actual events. This also applies to the ten-day furlough that York was given to think things over, although apparently there was no overt sign from God as depicted in the movie, just York's conscience.

The actual fighting in the Argonne is very precise and true to the actual events. Granted, there is no CGI (computer-generated imagery), dismembered bodies, or huge special effects, but that aside, the depiction of the story is incredibly well done. The No Man's Land set was constructed by three hundred workers, and during the filming they used five tons of dynamite and defoliated four hundred trees. In the movie York uses a 1903 Springfield, but the whole division would have been supplied with British 1917 Enfield rifles. The actual firearm used by York to dispose of a line of seven Germans was not a Luger, as shown, but rather a 1911 .45 ACP automatic. The Luger was preferred for the film because they couldn't get the .45 to fire blanks.

Sergeant York did indeed return to a hero's welcome in the United States; even the detail showing the picture of Mother York in his room at the Waldorf-Astoria was correct. A huge number of endorsement offers piled in, but they were all rejected because York refused to profit from killing. He didn't get the "dream home" at the point it was shown in the film (at the end)—that didn't happen until many years later—but it made a good ending for what is on the whole an extremely accurate and convincing movie. Gary Cooper was chosen to play the role of Alvin York by the man himself. Cooper was initially reluctant to play the part, due to the twenty-five-year age gap between him and Joan Leslie, who played Gracie. The actual age gap between York and his eventual wife was thirteen years. Cooper was almost forty when he played the role, ten years older than York; nevertheless, he brought a unique sensitivity, almost a naiveté, to the role that was incredibly convincing.

The movie premiered in September 1941, but a Senate committee forced it to be withdrawn after a month, saying that Hollywood was trying to coerce the United States into entering a war it didn't want. This picture was shown on the deck of the USS *Enterprise* to the officers and crew on the evening of Saturday, December 6, 1941, when the carrier was anchored off Hawaii. The next day the Japanese attack on Pearl Harbor brought the United States into World War II, and all bets were off. When *Sergeant York* reopened in 1942, everything had changed. The criticism had dissipated, and it became the highest-grossing film of the year. There were even stories circulating at the time of young men leaving the movie theaters after seeing the film and immediately signing up.

In 1952 York suffered a cerebral hemorrhage and became bedridden. He died at the Veterans Hospital in Nashville, Tennessee, on September 2, 1964. After a funeral service in his Jamestown church, with Gen. Matthew Ridgway representing President Lyndon Johnson, York was buried at the Wolf River Cemetery in Pall Mall.

### *The Fighting 69th* (1940)

This movie, directed by William Keighley, is loosely based on the exploits of New York City's famous 69th Infantry regiment during World War I. It has an all-star cast including James Cagney, Pat O'Brien, George Brent, Jeffrey Lynn, Alan Hale, Frank McHugh, Dennis Morgan, Dick Foran, and William Lundigan. With a cast like this, you can only expect the best, and this movie delivers precisely that. Pat O'Brien, renowned for donning the cloth to portray priests in a number of movies, plays Father Duffy, basically the stoic patriarch of the unit, the man the troops could turn to for solace and sound advice. George Brent portrays Maj. "Wild Bill" Donovan, the officer who keeps the men in line and harbors a particular dislike for main character, Pvt. Jerry Plunkett, played by James Cagney. Cagney plays Cagney, as he always did, but he did it so well that it's remarkably convincing. He comes across as a smart-mouthed, tough-talking New Yorker from Brooklyn with a strong instinct for self-preservation that initially manifests as cowardice.

The movie depicts Plunkett's transformation from a sneering, scowling chicken to a hero. One particular actor, Jeffrey Lynn, plays poet Sgt. Joyce Kilmer, the base's local celebrity, who even gets asked to sign books. The manner in which Lynn portrays the character of Joyce Kilmer is magnificently underplayed and ultimately convincing, as Jeffrey Lynn always was. Among the cast of characters is a slightly confusing one called Mischa Moskowitz, who is known for some inexplicable reason as Mike Murphy to his regiment friends. He speaks Yiddish, prays in Hebrew, but fights like an Irishman. When this character is wounded, Father Duffy prays with him, first saying the "Our Father," but then reciting the "Shema Israel," continuing in Hebrew.

Despite the references to the Jewish faith—probably done to appease the Warner (Wonskolaser) Brothers producers, Hirsch, Abraham, Schmuel, and Jacob (who became Harry, Albert, Sam, and Jack), this could be regarded as the most Catholic film that Warner Bros. produced during the 1930s and '40s. It's the only film that ends with the words, "Through Christ our Lord, Amen." Although it's packed with religious iconography, this doesn't detract from the actual fighting scenes, which are rather convincingly staged despite the lack of contemporary blood and gore. This was, after all, considered a "family" film in its day. If you love a good old war movie, this is precisely that, with no pretentions. It's character-driven, a little patronizing by today's standards, but thoroughly enjoyable, and a nice tribute to the Fighting 69th.

## *Flyboys* (2006)

This movie is about the adventures of the Lafayette Escadrille, a group of hormonally challenged young Americans who volunteered for the French military and became the country's first fighter pilots, before the United States even entered World War I. It's widely regarded as a poorly scripted exercise in rewriting history, carried on the shoulders of some particularly underwhelming performances and unconvincing CGI battle scenes. It fails on various levels. The antiaircraft artillery depicted as being used by the Germans was not of any type used by any side in the Great War. Also the maneuverability of those biplanes is greatly exaggerated. The movie is supposed to play out during late 1916 and early 1917 (the Fokker Dr.I triplane that appears in the film wasn't used until September 1917).

It's true that the pilots were given pistols to shoot themselves in case their planes caught fire, because they didn't have parachutes. In all fairness, most of the basic information is on the level. The character of Skinner is clearly based on African-American pilot Eugene Bullard, mentioned in chapter 4 of this book.

Although the film is supposed to tell the story of the Lafayette Escadrille, it's actually more of a composite—a generic World War I aviation film that just happens to feature Americans fighting for France. The original film, titled *Lafayette Escadrille* (1958), is probably a better option. Even though it's more of a love story than a war film, producer William Wellman did actually serve with this historic unit.

### *All Quiet on the Western Front* (1930)

This is an antiwar movie masterpiece, adapted from the novel by German author and Great War veteran, Erich Maria Remarque, that shows the Great War from the German perspective, and still resonates today. Such was the antiwar sentiment at the time that when the book was published in 1929, as *Im Westen nichts Neues*, it sold over 2.5 million copies in twenty-two languages, in its first eighteen months in print alone. The film, which is accurately based on the book, tells the story of a group of patriotic young German schoolboys coerced into enlisting at the start of World War I by their jingoistic teacher. The narrative is related almost entirely through the experiences of the character Paul Bäumer, wonderfully played by American actor Lew Ayres.

As the storyline develops, the boys reach the front lines and witness the reality of industrial war, surrounded by death and mutilation. The movie then engages in a two-and-a-half-hour-long process of elimination, as all preconceptions about the enemy and principal reasons for fighting dissipate in the heat of battle, leaving the protagonists disillusioned and angered by what they witness. There is one captivating scene (among many) where Paul mortally wounds a French soldier, and then sobs bitterly as he fights to save his life while trapped in a shell crater with the dying man. The film fervently refutes ideologies about heroism and patriotism, and emphasizes the real terror and futility of war.

Superbly acted, it really does focus on the premise that the Great War was the "war to end all wars," and that it should never be allowed to happen again. When the film opened in Germany eight months after the US screening, it was strongly condemned by Joseph Goebbels, Adolf Hitler's future propaganda minister, who publicly burned Remarque's novel. There were street riots generated by Nazi gangs, and Goebbels broke up the Berlin premiere screening by throwing stink bombs and releasing mice and sneezing powder into the cinema. A few weeks later, the picture was completely banned throughout Germany, considered "prejudicial to German national prestige." *All Quiet on the Western Front* was not shown in Germany again until the early 1950s.

Despite the obvious technological limitations of the time, the unrelenting realism of the battle action sequences is compelling even by today's standards. It was also groundbreaking at the time for being the first talking picture to use a giant mobile crane for filming. As the shells demolish underground bunkers, you can't help but be struck by the shrieks of fear and the incessant rat-tat-tat of machine guns, fizzing trench mortars, and whining shells. This film gets uncomfortably close to what it must have actually been like to be a soldier in the Great War. Sadly, the 1979 remake didn't capture the authenticity or immediacy of the original. As this book goes to press, there are plans for a remake of the remake of the original; hooray for Hollywood.

### Paths of Glory (1957)

This film was directed by Stanley Kubrick, and starred Kirk Douglas in what many consider to be his finest role. Based on an actual event that occurred in the French Army and related in the excellent novel by Humphrey Cobb, this film refuses to be obsequious or idealistic in its depiction of French soldiers in the Great War. Cobb served in the Canadian Army during World War I, and wrote this novel as an antiwar statement.

It's one of the few world war genre movies that doesn't actually show the Germans at any given time, except for a civilian or two. Kubrick masterfully created the claustrophobic, asphyxiating atmosphere of battle, and heartily condemns the antics of corrupt, callous, warmongering generals, superbly portrayed by Adolphe Menjou and George Macready.

The story revolves around a ridiculous order given by Gen. George Broulard (Adolphe Menjou), a member of the French General Staff, to his subordinate, the ambitious General Mireau (George Macready), to send his division on a suicidal mission to attack and take a German position during the Great War. The attack is repelled, leaving General Mireau furious and anxious to assign blame for the failure. Three French soldiers are randomly chosen to be executed for cowardice to compensate for the shame of the regiment. Colonel Dax, played by Kirk Douglas, is disgusted with his superiors' arrogant incompetence and attempts to defend these innocent men.

Kubrick's wonderful juxtaposition of battle scenes and gut-wrenching petty tyranny behind the lines is both moving and absolutely riveting. Moments before his execution, one of the three condemned man utters that he has not had "one single sexual thought" since the court-martial. The movie has a tremendous redemptive final sequence, in which a German civilian woman, a mysterious beauty, is forced to sing to the troops. Kubrick nails it when he combines compassion, cool detachment, and control in what quite possibly is one of the most powerful antiwar films ever made, a real must-see cinematic gem.

### The Harlem Hellfighters

Hollywood actor Will Smith plans to produce and maybe even star in the film version of World War I graphic novel *The Harlem Hellfighters*, by Max Brooks, for which Sony Pictures recently picked up the rights. Smith's production company, Overbrook Entertainment, along with partner James Lassiter, will produce an adaptation of the graphic novel, which is an interpretation of the real-life story of the 369th Infantry Regiment of the US Army, which saw action in World War I and World War II.

As discussed in chapter 4, the 369th Infantry is known for being the first African-American regiment to serve with the AEF during World War I, and was nicknamed "The Harlem Hellfighters." Max Brooks has taken some poetic license with his novel about the 369th; one difference between the book and reality is that while the Hellfighters received a parade in Paris and were feted heroes to the French, apart from a parade in New York City on February 17, 1919, they were not honored with accolades when they returned home (as depicted in the book). The book doesn't mention that many Hellfighters returned home badly injured or suffering from PTSD, and they all endured discrimination in the democracy they had fought for. It was for this reason that quite a few of them chose to remain in France after the war was over, where attitudes toward black people were considerably less demeaning, rather than return to a segregated America, where they would be expected to resume their place at the very bottom of the social ladder.

## VIDEO GAMES
### Battlefield 1
This video game about World War I introduces the subject to a new generation and a new audience. Internet sensation and video-gaming expert Alex Khan reviews the game exclusively here.

# Battlefield 1: My Armchair Experience of World War I
# By Alex Khan, the Prince of Macedon

I am by no stretch of the imagination a soldier, nor have I ever witnessed the horrors of war firsthand. All of my perceptions of war come from documentary footage, news coverage, cinema, and video-gaming. The first three mediums offer me a glimpse of war either from true reality or from the more-artistic moviemaking viewpoint. They are all very visceral, and allow me to observe the action from a passive spectator position (one in which I cannot actively take part in what I am seeing onscreen). The last category (and newest medium), video-gaming, is a far cry from reality, but it has the advantage of allowing me to achieve the sensation that I am taking part in warfare in all of its horrific carnage. "War is hell," indeed, but there is no denying that the topic of historical violence has fascinated noncombatants ever since war was first recorded.

The depiction of historical warfare in video games has manifested itself in many different formats (first-person shooter, real-time strategy, flight simulator, etc.), ranging from the wars of Ancient Greece and Rome all the way up to the modern era of warfare. I have a gut feeling that World War II is the most heavily depicted war seen in the video-game industry. The abundance of World War II literature is near infinite; the sheer amount of movies and documentaries covering the war is staggering; and the video-game industry in turn has rightfully interpreted this popularity into many successful World War II titles. World War I, dubbed the "Great War," unfortunately has been largely neglected in the video-game world for one reason or another.

As a longtime gamer, I do have fond memories of a few great games set during the Great War. From the skies over Europe in the classic flight simulator *Red Baron*, to the first-person battlefields of *Verdun 1914–1918*, there have been only a few exceptionally great titles set in World War I. Having seen the likes of *Verdun* in 2015, it was quite the miracle for gaming fans to receive yet another great title in the minuscule hall of World War I gaming titles, *Battlefield 1*.

Released in 2016, *Battlefield 1* comes from a strong tradition of Battlefield FPS (first-person shooter) games set in miscellaneous time periods (World War II, the Vietnam War, the near future, modern times). EA DICE producer Aleksander Grøndal mentioned in an interview that *Battlefield 1* was aptly named, as game creators believe World War I was the "genesis of modern warfare."

As a predominantly dedicated strategy gamer myself, I tend to avoid the FPS genre, as the quick movements of the in-game camera plays too harshly on my motion sickness. But as a lover of history, my heart set me on a path toward playing *Battlefield 1*. The story and essence of this game is captured beautifully in its single-player campaign mode, where the player hops from one character to another, giving a broad perspective of the many different walks of life and cultures represented by those who fought in the conflict.

The prologue level, named "Storm of Steel," puts you in the boots of the famous African-American regiment known as the Harlem Hellfighters. This was an actual regiment composed of African Americans fighting for the United States of America. Whatever historical liberties were taken in depicting this regiment in a video game are quickly forgotten, as the game quickly throws you into 1918 in the most visceral and beautifully depicted World War I game I have ever played.

Aside from its stunning visuals, the game quickly sets the tone for an extremely brutal gaming session. The opening cinematic scene depicts the Harlem Hellfighters in ferocious hand-to-hand combat with German soldiers, where both sides resort to using whatever blunt object they can find to finish each other off. Bayonets, shovels, and makeshift clubs are all utilized mercilessly before the intro scene ends, and you find yourself dropped into an inferno of absolute hell. The game even proclaims that the player is not expected to survive the opening stage.

You immediately start the game off next to a fellow soldier of the Harlem Hellfighters regiment who is shouting to your character that the position is surrounded by enemy soldiers. Old, clunky World War I tanks rumble ahead while your comrades push forward through a war-torn, European town, looking for the enemy. Artillery shells fall randomly near you, and the urgent sound of trench whistles echo in the background. You run past two comrades helping each other toward safety while you look out into the abysmal overcast sky. Everything looks incredibly bleak. Fire and smoke are everywhere. The camera rocks back and forth every time an artillery piece strikes a nearby location. Seemingly out of nowhere, German soldiers rush toward you. There is no indicator to tell you that they are enemy soldiers, out to end your life. A close-up of their uniforms might clue you in on their intentions, but your character will surely be gunned down if you pause long enough to inspect their apparel.

As the prologue suggests, nobody is expected to survive. I controlled several characters during my run in the opening stage, and they all met gruesome deaths. Enemy soldiers gunned down Willie, age twenty-six, once he got separated from the group. Needham, age thirty-three, died horrifically when a German soldier set him ablaze. David, a twenty-nine-year-old British crewman, died without warning while operating his tank. Orville, age eighteen, was killed during a gas attack. My last character was just about to be impaled by a shovel-wielding German soldier when an artillery strike ended both of our lives.

After I developed an eye for the different German uniforms present (especially those soldiers wearing the spiked Pickelhaube helmets), I got more adept at quickly identifying and shooting at the appropriate soldiers. A good percentage of the German soldiers sport the more-advanced helmet of the Stahlhelm design.

There is a lot to take in as you run through this digital battlefield, which is filled with plenty of visual stimuli to admire. While you peek over to shoot enemy troops, zeppelins are burning overhead in spectacular fashion. Biplanes are soaring over your position to attack the enemy somewhere in the distance. Fellow soldiers are being blown to bits by enemy grenades. Artillery explosions send various bodies flying through the air like rag dolls. The game does not hold back on its graphic depiction of war. When I was forced on that rare occasion to go toe-to-toe with enemy troops, I had to use my trench shovel in order to survive. Gruesome amounts of blood spill out of the enemy soldiers during these melee encounters. The graphic violence turns your heroic kill into a moment of reflection as you realize you just brought down a fellow human being.

Although the single-player campaign does not put you in command of German troops, there is subtle compassion and humanity shown toward the opposing side. At the end of the "Storm of Steel" level, there is a tearful, cinematic scene shown where a Harlem Hellfighter comes face-to-face with a German soldier. Initially their weapons are pointed at each other, but after witnessing the opening carnage, both combatants lower their weapons and walk their separate ways, in an unspoken mutual understanding that they had both seen enough. It is a powerful scene that will move players toward questioning why all of that bloodshed was even necessary in the first place. The Great War was definitely real, and many people lost their lives because of it. The game makes you think about history, and how dangerous it can become if it repeats itself.

The next storyline, "Through Mud and Blood," introduces you to the British character known as Edwards. Edwards has been assigned to a Mark V tank which is revealed to be quite menacing; unfortunately, it's also quite unreliable. Initially you will appreciate the behemoth vehicle as you crash through buildings and blast away countless enemy infantry. There is even the option to drive over enemy troops, which is extremely brutal. Enemy troops will scatter while their less-fortunate comrades fall down in agony as their blood shoots upward from your tracks.

On the other hand, there are some immediate flaws shown during the "Beren's Crossing" objective: The mud will slow your tank down significantly when it should be driving full speed to avoid being hit by enemy artillery. During a later confrontation with a German *Sturmpanzer* tank, the Mark V becomes a dangerous target as it breaks down at an inopportune moment. This aspect of the campaign shows the less-glamorous side of tank warfare. Once a tank malfunctions, someone usually has to go out and fix it. As I ventured out to fix the Mark V, there were swarms of German infantry in the vicinity, which I had previously been able to ignore while inside the tank. It was a scary situation to be in, and I could only pray that friendly infantry support was nearby.

The other stories in campaign mode truly depict a world war fought from different perspectives. The game puts players in command of an adventurous American pilot who takes you on a mission escorting bombers. In the subsequent level, you take on the role of an Italian soldier of the "Arditi," which I later learned was an actual unit in the Great War.

Instead of the usual German soldier, the Austro-Hungarian Army confronts you. The last two levels take you from being an Australian soldier at Gallipoli all the way to the Arabian Peninsula as a Bedouin warrior, taking on the Ottomans. I cannot think of another World War I game which shows this many different theaters of the war in such cinematic magnificence.

In the realm of multiplayer, *Battlefield 1* adds even more depth to the gameplay. Although the enemy units in single-player acted almost human, I personally believe the best opponents always come from the multiplayer side, where humans face off against other humans around the world.

A lot of aspects of the multiplayer tradition seem extremely unrealistic compared to what I have learned from firsthand accounts of modern warfare. For example, the common practice in multiplayer mode is to keep your soldier constantly in motion to avoid being shot by unseen opponents. While it is generally accepted that most soldiers do not wish to be shot, there is also the real element of fatigue, which would prevent a human from constantly running at full speed up and down stairs while reloading their Lewis gun with seemingly no effort or strain. Real pilots would not purposely abandon their undamaged planes in midflight just so they could parachute behind enemy lines. That said, there are some elements that are definitely equally important both in multiplayer and in real-life combat situations: teamwork and communication. The side that works together the best will generally win. In most multiplayer sessions, there is sadly very little teamwork on display, and almost no communication.

But the most significant aspect of warfare that can never be replicated in a video game is the actual fear of death. A digital soldier will never have to worry about getting roasted alive by a German flamethrower or getting crushed by a British Mark V heavy tank. The lack of fear in a video game usually results in displays of reckless valor and unrealistic actions. In real combat, I suspect that most soldiers would think more carefully about their safety.

The types of weapons and vehicles seen in both single- and multiplayer modes are abundant. Without even attempting to compile a complete list, I was shot at or personally controlled several weapons and vehicles in *Battlefield 1*: MP 18, Lewis gun, Gewehr 98, M97 trench gun, auto revolver, C96 Carbine, Cei-Rigotti Factory, Gotha G.IV bomber, Mark V British tank, and a Selbstlader M1916.

With a game so beautiful—yet proportionally horrific—I believe this World War I title will succeed in bringing the Great War to life, pushing players into learning more about this tragic conflict. There are definitely many unrealistic aspects of *Battlefield 1*, but the game only needs to fascinate the mind into learning more about actual history. When I heard about the Arditi from the "Avanti Savoia" level, I immediately looked it up to see if it was a real unit or not. In this case, curiosity was all I needed to open up a new history book. *Battlefield 1* deals with historical fiction, but the history is still there.

## Chapter Nineteen

# Our Great War

The United States did not enter into the Great War to achieve material or territorial gain, but its contribution in men and materials influenced the outcome and made a significant difference. America didn't profit in any tangible way from the fighting, and didn't demand indemnities or compensation from any of the Central Powers. There were discernible benefits, however, as US economic status improved dramatically due to trade with, and loans to, Great Britain and other Allied nations. At the time of the war, the United States declared it was a net debtor in international capital markets, but following the war, the United States began investing large amounts of money internationally, particularly in Latin America, in some respects usurping the role traditionally played by Britain and other European capital exporters. As the United Kingdom worked to rebuild its shattered economy after the war, New York emerged as London's equal, possibly even superior in the contest to become the world's leading financial center.

More importantly, the United States flexed its muscles and asserted its position on the world stage, along with gaining massive international prestige. Prior to the war, the United States was undergoing a transformation—a fledgling nation seeking and attempting to impose its global identity. Its belated but welcome entry into the war in 1917 marked the beginning of its journey toward becoming a world power.

For some politicians in Washington, DC, this was what validated their country's participation. Treasury Secretary William Gibbs McAdoo, son-in-law of President Woodrow Wilson, had serious ambitions to replace the pound sterling with the dollar as the foremost international reserve currency. Wilson had even higher aspirations, and surreptitiously hoped that history would judge him as the man who cemented world peace. Sadly, just twenty years later these aspirations would be dispelled by another global conflict, but at least Wilson's penchant for idealism and stirring speeches earned him a Nobel Peace Prize.

By participating in the war, and in the peace talks after the war, the United States made itself a much more important country in terms of world affairs. Domestically the Great War transformed the status for women. The Nineteenth Amendment reflected the British suffrage movement by guaranteeing women the right to vote. Wilson had championed it as "a necessary war measure." In a male-dominated society there were well-grounded fears that women would make Prohibition their number-one priority, as indicated in the Eighteenth Amendment that authorized Congress to ban the sale and transport of intoxicating beverages, but by 1920 the law governing Prohibition had been enacted. In theory American servicemen were compelled to remain teetotal throughout their participation in the Great War, but in a country such as France, this would have been nigh on impossible.

Most of the doughboys had never left home prior to the war, but now they returned worldly wise, expecting to live the rest of their natural lives as heroes. It didn't take long for disillusionment and dissatisfaction to set in. More than 300,000 US soldiers returned home with physical or mental afflictions and spent time in veterans' hospitals. Some underwent reconstructive surgery, while others received prosthetic limbs; soldiers with facial injuries received prosthetic masks. Injured soldiers had to undergo a government-regulated test in order to receive a disability rating. It was based on the premise that the higher the rating, the more government money the veteran would receive. The military remained segregated, and due to this it was difficult for minorities to receive treatment and payment.

Most shell-shock victims were not treated at all because according to some so-called experts, it was difficult to adequately ascertain whether or not they were in fact mentally ill. Consequently, many soldiers were denied government benefits, and many of these unfortunates never attempted to reapply. Between eight thousand and ten thousand soldiers were treated annually for mental disorders.

Some American cities passed laws that required veterans with severe facial wounds to wear masks or hoods in public so their disfigured faces would not unnecessarily frighten women or children. There were many social and economic consequences resulting from America's part in the Great War, but despite being an affluent and prosperous country, the status quo governing inequality between black and white, and rich and poor, remained. African Americans returning home after the war were optimistic in the hope that their patriotic sacrifices would have a positive impact on race relations and expand the boundaries of civil rights. In October 1919, in the South, the number of reported lynchings rose from sixty-four in 1918 to eighty-three in 1919. At least eleven of these victims were soldiers who had returned expecting something more than the same old. For African Americans, the end of the war brought anything but peace.

Many soldiers began asking if their sacrifice had been worth it. When the United States declared war, it did so without signing any pacts or treaties with the Allies; it was simply guilt by association, as part of a combined effort to attempt to defeat the Central Powers. During the German Spring Offensive in 1918, the prospect of Allied collapse and defeat became a distinct possibility. German storm troopers opened up great gaps in the Allied lines and advanced dozens of miles toward the Channel ports. American involvement was imperative to help tip the balance. Granted, the AEF had to make numerous concessions, but once they began to appear in significant numbers, the fate of the Central Powers was sealed. By the end of the Great War the AEF occupied more of the Western Front than Britain and all of her Commonwealth of Nations combined.

Sal Compagno, president of the Great War Society, asserts that "without General Pershing's forces on the Western Front, Germany would have won the World War! By New Year's Day, 1918, the British Army had been bled before Passchendaele; the French Army had suffered both defeat and mutiny from the Nivelle Offensive; and Russia, then under Lenin, had withdrawn from the war. With its victory on the

Eastern Front, the German Army had available over a million additional men to transfer to the West. The key to Allied victory was morale. It was the intense and undiminished morale of the US military, combined with a staunch domestic backing, which convinced the Germans they could no longer continue. When their morale collapsed on all fronts, they sued for peace. The AEF with its operations broke the German morale."

After giving a rousing speech to Congress regarding the reasons for America joining the European war, Wilson returned to his office. According to his private secretary, Joseph Patrick Tumulty, Wilson was surprised by the positive reception to his speech. Wilson said to his loyal secretary, "My message today was a message of death for our young men. How strange it seems to applaud that." Then the president laid his head on the table and sobbed like a child.

Many more tears would be shed before the war was over, but America did its part and brought the Great War to an end—even though it wouldn't be the "war to end all wars."

# Epilogue

The Great War was over, and now it was time to rebuild—both the cities, towns, and villages that had in some cases been completely eradicated, and war-ravaged economies. The victorious European nations were in debt to the United States to the tune of around $10 billion. Whole populations on the European mainland were starving, and without food shipments from the United States, the exhausted continent would not have survived.

Meanwhile, President Wilson held firm to his support for the treaty—even though it differed from his original Fourteen Points plan—and continued to maintain his utopian ideology for a "League of Nations." Congress would eventually reject both of these. There is no doubt, however, that Wilson had greater insight than many of his contemporaries when he said, somewhat prophetically, "Our greatest error would be to give [Germany] powerful reasons for one day wishing to take revenge." It didn't matter. The damage had been done, and now the hatred would ferment in the hearts and minds of many Germans. Wilson continued to staunchly defend his anti-imperialist sentiments and support for the League of Nations, despite growing Republican calls for a more-isolationist approach to the matter. The Republicans would win, and Wilson would ultimately see his noble ambitions thwarted—in the short term, at least.

Thanks to Wilson's visionary ambitions, America's place in the world as the leader of democracy and liberal globalism would be cemented for generations to come. Many of those who were inspired and shared the opinions of this president, such as Franklin D. Roosevelt, Herbert Hoover, and John Foster Dulles, would in time pay homage to the man in many ways. Although Wilson's last year as president was overshadowed by his own inertia and ill health, his legacy would endure.

Those who participated, both willingly and unwillingly, in the Great War bore witness to the incredible destructive power of the human race. For all its evils, the war also generated many innovations in medical treatments, geopolitics, and social relations. American author, journalist, and lecturer Adam Hochschild said, "The First World War in so many ways shaped the twentieth century, and really remade our world for the worse."

Many women would have vociferously disagreed with the latter, seeing that the Great War helped to radically change opinions regarding gender stereotypes. Women had shown that they were more than capable of doing work that had previously been seen as part of an exclusively male domain. As for the men—well, the world would never again doubt or question the aptitude or ability of the American fighting man. The heroism, courage, and tenacity that these doughboys displayed in the seminal months of the Great War would ensure their place in history.

And what of the veterans who appeared in this book? While it wasn't possible to trace all of them, here is what we do know about some of them.

## World War I Veterans

After the war, **Arthur Guy Empey** wrote a tremendous book based on his experiences titled *Over the Top*, which sold over a quarter of a million copies and was made into a silent film in Hollywood. He became an actor and pulp-fiction writer, and developed friendships with some very influential Americans, including William Randolph Hearst and Gary Cooper. At one time he even had his own militia. Empey died at the age of seventy-nine in Kansas, on February 22, 1963, at a US military veterans' hospital.

**C. Harold Floyd** survived the war only to be killed in a house fire:

**Berkshire Evening Eagle**, *March 13, 1944: "Fire Takes Life of C. H. Floyd: Wife and Daughter Taken to Hospital"*

*Holder of Distinguished Service Cross in World War I Overcome by Fumes in Kenilworth Street Home*

*C. Harold Floyd, sixty-five, treasurer, sales manager, and purchasing agent of the G.C.A. Manufacturing Company, and holder of the Distinguished Service Cross and the Purple Heart for service in World War I, is dead of carbon monoxide poisoning, and his wife and thirteen-year-old daughter, Betty, are receiving treatment at St. Luke's Hospital for smoke inhalation, as the result of a fire which destroyed two rooms of the family residence at 22 Kenilworth Street early this morning. The family dog, a Chesapeake Bay retriever, also perished in the blaze. Fire Chief Thomas F. Burke said the cause of the fire has not been determined.*

Ever heard that the number thirteen is unlucky? Well, one of our veterans, **Charles C. Gerwitz**, may have agreed. He crossed the ocean in a convoy of thirteen ships, and the journey took thirteen days. He was wounded the thirteenth hour of the thirteenth day during the thirteenth month of his service in the army. He was taken to Aid Station B4110, also known as Hospital No. 13. He received thirteen stitches in his wound, and was awarded the Purple Heart on September 13. He had thirteen sisters and brothers, and died on Friday, August 13, 1982, at the age of ninety-three.

**James V. Leak** of the famous "Lost Battalion" was captured and taken prisoner by the Germans on October 4, 1918. He was returned to the United States in 1919, and died in June of 1942 in Longview, Texas, at the age of forty-one.

**Morris Albert Martin**, wounded at the Meuse-Argonne, was born in Elmont, Kansas, on February 10, 1895. He married Lela Alice Johnston when he returned from the war, and they lived a long and happy life together. He passed away on November 8, 1975, in Fresno, California.

**Norvel Preston Clotfelter** was born in Illinois, in 1894. He married Mattie Walters, and they had four children. He died on May 13, 1967, in Springfield, Missouri, just one year after his wife passed.

**Bruce G. Wright** returned to Massachusetts after the war and married Miss Lovette L. Harvey, to whom he'd often written during his time in Europe. His diary was not discovered until 1963, and his grandchildren decided to have it transcribed. We're glad they did.

### Guy Ichabod Rowe

**Guy Rowe** returned to the United States in December 1918. In April 1920 he returned to Europe for duty with the Graves Registration Service at Cochem, Germany, and Paris, Brussels, and Antwerp. In September 1921 he attended the Ecole de l'Intendance Militaire in Paris, France, graduating in September 1923. He returned to the United States in November 1923 for duty as Coast Defense Quartermaster at Fort H. G. Wright, New York. In 1926 he attended the Command and General Staff School, Fort Leavenworth, Kansas, and completed the course in June 1927 as a distinguished graduate. He was then assigned to Philadelphia, Pennsylvania, as an instructor in the Quartermaster School, for four years' duty. He also served as quartermaster at the Infantry School, Fort Benning, Georgia, for two years, and as the Sixth Corps Area Quartermaster.

Rowe entered the Office of the Quartermaster General, Washington, DC, in June 1940. Named brigadier general by President Franklin D. Roosevelt, he continued his service through World War II. In April 1942 he was named to command the Quartermaster Replacement Training Center, Camp Lee, Virginia, and in February 1944 he became the commanding general of the Jeffersonville Quartermaster Depot, Jeffersonville, Indiana, until he retired as a brigadier general in 1947, after thirty-nine years of service. Among the awards, decorations, and citations received by General Rowe are: the Distinguished Service Cross, the Purple Heart, the Legion of Honor, and the Croix de Guerre with Palm by the French government. Brigadier General Rowe died on August 27, 1969.

### George E. Leach

After the war, **Col. George E. Leach** remained in command of the 151st Field Artillery until 1921, and resumed his work in the insurance business as a manager for the St. Paul Fire and Marine Insurance Company. In 1923 he was promoted to brigadier general and given command of the 59th Field Artillery Brigade, Minnesota National Guard. Leach was elected mayor of Minneapolis as a Republican for six two-year terms: in 1921, 1923, 1925, 1927, 1937, and 1939. He twice ran for governor (1926 and 1938), but was not elected. While mayor, Leach fought hard against the spreading influence of the Ku Klux Klan in Minnesota.

Leach, a first-rate athlete and an excellent skier, managed the very first US Olympic Ski Team in 1924, and was the National Ski Association representative to the Ski Congress, which met during the Olympics, and led to the creation of the International Ski Federation. He was inducted into the National Ski Hall of Fame in Ishpeming, Michigan, fourteen years after his death.

In 1931 Leach was given the temporary rank of major general and appointed chief of the National Guard Bureau in Washington, DC. He served until 1935, when he resumed his rank of brigadier general and returned to Minnesota to again assume command of the 59th Field Artillery Brigade. In 1937 he was elected president of the National Guard Association of the United States.

Leach commanded the 34th Division from 1940 to 1941, and was again promoted to major general. The 34th received its notification of federal activation and underwent rigorous training and preparation for its eventual participation in World War II. Leach retired from the army in 1941, highly regarded by the many soldiers who had served with him over the years.

Leach owned George E. Leach, Inc., a vending machine company. He also served as chairman of the National Automatic Merchandising Association. In 1924 Leach married Anita M. Churcher, whom he had met in Germany after World War I while he was serving occupation duty and she was serving with the YMCA. They had two children. He passed away in Los Angeles, California, on July 17, 1955, age seventy-nine, and is buried at Fort Snelling National Cemetery.

**Benjamin F. Allender** was born on November 10, 1895, in Ottumwa, Iowa. He enlisted on April 30, 1917, in Ottumwa, and served in Co. G, 168th US Infantry. On May 17, 1919, he received an honorable discharge, returning to Ottumwa, where he worked as a foreman in a packing plant. Allender died on January 10, 1974, in Ottumwa, Iowa.

**George B. Dempsey, MD**, was born in Millerton, New York, on June 11, 1887. A graduate of Cornell University Medical College, he joined the army on August 17, 1917, as a first lieutenant in Fort Benjamin Harrison, Indiana. He served overseas from January 7, 1918, to April 18, 1919. Honorably discharged on May 6, 1919, he returned to the United States, where he was a prominent physician, establishing his own medical practice in the town of Cornwall-on-Hudson, New York, where he died on September 5, 1967.

Newly commissioned, **Col. Charles Whittlesey** was awarded the Medal of Honor for his role in leading the Lost Battalion during their time in the Argonne Forest. A national hero after the war, he became a sought-after speaker. He was troubled, however, and became deeply depressed by the fact that some of his soldiers did not survive the battle, and many were wounded or maimed. On November 26, 1921, during a trip from New York to Havana on the steamship USS *Toloa*, Whittlesey jumped overboard and was never seen again. He signed his final letter to a close friend "As One."

# NOTES

## POEM

1. Robert Cortes Holliday, Robert Cortes, trans. *Joyce Kilmer* (New York: Kennikat Press, 1918).

## CHAPTER ONE

1. "Takes Own Life with Gas at Home," *Berkshire Evening Eagle,* January 13, 1925.
2. Woodrow Wilson, *War Messages*, 65th Cong., 1st Sess. Senate Doc. No. 5, Serial No. 7264 (Washington, DC, 1917), pp. 3–8, *passim.*
3. Woodrow Wilson, *Message to Congress,* 63rd Cong., 2d Sess., Senate Doc. No. 566 (Washington, DC, 1914), 3–4.
4. Ulysses S. Grant, "Proclamation 192—Neutrality of Citizens of the United States in the War Between France and the North German Confederation," August 22, 1870.
5. Peter Alhadeff, "100 Years Ago Today: First Lethal Gas Attack at Ypres." www.centenarynews.com/article/100-years-ago-today-first-lethal-gas-attack-at-ypres, April 21, 2015.
6. Arthur Guy Empey, *Over the Top* (New York and London: G. P. Putnam's Sons, 1917), 187–92.
7. Theodore Roosevelt, *America and the World War* (New York: C. Scribner's Sons, 1915), ix.
8. Ibid., xiv.
9. "Several Americans Are Believed Lost in *Sussex* Disaster," *Birmingham Age-Herald*, March 26, 1916.
10. Thomas H. Russell, *The World's Greatest War and Triumph of America's Army and Navy* (L. H. Walter, 1919), 418.
11. "Wants United States to Put Pressure on Britain," *Birmingham Age-Herald*, March 26, 1916.
12. "Germany Acknowledges the *Sussex* was Torpedoed and Offers to Pay Indemnity," *Birmingham Age-Herald*, March 26, 1916.
13. Winston Churchill, *The World Crisis, 1916–1918*, Vol. 1 (London: Scribner, 1927), 696.
14. Theodore Roosevelt, "Peace and War" speech.
15. Theodore Roosevelt, "Un-hyphenated American" speech.
16. Woodrow Wilson, *War Messages*, 65th Cong., 3-8, *passim.*

17. Ibid.

18. *The World War Experiences of Charles Harold Floyd, First Lieutenant, 107th Infantry: Written During and Immediately After the War (1917–1919)*, Massachusetts Historical Society.

19. Ben Allender, *Diary of World War*, New York State Military Museum and Veterans Research Center, 1–2.

20. John Joseph Brennan Collection, Veterans History Project, American Folklife Center, Library of Congress.

21. *The World War Experiences of Charles Harold Floyd.*

22. George E. Leach, *War Diary, George E. Leach, Colonel, 151st Field Artillery, Rainbow Division*, (Minneapolis: Pioneer Printers, 1923), 7.

23. Hillie John Franz, Veterans History Project, American Folklife Center, Library of Congress.

24. William G. McAdoo, *Crowded Years: The Reminiscences of William G. McAdoo* (Boston: Houghton Mifflin, 1931), 418.

25. George Creel, *How We Advertised America* (Macmillan, 1920), 3–9.

26. Robert Marion La Follette, *The Political Philosophy of Robert M. La Follette as Revealed in His Speeches and Writings* (Robert M. La Follette Company, 1920), 237–38.

## CHAPTER THREE

1. Alice L. Duffield, Veterans History Project, American Folklife Center, Library of Congress.

2. Charles Gerwitz, *World War I Memories*, Veterans History Project, American Folklife Center, Library of Congress, 1–3.

3. George B. Dempsey, *Diary of George B. Dempsey, MD, December 7, 1917–May 5, 1918.* New York State Military Museum and Veterans Research Center, 1–6.

4. *The World War Experiences of Charles Harold Floyd.*

## CHAPTER FOUR

1. Library of Congress, Rare Book and Special Collections Division, African-American Pamphlet Collection.

2. Michael L. Lanning, *The African-American Soldier: From Crispus Attucks to Colin Powell* (New York: Citadel Press, 1997).

3. Bruce G. Wright, *World War I Memoir* (1921), Massachusetts Historical Society.

4. Tyler Stovall, *Paris Noir: African Americans in the City of Light* (Boston: Houghton Mifflin, 1996; reissued 2012), 3.

5. Freddie Stowers, Medal of Honor Citation, Congressional Medal of Honor Society, www.cmohs.org/recipient-detail/2595/stowers-freddie.php.

6. John Joseph Brennan, *My Own True Story of My Experience in the Army*, Veterans History Project, American Folklife Center, Library of Congress, 4.

7. Wright, *World War I Memoir.*

8. W. E. B. DuBois, ed., "Documents of the War," *The Crisis* 28 (1919), 16–18.

9. Emmett Jay Scott, *Scott's Official History of the American Negro in the World War* (Chicago: Homewood Press, 1919), 117.

10. Henry Johnson Medal of Honor Citation, Congressional Medal of Honor Society, www.cmohs.org/recipient-detail/3517/johnson-henry-aka-william-henry-johnson.php.

11. Reid Badger, *A Life in Ragtime: A Biography of James Reese Europe* (Oxford: Oxford University Press, 1995), 215.

12. Scott, *Scott's Official History of the American Negro in the World War*, 9.

## CHAPTER FIVE

1. Dempsey, *Diary of George B. Dempsey*, 6–9.

2. *The World War Experiences of Charles Harold Floyd.*

## CHAPTER SIX

1. Francis Patrick Duffy, *Father Duffy's Story: A Tale of Humor and Heroism, of Life and Death with the Fighting Sixty-Ninth* (New York: George H. Doran, 1919), 14.

2. Ibid., 18–19.

3. Ibid., 197–98.

4. William Joseph Donovan, Medal of Honor Citation, Congressional Medal of Honor Society, www.cmohs.org/recipient-detail/2518/donovan-william-joseph.php.

5. Michael Aloysius Donaldson, Medal of Honor Citation, Congressional Medal of Honor Society, www.cmohs.org/recipient-detail/2517/donaldson-michael-a.php.

6. Richard O'Neill, Medal of Honor Citation, Congressional Medal of Honor Society, www.cmohs.org/recipient-detail/2568/o-neill-richard-w.php.

## CHAPTER SEVEN

1. Allender, *Diary of World War*, 2–3.

2. Theodore Kohls, Veterans History Project, American Folklife Center, Library of Congress, 1.

3. The Allied Appeal for Rapid American Assistance, wwi.lib.byu.edu/index.php/The_Allied_Appeal_for_Rapid_American_Assistance.

4. Wright, *World War I Memoir.*

5. Roy Scow interview, Veterans History Project, American Folklife Center, Library of Congress.

6. *The World War Experiences of Charles Harold Floyd.*

7. Alice L. Duffield, Veterans History Project.

## CHAPTER EIGHT

1. Augustin F. Maher, *How Connecticut Stopped the Hun* (New Haven: Press of S. Z. Field, 1919), 2.

2. Ibid., 7–8.

3. Wright, *World War I Memoir.*

4. Sgt. Boleslaw Suchocki, 28th Infantry, 1st Division, First Division Foundation and Museum.

5. Theodore Kohls, Veterans History Project, American Folklife Center, Library of Congress, 2.

## CHAPTER NINE

1. Elton Mackin, *Suddenly We Didn't Want To Die* (New York: Presidio Press, 1993).

## CHAPTER TEN

1. Transcript of a Letter from Guy Rowe to General McAlexander (August 4, 1919).

2. Jesse W. Woolridge, *The Giants of the Marne: A Story of McAlexander and His Regiment* (Salt Lake City, UT: Seagull Press, 1923).

## CHAPTER ELEVEN

1. Longshaw Kraus Porritt, Veterans History Project, American Folklife Center, Library of Congress, 1–3.

2. "The Wolfhounds Pick a Winner," *American Legion Monthly*, Vol. 17, No. 3 (September 1934), 34.

## CHAPTER TWELVE

1. Norvel Preston Clotfelter, Veterans History Project, American Folklife Center, Library of Congress, 29.

2. *Waldo Heinrichs Papers, ca. 1895–2015*, University of Massachusetts Special Collections and University Archives.

3. *Blue and Gold Stars*, Vol. 1, No. 2.

4. Ibid.

5. Ibid.

## CHAPTER THIRTEEN

1. Ibid.

2. Morris Albert Martin, Veterans History Project, American Folklife Center, Library of Congress, 15–26.

3. "The Lost Battalion," After Action Report, 77th Infantry Division, National Archives, College Park, Maryland.

4. "The Lost Battalion," *Berkshire Evening Eagle*, November 15, 1918.

5. "The Experience and Meaning of the Lost Battalion," World War I.com, presented by James V. Leak, Company E, 308th Infantry, November 11, 1938, www.worldwar1 .com/dbc/leak.htm.

6. General Orders No. 20, 37th Division. National Archives, College Park, Maryland.

## Chapter Fourteen

1. "Means Used by the Nazi Conspirators in Gaining Control of the German State," *Nazi Conspiracy and Aggression*, Vol. I, ch . 7, The Avalon Project, Yale Law School, Lillian Goldman Law Library, http://avalon.law.yale.edu/imt/chap_07.asp.

2. John Maynard Keynes, *The Economic Consequences of the Peace: The Economist* (New York: Penguin, 1995).

3. Achim Kai-Uwe Lange, *George Frost Kennan und der Kalte Krieg: eine Analyse der Kennanschen* (Münster, Germany: LIT Verlag Münster, 2001).

# BIBLIOGRAPHY

## BOOKS

Badger, Reid. *A Life in Ragtime: A Biography of James Reese Europe.* Oxford: Oxford University Press, 1995.

Baggett, Blaine, and Jay Winter. *The Great War and the Shaping of the Twentieth Century.* New York: Penguin Studio, 1996.

Bull, Stephen. *Aspects of Trench Warfare.* Canton: PRC Publishing, 2003.

Churchill, Winston. *The World Crisis, 1916–1918, Vol. 1.* London: Scribner, 1927.

Creel, George. *How We Advertised America.* London: Macmillan, 1920.

Duffy, Francis Patrick. *Father Duffy's Story: A Tale of Humor and Heroism, of Life and Death with the Fighting Sixty-Ninth.* New York: George H. Doran, 1919.

Empey, Arthur Guy. *Over the Top.* New York and London: G. P. Putnam's Sons, 1917.

Harris, Stephen L. *Harlem's Hell Fighters: The African-American 369th Infantry in World War I.* Washington, DC: Potomac Books, 2005.

Hart, B. H. Liddell. *A History of the First World War.* London: Pan MacMillan, 1972.

Hart, Peter. *The Great War: A Combat History of the First World War.* Oxford, UK: Oxford University Press, 2013.

Holliday, Robert Cortes, trans. *Joyce Kilmer.* New York: Kennikat Press, 1918.

Keynes, John Maynard. *The Economic Consequences of the Peace: The Economist.* New York: Penguin, 1995.

La Follette, Robert Marion. *The Political Philosophy of Robert M. La Follette as Revealed in His Speeches and Writings.* Robert M. La Follette Company, 1920.

Lange, Achim Kai-Uwe. *George Frost Kennan und der Kalte Krieg: Eine Analyse der Kennanschen.* Münster, Germany: LIT Verlag Münster, 2001.

Lanning, Michael L. *The African-American Soldier: From Crispus Attucks to Colin Powell.* New York: Citadel Press, 1997.

Little, Arthur W. *From Harlem to the Rhine: The Story of New York's Colored Volunteers.* New York: Covici Friede Publishers, 1936.

Mackin, Elton E. *Suddenly We Didn't Want to Die.* New York: Presidio Press, 1993.

Maher, Augustin F. *How Connecticut Stopped the Hun.* New Haven: Press of S. Z. Field, 1919.

McAdoo, William G. *Crowded Years: The Reminiscences of William G. McAdoo.* Boston: Houghton Mifflin, 1931.

Neiberg, Michael. *The World War I Reader.* New York: New York University Press, 2006.

Roosevelt, Theodore. *America and the World War.* New York: C. Scribner's Sons, 1915.

333

Russell, Thomas H. *The World's Greatest War and Triumph of America's Army and Navy*. New York: L. H. Walter, 1919.
Scott, Emmett Jay. *Scott's Official History of the American Negro in the World War*. Chicago: Homewood Press, 1919.
Stephenson, David. *The History of the First World War*. New York: Penguin, 2005.
Stewart, Richard W., trans. *American Military History*. Washington, DC: Center of Military History, 2010.
Stovall, Tyler. *Paris Noir: African Americans in the City of Light*. Boston: Houghton Mifflin, 1996; reissued 2012.
Strachan, Hew. *The First World War*. New York: Penguin Books, 2005.
*United States Army in the World War, 1917–1919*. Washington, DC: Center of Military History, 1991.
Woolridge, Jesse W. *The Giants of the Marne: A Story of McAlexander and His Regiment*. Salt Lake City, UT: Seagull Press, 1923.

## DIARIES, MEMOIRS, AND LETTERS

Allender, Ben. *Diary of World War*. New York State Military Museum and Veterans Research Center.
Dempsey, George B. *Diary of George B. Dempsey, MD, December 7, 1917–May 5, 1918*. New York State Military Museum and Veterans Research Center.
Floyd, Charles Harold. *The World War Experiences of Charles Harold Floyd, First Lieutenant, 107th Infantry: Written During and Immediately After the War (1917–1919)*. Massachusetts Historical Society.
Heinrichs, Waldo. *Waldo Heinrichs Papers, ca. 1895–2015*. University of Massachusetts Special Collections and University Archives.
Leach, George E. *War Diary, George E. Leach, Colonel 151st Field Artillery, Rainbow Division*. Minneapolis, MN: Pioneer Printers, 1923.
Rowe, Guy. Transcript of a letter from Guy Rowe to General McAlexander (August 4, 1919).
Wright, Bruce G. *World War I Memoir (1921)*. Massachusetts Historical Society.

## ARTICLES AND REPORTS

Alhadeff, Peter. "100 Years Ago Today: First Lethal Gas Attack at Ypres." www.centenarynews.com/article/100-years-ago-today-first-lethal-gas-attack-at-ypres, April 21, 2015.
*Blue and Gold Stars*, Vol. 1, No. 2.
Du Bois, W. E. B. ed. "Documents of the War," *The Crisis* 28 (1919).
"The Experience and Meaning of the Lost Battalion," World War I.com, presented by James V. Leak, Company E, 308th Infantry, November 11, 1938, www.worldwar1.com/dbc/leak.htm.
General Orders No. 20, 37th Division. National Archives, College Park, MD.
"The Lost Battalion," After Action Report, 77th Infantry Division, National Archives, College Park, Maryland.

"Means Used by the Nazi Conspirators in Gaining Control of the German State." In *Nazi Conspiracy and Aggression*, Vol. I, ch. 7. The Avalon Project, Yale Law School, Lillian Goldman Law Library (http://avalon.law.yale.edu/imt/chap_07.asp).

"The Wolfhounds Pick a Winner," *American Legion Monthly*, Vol. 17, No. 3 (September 1934).


## NEWSPAPERS

*Berkshire Evening Eagle*
*Birmingham Age-Herald*


## ONLINE RESOURCES

The Allied Appeal for Rapid American Assistance wwi.lib.byu.edu/index.php/The_Allied_Appeal_for_Rapid_American_Assistance

Library of Congress: Rare Book and Special Collections Division, African-American Pamphlet Collection; www.loc.gov/rr/rarebook/coll/afam.html

Library of Congress: Veterans History Project; www.loc.gov/vets/

Medal of Honor Citations: Congressional Medal of Honor Society; www.cmohs.org

World War I Document Archive: Brigham Young University; wwi.lib.byu.edu/index.php/Main_Page


## SPEECHES

Grant, Ulysses S. "Proclamation 192—Neutrality of Citizens of the United States in the War Between France and the North German Confederation," August 22, 1870.

Roosevelt, Theodore. *Peace and War.* Naval War College, June 2, 1897.

———. *Un-hyphenated America.* Carnegie Hall, October 12, 1915.

Wilson, Woodrow. *Message to Congress,* 63rd Congress.

———. *War Messages,* 65th Congress, 1st Session, Senate Doc. No. 5, Serial No. 7264, Washington, DC, 1917.

# About the Authors

**Martin King** is an Emmy Award–winning British-military historian and former university lecturer. He has worked as a historical consultant for various History Channel productions and has made personal appearances at the Pentagon, West Point, and Valley Forge. He speaks German, Dutch, Italian, and French and is in frequent demand as a speaker. US military personnel presented him and Mike Collins with a "Services to Education" certificate. The Belgian municipality made Martin an Honorary Citizen and he is an elected European Cultural Ambassador.

**Michael Collins** is a military historian and author who has cowritten several books with Martin, including *Voices of the Bulge*, *The Tigers of Bastogne*, *The Fighting 30th*, *To War with the 4th*, and *Warriors of the 106th*. He specializes in twentieth-century history, specifically World War I and World War II. He lives in Western Massachusetts and is widely renowned as a leading archivist/researcher.